UNDERCO
POLICE SURVEILLANCE IN
PERSPECTIV

Ben Bowling April '97

UNDERCOVER

POLICE SURVEILLANCE IN COMPARATIVE PERSPECTIVE

Edited by

Cyrille Fijnaut
Gary T. Marx

1995
Kluwer Law International
The Hague-London-Boston

Published by Kluwer Law International
P.O. Box 85889, 2508 CN The Hague
The Netherlands
Tel.: +31 70 3081551
Fax: +31 70 3081515

Sold and distributed in the U.S.A. and Canada
by Kluwer Academic Publishers
101 Philip Drive, Norwell, MA 02061
U.S.A.

In all other countries, sold and distributed
by Kluwer Academic Publishers Group
P.O. Box 322, 3300 AH Dordrecht
The Netherlands

Library of Congress Cataloging-in-Publication Data

Undercover—police surveillance in comparative perspective / edited by Cyrille Fijnaut
and Gary T. Marx
    p.   cm.
  ISBN 9041100156
  1. Undercover operations. 2. Criminal investigation. 3. Police patrol—Surveillance operations. I. Fijnaut, Cyrille, 1946– . II. Marx, Gary T.
HV8080.U5U53   1995
363.2'32—dc20   95–18010
                                                                                                          CIP

Cover design: A-Graphics Design

ISBN 90 411 00156

© 1995, Kluwer Law International, The Hague, The Netherlands

All rights reserved. No part of this publication may be reproduced, stored in a retrieval system or transmitted in any form or by any means, electronic, mechanical, photocopying, recording or otherwise, without the prior written permission of the publisher.

Table of Contents

Cyrille Fijnaut and Gary T. Marx

INTRODUCTION: THE NORMALIZATION OF UNDERCOVER POLICING IN THE WEST; HISTORICAL AND CONTEMPORARY PERSPECTIVES 1

1. Undercover: An Enduring Ingredient of Modern Policing 2
   - 1.1. France 3
   - 1.2. Germany 6
   - 1.3. Great Britain 7
2. Developments in the United States 10
3. Undercover Returns to Europe 15
4. The Articles 16

Dominique Monjardet and René Lévy

UNDERCOVER POLICING IN FRANCE: ELEMENTS FOR DESCRIPTION AND ANALYSIS 29

1. Introduction 29
2. The National Police 30
   - 2.1. The Police Urbaine 31
   - 2.2. Compagnies Républicaines de Sécurité 32
   - 2.3. The Political Police 34
   - 2.4. The Police Judiciaire 38
3. The Other Police Agencies 42
   - 3.1. The Gendarmerie Nationale 42
   - 3.2. The Douane 44
4. Conclusion 46

References 50

TABLE OF CONTENTS

Heiner Busch and Albrecht Funk

UNDERCOVER TACTICS AS AN ELEMENT OF PREVENTIVE CRIME FIGHTING IN THE FEDERAL REPUBLIC OF GERMANY 55

1. Introduction 55
2. 'Undercover' in the German Debate on Preventive Crime Fighting 57
3. The Consequences for Police Organization 60
4. The Effects of 'Preventive Crime Fighting' on the Criminal Justice System 62
5. Conclusion 67
References 68

Jean-Paul Brodeur

UNDERCOVER POLICING IN CANADA: A STUDY OF ITS CONSEQUENCES   71

1. The Canadian Police Apparatus 72
   1.1. The Canadian Police Forces 72
   1.2. Government Security Intelligence Agencies 73
   1.3. Quasi-governmental Security Units 75
   1.4. Private Security Agencies 76
2. Undercover Operations in the Canadian Context 76
   2.1. The Canadian Context 77
   2.2. Political Surveillance 78
   2.3. Undercover Police, Informers and Delators 79
   2.4. Fields of Undercover Policing 81
3. Intention 81
   3.1. Laundering Unresolved Cases 82
   3.2. Blackmailing Informants 83
4. Consequences of Undercover Policing 85
   4.1. Consequences: Desirable and Intended 86
   4.2. Consequences: Desirable and Unintended 88
   4.3. Consequences: Undesirable and Intended 89
   4.4. Consequences: Undesirable and Unintended 92
5. Conclusions 95
   5.1. Active Deception and the New Surveillance: the State as an Undercover Agent 95
   5.2. Consequences Entailed in Undercover Policing 97
   5.3. Necessary Evil 98
References 99

Peter Klerks

COVERT POLICING IN THE NETHERLANDS 103

1. Introduction: Policing under the Lee of Public Trust 103
   1.1. Introducing Secrecy inside Police Organizations 105
   1.2. Research Methodology and Structure of this Chapter 105

TABLE OF CONTENTS

2.	The Criminal Intelligence Department	107
	2.1. Development and Structure of the CID	107
	2.2. Role in Strategic Planning	109
	2.3. The Concealment of CID Information in Court	110
	2.4. Controlling the CID	112
	2.5. He's Got the Look	114
3.	Infiltration	115
	3.1. Recent History and Regulation	115
	3.2. Civilians as Infiltrators	118
	3.3. The Growing International Dimension of Infiltration	118
	3.4. The Shift from Evidence-gathering to Intelligence	119
	3.5. The Risks: Lacking Accountability under the Rule of Law	121
	3.6. The Risks: Police Corruption	122
	3.7. The Risks: Psychological Effects on the Undercover Agent	124
	3.8. Infiltration in the Future	125
4.	Surveillance	127
	4.1. A Short History of Police Surveillance Teams	127
	4.2. Police Surveillance Exposed and Reorganized under a New Doctrine	128
	4.3. Surveillance Reports Kept out of Court	128
	4.4. Does Police Surveillance Require a Formal Legal Arrangement?	129
5.	Informants	130
	5.1. Motivation of Informants	130
	5.2. Risks Involved in Working with Informants	131
6.	Secrecy and the Fear of Corruption	133
	6.1. Attitudes among the Police toward Secrecy	133
	6.2. A Justified Fear of Corruption?	134
7.	Conclusions	135
References		137

Lode Van Outrive and Jan Cappelle

TWENTY YEARS OF UNDERCOVER POLICING IN BELGIUM: THE REGULATION OF A RISKY POLICE PRACTICE ... 141

1.	The Early History	141
2.	The American War on Drugs During the Nixon Administration	144
3.	The 'Americanization' of Belgian Investigation Procedures	145
	3.1. At the Level of Police Organization	145
	3.2. At the Level of Legislation	146
	3.3. At the Level of Police Tactics	146
4.	Police Provocation and its Legalization	147
5.	The New Policy Directives	149
6.	Covert Policing and the Failure of Belgian Police Services	150
7.	Evaluation of the Current Situation	152

TABLE OF CONTENTS

Louise Shelley

SOVIET UNDERCOVER WORK 155
1. Introduction 155
   1.1. A Comparative Framework 157
   1.2. Sources 158
   1.3. Objectives 159
2. Undercover Work and the Legal Framework 159
3. The Militia and Undercover Work 161
   3.1. Developing Informants 161
   3.2. Deployment of Informants 163
   3.3. Employing Informant Information 164
   3.4. Anonymous Tips and Denunciations 165
4. Undercover Work of the Security Police 166
   4.1. Technology and the Security Police 166
   4.2. Recruitment of Informants 167
   4.3. Surveillance Methods 169
5. Post-Soviet Developments 170
6. Conclusion 172
References 173

Gary Armstrong and Dick Hobbs

HIGH TACKLES AND PROFESSIONAL FOULS: THE POLICING OF SOCCER
HOOLIGANISM 175
1. Introduction 175
2. The Inheritance of Covert Policing 176
3. Leaders of Men 178
4. Tactical Persuasions 180
5. Trying Times 181
6. Paying for Admission 183
7. Hooligan Conspiracies: Playing Away 185
8. Conclusion 190
References 191

Michael Levi

COVERT POLICING AND THE INVESTIGATION OF 'ORGANIZED FRAUD':
THE ENGLISH EXPERIENCE IN INTERNATIONAL CONTEXT 195
1. Introduction 195
2. English Law and Undercover Work 195
   2.1. Provocation and Entrapment 196
   2.2. Disclosure Rules 199
3. The Contexts of Police Undercover Work 201
4. Covert Investigations of White-collar Crime in America 202
5. Covert Policing of White-collar Crime in Britain 204

6.	Justifying White-collar Undercover Work	207
	6.1. Intended Consequences of Undercover Work	209
	6.2. Unintended Consequences of Undercover Work	209
7.	Conclusion	210
References		211

Gary T. Marx

WHEN THE GUARDS GUARD THEMSELVES: UNDERCOVER TACTICS TURNED INWARD ... 213

1.	The Expansion of Covert Policing	215
2.	The Problem of Guarding the Guards	216
3.	Some Examples	220
4.	Some Consequences, Costs and Choices	225
5.	Some Additional Consequences	228
References		232

Helgi Gunnlaugsson and John F. Galliher

THE SECRET DRUG POLICE OF ICELAND ... 235

1.	Secret Policing around the World	235
2.	Crime in Iceland	236
3.	Evidence of an Icelandic Moral Panic	237
4.	History of Policing in Iceland	239
5.	Secret Policing in Iceland	240
6.	Examples of Covert Policing Practices	243
7.	Moral and Geographical Boundary Maintenance	244
References		245

Dennis Töllborg

UNDERCOVER IN SWEDEN: THE SWEDISH SECURITY POLICE AND THEIR MODI OPERANDI ... 249

1.	Direction and Data Sources	249
2.	The Swedish Security Police (*Säkerhetspolisen*): Its Organizational Structure and Tasks in the Nineties	250
3.	*Modi Operandi*	252
	3.1. Search	253
	3.2. Wire-tapping and Letter Control	254
	3.3. Bugging	258
	3.4. Enlisting and Crime Provocation	261
4.	Conclusions	265

TABLE OF CONTENTS

Ethan A. Nadelmann

THE DEA IN EUROPE 269

1. 'Americanization' of European Drug Enforcement 269
2. Undercover Operations 275
3. Controlled Deliveries 284
4. Wire-tapping 286
5. Conclusion 287

Nikos Passas and Richard B. Groskin

INTERNATIONAL UNDERCOVER INVESTIGATIONS 291

1. Introduction 291
2. Operation C-Chase 293
3. Operation Exodus 294
4. Preparing International Operations 296
5. Coordination with Domestic Agencies 299
6. Coordination and Collaboration with Foreign Agencies 301
7. Diversity of Methods and Procedures 302
8. Diversity of Substantive Laws 303
9. Other Political Considerations 304
10. Timing the Close-down of Undercover Operations 306
11. Arrests and Prosecutions 306
12. Conclusion 307
References 309

Gary T. Marx

UNDERCOVER: SOME IMPLICATIONS FOR POLICY 313

Gary T. Marx

UNDERCOVER IN COMPARATIVE PERSPECTIVE: SOME IMPLICATIONS FOR KNOWLEDGE AND SOCIAL RESEARCH 323

References 337

INTRODUCTION

Cyrille Fijnaut
Gary T. Marx

The Normalization of Undercover Policing in the West: Historical and Contemporary Perspectives*

In the last 25 years undercover policing has become a public issue in North America and Western Europe. Much of the discussion has to do with the 'necessary evil' character of this policing strategy within democratic societies. On the one hand it is increasingly seen as an efficient and even necessary strategy to combat major crime problems, on the other hand it is a risky business involving the invasion of privacy, the exploitation of trust, danger to third parties and the risk of police corruption and a compromised judicial system.

For many years we have been engaged in research on covert policing. Gary T. Marx, as part of a more general interest in the interdependence between rule breakers and enforcers, has written extensively on the topic and in 1988 published *Undercover: Police Surveillance in America*. Among the many publications of Cyrille Fijnaut is a book on the notorious '*François*' undercover police corruption case in Belgium.[1]

The present volume is an outgrowth of our shared interest in the topic and of the increased salience of covert and technological policing in the West. Filled with questions but not with the resources to answer them, we did the next best thing – turned to leading scholars and asked them to comment on covert policing within their country.

We organized an international working group through the Law and Society Association and the Research Committee on the Sociology of Law that met in Amsterdam in 1991, Boston in 1992, Hamburg in 1993 and Leuven in 1994.

---

* We are grateful to the National Science Foundation grant # SBR-9396101 and the Law and Society Association for support.
1. G.T. Marx (1988), *Undercover; Police Surveillance in America*, Berkeley, University of California Press/The Twentieth Century Fund, and C. Fijnaut (1983), *De zaak-François; beschouwingen naar aanleiding van het vonnis*, Antwerpen, Kluwer Rechtswetenschappen. This case encompassed the fall of two undercover units. One of these units had been established in 1971 in the Ministry of Justice, the other one at the same time in the staff of the national gendarmerie and was led by Captain François. Around 1980 it became clear that some members of both units were heavily involved in various forms of illegal activity.

CYRILLE FIJNAUT AND GARY T. MARX

The articles on undercover policing in France, Germany, Belgium, Great Britain, Canada and Sweden included in this volume were presented in Amsterdam. In addition we broadened the scope by commissioning papers on undercover policing in Russia, Iceland, the Netherlands and the United States.

In this introduction we note the historical background and spread of undercover policing throughout the West. We argue that in modern Europe undercover policing has never been a marginal phenomenon but, on the contrary, from the beginning was an essential feature of the modern French police system. As such it gradually became an accepted (if never statistically the most common) European police strategy. This is true even in countries like Britain where verbal opposition to the continental 'spy system' was strong.

We note how the historical development of undercover policing in Europe is linked to its later development in the United States. We then consider the renewal, extension and transfer back to Europe of new American undercover techniques seen in recent decades.

Finally, we introduce some of the central themes treated in the chapters that follow.

1. UNDERCOVER: AN ENDURING INGREDIENT OF MODERN POLICING

From the 16th century onward, the emerging nation-states in Europe made extensive use of undercover techniques to protect their political, military and economic interests. Authorities in special bureaus opened diplomatic correspondence, recruited informants, and sent spies to learn the secret intentions of their enemies and rivals.[2] The first modern police apparatus was created in Paris at the end of the 17th century. It defined public order as the protection of the political order of the city. A central feature of this was gathering information on potentially dangerous classes, families and individuals through covert means.[3] In 1790 P. Manuel, a merciless critic of the pre-revolutionary Parisian police system, published a book documenting this system's tyrannical nature and its extensive use of intrusive policing means.[4] Parisian police leaders wrote of the importance of undercover policing to their job.

---

2. See e.g. G. de Bruin (1991), *Geheimhouding en verraad; de geheimhouding van staatszaken ten tijde van de Republiek (1600–1750)*, 's-Gravenhage, SDU Uitgeverij; G.R. Elton (1972), *Policy and Police; The Enforcement of the Reformation in the Age of Thomas Cromwell*, Cambridge, Cambridge University Press; P. Frazer (1956), *The Intelligence of the Secretaries of State and Their Monopoly of Licensed News*, Cambridge, University Press; J.W. Thompson and S.K. Padover (1938), *L'espionnage politique en Europe de 1500 à 1815*, Paris, Payot.
3. C. Fijnaut (1979), *Opdat de macht een toevlucht zij? Een historische studie van het politieapparaat als een politieke instelling*, Antwerpen, Kluwer Rechtswetenschappen, I, 489–551, 580–593. For a summary: C. Fijnaut (1980), 'Les origines de l'appareil policier moderne en Europe de l'Ouest continentale,' *Déviance et Société*, 1, 19–41.
4. P. Manuel (1790), *La police de Paris dévoilée*, Paris, J.B. Garnery.

INTRODUCTION: THE NORMALIZATION OF UNDERCOVER POLICING

1.1. France

In 1770, at the request of the Austrian Queen Maria-Theresia, Le Maire wrote a comprehensive overview of the way the police of Paris was organized and functioned.[5] The 20 *inspecteurs de police*, all members of the notorious *bureau de sûreté* are of particular interest. These police officers were a well-developed undercover unit. They were charged with secret investigations and the gathering of information on the private and public life of citizens in both political and criminal matters. The *inspecteurs* regularly operated as undercover agents themselves and also made use of three categories of informants: *observateurs* (observers), *espions* (spies), and *basse-mouches* (informers). These secret assistants of the *inspecteurs* were paid for keeping influential persons continuously under observation, for passing on rumours regarding political attitudes and social liaisons, for collecting information on sexual behavior, and for conducting the equivalent of 'buy-bust' operations. In the Paris area in 1753 their number was estimated to be 3,000.[6]

Commissaire Le Maire notes that the Parisian police inspectors kept authorities informed of the most secret aspects of citizens' lives. More recent authors have also emphasized the intrusiveness of the Parisian police in both private and public life.[7]

Outside of Paris the *sûreté* also made use of secret agents, particularly when national interests were believed to be at stake. Other city police forces and even the rural military police force, the *gendarmerie*, also used them to maintain public order and to investigate particular crimes, although to a lesser degree.[8] Chassaigne estimated that in the mid-eighteenth century there were 10,000 informers throughout all of France.

Revolutionaries like P. Manuel detested the pre-revolutionary undercover policing system, yet one of the ironies of the French Revolution is that after a

---

5. J. Le Maire (1879), 'La police de Paris en 1770,' in: *Mémoires de la Société de l'Histoire de Paris et de l'Ile de France*, Paris, 1–131 (mémoire éditée par A. Grazier). See for an original description of the system also M. Guillaute (1974), *Mémoire sur la réformation de la police en France, soumis au Roi en 1749*, Paris, Hermann (edited by G. de Saint-Aubin).
6. M. Chassaigne (1906), *La lieutenance générale de police de Paris*, Paris, Arthur Rousseau, 235 et seq. Other more or less important and/or informative, but somewhat traditional books on the police of Paris in the seventeenth and eighteenth century are: P. Clément (1866), *La police sous Louis XIV*, Paris, Didier; H. De Montbas (1949), *La police parisienne sous Louis XVI*, Paris, Hachette; M. de Sars (1948), *Le Noir; lieutenant de police, 1732–1807*, Paris, Hachette; E. Le Nabour (1991), *La Reynie; le policier de Louis XIV*, Paris, Perrin; C. Piton (1906), *Paris sous Louis XV; rapports des inspecteurs de police au Roi*, Paris, Société du Mercure de France; J. Saint-Germain (1962), *La Reynie et la police au Grand Siècle*, Paris, Hachette; E. Vaillé (1950), *Le cabinet noir*, Paris, Presses Universitaires de France.
7. See e.g. E-M. Benabou (1987), *La prostitution et la police des moeurs au XVIIIe siècle*, Paris, Perrin, and A. Williams (1979), *The Police of Paris, 1718–1789*, Baton Rouge, Louisiana State University Press.
8. *Cf.* I.A. Cameron (1981), *Crime and Repression in the Auvergne and the Guyenne, 1720–1790*, Cambridge, Cambridge University Press, 60–69. See further e.g. J.R. Ruff (1984), *Crime, Justice and Public Order in Old Regime France; the Sénéchaussées of Libourne and Bazas, 1696–1789*, London, Croom Helm.

brief period this system was rebuilt and strengthened to fight perceived enemies from within and without. A national police system emerged in the struggle against political opposition. This development found its clearest expression in the establishment of the *comité de sûreté générale* in 1792. It was charged with the direction of the so-called *police révolutionnaire* throughout France and of the *bureau de police* of the *comité de salut public* in 1794. The latter was entrusted with the political control of all agents of the new regime. Both *comités* made extensive use of informers and undercover agents in search of enemies of the Revolution.[9]

However it was Joseph Fouché, Napoleon's Minister of Police, who constructed the first modern police-state apparatus. While drawing on the previous system, he adjusted it to the revolutionary nation-state. Until World War I his model was used by reformers as a negative example of how not to restructure a national police system. In 1799 when Fouché first headed the *ministère de la police générale*, he formulated his ideas about the purpose, functioning and organization of the modern police. The police – in contrast with the administration – should make its influence felt without showing itself. The police must always be alert and take action – but surreptitiously. Fouché saw the police as a ministry for action (*'ministère d'action'*) – a secret but powerful driving force which was the indispensable arm of government (*'C'est un levier secret, mais puissant, mais indispensable entre les mains du Gouvernement'*).[10]

In conformity with this policing philosophy which in other ways resembled the principles of pre-revolutionary policing in Paris, Fouché organized his *ministère de police générale* into specialized roles across the Napoleonic empire. He created relationships with the ministries for internal and external affairs and with the ordinary administrative authorities *(conseillers, directeurs et commissaires généraux de police,* and *commissaires spéciaux de police)*. This state police apparatus drew upon, but also extended the traditional French undercover policing system. Based on the notion that policing amounts to continuous surveillance in all parts of society, the several departments and bureaus of the ministry, particularly the second department *(la sûreté générale et la police secrète)* daily collected information from all over the empire, emphasizing political opposition, public order and crime. This information was summarized for Napoleon Bonaparte in a secret daily *bulletin de police*. This was the first European police information system.

While Fouché's organization represented a breakthrough in policing large parts of the continent, the way the secret information was collected remained very traditional. As in pre-revolutionary times, the officers of the police ministry and their official collaborators depended heavily on actions of *observateurs, espions* and *basse-mouches*. This was the case in France, and within, and even beyond, the borders of the Napoleonic Empire. Their goal was to contain the

---

9. A. Ording (1930), *Le bureau de police du comité de salut public; étude sur la Terreur*, Oslo, I Kommisjon Hos Jacob Dybwad.
10. J. Fouché (1879), 'Organisation de la police,' *Revue des Documents Historiques*, 7–8, 102–105.

INTRODUCTION: THE NORMALIZATION OF UNDERCOVER POLICING

threat they saw from *emigrés* and to counter the political, economic, and military actions of the forces aligned against them.[11]

Eugène Vidocq played an important role. In spite, or perhaps because of his criminal background, in 1811 he became head of the *bureau de sûreté* in the *préfecture de police* of Paris. Vidocq and his numerous admirers portrayed him as the founder of this *bureau* and the inventor of undercover policing, but that is exaggerated. His bureau was the continuation of the *bureau de sûreté* that was established in the beginning of the eighteenth century within the Parisian police. His numerous and varied undercover techniques were similar to those his predecessors had used for a century. The difference between them and Vidocq was his skill. He was a creative and courageous master of covert behavior and he gave it greater formal recognition. His exploits are described in his own self-serving books and in biographies.[12]

Despite changes of political regime, undercover policing in Paris continued to be practised in an equivalent fashion in the first part of the nineteenth century. As head of the *bureau de sûreté* Vidocq survived the fall of the Napoleonic Regime in 1815 and the *coup d'état* of Charles X in 1824, as well as the take-over by Louis Philippe in 1830. In the political, as well as the criminal field, the police of Paris remained dependent upon the services of all sorts of unofficial agents.[13] Details of undercover policing are given in the memoirs of several *préfets de police* and heads of the *bureau de sûreté*. More recent academic research also shows that other large cities also relied upon covert policing as a general strategy.[14] In 1855 the French government estab-

---

11. See above all L. Madelin (1903), *Fouché, 1759–1820*, Paris, Plon, I, 276–309, 449–508. Apart from *Les mémoires de Fouché* (Paris, Flammarion, 1945, introduction et notes par L. Madelin) there are a lot of (other) interesting books on J. Fouché and the Napoleonic state police system, e.g. H. Buisson (1968), *Fouché; duc d'Otrante*, Paris; H. Cole (1971), *Fouché; The Unprincipled Partriot*, London; E. d'Hauterive (1943), *Napoléon et sa police*, Paris, Flammarion; H. von Hentig (1919), *Fouché; ein Beitrag zur Technik der politischen Polizei in nachrevolutionären Perioden*, Tübingen, J.C.B. Mohr; S. Zweig (1932), *Joseph Fouché; Bildnis eines politischen Menschen*, Leipzig, Insel-Verlag. One of the most remarkable spies has been Charles Schulmeister. See A. Elmer (1932), *Schulmeister: l'agent secret de Napoléon*, Paris, Payot (traduit de l'allemand).
12. In order to get some insight in the rather complicated story of Vidocq one could consult his more or less personal works: *Vidocq; The Personal Memoirs of the First Great Detective*, Cambridge, Mass., The Riverside Press, 1935 (edited and translated by E.G. Rich); *Vidocq; les voleurs*, Paris, Editions de Paris, 1957 (textes restitués et présentés par J. Savant); *Histoire de Vidocq; écrite d'après lui-même par M. Froment*, Paris, Laffont, 1967 (préface de Georges Neveux). See further a.o. J. Savant (1957), *Le vrai Vidocq*, Paris, Hachette, and Ph. J. Stead (1953), *Vidocq; A Biography*, London, Staples Press. An important source also is *Le procès de Vidocq; documents originaux présentés et commentés par Jean Savant*, Paris, Club du Meilleur Livre, 1956.
13. M. Gisquet (1841), *Mémoires*, Bruxelles, Société Belge de Librairie, II, 213–267, 273–282.
14. As far as the first category of publications is concerned, see L. Andrieux (1885), *Souvenirs d'un préfet de police*, Paris, Jules Rouff; M. Goron (1929), *Mémoires*, Paris, Jules Rouff, s.d., 2 T.; L. Lépine, *Mes souvenirs*, Paris, Payot; G. Macé (1891), *Le service de la sûreté*, Paris, Bibliothèque-Charpentier. In relation to more recent academic research one may refer to J.M. Berlière (1992), *La police des moeurs sous la IIIe République*, Paris, Seuil, and G. Bollenot, *Police politique et police secrète à Lyon (1831–1835)*, Toulouse, Centre d'Etudes et de Recherches sur la Police, s.d.

lished a national 'special police' to enlarge the surveillance of political opponents. To cover its true purpose it was called the *service spécial de surveillance des chemins de fer* (special service for the supervision of the railroads).[15]

1.2. Germany

The French Revolution and the Napoleonic Empire led authorities beyond France to organize their police surveillance in the French manner. For example, in Berlin in 1809 Justus Gruner was appointed *Polizeipräsident* (commissioner). He completely reorganized the police system and adapted the internal structure of the central bureau to the structure of the main office of the *préfecture de police*. This adaptation entailed the establishment of a *Sicherheitsburo* or safety bureau whose official members immediately started recruiting *Vigilanten* (informers) throughout the underworld. And when Gruner in 1811 was given authority over the *Höhere Polizei* (high or political police) for Prussia as a whole, he organized a secret police network inside the country and also sent his spies into foreign countries.[16]

The Vienna Treaty of 1815 created a new order. After the fall of the Napoleonic Empire, all the German states in one way or another created a police system to surveil political movements perceived to be a threat. They engaged in secret information exchanges that met with varying degrees of success.[17] The revolutionary movements in and around 1848 were a further stimulus for the strengthening of the political police in the relevant states and increased cooperation. In 1851 they established a *Polizeiverein* (police association) that for several decades was rather effective in combatting the communist movement.[18] The driving force behind this development was the Berlin *Polizeidirektor* (police director) Wilhelm Stieber. Starting in 1852 he transformed the existing *Sicherheitsburo* into a comprehensive and separate *Kriminalpolizei* (criminal investigation department) within the Berlin police force.[19]

The publications on the life and work of Stieber, as well as on the police of Berlin in general in the second half of the nineteenth century, clearly show that undercover tactics were an integral part of political and criminal policing. Stieber and his officers frequently operated as undercover agents, and they also

---

15. See G. Carrot (1984), *Le maintien de l'ordre en France depuis la fin de l'Ancien Régime jusqu'a 1968*, Toulouse, Centre d'Etudes et de Recherches sur la Police, II, 651. With respect to the functioning of these 'specials' see M. Mathieu (1987), 'Le rôle politique des commissaires spéciaux de la police des chemins de fer dans la Vienne entre 1874 et 1914,' in: *Maintien de l'ordre et polices en France et en Europe du XIXe siècle*, Paris, Créaphis, 151–166.
16. See W. Obenaus (1940), *Die Entwicklung der preussischen Sicherheitspolizei bis zum Ende der Reaktionszeit*, Berlin, W. de Gruyter, 68–108. Also important is: U. Veit (1937), *Justus Gruner als Schöpfer der Geheimen Preussischen Staatspolizei*, Coburg.
17. W. Siemann (1985), *'Deutschlands Ruhe, Sicherheit und Ordnung'; die Anfänge der politischen Polizei, 1806–1866*, Tübingen, Max Niemeyer Verlag, 72–241.
18. W. Siemann, *op. cit.*, 242–468.
19. W. Obenaus, *op. cit.*, 132–136.

made extensive use of informers to collect information, prevent disorder and even to arrest suspects.[20] Operational manuals discuss police surveillance and undercover policing in particular as an indispensable tool of urban criminal investigation. They discuss covert operations, the handling of informers and how to prevent them from turning into *agents provocateurs* and from cheating on police.[21] Several books on big-city police forces at the time (e.g., the police of Hamburg) include pictures of disguised members of undercover units.[22] In their autobiographies leading German police openly reported on their undercover operations in their country and beyond its borders.[23]

1.3. Great Britain

Although Continental rulers reorganized their medieval police systems after the modern French model or had this model forcefully imposed by Napoleon Bonaparte, changes in the British system were less pronounced, but not as distant from the French model as has traditionally been believed. Apart from some minor changes, e.g. Henry Fielding's replacement of the traditional system of decentralized parish policing, until 1829 and the passage of the Metropolitan Police Improvement Act, it remained the traditional system of decentralized parish policing.[24] To be sure there was discussion about reform. Henry Fielding, Jeremy Bentham, Edwin Chadwick, William Mildmay, William Pitt and Patrick Colquhoun among others developed very detailed plans for reform. They believed that the existing medieval arrangements were not appropriate for the problems of crime and public disorder in their industrializing society.[25] The proposals they made drew from the French model of modern policing. For this reason they met with strong opposition. To many persons the introduction of a French police system would amount to the establishment of executive tyranny.

---

20. Reference can be made to a.o. *Denkwürdigkeiten des Geheimen Regierungsrathes dr. Stieber*, Berlin, Julius Engelmann, 1884 (aus seinen hinterlassenen Papieren bearbeitet von dr. L. Auerbach); D. Fricke (1962), *Bismarcks Prätorianer; die Berliner Polizei im Kampf gegen die deutsche Arbeiterbewegung, 1871–1898*, Berlin, Rütten und Loening, 22–55, 89–144; V. Tissot (1884), *La police secrète prussienne*, Paris, E. Dentu; C. Wermuth and W. Stieber (1853), *Die Communisten-Verschwörungen des neunzehnten Jahrhunderts*, Berlin, Hayn.
21. See e.g. F. Kleinschmidt (1953), *Lehrbuch für den praktischen Kriminaldienst*, Lübeck, Verlag für Polizeiliches Fachschriftum; A. Lichem (1935), *Die Kriminalpolizei; Handbuch für den kriminellen Polizeidienst*, Grasz, Lenkam-Verlag, 62–64, 66–68; W. Stieber (1921), *Praktisches Lehrbuch der Kriminalpolizei*, Potsdam, Hayn (zweite, völlig umgearbeitete Auflage herausgegeben von H. Schneikert) 20–24, 58–59.
22. G. Roscher (1912), *Groszstadtpolizei; ein praktisches Handbuch der deutschen Polizei*, Hamburg, Otto Meiszners Verlag, 161–162.
23. See above all G. Steinhauer (1930), *Der Meisterspion des Kaisers; was der Detektiv Wilhelms II. in seiner Praxis erlebte*, Berlin, Karl Voegels Verlag.
24. J.J. Tobias (1979), *Crime and Police in England, 1700–1900*, Dublin, Gill and MacMillan, 25–56.
25. See L. Radzinowicz (1948–1956), *A History of English Criminal Law and its Administration from 1750*, London, III, 417–522.

The memory of Cromwell's New Model Army in the seventeenth century that had been fashioned into a domestic police force also created opposition.[26]

In spite of the public rhetoric, the functioning of the thief-taker system clearly resembled the operations of the *inspecteurs* of the *bureau de sûreté* in Paris. The thief takers – most of whom were themselves notorious figures in the urban underworld – also relied upon intelligence networks among thieves, prostitutes, and receivers. They made use of undercover techniques.[27] Even their more 'civilized' counterparts (Fielding's Bow Street Runners) used covert means in the criminal, as well as the political field.[28] The Home Office also used informers and spies to infiltrate rebellious movements and to observe disorders such as the Gordon Riots in London (1780) and the Luddite Riots in the Midlands (1811–1817).[29]

The Metropolitan Police Improvement Act was accepted by the Parliament because the ruling parties had gradually concluded that the army was no longer an appropriate or efficient instrument for restoring and keeping public order: it lacked the infrastructure and numbers to provide for troops all over the country and soldiers often sympathized with protestors and rioters. In addition, the traditional parish-based policing system could not keep up with rising crime rates.

In his original proposal for a police force of London, Home Secretary William Peel suggested a force that differed in important ways from the police of Paris. It would include neither a detective force nor a military type of organization. He sought to overcome the suspicion of a professional police service. The police of London were to be based on the principles of preventive policing.[30]

Yet the differences between the British and French police are not as great as is often believed. Thus Fouché also emphasized the preventive, as against the repressive function of the police. There were also structural resemblances. The London police were to be present 24 hours a day throughout the territory of London. In principle police would immediately spot any disturbance of daily life and react directly, with large numbers if necessary. Relative to the police of Paris the new police of London benefited from not being divided into so many different departments.[31]

The new police in the 1830s expressed its philosophy of preventive policing via a uniformed presence rather than a secret police presence. Yet after ten

---

26. S.H. Palmer (1988), *Police and Protest in England and Ireland, 1780–1850*, Cambridge, Cambridge University Press, 69–79. *See* further also C. Emsley (1983), *Policing and its Context, 1750–1870*, London, MacMillan, 8–75.
27. *See* R. Paley (1989), 'Thief-takers in London in the Age of the McDaniel Gang, 1745–1754,' in: D. Hay and F. Snyder, eds., *Policing and Prosecution in Britain, 1750–1850*, Oxford, Clarendon Press, 301–342.
28. *See* e.g. H. Goddard (1957), *Criminele recherche meer dan honderd jaar geleden; belevenissen van een Bow Street Runner*, Haarlem, Tjeenk Willink.
29. T.A. Critchley (1970), *The Conquest of Violence*, London, 95–113.
30. S.H. Palmer, *op. cit.*, 278–303.
31. *See* the publications of C. Fijnaut quoted in note 3, and also the comparisons C. Emsley has made piecemeal in his *The English Police; A Political and Social History*, Hemel Hempstead, Harvester Wheatsheaf, 1991.

INTRODUCTION: THE NORMALIZATION OF UNDERCOVER POLICING

years the police commissioners came to the conclusion that the newly established system was not effective enough. In 1841–1842 they created a small central detective office in Scotland Yard. Some years later they assigned two intelligence constables to each police division in order 'to observe all burglars and other felons throughout the police district and to prevent the commission of any crime by them.' There has been little research on these and related initiatives which eventually led to the creation of a criminal investigation department in 1878. Nevertheless, there is evidence to suggest that those early English detectives, like their forerunners at Bow Street, as well as their French and German counterparts, not only established close contacts with the criminals of the London underworld, but also infiltrated that world in disguise. In a memorandum of 1846 one of the commissioners stated '... no man shall disguise himself without particular orders from the superintendent.'[32]

As on the Continent, undercover policing in Britain became a routine strategy of the new police. This was encouraged by perceived threats to the political order from local social movements and Irish nationalists. Under government pressure the metropolitan police in the years 1881–1887 built up its so-called special (Irish) branch. The resemblance between its name and the French *police spéciale* founded in 1855 under the cover of a railway police system is not accidental. Howard Vincent, its main founder, was very familiar with the French police system. From the beginning the members of his branch used large-scale undercover policing to control the Fenians, to arrest Irish terrorists, to stop violent anarchism and to surveil political refugees from Russia, France and Germany. By the turn of the century the special branch was a reliable and effective part of the international net of similar continental police departments.[33]

Raymond Fosdick visited European police systems in 1912 in search of models for reform for the U.S.[34] His report *European Police Systems* was published in 1916.[35] Given the process of the normalization of covert means described above, it is surprising that Fosdick paid no attention to the phenomenon.[36] The reason for this could certainly not have been that he was unaware of it or was trying to protect trade secrets, since leading French and German

---

32. Cf. D.G. Browne (1956), *The Rise of Scotland Yard; A History of the Metropolitan Police*, London, George G. Harrap, 113–127, 182–196; P.T. Smith (1985), *Policing Victorian London; Political Policing, Public Order, and the London Metropolitan Police*, Westport, Connecticut, Greenwood Press, 61–112; H.L. Adam, *C.I.D.; Behind the Scenes at Scotland Yard*, London, Sampson Low, s.d., 45–51, 164–197.
33. R. Allason (1983), *The Branch; A History of the Metropolitan Police Special Branch, 1883–1983*, London, Secker and Warburg, 1–37, and B. Porter (1987), *The Origins of the Vigilant State; The London Metropolitan Police Special Branch before the First World War*, London, Weidenfeld and Nicholson. See further e.g. the memoirs of H.T. Fitch (1935), *Memoirs of a Royal Detective*, London, Hurst and Blacket; and B. Thompson (1933), *La chasse aux espions; mes souvenirs de Scotland Yard, 1914–1919*, Paris, Payot.
34. See R.M. Fogelson (1977), *Big-City-Police*, Cambridge, Mass., Harvard University Press, 67–192, and E.H. Monkkonen (1981), *Police in Urban America, 1860–1920*, Cambridge, Cambridge University Press.
35. The book was published in New York by the Century Co.
36. See notably the Chapters 8, 9 and 10.

officers had written about it. Perhaps the reason was that he felt it would be shocking to his American audience and that a negative reaction to this aspect of policing in Western Europe might get in the way of the transfer of other less controversial aspects to the U.S.

2. DEVELOPMENTS IN THE UNITED STATES

The United States traditionally shared with England the fear of a centralized permanently organized police force and in the words of a Congressman the associated 'informers, spies and delators' that accompanied despotisms.[37] These concerns were even more pronounced in the United States because of its struggle for independence.

The first municipal police force in the new nation consisted of non-uniformed and unarmed men, reflecting the country's anti-military attitudes. Fears of a strong central government with a well-developed standing army, along with budgetary concerns, accounts for this. Yet as the United States became more urban and ethnically diverse, it was no more able to resist the need for a formal, specialized police system than was Great Britain.

Imitating London, many large American cities had created uniformed departments by the 1850s. Most of the departments initially had limited or no formal provision for crime detection. They were clearly at a disadvantage in dealing with consensual crimes and those carried out by skilled conspirators. Again as in Great Britain, the latter part of the 19th century saw the development of detective bureaus and more systematic links between police and criminals, with greater reliance on the use of informers and undercover means.

The local bumbling gangs, street criminals, drunks, and relatively unorganized rioters who shocked upright citizens in the first half of the nineteenth century were supplemented in the last half of that century by skilled and inventive professionals using the latest technology and knowing how to manipulate the enforcement system. Deceit and trickery were seen as necessary to respond to the con artists, pickpockets, counterfeiters, safe-crackers, and ideologically inspired conspirators who were appearing in increasing numbers. New forms of criminality appeared, and greater enforcement priority was given to types of crime for which evidence is not easily gathered by overt means – counterfeiting and other monetary violations, fraud and narcotics. The planned and conspirational nature of these lend themselves to secret means of discovery.

Detective bureaus developed in most cities by the later nineteenth century. The first detectives came from civilian life – not infrequently its criminal fringe or even core. Scandals that resulted from this led to a policy of choosing detectives from the uniformed patrol. However, the detective's skill was based largely on his knowledge of, and contact with lawbreakers. The most common enforcement means were the licensing of vice providers, infiltration and a system for recovering stolen property known as 'compromises' involving deals

---

37. This section draws from G.T. Marx, *op. cit.*, 22–32.

INTRODUCTION: THE NORMALIZATION OF UNDERCOVER POLICING

with thieves. The meshing of detectives with criminals led to frequent scandals, even with recruitment from the uniformed ranks.

Under the impact of early twentieth century progressive reformers, local departments became more organizationally complex and special units that often relied on covert means were created for policing vice, alcohol, narcotics, labor, radicals and immigrants. Undercover policing also was encouraged by the growth of federal police agencies during the last half of the 19th century.

The Anglo-American tradition in the United States and paucity of federal criminal statutes worked against the establishment of a national police force of any significance until the twentieth century. In Europe, with stronger, more centralized states, national police systems were well developed by the nineteenth century. In the absence of anything but the most minimal federal-level police, private agencies filled the void. Burns, Pinkerton, and other agencies were established primarily on behalf of private industrial interests such as railroads, banks, mines and factories. Undercover means were central to their operations. Before the Civil War, the Post Office and Treasury Department relied on private agencies such as Pinkerton's. In testing employees and looking for theft, Pinkerton introduced a more modern rationalized form of undercover work where investigation was not dependent on a specific complaint.

The post-Civil War reconstruction era spurred the growth of federal law enforcement to police the vanquished South. Undercover means were used to ensure compliance with measures that met with popular resistance such as enforcing civil rights for blacks and chasing illegal brewers of alcohol.

In the early 1900s postal authorities began using the tactic to gather evidence against pornographers. The Harrison Act of 1914 (making the distribution of nonmedicinal drugs a federal crime) and the 1920 Eighteenth Amendment to the United States Constitution (mandating Prohibition) resulted in the creation of narcotics and alcohol enforcement units within the Treasury Department. Within a few years the number of federal prohibition agents reached 4,000, a figure that dwarfed all previous federal detective forces. The ban on narcotics and alcohol was accompanied by inventive and sometimes questionable covert practices.

The Bureau of Investigation (later called the FBI) was created in 1908 by Theodore Roosevelt against the wish of Congress. The FBI made extensive use of informants and passive surveillance in its search for fugitives and information. For example, after the 1934 escape of John Dillinger, the FBI:

> began as organized a search as was possible, making new contacts, utilizing new underworld informers. Every spot where he had ever been was covered or planted. A plant is the covering of a spot from another point, usually by the renting of a room or an apartment across the street from the place under observation. Many addresses where Dillinger had previously been seen or where any member of his gang was known to have been seen were covered night and day, week after week. His relatives in Mooresville were placed under surveillance.[38]

---

38. M. Purvis (1936), *American Agent*, New York, Garden City Publishers.

FBI agents sometimes might play a modest undercover role in crime, for example posing as a cab driver to deliver ransom in a kidnapping, infiltrating a workplace to observe a suspected extortionist or saboteur, or infiltrating a mental hospital as a patient to gather evidence on a suspect feigning insanity to avoid trial. But until quite recently, the FBI, unlike the Department of the Treasury or the Bureau of Narcotics, made little use of complex undercover activities for investigating conventional crimes.

Covert means were used, however, in political cases, and the FBI faced early criticism because of the 1919–1920 'Palmer Raids' (an illegal roundup and deportation of suspected radicals). Covert practices took on new life for the FBI in 1936 when President Franklin Roosevelt charged it with the investigation of Communist and Fascist groups in the United States. As part of its domestic intelligence goals, the FBI was given responsibility for combatting espionage, sabotage, and subversion.

In the postwar period the FBI's attention was focused primarily on the heavily infiltrated Communist party. As political unrest, social movements, and civil disorders increased during the 1960s, it broadened its domestic intelligence concerns to include the New Left, Black, Antiwar and Ku Klux Klan groups. Its activities went beyond gathering intelligence to counterintelligence actions. These activities drew on traditional techniques for dealing with vice and were aided by the Cold War ethos and the presence of former military intelligence agents in police departments.

Yet even with these developments, undercover policing was viewed ambivalently by the FBI and was not the major tactic it was to later become. While supporting an extensive system of civilian informers in political matters, particularly during the cold war, J. Edgar Hoover was hesitant to see the tactic used against organized crime and narcotics. It was simply too risky and the ever present danger of scandal and overzealousness might harm the image of the FBI.

Congressional hearings on the FBI's COINTEL program revealed an extensive program of surveillance, infiltration, disruption, and provocation, much of which was ethically questionable and some of which was clearly illegal.[39] Revelations of such abuses in a context of post-Watergate morality led to reforms and a significant reduction in the secret policing of politics by the 1970s.

As protest movements subsided, some of the covert resources that were developed or strengthened in the 1960s were redirected into conventional crime and a high priority was given to combatting drugs. The 1970s thus saw a greatly expanded federal crime control effort, including the pursuit of nonpolitical undercover activities on an unprecedented scale.

In the early 1970s, with the death of FBI director Hoover, undercover work changed significantly, expanding in scale and appearing in new forms. Covert tactics were adopted by new users and directed at new targets and new offenses. Applying ingenuity previously found only in fiction, law enforcement agents penetrated criminal and sometimes non-criminal milieus to an extraordinary degree. Even organized crime, long thought to be immune, was infiltrated. What

---

39. U.S. Congress, Senate (1976), *Final Report of the Senate Select Committee to Study Governmental Operations With Respect to Governmental Activities*, Washington.

was traditionally viewed as a relatively marginal and insignificant tactic used only by 'vice' and political 'red squads' became a cutting-edge tactic both locally and nationally.

This change is evident in comparing the 1936 words of leading FBI agent Melvin Purvis: 'no government operative may enter into illegal compacts or pursue illegal courses of action; it does not matter what desirable ends might be served,' with the words of another FBI agent four decades later: 'undercover operations have become the cutting edge of the FBI's effort to ferret out concealed criminal activity.'[40]

In 1973 there were approximately 30 FBI undercover investigations; by 1983 this had increased to almost four hundred and it has remained at about that level. Yet the issue goes beyond a mere increase in the prevalence of traditional forms. These have been supplemented by new and more complex forms and changing emphasis. We have seen an expansion from:

1. the lone undercover worker making individual arrests to highly coordinated team activities involving complex technology, organizational fronts and multiple arrests;
2. the traditional offer to buy contraband (the 'buy bust') to authorities offering to sell it (the 'sell bust');
3. using undercover means only against those who provide vice to using it against those who consume it as well;
4. using covert means primarily for organized vice or political groups, where there is no complainant other than the state, to using it for offenses where there is a complainant, as with relatively unorganized street crime;
5. using the tactic against lower status and marginal groups to its use against white collar offenders, including those in government and even in the criminal justice system;
6. using the tactic in a reactive way as part of an investigation of a crime that has already occurred, where apprehension is the goal, to using it in a proactive way in efforts to anticipate crimes not yet committed where deterrence and intelligence gathering emerge as important goals;
7. focusing on specific crimes to focusing on networks, organizations and individuals believed to be involved in crime;
8. asking the question 'is he corrupt?' to asking 'is he corruptible?';
9. agencies whose primary goal is criminal law enforcement to other agencies for whom this is a minor goal such as those concerned with agriculture, housing, customs, immigration, motor vehicles and forests and wildlife;
10. a relatively clear line separating public from private law enforcement to a blurring of this line with joint investigations and exchanges.[41]

---

40. M. Purvis, *op. cit.* and M. Riley, 'Confessions of a Harvard Trained G-Man,' *Harvard Business School Bulletin*, October 1982.
41. This theme is developed in G.T. Marx (1987), 'The Interdependence of Private and Public Police as Illustrated by Undercover Investigations,' in: C. Shearing and P. Stenning, eds., *Private Policing*, Newbury Park, Sage Publications, 172–193.

The United States has moved far in a short period of time with respect to the acceptance of secret police practices. What once occurred infrequently and was viewed with disdain as a characteristic of continental despotism is now routine administrative practice.

In its gradual embrace of covert practices over the past century, the U.S. has broken sharply with its previous attitudes. There has been a move away from the early British notion of a clearly identifiable citizen- or community-based police, where control agents do not have significant power beyond that of the ordinary citizen, toward the idea that police agents have much greater power than citizens and that policing is a function of the state, not the citizen. Elements of what Brodeur refers to as a 'high' or 'absorbent' political policing involving a comprehensive surveillance have been adopted and extended into nonpolitical spheres.[42] Fear of crime has partly replaced fear of a militaristic police. The secret agent, whether enshrined in film or television, literature or song, has become something of a cultural hero.

The above is related to changes in social organization, the nature of crime, the significant expansion of law and regulation, the relation of police to law and new surveillance technologies.

The broad increase in covert means over the past century is part of a gradual shift in the United States from a largely rural, unpoliced society to an industrial, policed society. The significant increase in the number and power of the police is part of a larger trend involving the growth of the modern bureaucratic state. In the United States it is ironically related to the growth of civil liberties and protections for citizens from police. As police have come to be more bound by the law, particularly after an arrest is made, they have given greater emphasis to the relatively unregulated (at least from a legal standpoint) use of covert means. In Europe, where police generally have greater powers to search, arrest and interrogate, these means are not as well developed.

More sophisticated covert practices are one part of an extension and redefinition of social control, which together with other practices, constitute what can be called the 'new surveillance.'[43] The rationalization of crime control that began in the nineteenth century has crossed a critical threshold involving changes in social organization and technology. Technology has enhanced the power of social control. The information-gathering powers of the state and of private organizations have torn asunder many of our conventional notions of privacy. Traditional lines between private and public and between the rights of the individual and the state are being redrawn.

One factor in a stronger national police presence is the weakening of boundaries between the states. The boundaries between nations have also weakened, giving rise to crime and social control on a global scale. This has led to increased social control across borders and the 'export' of many U.S. techniques, including covert surveillance.

---

42. J-P. Brodeur (1983), 'High Policing and Low Policing; Remarks on the Policing of Political Activities,' *Social Problems*, 30, 5, 507–520.
43. M. Foucault (1977), *Discipline and Punish*, New York, Pantheon; S. Cohen (1985), *Visions of Social Control*, Cambridge, Policy Press, and G.T. Marx, *Undercover*, ch. 10.

3. UNDERCOVER RETURNS TO EUROPE

This review suggests that in the course of the nineteenth century undercover policing became a normal policing strategy in Western Europe and gradually was adopted in North America as well. Yet the pendulum swings in two directions. Innovative United States' practices were then exported back to Europe.

European receptiveness was conditioned by events of the twentieth century. The experience and legacies of the Soviet Union and Nazi empire played an important role in the expansion and eventual de-legitimization of covert policing tactics.[44] Both regimes generalized and systematized the use of these tactics in all fields of policing, blurring the line between the criminal and the political and linking them to the unrestricted use of violence.

After the Second World War undercover policing was highly suspect and became a strategy to be used only in extreme cases, with the exception of the special cold war intelligence services.[45] Not surprisingly, in the 1960s and 1970s most of the European police forces were rather reluctant to take over the new undercover techniques propagated by the American federal police. When they did participate, they were generally silent about it. They were concerned that the sudden use of these techniques could create personal, organizational and legal problems and that the public would not be supportive.

Yet under active lobbying and the offer of resources from President Nixon's 'war against drugs,' significant changes occurred within the operational, training, equipment, organizational, and legal areas. Given its generally low visibility, the 'Americanization' of undercover policing in Western Europe faced only modest opposition. One can quibble over whether this is fundamentally new, or simply innovations on tactics that came from Europe. But what is clear is that covert means received new vigor and systematization, came to be used more aggressively and again became routine European police activity, migrating from politics to crime. This was not stopped by the sometimes serious problems of fitting the 'new' undercover policing into the old, as in Belgium.[46]

---

44. *See* Shelley's paper in this volume as far as the Soviet police system is concerned and G. Leggett (1981), *The Cheka; Lenin's Political Police*, Oxford, Oxford University Press. Important publications with respect to the SS-police apparatus are G.C. Browder (1990), *Foundations of the Nazi Police State; The Formation of Sipo and SD*, Lexington, Kentucky, University Press of Kentucky; R. Gellately (1990), *The Gestapo and German Society; Enforcing Racial Policy, 1933–1945*, Oxford, Clarendon Press; H. Krausnick and H-H. Wilhelm (1981), *Die Truppe des Weltanschauungskrieges; die Einsatzgruppen der Sicherheitspolizei und des SD, 1938–1942*, Stuttgart, Deutsche Verlags-Anstalt; J. Tuchel and R. Schattenfroh (1987), *Zentrale des Terrors*, Berlin, Siedler Verlag.
45. In the English literature the aversion to totalitarian policing is vividly expressed in the books of Ch. Reith (1943), *British Police and the Democratic Ideal*, London, Oxford University Press, and (1952), *The Blind Eye of History; A Study of the Origins of the Present Police Era*, London, Faber and Faber; and of E.K. Bramstedt (1945), *Dictatorship and Political Police; The Technique of Control by Fear*, New York.
46. *See* the book of Cyrille Fijnaut, quoted in note 1, and the chapter in this volume by Van Outrive and Cappelle.

Yet we also see convergence. As Ethan Nadelmann notes in his article in this volume, there has recently been some 'Europeanization' of American law enforcement (although independent of facilitative actions on their part).[47] U.S. Supreme Court decisions from the 1980s into the 1990s brought the U.S. closer to European practices for such things as a broader scope for warrantless searches, narrowing of the exclusionary rule, circumscribing the right to counsel, and lengthening the allowable time of detention. The cumulative consequence of developments on both sides of the Atlantic since the 1970s has been a convergence toward similar and greater police powers.

4. THE ARTICLES

The articles which follow go from general overviews on France, Germany, Canada, the Netherlands, Belgium, and Russia to specific case studies of using covert means against white collar crime and soccer hooliganism in Great Britain, against police themselves in the United States, for narcotics enforcement in Iceland and security concerns in Sweden, and as part of international investigations.

France

Dominique Monjardet and René Lévy offer a broad account of the varieties of undercover policing in France. Their article is a needed caution against the sweeping generalizations that we are prone to make in contrasting countries. They identify significant differences depending on the agency in question. One cannot speak of the French police, but must discuss distinctive units such as the *Police Nationale*, the *Gendarmerie Nationale*, and the Customs. Within these there are important divisions. For example, the *Police Nationale* involves the *Police Urbaine*, the *Compagnie Républicaines de Securité*, the *Police Judiciaire* and two types of political police – the *Renseignements Généraux* and the *Direction de la Sûreté du Territoire*, with different tasks, operations and formal controls.

Their article makes clear the need to go beyond a simple description of 'undercover tactics' to a consideration of the varied organizational, juridical and political contexts in which they are used. Depending on the setting the use of covert means can be secret or public, legal, illegal or in a legal vacuum and codified or uncodified. This suggests a rich variety of situations in which the tactic is used and works against any simple conclusions. Generalizations are best restricted to a particular type such as legal and codified vs. illegal and codified operations. The latter seems to be a distinctively French phenomenon and suggests a degree of moral pragmatism relatively alien to Anglo-American and Germanic traditions. The idea of bureaucratically regulating illegal actions and by so doing implicitly permitting them, strikes those not in the Latin tradition as curious to say the least. It is not that people do not often behave in

---

47. *See also* E.A. Nadelmann (1993), *Cops across Borders; The Internationalization of U.S. Criminal Law Enforcement*, Pennsylvania, The Pennsylvania State University Press, 196–197.

questionable ways to get a job done, as Everrett Hughes noted in his important article on 'Good People and Dirty Work'; it is the effort to control it via formal expectations that is notable.[48]

In France to a greater extent than in the Anglo-American tradition, covert means (and policing more generally) have been used in partisan political conflict by the central government. This alerts us to one of the greatest dangers of covert means – the constant temptation to use the tactic for political, rather than criminal enforcement ends. The issue is one of degree, since in a sense all rules are political and represent the interests and values of those in positions to make the rules. Yet there is a clear difference between using restricted police powers to enforce democratically arrived at criminal laws and evaluating the outcome in a public judicial setting, as against using unregulated or minimally regulated covert means to spy on, and harm one's political opponents.

Monjardet and Lévy go beyond descriptive classification (as important as that is in helping us see variation and understand what it is that needs to be explained), to identifying an important social and dialectical process involving police behavior and law.

When a new and attractive technique appears they see a move from the absence of both bureaucratic and legal rules, to internal rules (with the paradox of the apparent legitimation of a tactic that may be legally prohibited), to the eventual legalization of the tactic. Yet this binding in and formalizing may encroach on the police efforts to get the job done, which then leads to new unregulated techniques and shortcuts, with a continuation of the cycle. In such contexts of control and challenge (which apply to police and criminals as well), behavior is dynamic and to understand it we need a longer time frame and a focus on process, rather than a static account in one time period.

Germany

Heiner Busch and Albrecht Funk locate the expansion of covert means in Germany in recent decades within a broader context of social and legal changes in policing. They stress the organizational context of policing and changing patterns of criminal investigation. They organize their paper around three aspects involving undercover means as part of a more general change in criminal investigation based on 'preventive crime fighting,' and they consider the impact of this on police organization and on the relationship between police, prosecutors and courts.

They report that the English 'undercover means' is not adequate to describe the scope of preliminary investigations (*'Vorfeldermittlungen'*) or of preventive crime fighting (*'Verbrechensbekampfung'*). This helps us locate undercover means against a backdrop of broader social changes and in relation to other recent innovations in police techniques.

Police discretion with respect to covert means has increased as a result of a new emphasis on, and vague definitions of, 'organized crime' and 'preliminary crime fighting.' With this comes new resources for prevention and the creation of units specializing in covert means.

---

48. E. Hughes (1962), 'Good People and Dirty Work,' *Social Problems*, 10, 3–10.

Here, in Max Weber's terms, they identify a shift from formal-legal definitions of crime to definitions that are more utilitarian and ad hoc. The vagueness of the latter give police as administrative experts more flexibility. While this can be instrumental in responding to quickly changing events and new situations, there is a danger in lessened accountability and bureaucracies becoming a law unto themselves.

Canada

Jean-Paul Brodeur presents an overview of undercover work in Canada and considers the consequences of covert means with respect to their intended and actual outcomes. As in the United States there are many police agencies. In addition, things are complicated because of some blurring of the public-private line as a result of security units which are part of large companies owned by the government. Unlike the United States there is no police agency made up entirely of plainclothes investigators. Relative to most countries there is considerable public information available on Canadian intelligence and security agencies, although little is known about the use of undercover means in traditional criminal matters.

Brodeur notes that while Canada has a reputation as being a liberal country, in absolute terms it has more than twenty times the amount of wire-tapping found in the United States, at least as judged by official statistics. Canada also appears to have proportionally less undercover investigations than the United States. It is possible that the much greater reliance on wire-tapping is a functional alternative making reliance on undercover investigations seem less necessary.

Brodeur suggests a distinction between undercover policing which is personalistic and dynamic, as with a property sting, and that which is more passive and based largely on wire-tapping and video-taping and other forms of intelligence gathering.

When actions are carried out in secret in environments which can only be partially known and controlled, surprises are constantly present. Brodeur notes the usefulness of the distinction between the intended and unintended consequences of undercover work, but argues that it does not go far enough. Intention can be differentiated into premeditation, cognizance and purposiveness. In attending to the frequent conflict between the formal and informal aspects of organizations, Brodeur offers a helpful analytic framework for considering these varied consequences based on two variables – whether the outcome was intended or not and whether it is desirable or not. This is an important, if opaque, area which forces us to confront questions such as 'how do we determine intentions?' and 'how do we determine if outcomes are undesirable or desirable?'

In an example of the kind of analysis that independent scholars are well situated to make, but not always well disposed to undertake, he argues that publicly undesirable consequences may nonetheless be intended as formal law enforcement policy. He suggests the concept of entailed consequence (one that is short of, or goes beyond that which is intended), as a means of dealing with this. He notes that police behavior (unlike that of criminals) tends to be judged on the basis of motives, not outcomes. In a provocative conclusion he argues for a symmetry in which if we deny to criminals the argument of a necessary evil, we ought also to consider denying it to authorities.

The Netherlands

Peter Klerks draws on interviews and documents to offer a detailed description of four aspects of covert policing: the Criminal Intelligence Department, police infiltration, surveillance teams and informant handling. The Netherlands are particularly interesting in that the new surveillance appears to have been taken further here than in the rest of Europe. This partly results from strong encouragement by the United States which in the 1970s identified the Netherlands as the major European distribution point for Asian heroin. A special national undercover bureau was created in 1987 and about 100 operations a year against money laundering, and weapons and drug trafficking occur. There are 20 special surveillance teams and new CID interregional serious-crime teams that for security reasons operate in isolation from the rest of the force. The Parliament has approved undercover guidelines involving principles of proportionality and subsidiarity. This occurs in a context of relative police openness more reminiscent of the United States than of Europe.

As elsewhere anticipatory techno-policing relies on the collection and analysis of intelligence data for strategic and tactical purposes.[49] As in the German case, there is an emphasis on prevention and on understanding networks and organizations. There is a shift from evidence gathering to intelligence gathering. Much of this occurs before a formal preliminary inquiry. As such police have exceptional discretion.

This approach is quite different from the traditional conviction-oriented methods that rely so heavily on citizen reporting as the main factor for initiating an investigation. To rely exclusively on citizen mobilization in our complex world is clearly unwise and the changes in policing witnessed in recent decades are a response to this, yet such mobilization at least involves a type of democratic accountability and lessens the chance of one kind of official abuse – prejudicial or self-serving targeting.

Klerks confronts the central dilemma and balancing issue of covert means in a democratic society – how to respond effectively to sophisticated violators while at the same time retaining police accountability, civil liberties and citizen confidence.

The combination of public confidence in police, lenient judges and concern over serious organized crime creates an optimal climate for covert policing. Yet Klerks notes the dangers in this such as lack of accountability to the law, threats of corruption, and damaging effects on the agent. The gradual merging of two aspects of internal security – policing and national security – falls between the traditional controls of police management and the judiciary on the one hand,

---

49. On techno-policing for example *see* D. Nogala, 'The Future Role of Technology in Policing,' in: J.P. Brodeur, ed., *Comparisons in Policing: An International Perspective* (forthcoming) and G.T. Marx (1995), 'The Engineering of Social Control; The Search for the Silver Bullet,' in: J. Hagan, ed., *Crime and Inequality,* Stanford, Stanford University Press, 225–246

and the oversight apparatus that monitors security and intelligence services on the other. Accounts of covert police activity rarely enter the courtroom. Klerks argues that in the long run these dangers can be lessened and police effectiveness might even increase, if the new secretive sections were matched by new forms of accountability to parliamentary and judicial bodies.

Belgium

Lode Van Outrive and Jan Cappelle describe the recent Belgian experience with undercover policing. As in the Netherlands and Germany, they note a sharp increase in the practice and changes in Belgium law and policy as a result of U.S. influence. They raise issues which will become increasingly important as cross-border social control gains in influence, particularly among nations with unequal power.

They offer examples from Belgian history involving the state security's 'high police' of Fouché. In Belgium there is the common distinction between the state civil intelligence agency (the political 'high police') and the police service. As a control, the former was deprived of judicial authority, but it did adopt the French tradition of covert tactics.

While there were occasional uses of such means by criminal police, since the French revolution there has been resistance to this. As in England the idea of undercover implied the distasteful *agent provocateur*. Yet under U.S. pressure, this was to change in the early 1970s, as new elite units were established and laws and practices were gradually changed.

The importation back to Europe resulted in innovations. Unlike in the United States, the undercover agent involved in buying or selling drugs was himself guilty of a crime. To avoid such complicity, a 'pseudo-buy' tactic was used in which, after arranging to participate, the agent exits at the last minute and police then swoop down and seize drugs. The court record may make no reference to the role of the agent.

Over several decades the courts came to be more approving of American methods. As in several other European countries principles of proportionality (the more serious the offense the farther police can go) and subsidiarity (the unavailability of lesser means) guide the use of covert tactics. The pseudo-buy, the test-buy, accompanied shipment, short-term infiltration and privacy destructive observations are permitted, although long-term, deep-cover operations are not. Penalties for drug dealing were increased, making it easier to gain the covert cooperation of suspects in subsequent transactions. Police are permitted to conceal the name of the informer in the interest of crime control, although they are to report to the court in general how they gained their information. Ironically these secret tactics are governed by secret directives not subject to parliamentary approval or oversight.

But this transference has not been without problems. Two of the leading figures in the use of covert means for crime control have been arrested on corruption charges. They were among an elite group trained in covert means by the DEA in the 1970s. The cycle of scandal and reform in which misbehavior by police becomes public, triggering a clamor for reform, is well known to students of police.[50] This leads to name changes and organizational and personnel shifts, but generally not to a fundamental questioning of the tactic that produced the problem. What Peter Manning (1994) uncharitably refers to as the 'management conceit' assumes that organizational tinkering will solve the problem.[51] What is seen to be flawed is not the means, but the context in which it is used.

Their article implicitly raises concerns over the danger of a new police colonialism which may accompany cross-border social control. They are concerned that the incorporation of American anticipatory tactics into the Belgian system has occurred without sufficient regard for differences between the U.S. and Belgium societies and criminal justice systems.

What is best for the more powerful nation exporting police techniques may not be best for the importer. For example, they note that in the U.S. the emphasis was on combatting cocaine, while heroin traffic from Pakistan and Afghanistan was given a lower priority. However, Belgium's problem with addiction centered almost exclusively on heroin.

Soviet Union

Louise Shelley considers covert means in the former Soviet Union and recent changes in its Russian aftermath. The former U.S.S.R. is an ideal example of the type of society those concerned about the risks of undercover means seek to avoid. She argues that an ideology which justified state intervention in daily life together with the lack of an inhibitory legal framework, led to the penetration of all sectors of Soviet life by the state. Policing was based on a comprehensive world view which mandated control of all aspects of society. The state's secret intrusion into personal, social, economic and political life received unqualified ideological justification. This fits perfectly with the undercover technique's omnivorous, panoptic, anticipatory appetite for information.

Unlike in the West, secret police were not considered a necessary evil challenging basic societal values, but an essential and unambiguous tool. The concept of citizenship with the idea of rights for individuals against the state was non-existent. Laws were designed to protect the state against the individual, not the reverse. There was no concept of privacy as we understand it. Efficiency (defined as serving the ends of those in power), not the rule of law, was the operative standard. Duplicity was a central feature of the relationship between the state and the citizen and the latter's complicity with the security forces was common. The word undercover (with its connotation of skulduggery) does not exist in Russian and operational techniques for controlling politics and crime were not subject to close scrutiny. Given this legacy, the transition to democratic controls of covert means in the new Russian state has been slow. While laws have been passed regarding electronic surveillance and covert means, adequate enforcement mechanisms are absent.

---

50. L. Sherman (1978), *Scandal and Reform*, Berkeley, University of California Press.
51. P. Manning (1994), 'Politics and Metaphors in Police Studies,' *Sociological Forum*, 9, 4, 673–680.

The Soviets took over the Tsarist tradition of undercover work which, as on the Continent, had long been used successfully against political dissidents. In addition, the line between the political and criminal was much more blurred than in the West. Unlike the autocratic states of Europe in which police nonetheless became in principle, and to a significant degree in practice, accountable to legal norms and bureaucratic practices, in the Soviet Union the ultimate power was the Party. In the West the use of informers and other covert means exists along with basic civil liberties (if often uneasily). That was hardly the case in the Soviet Union in which the concept of police accountability to the citizens or the state was lacking. This calls for a Hobbesian or Machiavellian model of social control in which bureaucracy and law are subordinated to an ideology mandating maximum control of society. This contrasts with the more familiar modern model suggested by Weber.

The degree of citizen mobilization via covert means greatly exceeded that in the West. The emphasis was on individual informants rather than on technology (not out of principle, but through lack of availability). This offers a reminder that repressive regimes are not caused by high technology, nor is the latter necessary for them. Yet as the technology becomes more available, cheaper and easier to use, it will become more commonplace and enhance the surveillance capability of the state, without necessarily reducing reliance on humans. Shelley also notes that the extensive repression and thorough infiltration of daily life during the Stalin years meant that there was less need for the regular police to employ high levels of violence. Shelley suggests that the strong reliance on covert means inhibited the development of more open police detection techniques. This serves to qualify any too easy generalizations about the necessary links between use of covert means and technology and the development of overt and covert means in tandem. There are relations but they are complicated and vary depending on the circumstances.

United Kingdom

Gary Armstrong and Dick Hobbs consider police response to soccer hooliganism. They argue that politicians and the media helped create a moral panic which justified the creation of specialized police surveillance units directed against a marginal group. The low status of the group made possible police actions that would not have been publicly supported against other groups such as labor unions.

They also note how covert means lend themselves well to the dramatization of the fight against crime and a struggle between good and evil. Heroic police facing great peril is well suited to mass media glorifications.

They illustrate some of the potential dangers of a secret police interacting with presumed culprits on their own turf such as the danger of: creating (or lying about the appearance of) the very phenomena they are charged with stopping; of falsifying records; of police becoming what they pretend to be and of being arrested themselves; and of cases being rejected by the courts because of the vagueness of conspiracy charges or because police step over the line. Of course these don't occur to the same degree or in the same places. The empirical research task is to understand the varied consequences of covert means.

INTRODUCTION: THE NORMALIZATION OF UNDERCOVER POLICING

In 1985 Scotland Yard's Public Order Branch began undercover operations directed at soccer hooligans. In 1990 a National Football Intelligence Unit was created linking data from across the U.K. The information it gathered was computerized and among other data includes profiles of persons 'known to keep the company of hooligans.' An anonymous 'Hooligan Hotline' was also created. This serves to normalize the tactic and, once institutionalized, makes it easier for it to spread to other targets.

Their case study also has implications for social control across borders. Beyond infiltrators, British detectives known as 'spotters' traveled with fans to the Continent to assist local police. In Italy the identification and expulsion of British fans appears legally very questionable.

Michael Levi considers some constraints on covert policing in the United Kingdom and offers an overview of the legal rules. There is no general defense of entrapment the way there is in the United States and suspects in a sting can be questioned about an offense absent a caution. However, unlike in the United States, entrappers may be prosecuted as accomplices. One might think that covert means in the United Kingdom would have spread more rapidly and be closer to those in the United States than on the Continent, but that appears not to be the case.

Given the cultural similarities, it is interesting that the development and spread of American covert means seem to have had a lesser impact in the United Kingdom than on the Continent. While United Kingdom law generally tolerates such work, beyond drugs, terrorism, intelligence gathering and specialized instances such as contract murders, soccer hooliganism or the occasional property sting, relatively little undercover work occurs. Michael Levi suggests three reasons for this: 1) cultural, 2) cost and 3) legal uncertainty.

It appears that to a much greater extent than on the Continent senior police managers are inhibited in their use of covert means by concern over potential criticism from politicians and the mass media that they are behaving in an unfair, 'Un-British' fashion and acting as provocateurs and undermining public confidence in a hallowed British institution.

Levi identifies several other unstudied areas where covert means are used. The Post Office Investigation Department, for example, infiltrates offices in order to observe the activities of postal workers. HM Customs and Excise agency uses covert means in looking for Value-Added Tax fraud. These tend to be passive and short-term, rather than the long-term, deep-cover operations seen in the United States. He also notes that covert white-collar operations have been carried out by private detectives such as during takeover battles, in spying on rivals, in random tests of employees and in product counterfeiting.

The fact that information must be disclosed to the defense about police actions may create a pressure to 'launder' such information, as on the Continent. Police may prefer not to call an informant and may offer inaccurate information regarding how they came to suspect the accused person.

United States

The American President James Madison has written: 'you must first enable the government to control the governed; and in the next place, oblige it to control itself.' This is part of a broader problem in which organizations must control both their external and internal environments. Undercover means offer a powerful means for doing both.

The expansion of undercover means in the United States has not been restricted just to 'the usual suspects' (the target of a roundup in the film Casablanca), or to powerless and known public enemies. Gary T. Marx offers a case study of undercover tactics turned inward against the most (from a cynical view of politics as a game of mutual back-scratching and intimidation) unlikely of targets. He gives a number of examples of the tactic used to find corruption among police, prison officials, prosecutors, defense attorneys and even judges and legislators.

He notes that the civil rights movement helped call attention to the inequality in law enforcement that exists when government focuses only on the violations of the poor, while ignoring the rich and powerful. Covert means are ideal for the discovery and documentation of corruption (often a cooperative white collar crime with the absence of a complainant) and one in which a citizen making a claim against authorities may have difficulty being believed.

While the lack of a system of lateral entry in the United States might be thought to work against strong internal control, this is compensated for by the diversity of law enforcement agencies. The United States with its federal, decentralized system involving multiple, competing law enforcement agencies is more likely to see such efforts than is the case with the generally more homogeneous and monolithic police agencies of Europe.

That there is rich irony in using undemocratic means to protect democracy is apparent. The very power of the tactic can also be its undoing. Marx notes a number of the risks that such use entails and the greater difficulties that are present when the tactic is turned inward.

Iceland

Helgi Gunnlaugsson and John Galliher write on the drug police of Iceland, a small country of 250,000 that has an exceptionally low crime rate and few of the factors that have pushed larger countries into the use of sophisticated covert means. Yet Iceland has a drug police. They note that although drug use in Scandinavia has been decreasing since the early 1970s, narcotics enforcement has expanded. Their story partly reflects outside pressure and role models and fear. A culture that until recently supported a prohibition on beer can easily be upset by fear of drugs. Their account also illustrates the link between the activities of control agents and the kinds of deviance that is processed. It is likely that if the drug police of Iceland were suddenly to expand significantly in size, the number of persons arrested for drug offenses would expand correspondingly. Not only would police be looking harder in order to be productive, this would likely be accompanied by an ever lower tolerance for any drug infractions, as the moral boundaries became more constricted. Events that in the past might have been ignored as trivial would become officially processed. Police might also increase the pressure on informants to produce cases and covertly offer opportunities to easily tempted persons, who would not commit a drug offense were they not given the chance to do this by police.

INTRODUCTION: THE NORMALIZATION OF UNDERCOVER POLICING

In spite of its isolation, Iceland is drawn into an international web of markets and culture. This affects the practices of police (the DEA trained Iceland's narcotics unit) and the supply and demand for contraband. In responding to a presumed threat before the problem becomes widespread, we again see the logic of prevention so often drawn upon in the use of anticipatory covert means.

Sweden

Dennis Töllborg offers a careful description of the Swedish security police's organization and tasks. As in other countries there is a trend toward the centralization and systematization of information in various police search registers. The work of the security police involves processing and analyzing information found in the registers. By law police are permitted to collect all information needed to prevent or disclose crime, but this is not to be based solely on the expression of opinion. Among the covert means of information collection he considers are searches, wire-tapping and letter control, bugging and enlisting, and crime provocation.

There are of course risks with using such tactics, particularly with the greater leeway often allowed for state security cases. Supposed political threats can serve as the reason for investigating persons of interest to authorities who can not otherwise be investigated. There are dangers of provocation and of finding even the innocent guilty in order to justify use of a risky and expensive tactic. The innocent may be harmed as a result and the integrity of the police undermined. The presumption may be that persons subject to such severe means must be guilty, or else they would not have been treated in such an extraordinary fashion.

Töllborg also notes the problems of information overload and the reliability of information – particularly when it must be translated from a foreign language by translators who themselves may be viewed suspiciously.

There is the danger that political groups subject to intensive surveillance may be driven underground and may in fact become the subversives of the initial police vision. It is exactly this danger that an open society seeks to avoid. It is ironic that such a system may create the very security problems it is intended to protect against and 'this puts democracy at risk of committing suicide in fear of death.'

Töllborg discusses several scandals involving high ranking police officials accused of illegal listening and the smuggling in of bugging equipment. While he notes various controls around covert means, he raises classical issues about effectiveness when the oversight is internal or the overseers are unduly impressed with the importance of the police job. Those charged with keeping police accountable often don't want to look too closely for fear of damaging national security or crime control, or for fear of embarrassing police and the state. Reminiscent of the three monkeys avoiding knowledge of evil, Töllborg reports a desire on the part of some of those responsible for oversight to not 'know too much' when the 'security of the nation' is involved.

This involves questions of means and ends. The overwhelming importance of the goal may mean that 'it might not always be possible to maintain normal standards.' Implicit here is the idea that the end justifies the means. This of course runs contrary to the very basis of the constitutional state.

DEA and IRS

Our final two articles consider interaction between countries rather than practices within a country. The international character of violations involving borders (such as the importing and exporting of contraband and international financial dealings) means that customs and drug enforcement agencies would be more involved in international efforts than agencies concerned with purely domestic violations. Yet in operating beyond national borders many new issues appear.

Ethan Nadelmann discusses the activities of the United States Drug Enforcement Agency in Europe. He argues that there has been an 'Americanization' of European drug enforcement (and a reciprocal, although weaker move the other way). He argues that the United States Drug Enforcement Agency behaves much like a large private transnational organization. Rather than working towards the freedom to carry out its own drug enforcement operations abroad, it sought to enhance the enforcement capability of foreign countries. Emphasis was placed on influencing its foreign environment and shaping the institutions it deals with. The changes in Europe Nadelmann notes result from active lobbying, the provision of incentives and resources, and from the provision of a model.

Nadelmann argues that between the late 1960s and the late 1980s three broad changes took place. First, most European nations created specialized drug enforcement squads and prosecutors who emphasized such cases. There were also operational changes such as the 'buy and bust,' more extensive covert operations and electronic surveillance, the controlled delivery of contraband, and efforts to turn drug dealers into police informants. A final change involved the gradual legalization by both courts and legislatures of many of these practices.

As several of the earlier articles note, these changes are very controversial and the issues have hardly been resolved. For example, in many European countries police were not permitted to engage in crimes on behalf of law enforcement the way they were in the United States. This would appear to preclude many forms of undercover activity. Yet innovations have appeared to get around this. As noted above, rather than actually carrying out the direct purchase of drugs, the undercover agent disappears at the last minute and uniformed police enter and seize contraband. This charade often resulted in police lying in court about what actually happened. Not only did these practices raise fears of *agents provocateurs*, but they were seen to reflect the priorities of the United States rather than the host countries.

While Nadelmann speaks in general terms, as a careful observer, he also notes variation. Thus, these changes with respect to the use of covert means for criminal, rather than national security concerns, have been most characteristic of Germany, the Netherlands and Belgium, while there has been greater resistance in Italy, France and Spain. This likely represents cultural differences between the Mediterranean and Northern Europe as well as differences in the perceived seriousness of drug problems in the country.

INTRODUCTION: THE NORMALIZATION OF UNDERCOVER POLICING

Nikos Passas and Richard Groskin focus directly on an aspect only hinted at in the other papers – undercover investigations that literally cross borders. Little is known about the social structures and processes involved in law enforcement across international borders. Current social, economic, and technical changes are weakening, blurring or eliminating legal, spacial and temporal borders. In an increasingly interdependent world, the cross-national aspects of rule enforcement and violation offer a rich field for exploration.[52]

Passas and Groskin draw inferences about social control across borders from two controversial cases involving the laundering of drug proceeds and illegal arms trafficking. They note how the increased ease of movement of persons, capital and goods and services across borders has facilitated the internationalization of trade and along with this, the increased internationalization of crime. The demands of new international markets are met in both legitimate and illegitimate ways. In response there has been an increase in the internationalization of control.

In their paper they contrast domestic with international investigations and note the complicating issues and risks present with the latter. There is a general absence of international structures and principles for guiding such investigations, even among closely allied countries. Problems and conflicts may emerge as a result of differences in laws and legal culture (e.g., a crime in one country may not be a crime in another), methods and procedures; cultural conflicts and misunderstandings; logistical needs for resources and protection in foreign, often distant settings; differences in the level of supervision, accountability and integrity and in criteria for evaluation; differences in the relations and location of control agencies to government; difficulties of coordination both within and between countries; disagreements about when a case should be terminated and where it should be prosecuted; conflicts with other law enforcement agencies and with intelligence agencies; and conflicts between the goals of law enforcement and foreign policy and diplomacy. When the investigations are of a covert nature additional problems are present. Cooperative and (the much rarer) truly joint, multi-national investigations are means by which United States covert practices diffuse internationally.

In the final chapters Gary T. Marx offers some general ideas that can help order the rich variety seen in the preceding articles. His concern is with both policy and social research. Drawing from his book *Undercover*, he (1) suggests some criteria to use in considering whether or not the tactic is justified, (2) identifies some assumptions about the empirical world that should be met before the tactic is used, (3) notes some types of undercover operations and some dimensions along which they may vary and (4) notes some tensions that accompany even the most clearly and carefully developed policies. He then considers some implications for the comparative understanding of social control, in particular in so far as this involves the new surveillance, and he identifies issues for future research.

---

52. G.T. Marx (1993), 'On Policing Across National Borders,' *Onati Proceedings in Law*, 14, 77–88.

Dominique Monjardet*
and René Lévy**

Undercover Policing in France: Elements for Description and Analysis

1. INTRODUCTION

The eighteenth-century memorialist, Louis-Sébastian Mercier, tells us in his *Tableaux de Paris* that 'whenever two citizens start whispering, a third comes sneaking around to hear what they are saying' (quoted by Chassaigne, 1975, 244). And Rowan and Mayne, the first commissioners of London's New Police, were notoriously anxious to avoid anything that might lay their institution open to comparison with the 'continental' (read: French) system, abhorred by their countrymen (Reiner, 1985, 58; Emsley, 1987, 190).

In fact, due to a precociously centralized and centralizing state, the police was a creature of the reigning power, first and foremost a political body in the form of a political police: the Lieutenants general, then Fouché and his machine comprised mainly of informers, stool pigeons and *agents provocateurs* of every stripe. They left their stamp on the popular imagination, and not only on that of the nineteenth-century English gentry. Similarly, Vidocq became famous as the symbol of a movement that built a police force out of gangsters, on the pretext that they made the best underworld agents. The French police acquired a thoroughly bad reputation, illustrated by the reaction, at the end of the nineteenth century, of an army officer: 'I don't want junior officers of the 10th Chasseurs to have anything to do with the police, who are commonly chosen from the dregs of the population' (Forestier, 1983, 42).

Despite codification, selection, training and professionalization, which have brought the French and the English police closer together, the French police has retained certain distinctive features, the importance of which should not be underestimated.

---

* *Directeur de recherche* at the C.N.R.S. 'Travail et Mobilité' (C.N.R.S. and Université Paris X-Nanterre).
** *Chargé de recherche* at the C.N.R.S. Centre de Recherches Sociologiques sur le Droit et les Institutions Pénales (C.N.R.S. and Ministère de la Justice).
  The authors wish to thank Gary T. Marx, Cyrille Fijnaut, Philippe Robert, Frédéric Ocqueteau and Renée Zauberman for commenting on an earlier draft of this article.

The French police is a state police (and a highly centralized state at that), entirely under the command of the executive and, while the judicial policing it does is theoretically monitored by judicial agencies, the police force as a whole answers neither to parliament nor to local elected officials. Moreover, certain sections of the police comprise an explicitly political arm: the *Service des Renseignements Généraux* (RG), which is an intelligence service, and the *Direction de la Sécurité du Territoire* (DST), secret services whose activities are formally restricted to counter-espionage but who, because of the clandestine nature of their work and because they are under the exclusive control of the Interior Ministry, can intervene *ad libitum* in the internal politics of the country (Levergeois, 1978).

In the same context, the notion of 'undercover police tactics' also has an entirely different history in England and France. Far from being some modern invention, it is an age-old French tradition. One might even maintain that policing was entirely 'undercover' before it became organized and came out into the open as part of the public administration, employing for the most part uniformed functionaries.

It is not our intent, however, to begin with a formal definition of undercover policing. Rather, we will try to describe the tactics as they are employed in the various French police services, returning only at the end of our examination to the twofold question raised by the very notion of undercover policing: Is an exhaustive definition possible? Are these entirely separate tactics or only a special instance of police practices in general?

One cannot speak of *the* French police; the notion must be broken down into several branches. The first basic distinction splits the police into two major forces: the *Gendarmerie Nationale*, which is part of the armed forces and reports to the Defense Ministry, and the *Police Nationale*, made up of civil servants and organized into one *Direction*, or large department, of the Interior Ministry. This difference in status has some important consequences. We will look first at the National Police, which itself is a single organization in appearance only. Then we will cover more rapidly the National Gendarmerie. Finally, we will see a third institution which has received too little attention in policing studies, but whose recent activities have revealed police-like ambitions: the Customs.[1]

2. THE NATIONAL POLICE

Although the National Police is centralized and directed from the top, this does not mean that it is homogeneous: its some 125,000 members are spread among very different services that have distinct targets or functions. While members of the force rotate to a certain extent through a number of services in the course of their career (taking with them the customs and practices of the former department, a matter to which we will return), these different services are

---

1. An overview of all the French intelligence services as well as information on a number of recent 'affairs' can be found in Guisnel and Violet (1988).

guided by equally different logics. Because of this, a general notion such as 'undercover tactics' does not apply across the board, but must be considered separately for each service.

The National Police can be represented by a flow chart. But we have chosen to take a more sociological approach; we will attempt to identify each of the subunits by its official target and the corresponding rules it plays by. The term 'game rules' designates both the rules prescribed in the regulations and the set of customary practices. The rules are not the same for maintaining order, policing drug traffic or counterespionage. Likewise, customary practices may at times be seen as legitimate and openly stated to be so, at times simply tolerated or even kept secret; they may be strictly legal or illegal, or be employed in a 'legal vacuum.' It is in the light of these separate sets of rules that the notion of 'undercover tactics' takes on meaning.

Our approach breaks the National Police into four major divisions (which, it must be kept in mind, are under a single command: the Directorate General of the National Police, a highly political position filled by government appointment upon decision of the *Conseil des Ministres*, or Cabinet. The Director General works directly and constantly with the Interior Minister).

2.1. The Police Urbaine

The first division, which accounts for 70 per cent of the total National Police, is the *Police Urbaine*. Made up in the main of uniformed officers, spread throughout France (principally in towns of over 10,000 inhabitants), this is the 'everyday police,' which staffs the commissariats and police stations, walks the beat, drives patrol, maintains public order in towns and cities. Its officers police traffic, outdoor markets, the sale of alcoholic beverages and petty crime, and provide emergency aid. Its far-flung and to some extent unlimited tasks are largely conditioned by public demand, with the exception of duties such as guarding public monuments, transporting prisoners and policing sporting events. As a public service available night and day, it can be called at any time for any reason. Its activity is generally visible, its members work for the most part in uniform, in marked vehicles and in a primarily preventive or dissuasive role. Accordingly, the notion of 'undercover tactics,' does not make much sense here: they are probably little used except by overzealous officers. This does not mean that the Urban Police always operates within the law, however; viz. brutality (not unusual), or corruption (rarer), or even out-and-out criminal behavior; but these are clearly cases of deviancy and are usually punished when discovered.

From the standpoint of Urban Police practices, the problem is not 'undercover tactics,' but real and effective hierarchical control within the force. This branch of the police has what is probably the most extensive and explicit set of internal regulations and codes, but the number of texts in no way implies that their application is closely monitored. For many and complex reasons having to do with both the nature of the task (variety, unpredictability, uniqueness) and hierarchical organization, police on the beat and first-line supervisors enjoy a high degree of autonomy in their work; their superiors oversee operations from a distance and exercise sporadic and for the most part purely formal command over everyday operations.[2] More exactly, supervision oscillates between picky formal control (written reports on every intervention, records of all activities) and a real on-the-spot supervision that is very relaxed. We thus see a highly uneven system of sanctions bearing essentially on internal administrative rules and regulations, while what the French call *'bavures'* (cases of misconduct) in dealings with the public are often 'covered up' by superior officers. The latter are not overly eager to lessen the actual autonomy of their subordinates by imposing sanctions (Monjardet, 1985).

2.2. Compagnies Républicaines de Sécurité

The uniformed mobile police units specializing in the 'maintenance of public order' are the largest branch of the National Police. The bulk of this branch is comprised of 61 squads of *Compagnies Républicaines de Sécurité* (the French riot police), known as 'the CRS.' To these must be added a few permanent special detachments or squads of Urban Police, making a total of some 15,000 agents who, at least in principle, act in uniform and as a unit. Except when work is light and reinforcements are loaned to the Urban Police, their task is almost exclusively the maintenance of order (MO). This activity covers two areas:

- maintaining order at major public events (festivals, sporting events, rock concerts, etc.);
- maintaining order *stricto sensu*, i.e. crowd control and, if need be, dispersing and repressing political or social street demonstrations.

In France this latter activity has two faces. One visible, made to impress, which is the use of police *force*, is seen in the deployment and manoeuvring of powerfully equipped and specially trained units. As the primary goal is to intimidate and dissuade, emphasis is placed on the visibility of a force that looks for all the world like an army on the march. But maintaining order can wear and often has worn another face, when the goal is not only to control a crowd, but to punish demonstrators, and to discredit the organizers and the cause they are supporting. The history of the maintenance of order in France is replete with 'undercover' resources and tactics, illustrating the thousand-and-one ways of infiltrating demonstrations with plainclothes police used as informers, provocateurs and hooligans, whose instructions run from identifying and neutralizing the 'leaders' to directly provoking the police, looting stores, burning cars, etc.

While France can boast nothing as exemplary and dramatic as the case of the priest Gapone leading the St. Petersburg demonstrators to slaughter, the French 1970s provide numerous examples of street demonstrations degenerating into rioting and looting due to police provocateurs in disguise – young recruits from

---

2. Superior officers rarely come from the rank and file; the majority come from specific lateral recruitment. Moreover, they are present only during the day.

police academies momentarily cast as students or hoodlums, or ideologically motivated experts recruited from special sections of the RG (Sarrazin, 1974; Picant, 1979; Hamon and Marchand, 1984; Brunet, 1990; Favre, 1990). The only thing these had in common with the police activities was the workforce used, and even this could overspill the boundaries of the police to encompass private surveillance companies, for instance (Vaujour, 1990, 35). We are dealing here with a direct balance of political powers and even open class warfare, which does not bother with such trifles as legality or legitimacy. Once the Interior Minister judges that any sign of unrest in the streets is a challenge to the state and that the power in place, the institutions and the government are directly threatened by what he now designates as 'subversive activities,' anything goes, all means are effectively used and most often explicitly justified (Marcellin, 1978).[3]

And yet these tactics also had some unexpected consequences. While repeated violent demonstrations provided the police with an opportunity for a show of force, they also attested to their inability to predict or prevent trouble. The disruption caused by the circulation and deployment of large contingents of police exasperated the public. Finally, the priority given to the maintenance of order cut into the resources allotted to the fighting of crime, which seemed at the same time to be rising steeply. As a result we saw an increasingly low esteem for the police on the part of the public and a feeling among many police that their use as mercenaries was widening the breach between the police and the population at large. There followed a series of sharp debates within the police, the voicing of the first objections to government policy, growing politicization and, consequently, polarization within the force.

The massive use of tactics which, if they were to be effective, demanded a force that was dedicated, homogeneous and consenting, resulted in accentuating internal divisions and conflicts, and thus in weakening the police: 'Police in Shreds,' read one headline (Sarrazin, 1974). The lesson took a long time to learn. Such dubious tactics still resurface from time to time in the course of some law-and-order operation deemed vital by and for those in power. Yet since the end of the 1970s one can no longer speak of their generalized use. The last case in which the whole panoply of tactics was employed (the student demonstrations of November-December 1986) showed that public opinion and major police unions alike were against such tactics, which often backfired. By trying to shift its conflict with the student movement into the arena of public order, the government brought down a resounding political defeat marked by the withdrawal of a controversial draft law and the resignation of one minister.[4]

In short: here 'undercover police tactics' are defined not so much by a logic of policing (even from the standpoint of techniques of order-maintenance) as by

---

3. An expression that, in the broad definition of the term used by the Minister of the Interior, R. Marcellin, from 1968 to 1974, encompasses everything from violent political street demonstrations to union-sponsored marches for pay increases.
4. For once two parliamentary investigation commissions were formed; while they did not clearly allocate responsibilities, they at least produced documentation of a high quality (Monjardet, 1990).

the directly political use of police resources within a well-defined area, that of a type of political conflict in which the aim is to paint the opponent as a criminal.

2.3. The Political Police

The aim of the third branch of the National Police, the political police, is different again. This arm is an intelligence service, comprised of, on the one hand, the *Renseignements Généraux* (RG) and, on the other, the *Direction de la Sûreté du Territoire* (DST).

2.3.1. The Renseignements Généraux

The Director of the *Renseignements Généraux*, or RG, commands 3,600 functionaries (300 in the Central Directorate, 650 at the Paris Police Prefecture and the rest posted around the other departments of the country).

The RG's main mission is entirely open and above board: 'the service is an intelligence agency at the disposal of the entire government for everything concerning the political, social, economic and financial activities of the country' (Aubert and Petit, 1981, 144). The primary task of the members of the RG, which form a nationwide network (the service is descended from the railroad police), is to compile press reviews, keep tabs on public opinion (especially in periods leading up to an election), attend public meetings and congresses of all kinds, keep an ear tuned to public reactions to various government projects, in sum, to keep a thumb on the nation's pulse and to draft memoranda to the prefects and the central government.

Certain specifications of this task involve more direct policing: for instance, the prefect depends on the RG to keep him informed about the likely reactions of union leaders and workers in a factory planning lay-offs in order to forestall, if need be, occupation of the factory floor or to call in the necessary police forces if a 'hardline' demonstration seems imminent. From collecting public information that actually exists, it is easy to slip gradually into collecting less obvious information and to digging for hidden information, which implies disguising the nature of the inquiry and the use of a battery of undercover tactics: wire-tapping, electronic surveillance, spies, informers, infiltration: the gathering of information becomes internal espionage.

There seem to be two identifiable logics behind the use of such tactics. One flows from the needs of policing, as, for example, in the case of impending factory lay-offs; information is gathered with an aim to plan for the possible intervention of other police forces in the context of their normal activities: in this instance, to prepare the intervention of riot police.

More frequently, the aim is to provide judicial police agencies with information that will give their intervention legal justification. In effect, the *Renseignements Généraux* have generally lacked the power to repress or coerce: in principle, members of the RG are not part of the Judicial Police (OPJ: *Officiers de Police Judiciaire*) and consequently may not stop someone, or conduct searches, or interrogate someone, or detain someone in custody (Aubert and

Petit, 1981, 265).[5] In fighting terrorism, for instance, they must restrict their activities to infiltration and the identification of suspects, but they cannot make arrests. This is a logic, then, governed by a concern for 'rationality' (division and specialization of tasks), which distinguishes the RG from the 'political police' of dictatorships, for the RG is limited by the internal or external controls (in particular judicial controls) to which police forces are normally subjected.

In France these limits are elastic, but not infinite, and the police may be prosecuted when they employ blatantly illegal means. Or at least this was the situation until the Doucé affair, which revealed deviations from traditional doctrine that were as discrete as they were serious. In July of 1990, a somewhat off-beat Baptist minister known for his work with homosexuals vanished. On 13 September, the papers reported that four members of the Paris RG were being held on suspicion of being involved in the disappearance. The scandal occasioned a number of revelations, in particular concerning reforms within the Central Directorate of the RG and the Paris RG since 1989. In the main, these tended to leave general intelligence-gathering to the media, which had long since taken over the job from the RG, and concentrate on fighting terrorism, fraud, drug trafficking, illegal labor, etc. At the same time, the RG, and the Paris offices more particularly, received a greater number of authorizations to act as OPJ, and this included the most 'polyvalent' brigades (*cf.* for instance: Inciyan, 1990d).

The reformers no doubt intended to balance the repressive emphasis on certain well-defined targets by the internal rationalization of the use of 'undercover tactics.' A strict formal procedure was thus laid down for using informers: individual files, trial-period forms, registration, systematic notes on all contacts, verification of costs, etc. It would seem, however, as is always the case when dealing with the police, that it is easier to extend powers than to tighten controls.

In the same services (or in some cases, in specially created ad hoc sections) is a second, and properly political, logic that goes into gear when the aim of gathering information is not to prepare a police intervention but directly to intervene in the political arena. In this case, the information is not collected in order to forestall a crime, public disorder or a government slip-up, but to provide a hold on a politically important individual or group (in most cases, someone from the opposing camp or an overly independent crony) by second-guessing his plans or by publishing one or another of the activities they would prefer to keep under wraps. The object is intimidation, blackmail or public disgrace: the target is regarded as an adversary who must be put out of action.[6] Few French governments have disdained this path, in which, once again, anything goes, and not only are the police tactics kept undercover, they are definitely used for purposes other than official missions. The French 1970s

---

5. Except in the areas of racing and gambling (monitoring casinos, and clandestine gambling circles and clubs), which is in itself a hotbed of 'undercover practices.'
6. For an unvarnished description of 'twenty years of political policing' marked by 'special missions,' *see* the memoirs of Commissioner Harstrich (Harstrich and Calvi, 1991); for the recent period, *see* also Quadruppani (1990).

abound in examples: the covert police actions taken against the satirical weekly, *Le Canard Enchaîné*, which was found guilty of being too well informed (Plume and Pasquini, 1980); another famous example is the surveillance of the son of an opposition leader of the time (F. Mitterrand) in order to keep the authorities informed on his private life with the obvious intent of using this information as yet another weapon against the father (Picant, 1979; for the recent period, *see* Plenel, 1992).

Both of these cases have a twofold interest, for, if they made headlines, it is because they engendered their own perverse effects. Luck had it that a journalist working for the *Canard Enchaîné* (on a tip-off?), walked in on the operatives installing listening devices in the paper's offices: the agents were duly identified, and a complaint was lodged by the newspaper. Having denied everything, the minister was forced to invoke the National Security clause and find himself a particularly accommodating judge to dismiss the case. The price of police impunity was a political scandal. In the Mitterrand case, the operative tailing the son 'naively' followed the trail to certain powerful figures who could be seen at the National Police Firing Range. He requested further instructions from his superiors just as news of his report was leaking out. The action was promptly abandoned.

Above and beyond the particularities of these cases, they illustrate two possible limits on these types of undercover practice. In the first place, such practices carry a risk: they are effective only if kept secret; if the secret is discovered, they backfire, and the backlash may be more damaging than the advantage originally sought: the risk must therefore be in proportion with the expected result. Police behaviors incapable of making this calculation may self-destruct.

In the second place, when the action too obviously oversteps the bounds of the legitimate logic of policing and uses members of the force and policing techniques as mere means to unavowable political ends, the loyalty of the operatives must be beyond question. But this cannot be systematically guaranteed in a large, highly unionized police force recruited from a variety of backgrounds; and it is all the more difficult as another logic – just as pressing – tends to foster the professionalization of the personnel. Whence another alternative and one which is periodically tried: the old-boy network of the specialized external organizations, private security agencies or political security services which employ a large number of policemen and ex-policemen (or gendarmes).[7] The use of private services protects the client, but carries with it the disadvantage of dubious technical reliability. Here, too, the limits imposed by the very notion of undercover *police* tactics are evident. By definition, the

---

7. Recently the news carried the case of the 'plumbers of the Conseil Supérieur de la Magistrature', a team of retired gendarmes arrested by the police as they were illegally tapping the telephone of a government employee suspected of certain indiscretions implicating the President's Office (Henry, 1992). The best-known case is that of the former Gaullist Party security service, the *Service d'Action Civique* (SAC) of which 10–15 per cent of the 8–10,000 members are alleged to have been from the police (Commission d'enquête sur les activités du SAC, 1982, *passim*); concerning wire-tapping by private security agencies, *see* e.g. Besset, 1988; Guisnel and Violet, 1988, 263–265; Inciyan, 1990b and c).

use of dubious private services negates official *police* involvement in the tactic used; it does not change its character, but it does set limits on the possible recourse to a complex bureaucracy.

2.3.2. The Direction de la Surveillance du Territoire

One alternative is to use another official service of the political police, the *Direction de la Surveillance du Territoire*, or DST, whose highly selective recruitment and discrete mode of operation, guaranteed in all legality by the National Security clause, offers better insurance of loyalty and secrecy. Moreover, unlike the traditional RG units, the DST controls the policing process from start to finish, since it also carries out the operations suggested by the information it has collected. It has the exclusive right to conduct investigations of a judicial nature in cases of espionage, treason and breaches of national security (Arrighi and Asso, 1979), domains which it sometimes defines very broadly, since it turns out that, in a recent terrorism case, the DST failed to communicate information collected three years earlier on a suspect wanted by the judicial police. This service, whose internal organization is a closely guarded secret, employs 1,240 officers (Interior Ministry figures).

Legend has it that the French DST has been mixed up in a good many nebulous operations involving the police and politics that have never been elucidated. Nevertheless, it is now commonly acknowledged that the conception it had of its official task of surveillance and infiltration of actual or suspected terrorist groups was carried very far indeed. For instance, the bombs that destroyed the Brittany vacation home of a large construction boss, in April 1972, are thought to have been supplied to the Autonomous Breton Movement (FLB) by DST agents themselves. The story even suggests that they were overly zealous, since the 'victim' of the attack, forewarned by the police and in agreement with the principle of a symbolic attack, protested to the Ministry when he saw the extent of the real damage (Hamon and Marchand, 1984, 179–181).

With the DST or any ad hoc service put together for a discrete one-time mission, come all the compromises and spillovers inherent to internal counterespionage. This is the heartland of 'undercover policing tactics,' of frame-ups; the layman and even some participants see only the tip of the iceberg. To hear one ex-employee of the *Service de Documentation et Contre-espionnage* tell it, undercover is the be-all and end-all of counterespionage (Bernert, 1980).[8]

But there may be a moral to this tale as well, or at least some sort of self-regulatory mechanism that strips off the masks when things get out of hand and even the internal hierarchy loses control of the operation. Two affairs that made international news might suggest as much: the so-called 'Ben-Barka' affair, in 1965, and the Greenpeace Rainbow Warrior case, in 1985, which cost the minister and the heads of the services involved their jobs (Derogy and Pontaut,

---

8. The SDECE, now called the *Direction Générale de la Sécurité Extérieure*, is the equivalent of the DST, but responsible for foreign intelligence to the Defense Ministry (*see* Guisnel and Violet, 1988; concerning the history of the secret services, *see* Faligot and Krop, 1985).

1986). The Ben-Barka affair, named after a Moroccan opposition leader kidnapped and killed by Moroccan special services with a little help from the French, unleashed the punitive incorporation of the whole of the Paris Police Prefecture, with its 30,000 agents, into the National Police (Faligot and Krop, 1985, 293–301; Bernet, 1980). Of course, it would be naive to think that any regulatory mechanism works automatically, since, by definition, successful manipulation leaves no trace; but when one does happen to function, it can serve as a useful reminder: the vicious circle of manipulation and suspicion can spin so fast that it swallows up its authors.

Another interesting example is the affair of the 'real-fake' passport. Just after the March 1986 elections that pushed out the socialists, an affair of embezzlement hit the papers: in the firing line was the handling of public funds by an ex-socialist minister, C. Nucci, and his chief of staff, Y. Chalier. Chalier vanished, an order to appear was issued against him by the examining judge. All police forces received orders to locate and arrest him. He was spotted in Brazil; he returned to France and, arrested as he left the plane, was found to be in possession of an official passport bearing a false identity. The examining judge identified the passport as one of a number of 'blank' passports delivered by the passport service to the DST. How did this document, duly listed in a special DST register and signed by its Director, come, complete with a real photo and a false identity, to be in the possession of a fugitive from justice? The examining judge discovered a circuit involving a chief superintendent, head of another service, who was indicted, the Director of the DST and his assistants and, in all probability, the minister's staff, if not the minister himself. At that point the inquiry was blocked by the minister in question, on the grounds of the famous National Security clause. When the socialists returned to power, in 1988, they lifted the ban, and allowed the DST director to testify before the investigating judge that he had acted on personal orders from the previous Interior Minister (Plenel, 1989). This affair is of interest because, once again, it shows the resources and the limits of this type of tactic. 'Real-fake' passports are commonly used for secret agents whose true identity needs concealing; from this standpoint, the practice is regarded as licit and is *codified* by very precise internal police regulations: official register, forms to fill out, authorized signatures and return of passport after use. When the procedure is sidetracked to support some political manoeuvre, it becomes illicit, but the codified procedure does not disappear for all that: proof of the clandestine operation exists, then, and all the minister, caught in the bureaucratic trap of his administration, can do is to invoke the National Security clause, which fools no one.

2.4. The Police Judiciaire

The fourth and last important branch is the *Police Judiciaire*, responsible for fighting declared crime. This branch is comprised of the judicial police agencies proper, both the specialized central offices and regional services, to which must be added units known as *Sûretés* or *Unités de police judiciaire et administrative* (urban police judicial and administrative units belonging to the above-mentioned *Police Urbaine*). Unlike the uniformed employees, these agents are most often identified as the 'civilian' arm of the police. Compared with the foregoing branches, the Judicial Police is characterized by some fairly specific features:

- a relatively clear target: crime, explicitly defined by an established list of behaviors (felonies and misdemeanors) described by the law;
- prescribed techniques and methods (the *Code de Procédure Pénale*: the Criminal Procedure Code);
- a double system of controls: the Judicial Police is monitored by an internal hierarchy, as are the foregoing services, but it is also overseen by the courts.

This monitoring is done, in the first place, on the operational level: according to the Criminal Procedure Code, the *Procureur de la République* (public prosecutor) is, in theory, the true head of the Judicial Police, which he directs and coordinates. When a judicial inquiry is opened, the police no longer intervenes, except when ordered to do so by the investigating magistrate. Moreover, in order to exercise their judicial policing powers, the agents must be specially authorized by their court of appeal. This authorization may be withdrawn if the powers are abused. In practice, this is extremely rare and happens only in serious cases. Usually the magistrate in charge informs the police administration, which takes the preventive step of transferring the agent.[9]

Thus, although this branch of the police is not necessarily more transparent than any other, it is perhaps the most open to professionalization, in the sense that it is likely to become increasingly technical and as such difficult to monitor from within. While the use of 'undercover tactics' is no easier to detect, describe and interpret here than elsewhere, it is the object of internal discussion and information from both sides. Some authors explain their use at length in books for the general public (Cathala, 1977), and technical descriptions or Police Academy courses dwell on them, though not in official publications; others protest virtuously that, in their whole career as senior Judicial Police officials, they have never seen a policeman operate other than strictly by the Criminal Procedure Code (Denis, 1976; 1979).

Nevertheless, inasmuch as the aim of Judicial Police investigations is the repression of crime, which must go through the courts, there is public debate and external, judicial monitoring of police tactics.[10] The use of 'undercover tactics' is therefore relatively easier to detect in this instance than in the other branches of the police, and has given rise to discussions of jurisprudence and doctrine, which, to a certain extent, clarify the legal 'rules of the game'.

---

9. *Cf.* the extreme case of the head of the Criminal Brigade at the Paris PJ, the most prestigious of all units in this area, who, when threatened with such a sanction found refuge in a promotion-sanction to Inspector General of the National Police (Ottavioli, 1985). Which, let it be said in passing, says a lot about the reliability of the internal control exercised by this 'Inspectorate.'
10. Which does not exclude a few extras: for instance the vice squad's 'white notes' which, written on paper without a letterhead and unsigned, transmit directly to the Paris Police Préfecture (and doubtless the prefectures of other major towns), information on the private lives, particularly in the area of sexual conduct of various sorts of public figures; *see* Ottavioli (1985, 118 ff) for numerous examples of vice squad methods.

Here some distinctions need to be made. First of all, there are a few absolute taboos: the person must not be physically harmed in obtaining proof of a crime (chemical means, lie-detector tests, hypnosis, ill-treatment); nor can privacy be infringed upon (inviolability of the home, of a person's private life and mail, of the right of ownership, within the limits set by the law, except with the consent of the interested parties), nor can the right to defense be violated (respect for legal formalities in case of a search of business premises or home, seizure of goods, police custody: Besson, 1958, No. 29–30; Bouzat, 1964, 162–164; Merle and Vitu, 1979, No. 952; Lassalle, 1981, No. 57–59).

That being said, it is generally accepted that police inquiries are not as tightly bound by the principle of fairness of proof as are judicial inquiries, but this does not mean that anything goes. Police are allowed a certain amount of elbowroom, on the condition that the individual's rights and the dignity of the courts are respected, and it is left to the judge to decide the admissibility of the proof (Bouzat, 1964; Merle and Vitu, 1979, No. 950). And indeed the courts have been left to make the final decision in a number of cases. Without entering into the details of this jurisprudence – often contradictory because it is closely connected with the circumstances of each case – two distinctions must be made: cases in which the police intervene after the offense has been committed and are looking for proof, and those in which the police act before the offense is committed.

In the first case – in which an offense has already been committed –, the authors feel that cunning and trickery must remain exceptional means and that the necessity of such tactics must be assessed by two criteria: on the one hand, the seriousness of the crime and the disturbance it causes to public order (the more serious the offense, the less the means matter) and, on the other hand, the offender's personality (an occasional offender should not be dealt with in the same way as a professional): the harm occasioned by the offense is weighed against the harm caused by an unfair investigation (Blondet, 1958, No. 2; Parra and Montreuil, 1975, 430–442; Lassalle, 1981, No. 49; for a recent up-date, *see* Maistre du Chambon, 1989). In consideration of which, manipulation, disguises, infiltration (which is simply an extension of the preceding), ambushes and the use of informers (whose identity may be concealed even in court on the grounds of professional secret) are regarded as acceptable practices. Likewise, provocation, if it aims simply at bringing to light a crime already committed (e.g. when a police officer poses as a buyer for gold, drugs, conterband, the simple possession of which is illegal), is acceptable.

In the second case – intervention before the crime has actually been committed – the basic distinction in jurisprudence revolves around knowing whether the police manoeuvres did or did not play a decisive role in the committing of the offense that lead to the offender's arrest:

- if the police agent effectively incited someone to commit an offense that he or she would probably not have committed otherwise, the evidence is not admissible (Lambert, 1952, 486; Blondet, 1958);
- conversely, if the effect of the police manoeuvre was simply to give the offender the long-awaited chance, it is admissible (Blondet, 1958).

But we repeat, this is merely a summary of the jurisprudence and doctrine on the question and not an official table of what is and is not allowed: all types of proof may be questioned by the parties before the court, and the lawfulness of the proof depends on the principles and circumstances of the case.

Therefore, while such tactics are widespread, because of their uncertain legal status they must always be justified by the agents involved. Beyond all attempts at enumerating and describing 'undercover police tactics,' there is a form which can be defined as any police tactic which elicits from its authors denial, dissimulation or justification, suggesting that the practice is neither on solid legal footing nor automatically legitimate and must therefore be rejustified each time to all who would spoil the police's sport. 'Undercover policing' is that portion of policing which, in the perpetual game of 'cops and robbers,' is so shadowy that the practitioner no longer quite knows whose side he is on, or may end up being on.

This is clear in the treatment of informers insisted upon by the Interior Minister when he announced an increase in the budget for their remuneration, the implementation of which has always posed problems of limits and bounds.[11] Law and jurisprudence no doubt stipulate a number of rules governing the use of informers, their anonymity, their remuneration and the use of the information they provide as proof, but they leave open questions of recruiting, manipulating and monitoring informers and the compromises that necessarily come with these activities (*see* Di Marino, 1990, for an exhaustive discussion of this issue). In countless cases policemen have been formally sanctioned or discretely transferred for having misjudged the limits of what would be tolerated and the dangers of publicity: one Marseille police inspector was convicted of harboring a criminal because he had housed his informer,[12] a gendarme was accused of having shielded a bank robber to simultaneously remunerate and compromise him,[13] a chief of the *Office Central de Répression du Banditisme* (Central Office for the Repression of Banditry) was transferred after a photo showing him standing with a notorious crook appeared in major newspapers.

This type of affair was nicely described by an ex-department head when he admitted (speaking of police brutality during interrogations): 'a department head is frequently unaware of what goes on' (Chenevier, 1976): a fundamental conclusion because it underscores the twofold dimension of police secrecy. Policing activities are kept secret from laymen, that is the traditional meaning of 'undercover police tactics.' But they are kept just as secret *within* the police force itself: subordinates hide practices from their superiors at every echelon. In certain cases, secrecy is simply functional; it used to be the accepted, if not prescribed, rule, except in the DST, that the police officer took sole responsibility for his informers and was the only one who knew their identity (which sometimes produced the above-related consequences); but secrecy also covers

---

11. This announcement was justified by the disappearance of the *condés*, police who protect a criminal or a prostitute in exchange for information, and of bans on entering certain areas and localities, both traditional means for police to put pressure on unwilling informers (Plenel, 1986).
12. See *Le Monde,* 14 June 1985; Di Marino, 1990, 92.
13. *See* 'L'Elysée et ses gendarmes; les six "affaires" Barril,' *Le Monde,* 16–17 October 1983.

clandestine tactics properly speaking, some of which are motivated by departmental interests, others by the operative's personal interests (sometimes the two combine when a successful operation earns its author a promotion), and some by other motives altogether. The Doucé affair is a good example of interwoven motives, when the decision of the Parisian RG chief to rationalize and regulate the use of informers was met with his subordinates' desire to retain the old practices. This is also how it happened that inspector Dufourg conscientiously produced false reports on the recruitment of an informer. In such cases there is an extremely complex interweaving of the police logic of secrecy and the organizational logic of hierarchical authority which allows constant shifting from one to the other providing a mutual, alternating 'cover.' The need for police secrecy can cover deviant organizational behaviors, and organizational opacity can shield dubious policing initiatives. In some cases imbroglios are created in which no one can tell the victim from the criminal, or who is manipulating whom.

3. THE OTHER POLICE AGENCIES

3.1. The Gendarmerie Nationale

The *Gendarmerie Nationale* employs 96,000 men and women and comprises two major divisions:

- The *gendarmerie mobile* (some 20,000 officers), responsible for maintaining order and provided with heavy equipment. The Gendarmerie is usually deployed in tandem with the *Compagnies Républicaines de Sécurité* in accordance with the same rules by which the decision to call in the Gendarmerie is taken by a civil authority. The operations are commanded by a judicial police officer.
- The *gendarmerie départementale* (some 60,000 officers), whose divisions correspond to France's administrative divisions, called departments. The basic unit is the brigade, usually made up of a half-dozen officers; there are around 3,650 brigades. Although they form a grid covering the entire country, the bulk of their numbers is concentrated in rural areas where they are the major police presence.

Unlike the National Police, the Gendarmerie does not have an intelligence branch in peace time. Alongside their public safety missions and judicial policing, all territorial units are supposed to gather intelligence, something that is considered an essential mission and systematically carried out everywhere and at all times. Paradoxically, however, the Gendarmerie is expressly forbidden to dissimulate its activities.

The decree of 20 May 1903, strictly regulating the Gendarmerie's functioning is very clear on this. Gendarmes are to keep themselves informed of everything that happens in their district; they must inform their superiors and the competent civil authorities of any event or matter regarding public order. In practice, this means making a systematic record of all persons coming into contact, for one reason or another, with the Gendarmerie (Lafont and Meyer, 1980).

> A good brigade chief should know everything that is going on in his district. To do this he disposes of a network of volunteer intelligence agents (noteworthies of the community, functionaries, retired military men or civil servants, people of all backgrounds who have at heart the good of the community and public order) (Haenel and Pichon, 1983, 45).

In times of peace as in times of war, the circulation of this information is rigorously organized. But this multifarious intelligence-gathering – of which the majority of the population is unaware – is theoretically subjected to two formal constraints:

– Article 78 of the 1903 decree stipulates that 'under no circumstances' may the Gendarmerie 'interfere in matters having to do with politics';
– and Article 96 says: 'In no case, either directly or indirectly, may the Gendarmerie take on secret missions that might alter its true character. It is always to act openly, in military uniform and to do nothing which might bring dishonnor their branch of the service.'

In short, exactly the opposite of 'undercover tactics.' And yet, in 1987, gendarmes were authorized to carry out certain operations in civilian dress, and it would seem that the effect of this official authorization was to ratify and regulate some unofficial practices in a number of specialized criminal investigation squads.[14] To precisely what extent these stipulations are actually respected is not easy to judge. Certainly the bulk of the judicial policing done by the Gendarmerie is done in uniform, particularly on the departmental level. But it is possible that exemptions increase the higher one goes and the closer one gets to the specialized elite units. Such units are eager to emphasize their speciality and to obtain results at least as good as those of the National Police.[15]

In effect, between the Gendarmerie and the National Police there is a tradition of rivalry that was exacerbated by measures taken after the 1981 election of France's socialist president. Incidents in 1954 and later left him with good reasons to be wary of the police (e.g. *see* Guisnel and Violet, 1988, 42). It was for this that the gendarmes were delegated first to ensure the president's personal safety and then to coordinate the fight against terrorism. Serious

---

14. Director General of the Gendarmerie, Instruction No. 11 900 of 11 May 1987: gendarmes are not to act in civilian dress without written authorization bearing the agent's name, dates, places, and justification of the need for recourse to this method. In the event, they must be wearing an armband when making the arrest and carry official identification; in such cases, the right to use firearms is more restricted than when the agents intervene in uniform. But the legality of this instruction, which waives Article 96 of the 1903 decree, is dubious because it departs from what is, in principle, a superior norm (Dieu, 1992, 436–41).
15. Police unions allege that the Gendarmerie used this waiver to set up permanent non-uniformed units, in competition with the RG, and to the general satisfaction of the *préfets* (Guisnel and Violet, 1988, 96; Plenel, 1988).

missions warrant serious medicine, and the ensuing years saw the unfolding of an affair that cast doubt on some of the gendarmes' new methods: the manufacture of false proof and the buying of witnesses.

We are talking about the 'Irlandais de Vincennes' affair (the Irish terrorists of Vincennes), which began in 1982. In the immediate wake of a number of terrorist attacks in Paris and the creation of an anti-terrorist cell in the office of the President of the Republic, the special unit proceeded with much ado to arrest three 'international terrorists.' Eventually it turned out that they were well-known Irish activists and that the 'proof' and other 'exhibits' had been manufactured by the arresting officers, who went on systematically to lie to the judges with the support of the executive.[16]

3.2. The Douane

La Douane, or Customs, is not usually listed among the police agencies, something that stems perhaps not so much from its lower visibility as from a certain sociological nearsightedness. In terms of personnel (some 20,000 agents), organization, material means and the scope of their powers of investigation and coercion, the Customs services closely resemble the police (Thué and Porcher, 1990). The Customs has extremely broad powers of investigation and arrest, underpinned by a time-honored, albeit sometimes juridically fragile, tradition, which they implement independently of any judicial control. 'Undercover tactics' are part and parcel of their arsenal. Most familiar is their use of informers, euphemistically referred to as *aviseurs* ('spotters'), for whom the Customs code authorizes remuneration within certain bounds.[17] This is how, for example, they manage to procure files of the French clients of certain Swiss banks (e.g. *see* Pontaut and Szpiner, 1989, 94–95; Delberghe, 1990).

Such methods seem to have undergone considerable extension as of late, bolstered by a political will to step up the war on drugs and on the laundering of what the French call *narcodollars*, both of which come under the competence of the Customs. And the Customs services are under all the more pressure to demonstrate their efficiency in this area as the suppression of national borders within the EU raises the question of the validity of their traditional mission, and they feel the need to justify their existence. Furthermore, this policing has generated rivalry between the Ministries of the Interior and Finance, as each would like to see its own administration – i.e. the National Police and the Customs, respectively – play the leading role. The Finance Ministry has taken the first set, winning the right to monitor the circulation of 'dirty money,' since this assumes the collaboration of the banks, who are usually answerable to the Finance Ministry (Inciyan, 1990a).

Customs inspectors traditionally take an active part in the fight against drug trafficking, and a number of recent cases have put their methods in the spot-

---

16. For more on this, *see*: Derogy and Pontaut, 1986; Plenel, 1991, 1992; one of the officers implicated in the affair published his own version of the facts: Beau, 1989.
17. In principle, one third of the amount of the fine.

light. In particular, they make use of controlled delivery, which consists of infiltrating networks of drug traffickers and then acting as middlemen between them and the big French dealers in order to intercept the merchandise and catch the traffickers in the act. Several senior Customs officials have recently been prosecuted and even temporarily placed in detention by an investigating magistrate on charges of having overstepped their powers and having engaged in provocation: they not only presented themselves as potential buyers, but are alleged to have received the merchandise and handled money (Inciyan, 1991a and b).

The response of the Ministry in charge of Customs to the criticism of its agents was to trot out the traditional arguments of the police when caught in illegal activities: it pleaded vagueness of the law or 'legal vacuum,' invoking the necessities of the 'war on the "merchants of death", which should prevail over respect for the Criminal Procedure Code' (quoted by Inciyan, 1991, b); finally, the Ministry called for new legislation to regularize such practices. No sooner said than done: a law passed in late 1991 authorized police officers, gendarmes and Customs officials to 'acquire, hold or transport' narcotics or raw materials used in their manufacture for the purpose of documenting the traffic, identifying the offenders and effecting seizures.[18] The new law also allows officials to provide traffickers with whatever they need in order to operate: material means but legal ones as well (opening bank accounts, creating fictional societies). Customs officials having committed such acts before the law came into force were pardoned in passing. Thus was the 'legal vacuum' filled.[19]

On the sociological side, the basic distinction between the Customs and the other police agencies has traditionally been that Customs does not intervene in criminal activities within its purview with a view to prosecution, but aims to monitor its citizens in view of ensuring that they respect administrative regulations. Following this logic, judicial intervention depends on the good will of the administration, which is empowered to make settlements with offenders and resorts to prosecution only in cases of recidivists or to set an example (Barberger, 1985).

This seems still to be the prevailing logic behind the 'anti-laundering' policy, the aim in this case being to discipline the banks and recover the sums in question – while the account holders often remain out of reach. In the war on drugs, however, Customs may be in the process of adopting a penal logic properly speaking, which would make it a third French police agency, alongside the National Police and the Gendarmerie. The fact that Customs is demanding its agents be made Judicial Police officers, which would place them on an equal footing with police officers and gendarmes in their dealings with the justice system, points in this direction. At present, however, Customs finds itself up against a powerful coalition in which the Ministry of Justice has joined forces with Defense (the Gendarmerie) and the Interior (the Police) which, together with their personnel, are strongly resisting any such reform.

---

18. Law No. 91–1264 of 19 December 1991, *Journal Officiel*, 20 December 1991, 16593.
19. For a well-documented coverage of this, as well as the development of undercover Customs tactics, *see* Bordes, 1992.

4. CONCLUSION

The French police system is doubly determined by its historical origins. It is at the same time a state apparatus, and therefore an instrument of political power, and a social tool for the regulation and repression of crime. In this sense, undercover police practices point to a confusion between the political and criminal spheres and the constant temptation to slip back and forth between the two.[20]

The confusion or slippage are further stimulated by the 'politicization' and the internationalization of crime-fighting. When the increase in recorded crime figures is accompanied, as it has been in France since the late 1970s, by feelings of insecurity for which politicians keep shifting the blame to the opposition, there is politicization. Similarly, there is internationalization when, as can be seen in the anti-drug fight, methods are increasingly borrowed from other institutional contexts. The two mechanisms combine to muddle the overall picture and make it indecipherable.

Our overview of the French situation has been far too rapid, and yet we wanted to show that we need to go beyond a simple description of so-called 'undercover police tactics' and attempt to define who does what, according to what logic and in what organizational, juridical and political contexts.[21]

The case of police officers assigned to political intelligence operations is especially enlightening. In effect, they are not chosen on the basis of their political convictions. Moreover, career considerations as well as the need for administrative continuity over and above the vicissitudes of political life impose upon superiors as well as agents a certain degree of caution and neutrality. Because of their status and union laws, police officers are not entirely in the hands of the political powerholders. And even if the latter have no trouble finding agents for all manner of dirty work, motivated by conviction or opportunism, these activities cannot be hidden for long due to the very ideological diversity among police agents.[22] Which is why, in certain instances, those in power prefer to use outside agents, who are both freer to act and more dependent upon their clients.

This brings us to another distinctive feature of 'undercover police tactics' *à la française*, which is linked with the existence of a solid bureaucracy: in certain areas illegal activities are governed by strict regulations. We have already touched on these in the case of the 'real-fake' passport, which provides

---

20. In this sense, the French police fit the high-policing ideal type defined by Brodeur (1983, 512–514).
21. But our work does not embrace all of the official 'secret services' (*see* Guisnel and Violet, 1988; Faligot and Krop, 1985).
22. E.g. Guisnel and Violet (1988) report that the anti-terrorist cell created in the President's office, which was responsible for the Irish terrorist affair, also installed wire-taps without following the proper procedures; a fact other functionaries pointed out to the incoming right-wing government in 1986.

secret agents with an authentic document bearing false information, but whose delivery, use and restitution are precisely codified. The same is true of the authorization given gendarmes to operate in civilian dress, issued in the form of an internal directive exempting the agent from a regulation that is theoretically superior in the hierarchy of juridical norms to this directive.

But it is in the area of wire-tapping that secret regulations have become most widespread. Until the 1991 law, only court-ordered wire-taps were legal, although the way in which they were implemented was criticized.[23] But there were also parallel 'administrative wire-taps,' avowedly illegal and officially accepted; since 1960, however, these had been carefully organized and centralized by the creation of a paramilitary organization (the *Groupement Interministériel de Contrôle*, GIC) and an authorization procedure controlled directly by the Prime Minister.[24] It was the latter who decided how many wire-taps to authorize and divided them up among the ministries concerned, who in turn distributed them among the various services.[25]

This regulation was of an ambiguous nature. The original aim, colored by the Algerian war, was to bring under a single and politically reliable head, a number of (until then) widely dispersed practices employed without supervision by the various police and intelligence services. The rationalization targeted first of all individual (or even collective) strayings from the straight and narrow, and sought to preserve executive autonomy in its use of *Raison d'Etat*. This regulation of illegality has provoked numerous objections and draft laws since 1960; and yet it was not until France had been condemned twice in a row by the European Court of Human Rights (decisions in *Kruslin* and *Huvig*, 24 April 1990) that a law was actually passed. This was the Law of 10 July 1991, which stipulated the juridical conditions of judicial wire-taps

---

23. From 1980 on, Supreme Court jurisprudence placed growing restrictions on the conditions under which wire-taps could legally be carried out: telephones could be tapped only with an order from the examining magistrate, in view of establishing proof of an offense. And yet this jurisprudence was based on texts the vagueness of which had been criticized by the European Court of Human Rights in the *Kruslin* and *Huvig* decisions. Concerning French jurisprudence, see Pradel, 1990; Kayser and Renoux, 1990; and Jeandidier, 1990, who analyzes the repercussions of the European Court decisions on French legislation.
24. Each time one of the authorized services requests permission to install a wire-tap, the application had to be signed by the head of the service in question, and then endorsed by the minister responsible for the service (Interior, Defense, Treasury), the Telecommunications minister and the Prime Minister. Concrete reasons must be listed. The telephone line is then tapped by the PT (*Poste et Téléphone*) and the surveillance carried out by the GIC, whose organization is a secret (concerning the establishment of this agency, see Ditreau, 1963; Guisnel and Violet, 1988, 263 ff).
25. According to a 1981–1982 report by the then First President of the Supreme Court (Rapport Schmelck, unpublished), at the Prime Minister's behest, 930 wire-taps were authorized at the end of 1981: 730 for the Interior Ministry (Judicial Police, 280; DST, 240; RG, 210); and 200 for Defense. They were left in place for an average of 2.5 months (Guisnel and Violet, 1988, 275; Inciyan, 1991c).

and legalized administrative ones, which it placed under the control of an independent commission.[26]

Wire-taps are an excellent illustration of some more general mechanisms. Prior to 1960, illegal wire-tapping had grown immensely; in 1960, the aim was not at all to legalize the practices but to coordinate their administration; the administrative codification was not affected by the law of 17 July 1970 (Article 368 of the Criminal Procedure Code) prohibiting wire-tapping; in the end it would take thirty years of scandals and growing pressure for the practice to be legalized.

This gradual process highlights two dimensions of the codification of police tactics. As already illustrated by the 'real-fake' passports, the two aspects are independent and therefore allow us to suggest a general typology of police practices. The first dimension is the degree of internal codification, which goes from no rules at all to an explicit, formal set of regulations, sometimes secret, via customs specific to one service or another. The second dimension is the legal status, which goes from formally forbidden to formally authorized, via the so-called 'legal vacuum'. The real-fake passport is an example of an administratively codified, forged legal document (i.e. legally a crime), while Urban Police use of informers is legal practice, but left to the discretion of the functionary. The following diagram illustrates these two dimensions.

Diagram 1: Typology and evolution of undercover police practices

Internal Codification	Legal Status		
	Legality	'Legal vacuum'	Illegality
Formal rules	Wire-taps > 1991 Controlled deliveries > 1992 DST informants Files > 1991		Wire-taps 1960–1991 Real-fake passport Plainclothes Gendarmerie > 1987
Customary practice	RG informants	Files < 1978	Plainclothes Gendarmerie < 1987
No rules	Urban police informants		Controlled deliveries < 1992 Unofficial files > 1978 Wire-taps < 1960

This figure is not so much a classification as an illustration of the dynamic relations between police tactics and the law. The case of wire-tapping is particu-

---

26. Following the Schmelck report, the law sets out two principles. First of all, it upholds state monopoly on wire-tapping, which had been supplanted by the development of private operations (which, so it seems, the police and the courts often used to install judicial wire-taps!). And second, it defined the legal motives for installing non-judicial wire-taps, while retaining the earlier authorization procedure: henceforth, telephones could be tapped only for reasons of 'national security,' organized crime, terrorism, or 'the protection of national economic and scientific interests.' The recently published *Commission Nationale des Interceptions de Sécurité* first annual report states that wire-taps are now indeed monitored, but stresses, on the other hand, the difficulty of controlling illegal wire-taps, whether instigated by government employees or private parties.

larly instructive here. Technological progress brings wire-taps into the picture by way of the box 'no rules/legal status: forbidden'; they then advance first of all by way of 'internal codification' until – when the contradiction between bureaucratic codification and legal prohibition becomes too blatant – they are finally legalized. Even more complex mechanisms could be illustrated, e.g. the keeping of records on private citizens (*fichage*), which bifurcates along the way: the absence of internal regulations and legal status gives way to internal rationalization, following the pace of computerization: the 1978 law on 'computer records and liberties' then ratifies some aspects of this evolution and prohibits others.[27] Finally, in the case of controlled deliveries, which also grew up with no internal or external regulations, legalization very likely preceded internal codification.[28]

All of which confirms Brodeur's 'law' (1984, 36), which states that whenever a contradiction arises between police practice and legality, it is usually the law that is modified, not the practice. But once a practice has been both legalized and codified, it becomes surrounded with so many restrictions that there is a great temptation once again to look for more flexible practices. Accordingly, legal, regulated wire-taps are meeting with competition from private illegal wire-taps free of control (as illustrated by diagram 2). It is even likely that the numerous restrictions surrounding computer files have given rise to countless clandestine personal files that also escape control.

Diagram 2: The cycle of legalization of police practice

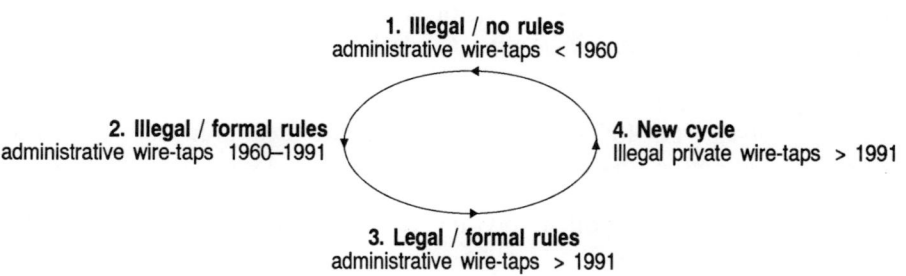

---

27. This internal rationalization of files can be seen in the Interior Ministry repertory established in 1968, which was sent to all courts bearing the warning: 'Confidential. Do not divulge or publish' (*Secrétariat général pour la police*, 1968). Law No. 78–17 of 6 January 1978, 'on computer files and liberties', places the recording and use of personal information under the strict control of the *Commission Nationale de l'Informatique et des Libertés* (CNIL), a national commission monitoring the use of computer files, which publishes an annual report and is presently presided by J. Fauvet, former Director of the highly respected French daily *Le Monde* (Flaherty, 1989, 165–238). And yet it was not until 1991, and then not without difficulty, that the decrees governing RG files were published (Inciyan and Paris, 1990; Inciyan, 1991d). Recently, the CNIL reprimanded the Gendarmerie for illegally keeping records on racial origins and political and religious opinions (Inciyan, 1992).
28. Indeed it seems that no strict accounts were kept of either the use of public funds or the fate of the 'merchandise.'

Thus we see that these two opposing tendencies are constantly present in both the profession and the institution of policing: a tendency towards internal codification and legalization born of both bureaucratic compulsion and the will of the police to cover their tracks; and a reaction, in the name of efficiency, characterized by a desire for autonomy, flexibility and personal discretion.[29] Concomitantly, these opposing tendencies ensure a dynamic relationship with the law which engenders a continuous succession of legalizations and new illegalities. 'Undercover police tactics' are merely one example.

REFERENCES

Arrighi, J.P., Asso, B. (1979), *La police nationale, missions et structures*, Paris, Ed. de la Revue Moderne.
Aubert, J., Petit, R. (1981), *La police en France; service public*, Paris, Berger-Levrault.
Barberger, C. (1985), 'Justice pénale et administration; le droit de la discipline des codes administratifs,' *L'Année Sociologique*, 35, 167–177.
Beau, J.M. (1989), *L'honneur d'un gendarme*, Paris, Ed. Sand.
Bernert, Ph. (1980), *SDECE, Service 7*, Paris, Presses de la Cité.
Besset, J.P. (1988), 'Les privés ont des oreilles,' *Politis*, 11 February, 4–7.
Besson, A. (1958), 'La police judiciaire et le code de procédure pénale,' *Dalloz*, Chronique XXI, 129–144.
Blondet, M. (1958), 'Les ruses et les artifices de la police au cours de l'enquête préliminaire,' *La Semaine Juridique*, I, 1419.
Bordes, Ph. (1992), *Enquêtes aux frontières de la loi; les douaniers et le trafic de drogue*, Paris, Robert Laffont.
Bouzat, P. (1964), 'La loyauté dans la recherche des preuves,' in: Coll., *Problèmes contemporains de procédure pénale, Mélanges Hugueney*, Paris, Sirey, 155–177.
Brodeur, J.P. (1984), 'La police: mythes et réalité,' *Criminologie*, XVII, 1, 9–41.
Brodeur, J.P. (1983), 'High Policing and Low Policing; Remarks About the Policing of Political Activities,' *Social Problems*, 30, 5, 507–520.
Brunet, J.P. (1990), *La police de l'ombre; indicateurs et provocateurs dans la France contemporaine*, Paris, Seuil.
Cathala, F. (1977), *Pratiques et réactions policières*, Saverdun, Editions du Champ de Mars.
Chassaigne, M. (1975), *La lieutenance-générale de police de Paris*, Genève, Slatkine-Mégariotis Reprints (1st ed. Paris, 1906).
Chenevier, C. (1976), *La grande maison*, Paris, Presses de la Cité.
Commission d'enquête sur les activités du S.A.C. (1982), *Rapport remis à M. le Président de l'Assemblée Nationale*, Paris, Alain Moreau (2 vol.).

---

29. This is where what Brodeur (1984) calls the *chèque en gris* (a sort of semi-blank check) – which consists of an authority giving instructions that are sufficiently vague for the operative's interpretation to be disavowed – encounters its limits.

Commission nationale de contrôle des interceptions de securité (1993), *Rapport d'activité 1992*, Paris, La Documentation française.
Delberghe, M. (1990), 'Une relaxe pour non-déclaration de compte bancaire en Suisse,' *Le Monde*, 19 June.
Denis, G. (1976), *Citoyen policier*, Paris, Albin Michel.
Denis, G. (1979), 'La rationalité des conduites policières dans la marche de la justice pénale,' in: Coll., *Connaissance et fonctionnement de la justice pénale*, Paris, Ed. du C.N.R.S., 31–48.
Derogy, J., Pontaut, J.-M. (1986), *Enquête sur trois secrets d'Etat*, Paris, Laffont.
Dieu, F. (1992), *Gendarmerie et modernité; étude de la spécificité gendarmique aujourd'hui*, Thèse, Toulouse, Université de Sciences Sociales/Institut d'Etudes Politiques.
Di Marino, G. (1990), 'L'indicateur,' in: Aussel, J.M., Borricand, J., Di Marino, G., Normandeau, A., Pradel, J., *Problèmes actuels de science criminelle III*, Aix-Marseille, Presses Universitaires d'Aix-Marseille, 63–98.
Ditreau, J. (1963), 'Les écoutes téléphoniques,' *La Nef*, 14, 109–114 (Special issue: *La police en France*).
Emsley, C. (1987), *Crime and Society in England 1750–1900*, London/New York, Longman.
Faligot, R., Krop, P. (1985), *La piscine; les services secrets français, 1944–1984*, Paris, Le Seuil.
Favre, P., ed. (1990), *La manifestation*, Paris, Presses de la Fondation Nationale des Sciences Politiques.
Flaherty, D. (1989), *Protecting Privacy in Surveillance Societies; the FRG, Sweden, France, Canada and the U.S.*, Chapel Hill/London, The University of North Carolina Press.
Forestier, I.-E. (1983), *Gendarmes à la belle Époque*, Paris, France-Empire.
Guisnel, J., Violet, B. (1988), *Services secrets; le pouvoir et les services de renseignements sous François Mitterrand*, Paris, La Découverte.
Haenel, H., Pichon, R. (1983), *La gendarmerie*, Paris, P.U.F.
Hamon, A., Marchand, J.-C. (1984), *P... comme police*, Paris, Alain Moreau.
Harstrich, J., Calvi, F. (1991), *R.G.; 20 ans de police politique*, Paris, Calmann-Lévy.
Henry, M. (1992), 'Des "plombiers" et un bout de bretelle,' *Libération*, 28 March.
Inciyan, E. (1990a), 'Drogue: deux ministères pour une seule guerre,' *Le Monde*, 10 May.
Inciyan, E. (1990b), 'Les grandes oreilles de la société Century,' *Le Monde*, 12 September.
Inciyan, E. (1990c), 'Le PDG de Century est inculpé pour écoutes téléphoniques illégales,' *Le Monde*, 13 September.
Inciyan, E. (1990d), 'Les R.G. parisiens dans la tourmente,' *Le Monde*, 27 September.
Inciyan, E. (1991a), 'Les méthodes des douaniers dans la lutte contre les trafiquants de drogue sont mises en accusation,' *Le Monde*, 16 March.
Inciyan, E. (1991b), 'Les douaniers en pleine "querelle de bornage",' *Le Monde*, 20 April.

Inciyan, E. (1991c), 'Les écoutes téléphoniques feront l'objet d'une loi d'ensemble,' *Le Monde*, 16 May.
Inciyan, E. (1991d), 'Pour mieux garantir les libertés individuelles les deux décrets sur les fichiers des RG ont été sensiblement modifiés,' *Le Monde*, 16 October.
Inciyan, E. (1992), 'La gendarmerie est appelée à mettre de l'ordre dans ses fichiers,' *Le Monde*, 24 July.
Inciyan, E., Paris, G. (1990), 'Après l'annulation des deux décrets sur l'informatisation des fichiers des renseignements généraux; M. Rocard annonce un renforcement des moyens de contrôle de la Commission nationale de l'informatique et des libertés; la petite histoire d'une volte-face,' *Le Monde*, 6 March.
Jeandidier, W. (1990), 'Note to Cass. Crim. 15 Mai 1990,' *La Semaine Juridique (JCP)*, 38, IIème partie, No. 21541.
Kayser, P., Renoux, T. (1990), 'La Cour de cassation et l'art. 66 de la Constitution: à propos de l'arrêt de l'Assemblée plénière du 24 novembre 1989 sur les écoutes téléphoniques,' *Revue Française de Droit Constitutionnel*, 1, 139–147.
Lafont, H., Meyer, Ph. (1980), *Le nouvel ordre gendarmique*, Paris, Seuil.
Lambert, L. (1952), *Traité théorique et pratique de police judiciaire*, Lyon Desvignes, 3ème édition.
Lassalle, J.-Y. (1981), 'Enquête préliminaire (art. 75 à 78 CPP),' *Juriclasseur périodique de procédure pénale*.
Levergeois, P. (1978), *J'ai choisi la DST*, Paris, Flammarion.
Maistre du Chambon, P. (1989), 'La régularité des "provocations policières": l'évolution de la jurisprudence,' *La Semaine Juridique*, 51–52, I, No. 3422.
Marcellin, R. (1978), *L'importune vérité*, Paris, Plon.
Merle, M., Vitu, A. (1979), *Traité de droit criminel; vol. 2: procédure pénale*, Paris, Cujas, 3ème édition.
Monjardet, D. (1985), 'A la recherche du travail policier,' *Sociologie du Travail*, XXVII, 4, 391–407.
Monjardet, D. (1990), 'La manifestation du côté du maintien de l'ordre,' in: Favre, P., ed., 207–228.
Ottavioli, P. (1985), *Echec au crime*, Paris, Grasset.
Parra, C., Montreuil, J. (1975), *Traité de procédure pénale policière*, Paris, Quillet.
Picant, C. (1979), *Des flics pour faire quoi?*, Paris, Editions sociales.
Plenel, E. (1983), 'Vent de pureté aux renseignements généraux,' *Le Monde*, 17–18 April.
Plenel, E. (1986), 'Le ministre de la sécurité augmente la rémunération des informateurs,' *Le Monde*, 21 May.
Plenel, E. (1988), 'L'Inspection générale de la police critique la "politique d'expansion" de la gendarmerie,' *Le Monde*, 4 March.
Plenel, E. (1989), 'Entendu par le magistrat instructeur le directeur de la DST affirme que M. Pasqua lui avait ordonné de fournir un faux passeport à Yves Chalier,' *Le Monde*, 23 November.
Plenel, E. (1991), 'Irlandais de Vincennes: les cachotteries de l'Elysée,' *Le Monde*, 21 March.

Plenel (E. (1992), *La part d'ombre*, Paris, Stock.
Plume, C., Pasquini, X. (1980), *Une enquête de police sur le Canard Enchaîné*, Paris, Editions J. Picolec.
Pontaut, J.-M., Szpiner, F. (1989), *L'Etat hors-la-loi*, Paris, Fayard.
Pradel, J. (1990), 'Ecoutes téléphoniques et Convention européenne des Droits de l'Homme,' *Recueil Dalloz-Sirey*, Chronique IV.
Quadruppani, S. (1989), *L'anti-terrorisme en France ou la terreur intégrée, 1981–1989*, Paris, La Découverte.
Reiner, R. (1985), *The Politics of the Police*, Brighton, Wheetsheaf Books.
Revue de la Police Nationale (1984), Ministère de l'Intérieur, Paris, No. 120.
Sarrazin, J. (1974), *La police en miettes*, Paris, Calmann-Lévy.
Secrétariat Général pour la Police (1968), *Fichiers de police*, Paris, Ministère de l'Intérieur.
Thue, L., Porcher, R. (1990), 'Trois administrations en fiches: police, gendarmerie, douanes,' *Cahiers de la Sécurité Intérieure*, 2, 167–196.
Vaujour, J. (1990), 'Genèse et développements de la sécurité privée: le point de vue de M. Jean Vaujour (Interview by F. Ocqueteau),' *Cahiers de la Sécurité Intérieure*, 3, 31–60.

Translated by Nora Scott

Heiner Busch and Albrecht Funk* | **Undercover Tactics as an Element of Preventive Crime Fighting in the Federal Republic of Germany**

1. INTRODUCTION

The use of police agents operating in secret appears to have become a universal element of modern police work, for which the Anglo-American term 'undercover agent' seems to be universally accepted today. In the Federal Republic of Germany, the use of so-called 'covert investigators' has also become a commonplace procedure, although these agents have by no means become as prolific as in the United States. Indeed, this method of police work can look back upon a venerable past, as is evidenced by Karl Marx's description of a famous trial in 1852 against some 'communist conspirators' for high treason in Cologne, accused of having contacts with Marx and other immigrants in London.[1]

This should be reason enough to turn our attention to the police definition of 'undercover agents,' the scope and the areas of undercover policing and to ask what their intended and unintended consequences are. The best way to study the significance of 'undercover agents' in Germany would be a systematic empirical analysis of their part in different types of covert operations. We are quite certain that the consequences of undercover policing that Gary T. Marx has so meticulously found for the United States also holds true for the Federal Republic of Germany. Even the attempt to arrive at a cost-benefit analysis of undercover work in Germany would reveal similarities. What in one case appears sensible, becomes illegitimate or simply dysfunctional in a different operational setting (Marx, 1988, 108). Ultimately, every evaluation of a concrete situation is crucially dependent upon identifying the extent to which a particular mode of

---

* Members of the Arbeitsgruppe Bürgerrechte, Free University, Berlin, Germany.
1. A Prussian police officer travelled to London and try to adduce evidence of a conspiracy among German immigrants in London against the Prussian State, *cf.* Karl Marx (1852), 'Enthüllungen über den Kommunistenprozeß in Köln,' in: *Marx-Engels Werke*, vol. 8, 405, and Siemann, 1983, 517.

operation evokes changes in the organizational context of police work in general and in the practice of crime investigation in particular.

We have chosen a different approach. The access to facts and figures about concrete undercover operations in Germany is extremely limited. Only for the *Bundeskriminalamt* – roughly comparable to the FBI – is information about the number of 'covert investigations' between 1982 and 1990 available. It carries out about 70 operations every year.[2] Even this figure is unknown for most of the sixteen German *'Länder'* – states with their own police force. The occasional empirical evidence about undercover operations in some spectacular cases and trials does not allow a systematic analysis. Besides the general tendency of police forces to keep undercover operations secret, there is one very simple reason for this. Up till now most German state officials have even denied that we have 'undercover agents' in the American sense of the term. Police officers are supposed to strictly obey the law (*Legalitätsprinzip*). German criminal procedure does not permit 'covert investigators' to commit crimes in order to infiltrate a targeted group (*cf.* Lüderssen, 1985, 6; Körner, 1990, 108).

'Undercover operations' have a different significance in Germany, a country with a distinctive legal context and police tradition relative to the Anglo-American criminal justice system. The term 'undercover' insufficiently describes the scope of *'Vorfeldermittlungen'* (preliminary investigations) and *'vorbeugende Verbrechensbekämpfung'* (preventive crime fighting), which dominate the discussion of policing strategies in Germany. At the same time it is evident that the use of 'undercover agents' is becoming more important in Germany, too, as a result of the general and complex transformation of organizational structures, crime and policing strategies. Our approach, therefore, will be to deal with the question of the significance of 'undercover agents' within an analysis of the organizational context of policing and the changing patterns of crime investigations.

We organize our paper around three propositions. In section 2 we shall attempt to demonstrate that undercover methods must be considered as an element of changing methods of crime investigation within the broad concept of 'preventive crime fighting.' Then, in section 3, we shall attempt to deal with the effects this will have on police organization and, in section 4, on the relationship between the police, the public prosecutor, and the court.

In this manner we illustrate the effects and civil rights costs of the concept of 'preventive crime fighting.' The costs are not merely from the particular dangers of any specific undercover technique and its application to differing areas (drug trafficking, terrorism, etc.). It is our contention that the crucial problem lies in the institutionalization of policing strategies, in which police activities are increasingly linked to criteria such as 'organized crime' whose

---

2. During the same time – from 1985 to 1990 – the number of formally reported wire-tapping operations of the *Bundeskriminalamt* based on the Code of Criminal Procedure almost doubled (from 98 to 173). *Cf.* Deutsche Bundestag, 12. Session, nr. 12/1255, 2. Many of the sixteen state polices run even more wire-tapping operations; in Baden-Württemberg the number rose from 182 in 1984 to 520 in 1992. Altogether this results in a total number of wire-tapping operations in Germany – 3499 in 1993 – which is several times higher than in the United States.

interpretation and social concretization can only take place within the confines of the organization itself.[3]

2. 'UNDERCOVER' IN THE GERMAN DEBATE ON PREVENTIVE CRIME FIGHTING

In contrast to England, in the German police system in the 19th century there was no contradiction between the idea of preventive policing and undercover work. On the contrary, in the 'Higher Privy Police Forces' these concepts were inextricably interconnected. These police forces were 'higher' simply because they had, as agencies of the state executive, the task of 'preventing crimes against the state.'[4] These were secret police forces not only because they operated with covert techniques, but because they pursued the goals of the king and his Privy Council.

Political debate in Germany in the 19th century centered around defining the scope of these goals and thus of the legal limits on the police. This debate ultimately culminated in a strict legal limitation of police powers in the criminal procedure and in special police statutes (*Polizeigesetze*). The police was authorized – be it for the purpose of law enforcement or for the purpose of prevention – to interfere with the property rights and civil liberties of citizens only in the presence of a concrete suspicion of crime or in the event of impending danger. In other words, by law the police was tied to a reactive model of policing (Funk, 1985).

In this debate on legal control of the police in 19th-century Germany, the question of undercover investigations played only a minor role. Such methods were not only part of the tradition of the political police, in which, in the days of the German empire, 'undercover agents' were even used to keep track of moods and sentiments in working class pubs (Evans, 1989). Temporary covert activities were also an institutionalized element of detective work (*see* below). However, in the criminal department these operations had usually been restricted – in contrast to the political police – to focused investigations in criminal cases, in which the police tried to convict a suspect. Thus, 'undercover operations' were still part of the reactive model of policing and the typical German program for controlling police activity by binding them to impending dangers and/or concrete suspicion of a criminal offense.[5] Of course, no model of legal control provides a sufficient explanation for the concrete development of crime investigation and the role of 'undercover policing' in Germany. These remarks are merely intended to draw attention to the legal and political context

---

3. Our research group has an empirical project on the structural changes in criminal investigation (*cf.* the research proposal 'Strukturwandel der Verbrechensbekämpfung,' Berlin, 1992). We thank Norbert Pütter and Sabine Strunk for valuable suggestions.
4. Thus the formulation in a typical royal decree dealing with the establishment of a Higher Police Force in Westphalia in 1808, quoted in Siemann, 1985, 59.
5. It is precisely for this reason that Germany also has its own police statutes as an independent body of administrative law in which the preventive task of forestalling impending dangers is codified in addition to the code of criminal procedure.

in which the adjective 'undercover' played only a minor role until the 80's in the German debate on new investigation methods for the police war against crime.

The demand for overcoming the traditionally reactive pattern of police activity however can be traced back to the end of the 60's. The demand for reform arose on the one hand out of a constant increase in recorded crime, i.e. an increase in police input, and on the other hand out of the perception of 'a more mobile and thus more unstable order' (Herold, 1972, 133). As a consequence the reformers within the police tried to change the police 'from a mere instrument of enforcement' to an intelligent, proactive agency of crime control.

The goals of creating a police force superior to all other institutions in recognizing and identifying problems of social control, based upon a systematic analysis of its own input and the aim of exerting preventive control, was hardly achieved by the reform efforts of the 70's. Even if the massive expansion of police forces and the reform of police organizations in Germany during the 70's failed to meet the goal of wide-ranging prevention, the reform efforts would still have a profound impact on patterns of criminal investigation and policing strategies (Busch et al., 1985). Integrating federal and state police forces into and via a data processing network, the expansion of the *Bundeskriminalamt* (Federal Bureau of Investigation) and *Landeskriminalämter* (State Bureaus of Investigation) and increased specialization and professionalization, all helped to erode traditional reactive patterns of action and led to the development of proactive policing strategies. In legal circles they are referred to as methods 'of preventive crime fighting' (*cf.* Weßlau, 1989). During the 70's most of these methods were electronically based. These include:

- police surveillance, i.e. the (covert) registration of a person's location, companions, vehicle at police checkpoints (e.g. border, traffic check);
- the 'fishnet search,' i.e. the registration of all persons passing special checkpoints with the help of data files (e.g. wanted lists) in the shared computer network of the Federal and the state police;
- computer-matching, which was frequently used at the end of the 70's, and crime analysis. For the latter special types of data processing programs have been developed for general intelligence ('PIOS') and targeted investigations ('Spudok').

These techniques are 'covert' only in the sense that they include the collection and storage of data on persons by the police without their knowledge or without knowledge of what use the police are making of such data. Such new techniques in the hands of the police, used as proactive methods in the fight against terrorism, tended to be more a bone of contention in the political discussion in the 70's than the deployment of 'undercover agents.' The use of 'covert investigators' still played a minor role in the concept of preventive crime fighting. There were two reasons for this. On the one hand, the access to terrorist groups by 'undercover agents' is extremely difficult, even informers are hard to recruit. On the other hand, in the initial efforts to legalize proactive methods in the code of criminal procedure and police laws, the use of 'undercover agents' was the most sensitive point.

The first signs of the deployment of 'covert investigators' surfaced during the 70's in the drug and narcotics divisions of the criminal police of the *Länder* (states). In the State of Baden-Württemberg, for example, mobile drug units that predominantly employed informers have existed since 1973. So-called operational investigation groups, aimed at higher levels of drug trafficking, also used 'covert investigators' deployed on long-term infiltration assignments. All in all, 'undercover policing' still remained restricted to sporadic short-term operations up to the 80's, when the fight against organized crime led to a generalization and expansion of the concept of 'preventive crime fighting.' Defining organized crime as a work area for the criminal police legitimates reversing the traditional reactive structure of criminal investigation.

Yet a legal definition of the term 'organized crime' was lacking. Definitions, as a director of the *Landeskriminalamt* Hamburg (State Bureau of Criminal Investigation) argues, were of little help in everyday practice (Sielaff, 1983, 417). Organized crime, according to the guidelines of the Standing Conference of Secretaries of Justice and Interior, 'is the methodical commitment of crimes of considerable significance as a single offense or as a whole directed towards profit or power if and when more than two individuals cooperate a) using commercial or business-like structures, b) using force or other means of intimidation or c) exerting an influence on politics, press, public adminstration, the justice system or commerce and industry.' (*Gemeinsame Richtlinie*, 1990, 2.1.)

Within this concept of organized crime, the necessity for proactive 'undercover operations' beyond the realm of normal input-oriented police work can be defined only in general terms. The lack of charges, the way these criminals act (their *modus operandi*), and the intimidation of potential witnesses all contribute – as the supporters of the new concept would argue – to the failure of the traditional reactive model of detective work. While charges and complaints filed by citizens give rise to roughly 90 per cent of all police activity with regard to criminal acts, experts argue that it is different with respect to organized crime. Stümper, one of the representatives of proactive policing, summarized the goals of the police in the following way: 'This (type of) crime can't be effectively fought solely with the traditional methods of detective work. The police themselves must go underground – be it with their own personnel, by taping their own reliable and high-yield sources of information, or through the extensive use of technical means. It must recognize even the first signs of criminal activity and systematically develop information necessary for this end' (Stümper, 1985, 67).

In line with this position the methods of undercover investigation described by G.T. Marx – using undercover agents, buying stolen property, arranging mock deals, covert observation, etc. – have also become more important in Germany over the last ten years. Today, undercover operations are staged more systematically and more often on a broader scale than they were prior to the 80's. They are now combined with techniques of electronic surveillance and investigation that were limited to fighting terrorists by the political police in the 70's. This enlarged pattern of undercover operations centers around special areas of investigation, referred to as organized crime.

3. THE CONSEQUENCES FOR POLICE ORGANIZATION

Since 1984 there has been a significant expansion of specialized organized crime units in the criminal police. This resulted from agreement on a common proposal by a subcommittee of the Conference of the Ministers of Interior, which links the different police forces of the Federal Government and the sixteen states into an integrated system through recommendation and binding decisions. This agreement favored the establishment of special units and divisions for fighting organized crime with the additional task of both coordinating and implementing the use of covert operations. Units or divisions of this nature were set up:

- at the *Bundeskriminalamt* (Federal Bureau of Criminal Investigation) for special interstate cases and international organized crime;
- at the *Landeskriminalämter* (State Bureau of Criminal Investigation) for interstate crime;
- in major cities for regional organized crime to the extent that focal points of organized crime are located in these regions.

The agreement described the task of these units in the following way:

> 'Police officers specially trained for undercover and/or covert operations are to serve on a stand-by basis in these units. These units are to perform the following special or general tasks in the field of organized crime:
> - retrieval, collection, assessment and dissemination of information;
> - communication with their own agency, service or force and with the special units of other agencies, service or force;
> - covert investigation of individuals, criminal activities and individual crimes;
> - control and command of investigation in certain proceedings involving fields of crimes or, with special orders, in proceedings involving specific crimes up to and including the presentation of files in court proceedings.'
> (AK II, 1984, 79).

Meanwhile all states had built up such units in the State Bureaus of Criminal Investigation (*Landeskriminalämter*); at the same time the *Bundeskriminalamt* extended its corresponding departments. On the state level these units are still organized in various ways: some integrated the drug units in the Organized Crime Unit of their State Bureaus (as in Bavaria) others did not (i.e. Hamburg); some segregate these units totally from the other divisions of the criminal investigation department (Lower Saxony), others prefer a stronger integration (Nordrhein-Westfalen); some develop regional subunits (Bavaria), others concentrate organized crime investigation in the State Bureau of Criminal Investigation. Ignoring the peculiarities in different states, the general features of these units can be summarized:

1. The organized crime units form a new field of specialization in the criminal investigation departments, with sophisticated technology, increased financial resources and a higher level of personnel strength and professionalization.

In contrast to ordinary superintendents' offices, they exhibit greater flexibility and are subject to less time pressure in investigations. This applies equally to other specialized units in criminal investigation; it is a particular feature of the organized crime units however, that they integrate police intelligence, crime investigation and undercover methods.

2. These units build up their own information system, inaccessible to the rest of the criminal investigation department. Typically, the organized crime units use the same modes of operation used by the political units. In addition to the regional databanks maintained by the State Bureau of Criminal Investigation, they also maintain a national 'PIOS' databank at the *Bundeskriminalamt* (PIOS stands for Persons, Institutions, Objects – like buildings – and Things – pieces of potential material evidence), where all relevant information of potentially interstate interest is collected.[6] The 'evidence documentations' set up for individual cases or larger scope cases ('SPUDOK') basically function according to the same principle and are ultimately fed as far as necessary into the PIOS databank once the case investigation has been completed. By means of these databanks, 'relevant persons' as well as 'connections between persons, group of persons, institutions, objects and things' are to become recognizable and provide 'information for police investigation tactics.' (Sielaff, 1990, 71).

3. The data stored in these databanks are only partially the product of the investigations and covert operations performed by these units themselves. For the most part they are extracted from the information gained from the day-to-day activities of the police and the ordinary detective superintendents' offices (homicide, burglary, etc.). There is 'mainly a one way flow of information within the police force from the beat-level to the organized crime units ... i.e. policemen on patrol duty and detective superintendents pass on their information and tips without asking any feedback. There is a problem in convincing beat-level cops of the necessity of this one-way communication.' (Rebscher/Vahlenkamp, 1988, 156). Because of that, organized-crime units in the State Bureaus of Criminal Investigation established a net of liaison officers in many units of the criminal investigation department to ensure the flow of information.

4. In many states (e.g. Hamburg, Lower Saxony) the organized-crime units even exercise formal authority over the ordinary detective offices (e.g. burglary, car theft). In specific instances the chief of the organized-crime unit 'can give orders to other units to abandon investigations running counter to his own.' (Sielaff, 1985, 580). He also has the right to claim responsibility for investigations previously conducted by other detective units or to delegate responsibility for investigations to these ordinary units.[7]

---

6. Each and every piece of information is coded as a separate file containing pre-formatted data such as identity characteristics and open unformatted file extensions and cross-references to other files. This manner of organization is intended to facilitate maximal search capability. Searching either takes place according to regular search categories or according to the cross-references of current files.
7. In some states only after prior consultations with the chief of the *Landeskriminalamt* (State Bureau of Criminal Investigation).

5. The organized-crime units stimulated a growing demand for 'covert investigators.' Meanwhile, these agents form a group of professionals for covert investigations, in some states separate from the organized-crime unit responsible for intelligence and investigations. The dominant trend, however, appears to be that the organized-crime units get their own covert investigators and professionals for surveillance methods. On the one hand, integration facilitates taking control of covert operations; on the other hand, it's easier to keep covert investigations secret in the criminal investigation division (e.g. for Hamburg, Sielaff, 1990, 74).
6. As a result of the specific combination of sensitive case investigation and the use of covert techniques, organized-crime units are pledged to secrecy to a greater extent than in ordinary investigations. In some states (e.g. Hamburg, Lower Saxony) these units are even spatially separated from the rest of the criminal investigation department. According to one source: 'Particularly with reference to investigations of professional and organized criminals who may indeed have access to an inside view of police organization, we must pay special attention to maintaining security. In the case of undercover operations, this becomes even more imperative due to the potential dangers that could arise for our officers. Thus, it only makes sense that our (organized crime) unit is located at the *Landeskriminalamt* (State Bureau), completely sealed off from the rest of the force.' (Sielaff, 1985, 580).
7. Legally, these units possess no special police powers directly linked to organized crime. The so-called 'Organized Crime Law' (OrgKG) of 1992 – an amendment to the code of criminal procedure – avoids any definition of 'organized crime' (*cf.* Pütter, 1993, 161; Schoreit, 1991, 538). The label 'organized crime' only serves to define different areas of responsibility in the criminal investigation division. At the same time the assignment of cases to an organized-crime unit makes a real difference. It opens up the use of methods of 'preliminary investigations' codified in the criminal procedure and the police statutes. The range of crimes for which the use of techniques of electronic surveillance and covert registration is authorized is far-reaching. It even extends to wire-tapping and the deployment of covert investigators in cases of professional fencing or organized theft. As a result, these methods are even legally available to detective superintendents' offices occupied with routine investigations of burglary or theft. In actuality, however, techniques and methods of proactive, covert investigations are available only to the highly professional units of organized crime and drugs, terrorism and political crime.

4. THE EFFECTS OF 'PREVENTIVE CRIME FIGHTING' ON THE CRIMINAL JUSTICE SYSTEM

In the realm of organized crime, investigations go beyond the level of individual crime. The concept of 'preventive crime fighting' leads to the conclusion that not only are the police faced with the task of creating units no longer bound to specific crimes, but that the only meaningful investigation involves pro-active and covert methods to detect the criminal.

> 'The crime-fighting approach is predominantly pro-active; it transcends the level of the individual crime and deals with persons and/or organizations, The traditional principle of reacting to crimes, primarily individual crimes, is as best a flanking measure. It is not the investigation of an individual crime, but rather the uncovering of the underlying relationship and series of crimes that will put us on the track of the criminal organization, thus forming the pattern of combatting it effectively. In this sense, fighting organized crime is "network detection".' (Sielaff, 1990, 69).

Although this sounds like sociological research, in practice 'preventive crime fighting' reverses the traditional 'inductive' method of investigation to a 'deductive' one. At first, 'preliminary investigations' involve the collection of police intelligence to substantiate a general suspicion, they correspond to this extent to the 'anticipatory intelligence operations' described by Gary T. Marx for the United States (Marx, 1988, 61). In addition, they include preventive and facilitating undercover operations to reduce a general suspicion to a particular, specific, concrete suspicion and lead, last but not least, to an arrest of suspects. Compared with undercover operations in the United States, 'preliminary investigations' still rely more on techniques of electronic surveillance and databanks. Besides the reasons mentioned above – the heritage of technical optimism in the police reform of the 70's and the still existing legal uncertainty about the discretionary power of undercover agents (*see* below) – the different evaluation stems from enhanced chances of electronic identification and registration due to the existence of identity cards, the registration of residents and many other administrative databanks containing files of citizens (e.g. vehicle registration).

Consequently, in Germany the effects of undercover policing first became increasingly obvious in the growing informational capacities of police surveillance and registration. The increasing demand for other private and public data files of computer-matching and screening programs resulted in confrontations with data protection commissioners. Meanwhile all these methods have been introduced into the code of criminal procedure and police statutes (*Polizeigesetze*) as means of preventive crime fighting. In addition, 'preliminary investigations' inevitably require that many more persons be kept under surveillance and stored in databanks than in a traditional inductive investigation. This is a direct result of the instruments being used: maintaining surveillance of telephone booths suspected of being used by a potential criminal implies also surveillance of other persons using these booths. If a person is placed under 'covert police surveillance' (referred to in the Schengen Agreement as 'covert registration'), all his contacts are stored in a data file, even fellow passengers who are sitting in the same railroad compartment. For this reason, data protection commissioners have for years pointed out the fact, that 'PIOS' and 'SPUDOK' databanks contain numerous so-called 'other persons,' i.e. persons not even under preliminary suspicion of having committed any crime (*cf. Tätigkeitsbericht des BfD*, 1984ff). These persons thus are classified as 'not yet suspect' and they remain in this category until additional information result in a different conclusion or the investigation is terminated.

Meanwhile, the increased use of undercover operations in the 80's gave rise to a political and legal discussion about the wide range of police discretion inevitably linked with such methods. A Subcommittee of the Standing Conference of Secretaries of the Interior and of Justice pointed to the gist of the problem in 1978. 'The police officer involved in covert crime fighting will only be successful if given the opportunity, to unconditionally conduct surveillance for rather long periods of time without having to intervene.' (*Rechtsprobleme*, 1978, 70). This implies that organized-crime units have the right to delay arrests in order to infiltrate a network of criminals and to detect the hard core of criminal activities. This discretion poses only minor legal problems as long as the police are informed about potential crimes by means of electronic surveillance, wire-tapping or informers. In order to prevent or detect a more serious crime, the police have the right to suspend an arrest unless the life and integrity of people (or other outstanding interests protected by law) are put at risk.

The most contentious matter is the scope of discretionary powers permitted to investigators involved in criminal activities. The existence of undercover agents itself had been established in police statutes and finally in 1992 in the code of criminal procedure. They are described in § 110a of the code as:

> investigating officers who are given a modified long-lasting identity (legend). They have the authority to act on their own account in legal transactions using this identity. They have permission to produce, modify, and use documents insofar as it is indispensable to building and maintaining the legend.

There is nothing in the code, however, about the legal limits of action, the most disputed aspect of undercover work. Problems arise especially in two areas:

a. In 'facilitative operations' that try to provoke a criminal act (Marx, 1988, 65). Such methods are heavily used by German police in drug operations. In many smaller deals as well as in larger controlled deliveries carried out to detect international drug-trafficking, it is doubtful whether the targeted person would have committed the act without the agent's help. It is a punishable offense nevertheless. The limits of provocation are frequently under dispute; the courts' rulings on inadmissible provocations indicate at least the existence of rather dubious undercover operations in some criminal investigation departments (e.g. where the seller as well as the potential purchaser were informers or agents, or the agent put a drug laboratory at the disposal of a hesitating chemist, *cf.* Körner, 1990, 625ff).
b. Problems arise likewise in operations targeted to infiltrate organized crime. In order to live and move in a criminal environment, undercover agents have to adapt their behavior to that of criminals. They frequently have to commit crimes in order to maintain their own covers. One German agent acknowledged committing up to two hundred crimes during his career (Koriath, 1992, 370). Legally, however, these acts are still highly contentious. The 'principle of legality,' the ideal of strictly law-abiding police

agents is still central in the legal description of police work. The Supreme Court has justified the use of 'covert investigators' with constructions such as 'supra-legal emergencies' in accordance with the criminal code and the purported necessity of guaranteeing the 'ability of the penal system to stay in operation.' Even mainstream legal opinions have found it difficult to accept this line of reasoning and have demanded a clear codification of the activities of undercover agents in criminal procedure (*cf.* Hassemer, 1985, 71ff). In the political arena, however, there is no majority for such a solution and as a result codification still remains on the agenda of the lawmakers of the Standing Conference of Secretaries of the Interior.

The legal ambiguity of covert investigators is part of a more general problem of undercover operations: the functional and strategic approach to the rule of law. Special police units, two authors of the Federal Bureau admit, measure their effectiveness 'not only in terms of investigations completed, but also and particularly with reference to the gradual illumination of the structures' of organized crime (Rebscher/Vahlenkamp, 1988, 160). Undercover policing frequently combines a whole set of goals: gathering intelligence, considering criminal policy goals (e.g. not intervening in a controlled crime scene) and protecting information sources and the false identities of agents. This necessarily results in a police strategy that tries to use undercover operations mainly as a means of extracting a confession or finding other pieces of evidence, thus 'sparing investigating agencies the necessity of divulging their covert methods and evidence later in the court.' (Deckert, 1991, 1157).

In contrast to the police, public prosecutors cannot fully commit themselves to such a strategic concept in formal court proceedings. They must present legal evidence of guilt, above all, to the defense. Their effectiveness is a function of their ability to gain confirmation in court of charges brought under criminal law.

The institutionalization of this functional difference between police and public prosecutor as part of the legal system is complicated and it becomes even more so in the area of preliminary investigations. Formally the public prosecutor's office is in charge of the whole investigation process; the police operate only in accordance with instructions of the prosecutor. Legally, this competence is restricted to criminal prosecutions: the reactive detection of crimes regulated by the code of criminal procedure. The prevention of crime and the detection of impending dangers are the traditional purview of the police force as codified in police statutes. Neither public prosecutors nor the criminal courts have any authority in this area.

The concept of preventive crime fighting and undercover policing undermines this traditional separation in two respects. On the one hand, it dissolves the legal terms of 'impending danger' and 'concrete crime' into the notion of abstract 'risk' and general 'suspicion' requiring 'preliminary investigations.' On the other hand, it moulds proactive and repressive operations into a general task of 'preventive crime fighting.' From the beginning of the 70's, police authorities and the Standing Conference of Secretaries of the Interior have expansively interpreted the new methods of preliminary investigations as an integral part of traditional policing. An investigation falls within the competence of the public prosecutor's office only if the police succeed in identifying concrete suspects and gaining legal evidence as a result of undercover operations. In the legal debate, this position of the police could not gain acceptance. In actuality, however, the police have been rather successful. The criminal investigation departments have total control over the databanks; the police and not the public prosecutor runs the informants or undercover agents. In crime prevention – a rather large area of preliminary investigations regulated in the police statutes – the police in most states are only obliged 'to announce' the deployment of undercover agents. And even in targeted crime investigations for which public prosecutors are definitely responsible, they often remain at a disadvantage. Information is pre-shifted or simply not provided. By accepting the police argument that they have to protect their information sources and undercover operations, public prosecutors allow themselves to be transformed into the 'dancing bears' of the police (Spiegel, 1990, 10, 106).

This relationship of dependence has weakened in the last few years. On the one hand, procedural controls have been strengthened in the last amendment to the code of criminal procedure, codifying the use of covert investigators and other undercover techniques in 1992. The public prosecutor has to approve the application of measures like covert registration or investigation. On the other hand, public prosecutors have succeeded in setting up their own specialized organized-crime units. As a consequence, the problem of how to strike a balance between rather multifunctional undercover operations and criminal prosecution founded on the rule of law is incorporated increasingly into the public prosecutor's office. In many large cities, the organized-crime units of the police for their part set up special offices for maintaining liaison with the state attorney's office. The danger of such a liaison is that the state attorney's office may find itself being gradually drawn away from judicial criteria, becoming increasingly committed to the criteria of police efficiency.

However, as soon as public prosecutors bring a charge in court, undercover operations have to face the challenge of legal evaluation. The role of informers and undercover agents makes this particularly clear. The *Bundesgerichtshof* (Federal Court) has strictly upheld the principle of public trial in its rulings. Neither the defendant nor defense counsel can be removed from the proceedings during the testimony of informants or covert investigators. If being presented as witnesses, they may testify only if they are willing to reveal their identities (Weider, 1984, 29). And if the identity of an informer or agent is publicly known, they are obliged to testify; thus defense attorneys have a strong incentive to find it out.

For this reason the police try to keep undercover operations out of the scope of criminal procedure as far as possible. Covert operations, as an attorney has noted, 'shy away from being presented as evidence the way the devil flinches at the sight of holy water' (Deckers, 1991, 1257). Remarks and decisions on ongoing operations are preferably noted solely in the working files of the criminal police; informers or covert investigators are introduced only as hearsay witnesses. Most important is the fact that police administrations in the departments of interior and public prosecutors have the right to close police files if public security or the life of the witness is at risk, as well as to refuse to permit police informers or undercover agents to testify. Limitations imposed by police authorities in the testimony of informers and undercover agents definitely constrain the hearing of the evidence. They signify, as a public prosecutor put it frankly, 'that the executive power has to perform tasks that might collide with the duty to support criminal justice. These tasks may be more important than the ascertainment of the truth by the courts' (Körner, 1990, 685). Such restrictions are frequently found in trials, e.g. in cases of provocative drug deals with informers and agents. They indicate the dependence of the courts on evidence given by the police, that is submitted by prosecutors in cases evolving from undercover operations. It becomes the judge's responsibility to decide the extent to which he is willing to accept the police version of the facts.

5. CONCLUSION

The traditional reactive mode of crime investigation will remain intact for the majority of offenses and even be reinforced by a steadily increasing number of citizen reports and complaints. From this perspective the concepts of 'organized crime' and 'preliminary crime fighting' at first represent selection strategies that separate an area of intensified investigations from routine investigations. In such an organizational perspective, vague definitions of organized crime (severe crime, particular social damage) are functional. The administrative 'working terms' guarantee discretion in a selection process determined by a variety of goals: not only the control and investigation of specific areas of crime (e.g. drug-trafficking, the 'mafia') but also interests of and within the police organization and interest in the symbolic use of criminal politics. Simultaneously, the resources and legal instruments of preventive crime fighting available to the specialized and professionalized organized-crime units (terrorism, political crime) open up new possibilities of police surveillance and investigation in the most intimate spheres in the life of citizens.

This does not make it permissible to draw the conclusion that they have little impact on the criminal justice system as a whole, although these covert operations create serious problems in selected areas and cases. The concepts of 'organized crime' and 'preventive crime fighting' transform the legally defined 'reality' of criminal offenses into a world of crime defined by the police. Terms like 'organized crime' or 'crime of considerable relevance' and other blanket clauses do not provide clear normative criteria that guarantee legal accountability. In Max Weber's sense of the term, they are not 'formal-legal' concepts, but rather 'material-utilitarian' criteria, the definition of which becomes the responsibility of administrative experts: an activity Weber interprets and discusses as a step toward bureaucracies' assuming a life of their own (Max Weber, 1972, 128, 122; Schluchter, 1972, 122ff).

This shift to material-utilitarian concepts in the code of criminal procedure and the police statutes has far-reaching consequences. In Germany accountability of the police is established primarily by law. Consequently, increasing the flexibility of formal-legal norms erodes the traditional model of legal (*rechtsstaatlicher*) police control. In legislation this resulted in an increasing use of procedural regulations in the police statutes and the code of criminal procedure. The approval of public prosecutors or even of judges is required for many methods of preventive crime fighting (i.e. judicial approval of covert investigators or wire-tapping). However, it is doubtful whether these procedures could really balance the increasing discretionary powers of the police. As long as these approval procedures are handled as purely internal matters of the police, prosecutors and (special) judges and are shielded from public scrutiny, the impact of these procedural controls will likely be rather limited.

REFERENCES

AK II, 1984, Ad hoc – Ausschuß des Arbeitskreises II der Ständigen Konferenz der Innenminister der Länder und des Bundes, *Neue Methoden der Verbrechensbekämpfung*, reprinted in: *Cilip (Bürgerrechte und Polizei)* 1984/1, 11, 76–86.

Deckers, R. (1991), 'Verteidigung beim ersten Zugriff der Polizei,' *Neue Juristische Wochenschrift*, 18, 1151–1158.

Evans, R., ed. (1989), *Kneipengespräche im Kaiserreich; Stimmungsberichte der Hamburger Politischen Polizei 1892–1914*, Reinbek bei Hamburg, Rowohlt.

Funk, A. (1986), *Polizei und Rechtsstaat; die Entwicklung des staatlichen Gewaltmonopols in Preußen 1848–1914*, Frankfurt am Main/New York, Campus.

Gemeinsame Richtlinien der Justizminister/-senatoren und der Innenminister/ -senatoren der Länder über die Zusammenarbeit bei der Verfolgung Organisierter Kriminalität vom 13.11.1990, *Ministerialblatt für das Land Nordrhein-Westfalen*, 93, 21 December 1990.

Hassemer, W. (1985), 'Die Funktionstüchtigkeit der Strafrechtspflege; ein neuer Rechtsbegriff,' in: Lüderssen, K., ed., *V-Leute; die Falle im Rechtsstaat*, Frankfurt am Main, Suhrkamp, 71–91.

Herold, H. (1972), 'Gesellschaftlicher Wandel – Chance der Polizei,' *Die Polizei*, 5, 133–137.

Koriath, G. (1992), 'Straftaten bei verdeckten Ermittlungen,' *Kriminalistik*, 6, 370–389.

Körner, H.H. (1990), *Betäubungsmittelgesetz*, München, Beck.

Lüderssen, K., ed. (1985), *V-Leute; die Falle im Rechtsstaat*, Frankfurt am Main, Suhrkamp.

Marx, G.T. (1988), *Undercover; Police Surveillance in America*, Berkeley, University of California Press.

Marx, K. (1852), 'Enthüllungen über den Kommunistenprozeß zu Köln,' in: *Marx-Engels Werke*, vol. 8, Berlin (GDR), Dietz, 1953, 405–430.

Pütter, N. (1993), 'Verrechtlichung '92: das OrgKG,' in: Komitee für Grundrechte und Demokratie, *Jahrbuch 1991/92*, Sensbachtal, 161–168.

Rebscher, E./Vahlenkamp, W. (1988), *Organisierte Kriminalität in der Bundesrepublik Deutschland*, Wiesbaden, Bundeskriminalamt (Sonderband der BKA-Forschungsreihe).

Rechtsprobleme, 1982, 'Rechtsprobleme der Polizei bei verdeckten Ermittlungen. Ergebnisse einer von dem Innen- und dem Justizministerium Baden-Württembergs eingesetzten Arbeitsgruppe (1978),' reprinted in: *Cilip (Bürgerrechte und Polizei)*, 1981/1, 11, 63–72.

Schoreit, A. (1991), 'Bekämpfung der Organisierten Kriminalität und anderer Formen von Straftaten aus der Sicht der Polizei und der Staatsanwaltschaft,' *Strafverteidiger*, 11, 538ff.

Schluchter, W. (1972), *Aspekte bürokratischer Herrschaft*, München, List.

Sielaff, W. (1983), 'Bis zur Bestechung leitender Polizeibeamter; Erscheinungsformen und Bekämpfung der Organisierten Kriminalität in Hamburg,' *Kriminalistik*, 8/9, 417–422.

Sielaff, W. (1985), 'Verdeckte Ermittlung in der Sex- und Glückspielindustrie,' *Kriminalistik*, 12, 577–581.

Sielaff, W. (1990), 'Bekämpfung der Organisierten Kriminalität in einem Stadtstaat,' in: *Organisierte Kriminalität*, Schriftenreihe der Polizei-Führungsakademie, 3/4, 65–80.

Siemann, W. (1985), *Deutschlands Ruhe, Sicherheit und Ordnung; die Anfänge der politischen Polizei in Deutschland*, Tübingen, Niemeyer.

Stümper, A. (1985), 'Organisierte Kriminalität; ein ernstzunehmendes Problem,' in: Lüderssen, K., ed., *V-Leute; die Falle im Rechtsstaat*, Frankfurt am Main, Suhrkamp, 65–70.

Tätigkeitsberichte des Bundesbeauftragten für den Datenschutz, 1984 (Sechster Tätigkeitsbericht), Bonn.

Weber, M. (1972), *Wirtschaft und Gesellschaft*, Köln, Kiepenheuer & Witsch.

Weider, H-J. (1984), 'Verteidigung gegen Phantomgestalten; V-Leute im Strafverfahren,' *Cilip (Bürgerrechte und Polizei)*, 1984/1, 17, 29–35.

Weßlau, E. (1989), *Vorfeldermittlungen; Probleme der Legalisierung vorbeugender Verbrechensbekämpfung aus strafprozeßrechtlicher Sicht*, Berlin, Duncker & Humblot (Strafrechtliche Abhandlungen, Neue Folge, vol. 65).

Jean-Paul Brodeur* | Undercover Policing in Canada: A Study of its Consequences

Marx (1988) devotes three chapters to an examination of the intended and unintended consequences of undercover policing. The aim of this paper is to discuss the implications of the concepts of intended and unintended consequences of undercover policing and to identify some of these consequences within the Canadian context. In Marx (1988, 130), intended and unintended consequences of undercover policing coincide respectively with the desirable and undesirable consequences of this type of policing. I shall argue that a large number of the undesirable consequences of undercover policing can be viewed as intentional.

The paper is divided into three parts. First, I briefly describe the Canadian policing apparatus and I discuss specific features of the Canadian context of undercover policing. Second, I analyze the meaning of intended/unintended consequences in the field of undercover policing. Finally, I identify some of these consequences and classify them according to four categories, namely (i) consequences which are desirable, from a law enforcement perspective, and intended; (ii) consequences which are desirable and unintended; (iii) consequences which are undesirable and intended and (iv) consequences which are undesirable and unintended. In my conclusion I argue that the dichotomy between intended and unintended consequences is too narrow to account for the consequences of undercover policing.

Part of the research upon which this paper is based on comes from a study that I did for the *Board of Inquiry on Activities of the RCMP Related to Allegations Made in the Senate of Canada* (Royal Canadian Mounted Police, (RCMP) 1991b). This board of inquiry was appointed after Canadian Senator Michel Cogger had alleged on the floor of the Senate that he was being unjustifiably targeted by the RCMP for an undercover sting operation (this operation can be briefly characterized as a mini-ABSCAM type of uncover police work; the senator was subsequently charged with peddling influence and was acquitted in 1993).

---

* Director, International Centre for Comparative Criminology, Université de Montréal, Montréal, Canada.

JEAN-PAUL BRODEUR

This was the first time that such operations had been publicly scrutinized in Canada. The chairman of this board of inquiry was Judge René J. Marin, who is also the Chairman of the RCMP External Review Committee (I shall also refer to RCMP (1991a) as the Marin report).

1. THE CANADIAN POLICE APPARATUS

There are four kinds of policing organizations that operate in Canada: the public police forces, civilian governmental agencies involved in the collection of security intelligence, security units which are parts of large companies owned by the federal government or by one of the provinces and, finally, private security agencies. I will briefly describe these organizations from the standpoint of their effective or potential involvement in undercover operations.

1.1. The Canadian Police Forces

In 1990, there were 56,034 peace officers (public police) in Canada; the police forces also employed 19,330 civilian personnel, thus putting the sum total of persons working for police forces at 75,364. This number has remained fairly stable until now.

Canada is a federation of ten provinces and two northern territories. There are three kinds of police forces in Canada. A federal police force, which is the RCMP. Three provincial police forces, the largest of which being the Ontario Provincial Police, for the province of Ontario, and the Sûreté du Québec (SQ), for the province of Québec (there is a third much smaller force in the province of Newfoundland). The two largest forces number between 5,000 and 6,000 men (it varies slightly from year to year). In addition, there are municipal police forces in Canadian cities. In 1994, for example, there were 156 municipal police forces in the province of Québec; the figure is lower in Ontario, where there are now approximately 130 regional and municipal police forces.

Except for the smaller ones (e.g., a force of 5 uniformed officers in a small rural town), all Canadian police forces have basically the same mandate. This mandate comprises order maintenance, which is basically upheld by uniformed police, criminal investigation and the provision of certain services (e.g. ambulance). Criminal investigators are not part in Canada of a separate corps, as in certain European countries (Scotland Yard in the U.K. or the *Police Judiciaire* in France). Furthermore, there is no Canadian police force which is wholly comprised of plainclothes investigators, like the U.S. Federal Bureau of Investigation (FBI). The largest part of the personnel of the RCMP wears a police uniform.

The biggest police force in Canada is the RCMP, which today numbers approximately 14,500 peace officers and 1,800 civilians. On top of the traditional police mandate described above, the RCMP performs several other important tasks. First, it is charged with the enforcement of numerous federal statutes (e.g., customs, airport security, etc.). Second, it acts as a provincial police force for 8 of the 10 Canadian provinces and for the two territories.

Third, it has specialized in the investigation of certain kinds of crime such as narcotics, political corruption and corporate crime. Fourth, it provides technical support and training assistance for all other Canadian forces (the Canadian Police Information Centre, which is the main centralized data bank on Canadian offenders, is managed by the RCMP, which collects and processes data from all other police forces and from Courts and Corrections). Lastly, the RCMP is making a strong comeback in political policing. I address this last issue in the next section.

1.2. Government Security Intelligence Agencies

There exist a number of fairly recent and reliable descriptions of the Canadian intelligence and security community (Canada, Senate, 1987; Security Intelligence Review Committee (SIRC), 1987, Robertson, 1989 and Brodeur, 1990).

According to SIRC (1987), the pyramid of intelligence and security agencies is crowned by the Cabinet Committee on Security and Intelligence (CCSI). The Prime Minister and his Deputy, the President of the Treasury Board, the Minister for International Trade and the Minister of Finance are members of this committee. So are also representatives of the ministry of the Solicitor General and the departments of National Defense, External Affairs, Employment and Immigration, Transport, Revenue, Justice and the Customs and Excise branch. In sum at least 7 ministries and 12 members of Cabinet develop policy on security and intelligence and, by implication, on political surveillance and counterterrorism.

Although they may seem remote from the field and from undercover operations, these committees make decisions which affect operations in a very concrete way. It was recently revealed that Mohammad Mashat, Iraqi's ambassador in the U.S. at the time of the Gulf war, was permitted to immigrate to Canada (Windsor, 1991). This affair took the proportions of a major scandal in Canada, because the Conservative government tried to put the blame for the oversight on Mr. Raymond Chrétien, who was the second highest-ranking civil servant in the department of External Affairs. Mr. Raymond Chrétien also happened to be the nephew of Mr. Jean Chrétien, who was then the leader of the official Liberal opposition. According to what was revealed during the hearings of a House Committee appointed to investigate how the Iraqi-ex-ambassador got into Canada, decisions were taken at the highest level of government – the Privy Council Office – in this affair; in his testimony before the House Committee, Mr. Raymond Chrétien vigorously denied any responsibility in letting Mr. Mashat immigrate to Canada. In the 1993 federal election, Mr. Jean Chrétien was elected as the new Prime Minister of Canada and he subsequently appointed his nephew, Raymond Chrétien, as Ambassador to Washington, which is the most prestigious ambassadorship in Canadian foreign affairs.

There are several intelligence-gathering agencies in Canada. The departments of Foreign Affairs (DFA; formerly known as External Affairs) and of National Defense (DND) each have their own intelligence units. The three major federal organizations are the Canadian Security Intelligence Service (CSIS), the RCMP and the Communication Security Establishment (CSE). Little is known of the intelligence units of the DFA and the DND, apart from the fact that they are relatively small organizations. I will focus on the CSIS, the RCMP and the CSE, which are the three main components of the apparatus of political surveillance.

Previous to 1984, the Canadian security service was part of the RCMP, which investigated both politically-motivated and ordinary crime, like the FBI. Following a series of scandals similar to the uproar caused in the U.S. by the revelation of the 'dirty tricks' played by the FBI within the framework of the infamous COINTELPRO, the McDonald, the Krever and the Keable commissions were appointed to investigate undercover operations conducted by the RCMP and other Canadian police forces. Upon the recommendations made by the McDonald inquiry, the RCMP Security Service was abolished and the civilian CSIS was created to replace it. CSIS is not a police organization in the legal sense of the word. All Canadian police are peace officers, who have the legal power to make arrests. The members of the CSIS do not have peace officer powers and must rely on the police to make arrests and, more generally speaking, to enforce the law. The CSIS has about 2,800 employees and a budget of $207 million.

Among the police organizations on which the CSIS must rely for its operations, there is one force which is given priority by section 61 of the CSIS Act. This section gives the RCMP the prime responsibility for enforcing the law in the field of offenses against national security. In simple terms, the McDonald Commission's concept of political policing rested on the assumption that the CSIS would be the brain and that the RCMP – and other police forces with which the RCMP was to pass agreements – would be the arm. This concept was flawed from the start, because no police organization can agree to divorce intelligence from operations and vice-versa. Either the CSIS would get its own arm or the RCMP would grow another head. CSIS would have had to fight an uphill battle in order to develop its own arm, because its members lacked the legal powers to make arrests. The RCMP did not have any legal obstacles in its way, if it wanted to make a comeback into security intelligence. All it had to do was to wait long enough for its past sins to be forgotten. After 1988, the RCMP established a full directorate – the National Security Investigation Directorate – for its investigations into offenses threatening the national security of Canada and, in particular, terrorism. The RCMP is also responsible for the protection of Canadian Cabinet members and visiting dignitaries from other countries. It is firmly reestablishing its position in the field of the protection of Canadian national security. Cléroux (1990) makes a strong case that instead of being partners, the CSIS and the RCMP are actually competitors.

The third organization involved in security intelligence is the CSE, which falls under the governance of the Department of National Defense. Except for a few articles in the Toronto *Globe and Mail* (Sallot, 1984 and a more recent series by Moon, 1991), the CSE is a little known organization. In addition to its mandate of protecting classified federal government communications, the CSE collects signal intelligence (SIGINT), which is its primary function. It operates within the framework of the 1947 UK-USA Agreement, to which the U.S., the U.K., Australia and to a lesser extent New Zealand are also parties. The CSE monitors and analyzes telephone, telex, facsimile, data-transmission, cables and radio messages going to and from Canada and other countries. It also listens to radar signals. As can be seen from this description, the CSE is the Canadian equivalent of the U.S. National Security Agency.

The CSE has approximately 850 civilian employees and the military assigns about 1,100 specialists to operate the agency's monitoring stations in Canada, Bermuda and Germany. Its budget is estimated at $250 million (Moon, 27 May 1991, A4). The Canadian consumers of CSE intelligence include the military, the Privy Council Office, the federal departments of External Affairs, Transport and Employment and Immigration, the Customs and Excise branches, the RCMP and the CSIS.

1.3. Quasi-governmental Security Units

The province of Québec has not only invested high hopes but very large sums of money into transforming the north of Québec into a gigantic electrical powerplant that would provide energy to the whole of the eastern U.S. In order to achieve this goal, several dams will have to be built to harness the power of northern rivers and very large areas of land will as a result be flooded. For reasons of environmental protection, the Aboriginal peoples of northern Québec strenuously oppose this project, on which the whole economic future of Québec is said by politicians to rest. Indeed, it would be difficult to overstate the magnitude of what is at stake in the hydro-electrical development of northern Québec.

The provincial police force of Québec – the SQ – is not up to the task of controlling the Aboriginals in the North nor, for that matter, anywhere else in Québec. Hydro-Québec, which is owned by the provincial state, has recently created a security unit numbering over a hundred persons for the sole purpose of gathering security intelligence on Aboriginals that may oppose its projects and cause damage to its property and installations. This unit is different from an in-house private security agency, that would mainly recruit security guards. It is headed by a former high-ranking officer of the provincial police force with experience in the field of security intelligence. According to a Hydro-Québec confidential document that outlined the function of this unit, it was to embark upon a program of surveillance which implied infiltration and the use of undercover operatives. This document was leaked to a legal firm representing Aboriginal bands and I obtained a copy of it.

Hydro-Québec is not alone in creating its own security unit. The Québec Department of Social Security has hired investigators to track down people illegally receiving welfare money. There are numerous other government departments such as Internal Revenue which are using their own investigators. However, Hydro-Québec may be unique in fielding a unit with a mandate which parallels that of a state intelligence service. I am not aware of the situation prevailing in other Canadian provinces with respect to the control of Aboriginal bands, which are quite as militant as the Québec bands.

1.4. Private Security Agencies

Giving an account of the undercover operations of private security agencies extends far beyond the scope of this paper and could only be the object of a separate study. Since 1960, the growth of private policing in Canada has been massive. From adducing evidence for divorce cases to providing protection to business executives against terrorists, private security agencies are heavily involved in operations that imply the use of deception and of undercover tactics. They are also used by government to infiltrate organizations such as pro-abortion groups. The work of Shearing (1992) and of Shearing and Stenning (1981) provides an accurate picture of private policing in Canada. Marx (1987) and Johnston (1992) describe the interweaving of public in private police in undercover operations.

2. UNDERCOVER OPERATIONS IN THE CANADIAN CONTEXT

In this paper, 'undercover policing' is understood as policing operations which are covert and involve deception. This characterization is faithful to Gary Marx's concept of undercover policing (Marx, 1988, 12). There is a feature of Marx's account that deserves some discussion. Marx (1988, 12) characterizes undercover policing as *active* as opposed to passive surveillance. I believe that the line between active and passive undercover police operations is rather blurred and that the contrast between these two kinds of operations tends to be more salient depending on what model of undercover policing one is using.

I think that the model that Marx (1988) is using is that of police entrapment, a good example of which is a sting operation or a police controlled purchase of drugs ('buy and bust'). The following description of a true undercover operation is proposed by Marx (1988, 12).

> Unobtrusive surveillance does not directly intervene to shape the suspect's environment, perceptions, or behavior. (...) Undercover work is both *covert* and *deceptive*. (...) Unlike conventional police work ... the investigation may go on *before and during* the commission of the offense. It may start with the offender and only later document the offense. Discovery of the offender, the offense, and arrest may occur almost simultaneously. (emphasis in text)

Relying on this model involves a conception of undercover operations that I shall characterize as personalistic and as dynamic. By personalistic, I mean that undercover work is viewed as involving deceptive relationships between individual persons who hide their identities. By dynamic, I refer to the fact that deception is conceived to be more than artifice. It is artifice used to shape behavior, in other words, it is manipulation. According to this conception, secret electronic surveillance is covert, but it is not actively deceptive and consequently does not qualify as undercover policing.

This conception of undercover policing is certainly defendable. Yet, it runs into several difficulties. Being patterned on the action of peace officers engaged in criminal law enforcement, it neglects techno-policing, intelligence gathering and political surveillance and private policing. I shall illustrate the two first shortcomings.

In Canada, the Criminal Code, which forbids electronic surveillance unless it is authorized by judicial warrant, defines a private communication as 'any oral communication or any telecommunication made under the circumstances in which it is reasonable for the originator thereof to expect that it will not be intercepted by any person other than the originator thereof to receive it.' (s. 183). If activists involved in the protection of the environment suddenly learned that their telephone lines were tapped, I believe that they would feel they were deceived in their reasonable expectation that their conversations were private. The deception in this case could be said to be systemic. It is performed on behalf of the state by anonymous agents. This does not make it any less deceptive.

A second difficulty is that the collection of intelligence, can involve a fair amount of active deception, even if its purpose is merely to learn something and not to perform eventually the arrest of an individual offender. Actually, the collection of intelligence may in itself involve a great deal of undercover work – surreptitious entry, covert search and seizures, mail opening, etc. In a very elaborate operation, the RCMP Security Service stole a computer disk storing the list of all members of the autonomist *Parti Québécois* (PQ) in order to copy it (the disk was returned unbeknownst to its owner during the same night that it was taken). This operation, whose sole purpose was the collection of information, would surely qualify as undercover work. It involved actively deceiving many people (one locksmith, the personnel of the computer company where the disk was stored and eventually the police of Montreal, if anything went wrong during the operation; nothing did). The PQ was never aware of the operation until 5 years later. During this interval, the covert operation could not be said to have influenced the PQ's behavior in any fashion. Not having involved active deception with regard to its target, it would probably not qualify as a true undercover operation for Gary Marx, although it was certainly perceived as such in Canada.

I shall now provide some background on the Canadian context of undercover operations.

2.1. The Canadian Context

There are some general points that need to be made in order to understand the Canadian situation in relation to undercover operations. Some of these points are very general, such as the unjustified reputation that Canada enjoys of being a liberal country. For instance, in absolute numbers, the Canadian police intercepts private communications twice as frequently as the U.S. and, taking into account that the U.S. is ten times as populated as Canada, they do it twenty times more often than their U.S. colleagues. Such examples could be multiplied.

A second kind of consideration is more specific. Basing his assertions on the annual reports of the U.S. Sentencing Commission, Doob (1993, 19, note 3) estimated that drug offenses were described as being the 'primary offense category' for 47 per cent of defendants sentenced for federal offenses for the 12 months ending September 1990, thus accounting for 53 per cent of all federal custodial sentences. In Canada, for the years 1986–1987 to years 1989–1990, the percentage of federal admissions to prison for drug offenses was on average not higher than 1.5 per cent. The average percentage of admissions to provincial institutions for drug offenses was 4.5 per cent for the same period (Canada, 1991, 126 and 138; we can safely assume that the corresponding percentage of custodial sentences to U.S. state prisons would be much higher than that, since it is often claimed that the explosion in the number of persons incarcerated in U.S. state prisons is due in large part to the war on drugs). Since drug cases account for a very significant amount of undercover police work, we can infer from this brief comparison that there should be less undercover criminal law enforcement in Canada than in the U.S.

2.2. Political Surveillance

Not unexpectedly in view of what was just said, undercover policing was associated in Canada with political policing – particularly, counterterrorism – by both public and learned opinion. This situation is also owed to the fact that almost everything that is publicly known about undercover policing in Canada was learned through the revelations of public commissions of inquiry that dealt exclusively with aspects of political policing.

Canada experienced a wave of terrorism from the early 1960s until 1973. In order to counter terrorism and French Canadian separatism, the police had to rely on an aggressive style of undercover operations, which occasionally resulted in a breach of human rights. Many of the commissions of inquiry on the police were appointed to investigate these violations of human rights, as in the U.S. were the Church Committee, the Pike Committee and the Rockefeller Commission (*see* Johnson, 1985). From 1966 to 1981, there were no less than 6 major commissions that investigated the RCMP Security Service. These were: the Wells Commission (Canada, 1966a), the Spence Commission (Canada, 1966b), the Mackenzie Commission (Canada, 1969), the McDonald Commission (Canada, 1980 and 1981a and b), the Keable Commission (Québec, 1980) and the Krever Commission (Ontario, 1980). To the reports of these commissions must be added those of two Special Senate Committees appointed to investigate counterterrorism (Canada, Senate, 1987 and 1989) and, since 1985, the annual reports of the Security Intelligence Review Committee (SIRC). SIRC was created in 1984 to oversee the operations of the civilian Canadian Security Intelligence Service (CSIS), which was also formed in 1984, following the recommendations of the McDonald commission. These reports have generated an extensive literature, which is mostly journalistic, on police deviance (Cléroux, 1990) contains an extensive bibliography of this literature).

With the exception of the recent report issued by the RCMP External Review Committee (RCMP, 1991a) on allegations of entrapment by a Canadian member of the Senate, there is very little that is publicly known about undercover operations in fields other than political surveillance. RCMP (1991a, 92) actually recommends the establishment of a Central Registry for all coded informants used by the Force, which should put the RCMP in a position to assess the performance of its informers. This recommendation is an indication that the RCMP, which is the main police force in Canada, is not yet in a position to assess the impact of undercover policing, which is intrinsically linked to the use of informants. The situation is no better with respect to other Canadian police forces.

The other main source of knowledge about undercover policing is the jurisprudence. In Canada, this is a rather limited source, since there are few cases where judges explicitly refer to undercover policing. This jurisprudence was recently reviewed by Schiffer (1991) and Stober (1991).

To sum up: what is known in Canada about undercover policing deals almost exclusively with this kind of work in political surveillance, counterterrorism and subversion. Although we know that such tactics play an important part in other fields, such as the enforcement of laws against drug trafficking, few specific cases of undercover policing have been documented.

2.3. Undercover Police, Informers and Delators

Although they are frequently referred to, Marx (1988) does not devote many pages to informers (basically, 152–158), the focus of the book being a particular form of police surveillance rather than a particular group of surveillants. Actually, if a group had to be singled out in Marx (1988), it would be the police. Due to the fact that police informers were star witnesses in at least two of the major Canadian public inquiries on policing (the McDonald and the Keable), they were the object of much attention in this country. In Canada (1980 and 1981a and b; the McDonald report), the authors use the same phrase 'police (undercover) agents' to refer both to police officers working undercover and to police informers (sometimes referred to as 'agents of the police' instead of 'police agents,' in police testimony before the courts or commissions of inquiry). In RCMP (1991a, 35), 'undercover agent' explicitly refers to a particular kind of police informer. Furthermore, some of the most elaborate descriptions of undercover operations that were made by commissions of inquiry focused on the role played by informers. Finally, informers who got a lot of publicity, through their appearance before commissions of inquiry or as witnesses in sensationalized trials, have published books (e.g. Deveault, 1980). Hence, it is virtually impossible to speak of undercover policing in Canada without feeling the need to emphasize the part that is played by police informers in these operations. One could say that informers and their handlers are seen in Canada as the two pillars of any undercover operation.

Like Wool (1986), the Marin report defines a police informer as a person who provides information to the police without being obliged to do so by law. This definition is meant to counter the standard police claim that 'anyone who gives information to the police is a police informant' (*see* Kelly and Kelly, 1976, 322; William Kelly was a high-ranking officer in the RCMP). Many persons are required by statutes such as the Motor Vehicles Act to report a great deal of information to the police. Referring to them as police informants would be ludicrous.

Furthermore, Canadians draw a distinction between what are considered two very different kinds of police informants. We tend to distinguish between the informer, in the traditional sense of the word, and the delator (in French, *délateur*). Delators are Crown witnesses who are granted court and financial considerations to testify in open court against their former accomplices in extremely serious crimes, which are difficult to solve for the police (typically, an assassination perpetrated by a professional 'hit man' working under contract). A research project conducted on delators in Montréal has shown that 26 out of 42 court cases, in which 31 delators testified against 161 accused, involved charges of first-degree murder. All but four of these murder cases were related to gang slayings (Gravel and Bordelais, 1993, 59). In the U.S., a witness protection program was developed, following the adoption of the Organized Control Act in 1970. This program is managed by the U.S. Marshals Service, which is responsible for protecting the court system, that is judges, counsels, members of juries and also witnesses. A large number of the witnesses benefiting from this program are delators.

In Canada, delators are not usually given full immunity from prosecution; rather, they are offered an advantageous plea bargain and a reduced sentence (e.g., manslaughter instead of first degree murder). The crucial difference between informers and delators is that only the former can be said to work undercover, since the latter agree to blow whatever cover they may have by accepting to testify in open court. Canadian police made an extensive use of delators between 1972 and 1986. In a celebrated case, one delator, Mr. Yvan Beaupré, testified that he had committed perjury with the knowledge of the police and of the Crown prosecutor; he also testified that police had incited him to present false evidence. In a landmark ruling on this case, the Supreme Court of Canada ordered a new trial, blamed the behavior of the police and of the prosecution and implied that the use of paid delators tended to bring the administration of justice into disrepute (*R. v. Dufresne* (1988), 1 R.C.S., 1095).

Although, as I just argued, delators are different from informers, there are also important similarities between the two categories. They both refer to persons involved in criminal activities, who are 'flipped' or 'turned' by the police in exchange for court and/or financial considerations; both kinds of persons provide the police with information on crimes and their authors (often associates) and both are also protected by the police (delators are physically protected, since they have no cover). Furthermore, there is a two-way circulation between the two categories. A 'repentant' accused, willing to testify against former associates, may be offered complete immunity and returned into the criminal milieu, if the police and the prosecution believe that there is more to gain in having this individual as an informer than as a witness. Conversely, an informer may accept to reveal his identity and testify in open court, if the benefits that he or she may reap are substantial enough. For example, in the U.S., the former FBI informant Emad E. Salem is now being turned into a delator and a witness for the prosecution in the case against Sheik Omar Abdel Rahman (Bernstein and Blumenthal, 1993 and Blumenthal, 1994).

2.4. Fields of Undercover Policing

Although I previously said that most publicly known cases of undercover policing fell within the range of political surveillance and counterterrorism, this kind of police tactic is used in other fields of law enforcement such as consensual crime and, most particularly, drug offenses, parallel illegal markets (e.g. cigarette smuggling), political corruption and corporate crime, low clearance rate crime (e.g. organized burglary and theft of motor vehicle) and low visibility crime (e.g. tax evasion).

There is one recent issue in relation to fields of operation for undercover policing that must be mentioned, because of its particular relevance to Canada. It is the serious involvement of organized groups of Aboriginals in parallel illegal markets, and most noticeably in weapon, alcohol and cigarette smuggling and in managing outlaw casinos. Smuggling and illegal gambling are occurring on a massive scale without any police reaction; they are also highly visible, cigarette smuggling now enjoying a media profile comparable to drug trafficking and they are consequently becoming a mounting source of public indignation. Furthermore, some Aboriginal gangs are openly defiant of the police, publicly claiming that they could outgun any Canadian police force. The present situation is reminiscent of the apparent immunity that was enjoyed by Québec terrorists in the sixties and early seventies and it potentially is political dynamite, police spokesmen being increasingly vocal about the fact that they are kept in check by political interference. In the seventies, such a situation ultimately resulted in a wave of infiltration and of repression of the groups that openly threatened the prevailing order. It may again so result with respect to the Aboriginals, who appear unaware of their vulnerability to tactics of undercover policing.

The diversity of these fields of undercover operations raises finally the issue of the possibility of developing a unified theory of undercover policing, which can account for the differences between operations. This issue is particularly acute when we compare undercover operations in the field of political surveillance and criminal investigations (or instigations, to use the terminology of Wilson, 1978).

3. INTENTION

The concept of intention plays a large part in Gary Marx's work and particularly in Marx (1988), where one chapter is devoted to a description of the intended consequences of undercover policing and two others to its unintended consequences. In Marx (1988), the unintended consequences of undercover policing are seen as undesirable. The criterion used to determine whether a consequence is desirable is whether it benefits or not a formal law enforcement policy.

The concept of intention is notoriously fraught with difficulties and it involves logical, philosophical and legal notions. I cannot within the scope of this article undertake a thorough examination of the concept of intention. What I will do is identify its main dimensions. I will be in part guided by legal doctrine, although I want to make it clear that I am not undertaking a legal discussion. After having identified the main component of intention, I will discuss two cases to examine if it is conceivable to envisage effects of undercover policing which are both intended and undesirable.

There are three main dimensions to intention: *cognizance, purposiveness* and *premeditation*. The notion of premeditation – preparation or planning in advance – is clear enough. Cognizance, on the other hand, raises an issue. A distinction is generally made between knowledge of one's action and the knowledge of its consequences. For example, the offense of manslaughter is a kind of homicide where the offender wanted to cause serious harm to a person but had not anticipated that the person would die as a result of his or her injuries. Many factors intervene in assessing whether a person is justified is claiming not to have anticipated the consequences of his or her action. The most complex of these factors is the issue of common knowledge. A person accused fifty years ago of polluting a river with mercury may have argued that he or she was not aware that mercury contaminated fish, thus making their consumption a serious health hazard. However, it would be very difficult to present such a defense today, with all the knowledge that we have accumulated on water pollution by mercury. Hence, knowledge of the consequences of one's act tend to vary across time.

When it is divorced from the element of cognizance – a person knows that he or she is committing an offense, but does it for a good purpose, like Robin Hood who stole from the rich to give to the poor – purposiveness is almost never admitted by the courts as a sound defense. There is only one noted exception to this rule and it is when the police claims to have broken the law – e.g. by committing an offense against privacy or by submitting a suspect to a brutal interrogation – for reasons of efficiency in the struggle against crime (Brodeur, 1981).

I will now discuss two cases of undesirable consequences from the point of view of formal law enforcement policy to see whether any of these consequences could be said to be intended. One of these cases will involve the use of a delator and the other one the use of an informer. This discussion serves purposes of illustration and clarification and a more systematic analysis will be presented in the next section of this paper.

3.1. Laundering Unresolved Cases

One of the most notorious delators in the history of Québec courts, a fellow nicknamed 'Apache' (Mr. Yves Trudeau) was offered to plead guilty to 35 counts of manslaughter committed between 1970 and 1985 and involving 43 victims, in return for testimony against accomplices who were accused of first-degree murder. The 'deal' that this delator made with the prosecution was formalized through a contract (in French, a *convention*) between him and the prosecution. A copy of that contract was obtained by researchers (*see* the Appendix of Gravel and Bordelais, 1993). All the offenses of manslaughter to which he pleaded guilty were in truth cases of first-degree murder, since 'Apache' Trudeau was a professional assassin.

For having allegedly murdered 43 persons, Mr. Trudeau was awarded a sentence of life imprisonment, with the provision that the sentence would be administered by the Québec correctional authorities instead of the federal services, as should have been the case under Canadian law. As it is spelled out in details in the contract, this life sentence was reduced to 4 years of full imprisonment under the protection of the Québec provincial police and with money for expenses, followed by two years of partial incarceration with day passes to go working outside of the prison and two years in a half-way house. After fulfilling this part of the bargain, Mr. Trudeau would be put on full parole in 1994. Such treatment is incredibly lenient for someone who admitted having murdered 43 persons and who was known by the police to kill in cold blood.

Even though this man was a contract killer, it is very unlikely that he was actually responsible for all 43 murders to which he pleaded guilty. The police used him to close some of their unresolved homicide files and rewarded him with a super 'fix.' This practice of laundering their files of unsuccessful investigations is frequent when the police make a deal with a delator.

In this instance, the element of cognizance is obviously present. That premeditation is also present is at least plausible. Purposiveness, however, is clearly a factor. There can be little doubt of the willingness of the police to launder its files, when they have an occasion to do so. Hence, it would seem that the laundering of police files is an intended consequence of the use of delators.

Is this intended consequence undesirable from a law enforcement policy perspective? Since it entails that the police will stop looking for the real culprits of very serious crimes, such as homicide, this question can only be answered in the positive. Furthermore, it often entails making proposals to delators which totally debase justice. However, from the point of view of a police organization's bureaucracy, such a consequence of the use of delators may appear desirable because it increases the clearance rates for the most serious offenses in the criminal law.

It would then seem that we have found a consequence that is both intentional and undesirable with respect to law enforcement policy. Since it could be objected that the recourse to delators is a practice that is not at the core of undercover policing, at least as it is defined by Gary Marx, I shall try to provide another paradigm case.

3.2. Blackmailing Informants

In 1992, the McDonald commission on the RCMP transferred to the Canadian national archives several boxes of documents that it had previously used in its inquiry, completed more than 10 years before. Members of the Québec press began to examine these documents and in a series of damaging articles tried to revive the issue of federal surveillance of the separatist *Parti Québécois* (PQ). Despite being both public and legal and having elected members in the Québec legislature, this political party had its list of members stolen by the RCMP in 1973 and was the target of intensive surveillance since its creation in the sixties. In trying to embarrass the RCMP and the federal government, the Québec press opened a Pandora's box from which spilled elements that were to prove extremely embarrassing for the PQ itself.

Mr. Claude Morin is one of the best known political figures in Québec. He was a past vice-president of the PQ and by common assent its chief strategist to achieve the secession of Québec from Canada. When the PQ was elected to form the provincial Québec government in 1976, Mr. Morin became a senior cabinet minister responsible for provincial-federal relations. In an attempt to preempt the effects of an imminent national television broadcast on the French channel, Mr. Morin gave a television interview in May 1992 revealing that he had been a paid informer for the RCMP from 1975 until his resignation from government in 1981. By his own admission, he received approximately $800 during meetings with his RCMP handlers, these being held every 6 weeks or so.

Mr. Morin's explanations of his behavior were published in the 11 May issue of the Montréal daily *La Presse* (B1–3). Essentially, Mr. Morin claims that he accepted to meet with members of the RCMP who allegedly wanted to know whether the PQ was not infiltrated by foreign agents and radicals, in order to learn what the RCMP knew about the PQ and what it had in store for it. He also asserts that he informed Mr. Marc-André Bédard, the PQ Minister of Justice in the 1976 provincial Cabinet, of his activities. In other words, Mr. Morin's defense rests on his pretension having been a double agent. With some reservations, Mr. Bédard publicly corroborated Mr. Morin's account of his activities (*La Presse*, 13 May 1992, B3). Ms. Lorraine Lagacé, a Québec civil servant who became the *confidente* of Mr. Morin with respect to his activities as an RCMP informant and who revealed his role to PQ officials, claims that Prime Minister Lévesque was devastated when he learned in 1981 that Mr. Morin was in the pay of the RCMP and that he asked for his resignation (*La Presse*, 13 May 1992, B3).

There are many contradictions surrounding this affair, many persons being convinced that Mr. Morin became an informant for the RCMP much earlier than 1975 (Mr. Morin admits having been approached by RCMP Inspector Raymond Parent in 1969). The really crucial issue is whether Mr. Morin was only an informant for the RCMP or if he were not deliberately entrapped into becoming a paid informer in order to be blackmailed if the PQ took the provincial power in Québec (Gagnon, 1992, B3; Cléroux, 1992, D1 and D5). The weight of public evidence suggests the latter. First, not only were Mr. Morin's RCMP handlers very experienced officers, but his first RCMP contact, Inspector Raymond Parent, had a proven background in 'disruptive tactics' (RCMP jargon for dirty tricks; Inspector Parent's crucial role in the theft of the list of the PQ's members in 1973 was acknowledged by both the Keable and the McDonald inquiries into RCMP wrongdoing). Second, Mr. Morin was actually filmed by the RCMP as he was being handed money during one encounter with his control officers. Finally, Mr. Morin's code name – Q 1, indicating that he was one of the earliest informants of the RCMP's D Branch, responsible for chasing Québec separatists – was changed to 'French Minuet,' after he became a Québec cabinet minister in 1976. According to Cléroux (1992, D5), such a code designates a compromised target rather than just a paid informant. Cléroux asked one of his sources – a retired Mountie – why Mr. Morin was specifically given the new code name 'French Minuet' and he replied: 'Why not? We taught him how to dance.' Later, when Mr. Morin was no more an entertaining dancer, his activities as an RCMP informant were leaked to the press with a vengeance, precisely in a period when the media were trying to reassess the political surveillance exercised against the PQ. This made it seem that none was more eager to inform on the PQ than its chief strategist during the lost referendum campaign of 1980.

It is beyond doubt that the RCMP handlers of Mr. Morin knew what they were doing when they succeeded in compromising him and that they had planned and executed this operation over a long period of time. Furthermore, transforming 'Q 1' into 'French Minuet' was precisely what they wanted (why otherwise would have they filmed him accepting money from them?). It is no less clear that if such operations may appear justified within a power struggle against political 'enemies,' they have no relationship to law enforcement. Even if one views his behavior as reckless and even unsavoury, Mr. Morin was guilty of no crime whatsoever. In targeting him for blackmail, the RCMP was violating its commitment to uphold the law, if not the law itself; in publicly revealing or confirming his identity as a police informant, members of the RCMP, whether they were retired or still active, broke what police have always claimed to be the most cardinal rule of the book on handling informers.

The purpose of the above was to explore the concept of intended consequence and to prepare the ground for the classification that will be offered in the next part of this paper. In this section, I discussed the issue of whether consequences of undercover policing that were undesirable from a law enforcement perspective could also be said to be intended by persons actively involved in undercover operations. Although no firm conclusion can be drawn on the basis of the examination of two cases, I believe to have shown that it cannot be ruled out as a matter of principle that police may intend to operate in a way that will result in consequences they know to be wrong from a law enforcement perspective.

4. CONSEQUENCES OF UNDERCOVER POLICING

There are in Canada very few assessments of the collective impact of undercover policing. The basic sources of information on undercover policing are government reports, jurisprudence, press clippings and a few unreliable autobiographies. There is very little research field work on undercover policing and there is almost no quantitative research at all (what little field work we have was undertaken by commissions of inquiries and would not qualify as field work in the sociological sense on the word). Hence, any assessment of the consequences of undercover policing is based upon extrapolations made from a limited selection of cases, which to a certain degree involve speculation.

As previously announced, we generate four categories of consequences: desirable/intended, desirable/unintended, undesirable/intended and undesirable/ unintended. This categorization is more exploratory than firm and it is meant as an instrument to test the relevance of using such predicates to classify the consequences of undercover policing. This statement is particularly true with regard to the notion of intention, which is used here according to the criteria identified in the previous section. Cognizance and purposiveness will play a much larger role than premeditation in my discussion. Furthermore, I follow the legal tradition in giving to cognizance more weight than purposiveness. This means that *if it makes no sense to pretend that policing agencies are unaware of a given consequence, I will tend to classify it as being intended*. For reasons that will be apparent in the course of the discussion, this rule will not be consistently applied. Even if it is not consistently applied, it is bound to be controversial. I shall address the objections to this rule in the conclusion of the paper.

4.1. Consequences: Desirable and Intended

Justifiably or not, the use of informants is perceived to be at the core of law enforcement in the fields of consensual crime, corporate crime, political corruption and politically-motivated crime such as terrorism. Although Manning sees in the 'agent/informant mode of targeting' only one of such targeting modes in the field of narcotics, most authors, and particularly those with a police background, see the use of informers within the context of undercover operations as the main tool for making cases in narcotics and other consensual crimes. Officers in the field of security intelligence would also agree that infiltration is the only effective way of countering terrorism and other politically-minded deviance.

Manning (1980, 13) is critical of undercover operations using informers in the field of narcotics. Manning's assessment receives weighty support from the 1991 report of the Inter-American Commission on Drug Policy (IACDP) – a private group of experts from Bolivia, Canada, Colombia, Mexico, Peru and the U.S. –, which concluded that strategies aimed at the interception of drug shipments were extremely costly and did not produce the expected results (Campbell, 1991).

The intended desirable consequences of undercover policing can be classified in three categories.

Crime repression

Due to the complete lack of data on the impact of undercover tactics, it is impossible to provide any assessment which is not wholly speculative. Being perceived, as I just said, as the main tool of law enforcement in the field of consensual crime and related domains, undercover operations are automatically credited in part for any results achieved by the police in these fields. Hence, the RCMP provides us in its annual reports with the amount of seized drugs and gives no detail on how the seizures were achieved. We are left to speculate on the part played by undercover tactics.

The use of undercover tactics in drug law enforcement has two important consequences. It focuses law enforcement on the supply of drugs rather than on its consumption and on the treatment of addicts and it also allows police to target serious criminals, who are much less visible than their street hirelings. The first strategy is now coming under the fire of increasing criticism, as the above quoted report of the IACDP bears witness to. As for the second strategy, it rests in part on the assumption that illegal markets are managed by huge organizations shaped like pyramids, the top of the pyramid being what holds it together. Hence, the crucial interest of getting to the top of the pyramid. Reuter (1983a and 1985) has convincingly shown that this belief was mistaken and that organised crime is actually splintered into a variety of loosely organized feuding gangs.

The dearth of reliable data on undercover policing is indicated by the fact that the Marin report (1991a) was compelled to devote a few pages to detailing the results of the Crime Stopper programs implemented in Toronto. These kinds of programs, where anonymous callers phone in information related to a crime reenacted on television, are very distantly related to undercover policing. They are merely enticements to mass delation.

The impact of the use of 'professional delators' was investigated in a research project undertaken at the Université de Montréal (Gravel and Bordelais, 1993, 63–68). The research assessed the outcome of criminal procedures against 157 defendants, where paid delators were used to obtain a conviction, either through persuading a defendant to enter a plea of guilty or through obtaining a verdict of guilty from the court. For all offenses, the use of delators resulted in a conviction rate of 72.4 per cent as compared to a general conviction rate of 91.8 per cent for the criminal courts of the district of Montreal, for years 1982–1986 (85.3 per cent of these convictions were the result of a plea of guilty). The comparison is even more unfavorable for delators when only cases of first degree murder were considered. The recourse to delators only resulted then in a conviction rate of 63.2 per cent as compared to a general conviction rate of 81.1 per cent for the courts of Montreal (1982–1986). These results are not impressive and provide a weak justification for the enormous privileges which were granted to delators. In theory, the evidence provided by delators is of the strongest kind that can be presented in court – being an eye-witness to a crime. In practice, this evidence is often rejected because of the lack of credibility of a delator as an eye-witness. The evidence is not as much legally weak as it is tainted by its source.

Crime prevention

By providing advanced knowledge of impending crimes, the use of informers is in theory one of the few policing strategies which can be said to be preventive in a precise sense. Preventive policing is crucial in relation to crimes of violence, such as terrorism.

Unfortunately, it is close to impossible to assess the preventive impact of undercover policing. Prevented crimes are non-events and difficult to calculate. Furthermore, it is the security services which are the most prone to claim success for foiling terrorist plots. The validity of these claims cannot be assessed, as any checking is made impossible by the confidential nature of the operations aimed at protecting national security.

Criminal and security intelligence

The accumulation of criminal and security intelligence is a clear outcome of undercover operations. With regard to such agencies as the CSIS, it is the only legitimate outcome.

Criminal intelligence should play a decisive part against crimes of very low visibility, such as political corruption and corporate crime. Security intelligence is vital to the prevention of politically motivated violence and other crimes shrouded in secrecy. Both kinds if intelligence suffer, however, from two limitations.

First, their influence on government decision-making is too often marginal. Second, it would also seem that the police intelligence units have inadequate analysis capacity, which results in severe shortcoming in the quality of their product. The Marin report (RCMP, 1991a, 61) found that Senator Cogger was targeted by the RCMP's Special Federal Inquiries Unit only after 'several media alerted RCMP members of Senator Cogger's alleged involvement (in the acceptance of payment for political services) and the use of his office of Senator to influence government action' (RCMP, 1991a, 61). It is the Montreal *Gazette* that initially broke the story of Senator Cogger's alleged involvement in influence peddling, in 1988. One would expect investigative journalism to feed on the scraps from undercover policing rather than the police finding their targets in press clippings.

4.2. Consequences: Desirable and Unintended

The consequences that I am briefly going to describe are classified as unintended in the sense that they are usually not the specific purpose of undercover tactics. However, in certain circumstances which I shall indicate, they may become the goal that is specifically intended. I have tentatively identified four consequences which are both desirable and unintended.

Deterrence

With regard to certain groups or individuals, the knowledge that they may possibly be the target of undercover operations spearheaded by informants can be enough to produce a deterrent effect. Generally speaking, however, this deterrent effect is stronger on persons who are not hardened criminals. The underside of deterrence is what is called the 'chilling effect' that stifles the expression of legal dissent and which is undesirable. When a certain kind of criminal activity has never been the focus of police repression, undertaking an elaborate undercover operation – such as operation ABSCAM against corrupted politicians in the U.S. – may intentionally serve as a warning and help deter potential offenders. Due to the prohibitive costs of operations like ABSCAM, they could not be said to be worth their money, if it could be shown that they have no deterrent effect.

Disorganization

Hardened criminals may not be deterred by the knowledge that they are likely to be the targets of undercover operations. Nevertheless, this knowledge compels them to take elaborate precautions that can possibly become a severe impediment to their activity. In other words, undercover policing can be a major hindrance to the smooth functioning of a criminal operation. Disorganization of criminal schemes is a general side-effect of the use of informers rather than a specific goal and it cannot be measured with any degree of accuracy.

Maintaining police morale

It is obvious that police organizations do not resort to undercover tactics spearheaded by informers in order to boost the morale of the troops. Nevertheless, undercover tactics may be viewed at least as an anti-depressant. Indeed, if we try to predict what would result from a complete ban on the use of informers and undercover tactics in such fields as drugs, the demoralization of narcotic squads is an entirely foreseeable result. This raises an important issue. If it were shown that undercover tactics have only a marginal impact on drugs, would it be worth it to keep resorting to them just to prevent a collapse of police morale?

An alternative to escalation

In themselves, undercover operations and the use of informers are soft methods of social control, as compared to the militaristic mode of targeting referred to by Manning (1980). In some countries of Europe such as France, informers are irretrievably linked to the invention of policing and they have been systematically used since at least the 17th century (Brodeur, 1983). Yet the civil liberties are still very much alive in countries like France. As compared to military repression, which is undiscriminating in its violence, the use of informants remains a police strategy that may threaten civil liberties, but which does not abrogate them.

4.3. Consequences: Undesirable and Intended

This category is admittedly the most problematic. How, it may be asked, can the criminal justice system and particularly the police intend to produce consequences that are undesirable with respect to formal law enforcement policy? Actually, if we use the criteria of cognizance, all of the consequences described in this section are intentional. Nevertheless, those which are lacking true purposiveness are not intended in themselves. I will justify my classification in the course of presenting it.

Licensing criminals

No consequence of undercover operations has generated as much discussion in Canada as licensing informers (and undercover police) to commit crimes. This consequence of undercover operations was particularly emphasized by Reuter

(1983b). Reuter argues that the value of an informer depends upon the depth of his involvement in the crime milieu. In order to have their good informers maintain their position, police handlers have no other choice than to license them to commit crimes.

Described in this way, licensing criminals appears to be a pre-condition of undercover operations rather than a consequence of them. Actually, things are not so clear-cut in the field. All big police organizations have formal and informal guidelines on the handling of informers. They all proclaim that informers are not permitted to breach the law in the course of their assignment with the police (in certain police departments, this prohibition is set down in writing as part of a written agreement between the force and its informer; *see* Bozza, 1978 and Québec, 1992). However, the application of these guidelines is often progressively suspended as handlers get more deeply involved with their informers in risky operations. In Canada, an officer from the RCMP is appealing his conviction for drug trafficking on the grounds that he only accepted a part of the benefits that his informer was making in selling drugs (the informer apparently found it unfair that his handler should not get his piece of the cake).

It could then be said that licensing criminals is as much an ongoing consequence of undercover policing as a pre-condition to it. Granting that this consequence is undesirable, is it intentional? The police are fully aware that most of their valuable informers are involved in crime (several informants in the field of narcotics are known drug addicts, to take a banal example). Hence the element of cognizance is fully present. The case is different with regard to purposiveness. Unless the case officer is corrupted and wants a share of the profits, the purpose of licensing criminals is not to let them break the law with impunity; it is to develop valuable sources within the criminal milieu by licensing some criminals. There also may be cases where an informant is deliberately enticed to break the law to make him or her vulnerable to blackmail. In any event, since I decided to follow judicial practice and give more weight to cognizance than purposiveness (or lack of it), I classify this undesirable consequence as intended. I shall revisit this issue in my conclusion.

Statutory violations of confidentiality

The Krever commission of inquiry into the recruitment of doctors – particularly psychiatrists – as police informers revealing to the police the content of some of their patients' files in violation of their medical oath, issued its report in 1980 (Ontario, 1980). It revealed that the police practice of recruiting physicians to inform on their patients was widespread. With regard to intention, these cases are similar to the licensing of criminals. The element of cognizance is obviously present. Yet the element of purposiveness appears to be lacking, this practice being more of a means to achieve another goal, which is assumed to fall under law enforcement, than an end in itself. However, the element of cognizance is even stronger than in the cases of licensing criminals, since the police know that every time that a professional bound by an oath of confidentiality will give information about his clients/patients, he or she will be breaking the oath. Moreover, it is doubtful that persons accused of having conspired to have doctors break their oath would have been acquitted by a judge by pleading that they did it for a good purpose. Although this type of case may seem controversial, it could also be considered as another instance of a consequence of undercover policing that is both undesirable and intended.

Crime facilitation

I borrow from Marx (1981; *see* also Marx, 1982) the expression of crime facilitation to designate all aspects of crime incitement that are intrinsically linked with undercover policing. These aspects were described by several authors under the name of instigation, entrapment, trickery and even framing. These practices are seen as undesirable – and even illegal – by the courts (for early descriptions, *see* Donnelly (1951) for the U.S. and Devlin (1971) for the U.K.; since the reality of entrapment was not fully acknowledged in Canada before the 1988 Supreme Court ruling *Mack* v. *the Queen*, there are no early descriptions in Canada).

There is no doubt that the police are fully aware that sting operations are instigative and that instigating the commission of a crime under controlled circumstances is the explicit purpose of such operations. Needless to say, sting operations do target some very unsavoury characters. However, the systematic implementation of an all-out crime facilitation strategy would have massively disturbing effects on any law abiding community. Crime facilitation is undesirable, but it is also an intentional practice that is at the core of undercover policing.

The subversion of the due process of law

I am here referring to all the violations of criminal law procedure, the due process of law and Charter guarantees that result from undercover operations. Some of these violations, such as perjury, are criminal offenses. Others, such as the use of an unreliable informer to trick a judge into granting his authorization for the installation of an electronic listening device, as in the *Atwal* affair in British Columbia, involve deception of a non-criminal nature. It would be naive to believe that the police is unaware of some of their informers' misconduct in court and that they do not condone it. Contingent fee arrangements with informers or delators are an open invitation to perjury (e.g. *The Queen* v. *Dufresne*, 1988). In other cases (e.g. the *Atwal* affair), it is the police themselves who trick a magistrate in presenting him with affidavits justifying the use of electronic surveillance, which they know to be false. Hence, I believe once more to be correct in describing this consequence as undesirable and intentional.

The collection of intelligence damaging to personal reputation

While director of research for the Keable inquiry (Québec, 1981), I was asked to review all the informers' files of a large police force and to assess the value of the information provided by these sources. I concluded that a significant part of the information supplied by human sources could be described as malicious gossip, which devoted an inordinate importance to the sexual life of their targets. Such muck-racking is unrelated to any actual or potential criminal prosecution. Yet it may be used as leverage to influence the behavior of a perceived opponent and eventually to discredit that person (the FBI files on the extra-marital affairs of Dr. Martin Luther King is one of the better known instances of this practice). In Canada, ministers who wanted to keep large police forces on a tight leash were in a number of times forced to resign amidst rumours of scandal (e.g. Mr. Francis Fox, who was Solicitor General of Canada, and Mr. Gérard Latulippe, who held the same post in the Province of Québec were two such casualties). When a police agency decides to keep hoarding this kind of information, its practice can be described as both intentional and undesirable.

Targeting non-criminal opponents

This consequence is often described as political targeting. However, political targeting is just a particular instance of a wider practice that consists of targeting a person as the focus of a sting operation for reasons which are altogether extraneous to law enforcement or for the purpose of using persons who live highly visible unconventional life styles as scapegoats (e.g. artists or athletes). In Canada, the singer Claude Dubois, who was a heroin addict, was targeted by such an operation. Since sting operations rarely target a mere consumer of drugs, we may infer that Mr. Dubois was singled out more because of his popularity with youth than for his addiction.

Unwitting informants can be manipulated into acting as a screen for such targeting, by making it appear that it is they who are actually doing the targeting. In some other cases, informers will deliberately seek revenge by depicting an enemy as a real or potential criminal or as a threat to Canada's national security. From the viewpoint of their principal actors (informers or their handlers), these practices are deliberate. They are also quite unjustifiable.

4.4. Consequences: Undesirable and Unintended

If we use the criteria of cognizance, most of the consequences that I characterize as unintended in this section might also be described as intended. There are, however, two main differences from the cases classified under the previous category. The first one is the degree of purposiveness: the consequences that I will now describe are not even remotely produced for their own sake by police agencies. The second difference concerns cognizance. It can be argued that the police are *generally* aware of these consequences. However, they do not have specific and direct knowledge of the individuals involved in the undesirable situations potentially generated by undercover policing. An example will serve to make my point. It would not really be difficult for a police force to make a survey of all its informants who are drug addicts. The handler of an addicted informer usually knows of his or her addiction and decides not to interfere with it. However, a project to identify all the members of a police force who were corrupted by having too close a relationship with their informer(s) would be confronted with unsurmountable difficulties. Hence, even if the leadership of a police force is aware that *some* corruption is bound to be the result of undercover work, it cannot be said to condone the corruption of any particular officer (unless, of course the corruption of an individual is revealed).

I will now present what I believe to be the major unintended and undesirable consequences of the use of non-casual informers in the context of undercover policing.

Police corruption

Undercover operations using informers deeply involved in the criminal milieu tend to blur the differences between crime fighters and hired criminals. They become partners widely sharing the same expectations and, not infrequently, the same risks. Hence, they develop the strong ties that usually bind together people facing the same risky predicaments. Such situations favor loss of police identity (either partial or complete) and is conducive to police corruption. Police corruption may also be fostered by the fact that the kinds of crime for which informers are used entail (i) a high degree of secrecy; (ii) very large sums of money (when dealing with drugs) and (iii) are likely to produce the feeling that law enforcement makes little difference (the sinking feeling that one works in vain is a strong enticement to becoming cynical and, eventually, corrupted – *see* Brodeur, 1981).

A shield for misconduct

This consequence of the use of informers in undercover operations is closely related to the preceding one, although it is different from outright corruption. I have been a member of a civilian police review committee for more than three years. I was struck by how often police officers whose behavior was under review tried to justify the fact that they were at the wrong place (e.g. a strip joint), at the wrong time (being on duty) and doing the wrong thing (getting drunk) by alleging that they were 'meeting with an informer.' These claims being unverifiable, 'working an informant' provides a shield for all kinds of misconduct unrelated to any undercover operation. Unintended by a police organization, this consequence may be fully willed by individual officers.

Innocent casualties

Gary Marx provides examples of cases where mistaken identities come to a tragic end, as when undercover operatives are killed by police unaware of their true identity. There are also numerous cases where persons suspected rightly or wrongly to be police informers are executed by the persons they are supposed to be informing on.

These are dramatic cases. There are others, less dramatic, but involving dire consequences for innocent third parties. In the months that followed the 1970 October terrorist crisis, Mrs. Carole Deveault, a police informer working for the counterterrorist unit of the police of Montreal, drew a psychological profile of one of her professors, who exercised a charismatic influence on his students. In that psychological profile, the informer admitted that her professor was much too 'brilliant' to ever join such a terrorist organization as the *Front de libération du Québec* (FLQ). That seemed to settle the matter and the professor was never interrogated nor arrested. He eventually became a Québec deputy minister in the early 1980s, when the *Parti Québécois* (PQ) was elected to head the government of the province of Québec.

Eight years later, the police of Montreal were investigated by a commission of inquiry into police wrongdoing, which had been appointed by the PQ government. Mrs. Deveault was for a time the inquiry's star witness, having turned against her former handlers. Wanting to embarrass the government, the Montreal police lawyer cross-examined Mrs. Deveault on the profile that she had written many years before, during one of the public hearings of the Commission. The press picked up the story and the career of the deputy minister, who had never been involved in terrorism, was ruined. In this case, the action taken by the police was fully intentional.

Police disorganization

The cases of mistaken identity which may result from a lack of police coordination can foster disorganization. As is well-known all undercover operations are shrouded in a secrecy that can only be broken on a police 'need to know' basis. Operating on the basis of the need to know is like handing to actors scripts which are filled with blanks. The need to know basis is the weakest link in an operational chain of command.

Furthermore, the use of informers may strain the relationships between the police and the personnel of other components of the criminal justice system. Deals with delators are made without involving the parole boards, which have later to grudgingly abide by them. Probation officers find themselves into a similar predicament.

Cost overruns

There is yet another unintended consequence of undercover policing that deserves its own heading, but that I cannot discuss in detail because of the limited scope of this paper. It is often pretended that informers are not expensive (e.g. Bouza, 1976), although trial disclosures reveal that they receive payments in excess of a hundred thousand Canadian dollars. However, it is undisputed that some of the undercover operations that they trigger – such as ABSCAM – are enormously expensive, their cost running over several million U.S. dollars.

Whistle blowing

The Marin report (RCMP, 1991a) describes two undercover policing projects of the RCMP, project Albus and the Sack operation, which were related to tenders for a communication systems for the department of External Affairs (COSICS). It was suspected that Senator Cogger had used his influence on behalf of one company. The RCMP tried to approach a Montreal businessman to assist in creating an opportunity for Senator Cogger to exercise his influence in a criminal manner (RCMP, 1991a, 26–27). The Montreal businessman was not involved in crime in any manner; he was chosen precisely because he had complained of the unfairness of the procedure of tender in the COSICS contract.

Not only did he refuse to cooperate, but he informed Senator Cogger that the RCMP was 'trying to set (him) up.' This information led the Senator to make his allegations on the floor of the Senate and to the Marin inquiry.

Informers or potential informers turning against their employers is more frequent than believed. Gary Marx described the shifting allegiances of informants and *agents provocateurs* in one of his earliest publications (Marx, 1974). As I previously said, one of the key witnesses of the Keable inquiry was an informer who turned against his Montreal police handler. Needless to say, this consequence is both undesirable from a police perspective and unintended.

Delegitimization of the criminal law

One of the most damaging consequences of undertaking undercover operations that rest upon the use of paid informants is also the most easy to describe. It generates scandals which shatters the image of law enforcement and bring the whole criminal system into disrepute. In Canada, we have only to recall the elaborate operation undertaken by the SQ against a Québec chapter of the Hell's Angels (which turned into a circus), to realize how much the image of the criminal law can be stained by scandals involving paid informants. We should also remember that the Keable and McDonald inquiries, which led to the downfall of the RCMP's Security Service were both triggered by an undercover operation that misfired (a police break-in at the offices of a leftist news agency – the *Agence de Presse Libre du Québec*).

5. CONCLUSIONS

In this paper, I have tried to build on Gary Marx's conception of undercover policing. First, I provided background information on the Canadian police and intelligence security apparatus and I discussed some of the features of undercover policing in Canada. Second, I analyzed the main consequences of undercover policing and attempted to classify them according to four categories, established by the cross-tabulation of two pairs of predicates, namely desirable/undesirable and intended/unintended. These issues were approached within the framework of a dialogue of ideas, based on the work of Gary Marx.

In my discussion, I addressed two theoretical problems – whether undercover operations involve active deception, and whether undesirable consequences can also be considered as intended from a formal law enforcement policy perspective. I shall now sum up my conclusions with regard to these two issues.

5.1. Active Deception and the New Surveillance: the State as an Undercover Agent

According to Gary Marx, undercover policing is characterized by active deception, which is actually the hallmark of the sting operations serving as models for his conception of undercover policing. His position has two important implications. Since the purpose of a sting operation is to perform an arrest and to prosecute suspects, it would follow, first, that police operations which are limited to the collection of intelligence would not qualify as true undercover operations. Stopping short of an arrest, they would not be seen active enough to qualify. Secondly, this perspective also implies that the use of surveillance technology such as wire-taps and videotaping does not *per se* constitute undercover policing, since it does not involve active *interpersonal* deception.

I tried to show that both features of this account of undercover policing were problematic. When performed by agents of a security service, the collection of intelligence actually does involve a lot of active deception. Furthermore, the information collected serves eventually to perform mass arrests of political opponents in crisis situations. I also argued that electronic surveillance was perceived by the public as being deceptive. I would now like to show that this kind of surveillance also implies active deception in the sense proposed by Gary Marx. I shall use as my example the most powerful Canadian organization engaged in electronic monitoring, that is, the CSE.

The very powerful technology that Canada's CSE and the U.S.' NSA use makes it possible for them to monitor 'emanations' emitted not only at home but in the neighboring countries. Thus, it becomes possible for these two countries to circumvent their respective legislation protecting private communications from interception. In theory, Canada monitors what is transmitted through the air waves in the U.S. and the U.S. does the same for Canada. Since these countries share the intelligence that they collect, both are given access to the private communications of their own citizens, albeit indirectly, while being allowed to claim that they respect their home privacy laws (Canada does not monitor Canadian personal messages nor does the U.S. for U.S. messages). This at least is the theory. Former employees of the CSE revealed to the press that these agencies often do not go to the trouble of getting needed information on their own citizens through the co-operative system, and routinely break their own privacy laws. It would then seem that the distinction between passive surveillance and active undercover operations is largely irrelevant for agencies such as the CSE and the NSA. Whether the collection of SIGINT is a passive or an active undertaking is a rather spurious question. There can be no doubt that the way in which the CSE and the NSA circumvent the privacy laws of their respective countries is strongly deceptive.

How deceptive it is can be assessed from the efforts of the government to keep the lid on any information about the CSE. The Canadian government is actively engaged in a campaign of disinformation about the true nature of the CSE's operations. When Mr. Ward Elcock, deputy clerk for security and intelligence and legal counsel to the Privy Council Office (the most powerful office in the Canadian government), was called to testify on the CSE by a parliamentary committee reviewing the first five years of operation of the CSIS Act, he infuriated the members of the Committee by refusing to provide anything else than the most general information on the CSE. He also testified to the effect that the CSE did not violate the Canadian privacy laws.

This governmental culture of vague and misleading statements and of half-truths concerning the real activities of the state apparatus for political and criminal surveillance extends far beyond the CSE. All policing agencies are to some extent under its protective cover. However, when the operations performed by these agencies come into full light, the extent of the deception actively resorted to by the state to disguise them is disclosed and comes as a shock to the general public.

If we stop being fascinated by particular operations, and focus on the relationship between the state, its surveillance agencies and the public, the state is shown to be actively engaged into systematic deception of the public on behalf of these agencies. The state's action can consequently be described as undercover policing, in the strict sense of the word. It shapes beliefs and behavior through manipulation.

5.2. Consequences Entailed in Undercover Policing

In my discussion of the consequences of undercover policing, I broke down the concept of intention into premeditation, cognizance and purposiveness. I also adopted an impartial quasi-judicial perspective. My impartiality consisted of adhering strictly to the legal tradition of giving more weight to cognizance than to purposiveness in the assessment of intention. The critical stance adopted by the courts with respect to purposiveness manifests itself very clearly in the doctrine of 'constructive malice,' according to which an offender can be said to have intended all the consequences of the offense he originally intended to perpetrate, even if this offender did not will any of these consequences (e.g. if fleeing robbers accidentally kill a police officer by running into him with their getaway car, they can be prosecuted for murder, according to the doctrine of constructive malice). I would not go as far as to apply this doctrine to undercover policing. However, I strongly object against the double standard applied by the courts in judging police wrongdoing. When police wrongdoing is judged, notions such as motive and purpose (or lack of criminal motive or purpose) come to play an exculpatory role that they never play in the case of ordinary defendants.

The results of my analyses are admittedly exploratory. However, they clearly imply that all consequences that are intended from a formal law enforcement policy perspective are not necessarily desirable or, conversely, that some undesirable consequences are intended. Moreover, we found that some important consequences of undercover policing, such as licensing criminals, were particularly hard to classify with regard to intention. Actually, most concepts, including even the concept of consequence, proved to be fuzzy on the edges when applied to undercover policing.

The reason why I keep stressing the fact that some undesirable consequences of undercover policing are intended is the following. The idea of an unintended negative consequence carries with it the false notion that this consequence is *accidental* and that it could eventually be avoided, if proper precautions were taken. Such an implication is not to be found in the work of Gary Marx, but it might be fostered by the uncritical use of the terminology of unintended negative consequences.

The general outcome of my analyses with regard to intention is that the dichotomy between intended and unintended consequences is far too rigid to accommodate all the consequences of undercover policing. We propose that the concept of entailed consequence be introduced into the analysis.

A consequence that is entailed by undercover policing is short of or beyond intention. It could be likened to the unavoidable price that has to be paid for a certain kind of police practice. For example, the fact that doctors are in breach of their medical oath is the price to be paid to recruit them as informers. Whether this consequence is intended or unintended is beside the point. This consequence is simply necessarily entailed by the recruitment of doctors and other professionals as informers, unless the medical and similar oaths are amended (any proposal to amend the medical oath to permit doctors to be police informers would stir up medical protest and generate public indignation).

The benefits of viewing certain outcomes of undercover policing as entailed consequences is threefold. It permits a lucid cost/benefit analysis, that may purport to assess whether we want to pay the price for a certain kind of policing. For example, granting that undercover operations entail the licensing of criminals and that their efficiency is limited in enforcing anti-drug legislation, do we want to pay the price of granting immunity to criminals just in order to make the police feel good in its losing war against drug traffickers? It also gives us the possibility to weigh political, social and ethical issues in undercover policing from the dispassionate and uncompromising perspective of *Realpolitik*.

5.3. Necessary Evil

The main benefit of viewing certain consequences as being entailed is that it leads us into questioning one of the most powerful legitimation tools in the criminal law arsenal, that is, the doctrine of the necessary evil. Legitimation of abusive practices such as violations of privacy, infiltration, entrapment and torture, usually occurs in four stages. First, there is an official *recognition* by the state of the occurrence of a questionable practice. This normally happens after many public scandals, that were followed by as many official denials. That initial step is followed by a solemn condemnation of the abusive practice: the practice is unquestionably evil. Such posturing clears the politicians' conscience and reasserts that the state is still committed to uphold morality. Then comes the moment of *insinuation*: even admitting that the practice is evil, it is asked, can we do without it? Several arguments in support of the practice are dribbled (the other side is resorting to it, one has to keep in pace with technology, 'you have to drive faster than a speeding motorist in order to catch him or her,' there is no other efficient way to be achieve results, and so forth). Finally comes the *solution*: the practice is going to be allowed, but on a limited and *controlled* basis, the controls being either legal or administrative, or both.

What ought to be questioned is the extent to which the doctrine of necessary evil does not imply the worst kind of double standards. There are legions of criminal cases where the defendant could argue that he or she had no choice than to break the law. In all but the most exceptional circumstances, the courts reject this line of defense as a matter of principle, because it would lead to wholesale acquittals, most defendants being able to claim that they acted under one form or another of determination. However, if this is so – and there are strong reasons that validate the attitude of the courts in this respect –, does it not follow that allowing the doctrine of necessary evil to grant legitimacy to the state's most questionable actions will also result into acceptation of any abuse of its power?

REFERENCES

Bédard, M.-A. (1992), 'Déclaration de Marc-André Bédard,' *La Presse*, 13 May, B3.
Bernstein, R., Blumenthal, R. (1993), 'Bomb Informer's Secret Tapes Offer a Rare Glimpse into Dealings with the F.B.I.,' *The New York Times*, 31 October 1993, 16.
Blumenthal, R. (1994), 'Imad Salem,' *The New York Times,* 9 January, 1.
Bozza, C.M. (1978), *Criminal Investigation*, Chicago, Ill., Nelson-Hall.
Brodeur, J.-P. (1981), 'Legitimizing Police Deviance,' in: Shearing, Cl., ed., *Organizational Police Deviance*, Toronto, Butterworths.
Brodeur, J.-P. (1983), 'High Policing and Low Policing; Remarks About the Policing of Political Activities,' *Social Problems*, 30, 5, 507–520.
Brodeur, J.-P. (1990), 'Security Intelligence and Policing in Canada,' in: Gagnon, A.G. & Bickerton, J.P., eds., *Canadian Politics; An Introduction to the Discipline*, Peterborough, Broadview Press, 263–281.
Campbell, M. (1991), 'Billions Wasted on Drug War, Report Charges,' *The Globe and Mail*, 12 June.
Canada (1966a), *Rapport de la Commission d'enquête quant aux plaintes formulées par George Victor Spencer* (Dalton Courtwright Wells, président), Ottawa, Imprimeur de la Reine (available in English).
Canada (1966b), *Rapport de la Commission d'enquête sur certaines questions relatives à la dénommée Gerda Munsinger* (Wishart Flett Spence, président), Ottawa, Imprimeur de la Reine (available in English).
Canada (1969), *Rapport de la Commission d'enquête sur la sécurité* (Maxwell Weir Mackensie, président), Ottawa, Imprimeur de la Reine (available in English).
Canada (1980), Commission d'enquête sur certaines activités de la Gendarmerie Royale du Canada, *Premier rapport: Sécurité et information* (David C. McDonald, président), Ottawa, Approvisionnements et Services Canada (available in English).
Canada (1981a), Commission d'enquête sur certaines activités de la Gendarmerie Royale du Canada, *Deuxième rapport: La liberté et la sécurité devant la loi* (David C. McDonald, président), Ottawa, Approvisionnements et Services Canada, 2 volumes (available in English under the title of 'Freedom and Security under the Law,' Commission of Inquiry Concerning Certain Activities of the Royal Canadian Mounted Police, Second report, Ottawa, Minister of Supply and Services).
Canada (1981b), Commission d'enquête sur certaines activités de la Gendarmerie Royale du Canada, *Troisième rapport: Certaines activités de la GRC et la connaissance qu'en avait le gouvernement* (David C. McDonald, président), Ottawa, Approvisionnements et Services Canada (available in English).

Canada (1991), *Adult Correctional Services in Canada, 1990–1991*, Ottawa, Canadian Centre for Justice Statistics, Statistics Canada.

Canada, Senate (1987), *Terrorism; The Report of the Senate Special Commitee on Terrorism and Public Safety*, Ottawa, Minister of Supply and Services.

Canada, Senate (1989), *Terrorism; The Report of the Second Special Committee of the Senate on Terrorism and Public Safety*, Ottawa, Minister of Supply and Services.

Cléroux, R. (1990), *Official Secrets*, Scarborough, McGraw-Hill Ryerson.

Cléroux, R. (1992), 'Mountie Mischief and l'Affaire Morin,' *The Globe and Mail*, 11 July, D1.

Deveault, C. (1980), *Toute ma vérité*, Montréal, Stanké (avec l'assistance de Monsieur William Johnson).

Devlin, K.L. (1971), 'Informers, Spies, and Agents Provocateurs,' *Chitty's Law Journal*, 19, 65–68.

Donnelly, R.C. (1951), 'Judicial Control of Informants, Spies, Stool Pigeons, and Agents Provocateurs,' *The Yale Law Journal*, 60, 1091–1131.

Doob, A.N. (1993), *The United States Sentencing Commission Guidelines: If You Don't Know Where You Are Going, You Might Not Get There*, Paper prepared for the Colston International Sentencing Symposium, University of Bristol (England), April 1993 (revised version, to be published in the Proceedings of the Conference).

Ericson, R.V. (1981), *Making Crime; A Study of Detective Work*, Toronto, Ont., Butterworths.

Gagnon, L. (1992), 'French Minuet, suite ...,' *La Presse*, 12 May, B3.

Gravel, S., Bordelais, S. (1993), *Le recours aux délateurs dans le contexte de l'administration de la justice québécoise*, Montréal, Centre International de Criminologie Comparée.

Johnson, L.K. (1985), *A Season of Inquiry; The Senate Intelligence Investigation*, Lexington, Ky., The University Press of Kentucky.

Johnston, L. (1992), *The Rebirth of Private Policing*, New York, Routledge.

Kelly, R.J. (1978), *Organized Crime; A Study in the Production of Knowledge by Law Enforcement Specialists*, Ph.D. Dissertation, City University of New York.

Kelly, W., Kelly, N. (1976), *Policing in Canada*, Toronto, Ontario, MacLean-Hunter.

Lagacé, L. (1992), 'Déclaration de Loraine Lagacé,' *La Presse*, 13 May, B3.

Law Reform Commission of Canada (1986), *Electronic Surveillance*, Ottawa, Law Reform Commission of Canada, Working Paper 47.

Manning, P.K. (1980), *The Narc's Game; Organizational and Informational Constraints on Drug Law Enforcement*, Cambridge, Mass., MIT Press.

Marx, G.T. (1974), 'Thoughts on a Neglected Category of Social Movement Participants: Agents Provocateurs and Informants,' *American Journal of Sociology*, 80, 2, 402–442.

Marx, G.T. (1981), 'Ironies of Social Control: Authorities as Contributors to Deviance Through Escalation, Non-enforcement, and Covert Facilitation,' *Social Problems*, 28, 3, 221–246.

Marx, G.T. (1982), 'Who Really Gets Stung? Some Issues Raised by the New Police Undercover Work,' *Crime and Delinquency*, 28, 2, 165–193.

Marx, G.T. (1987), 'The Interweaving of Public and Private Police in Undercover Work,' in: Shearing C.D. and Stenning P., eds., *Private Policing*, California, Sage, 172–193.
Marx, G.T. (1988), *Undercover: Police Surveillance in America*, Berkeley, University of California Press.
Moon, P. (1991), *The Globe and Mail*, Series of articles from 27 to 30 May.
Morin, C. (1992), 'Pourquoi j'ai accepté de collaborer avec la GRC,' *La Presse*, 11 May, B1.
Ontario (1980), *Report of the Commission of Inquiry into the Confidentiality of Health Information* (Horace Krever, chairman), Toronto, J.C. Thatcher, Queen's Printer, 3 volumes.
Québec (1992), *Rapport du Groupe de travail sur l'Administration de la justice en matière criminelle*, Québec, Ministère de la Justice, Ministère de la Sécurité publique.
Québec (1981), *Rapport de la Commission d'enquête sur des opérations policières en territoire québécois* (Jean F. Keable, président), Québec, Ministère de la Justice.
RCMP (1991a), *Board of Inquiry on the Activities of the RCMP Related to Allegations Made in the Senate of Canada: Report* (The Honourable René J. Marin, Chairman), Ottawa, RCMP.
RCMP (1991b), *Board of Inquiry on the Activities of the RCMP Related to Allegations Made in the Senate of Canada: Research Studies 1991* (The Honourable René J. Marin, Chairman), Ottawa, RCMP.
Reuter, P. (1983a), *Disorganized Crime; The Economics of the Visible Hand*, Cambridge, Mass., MIT Press.
Reuter, P. (1983b), 'Licensing Criminals: Police and Informants,' in: Caplan, G.M., ed., *ABSCAM Ethics; Moral Issues and Deception in Law Enforcement*, Cambridge, Mass., Ballinger, 100–117.
Reuter, P. (1985), *The Organization of Illegal Markets; An Economic Analysis*, Washington, D.C., U.S. Department of Justice, National Institute of Justice.
Robertson, K.G. (1989), *Canadian Intelligence Policy*, Graduate School of European and International Studies, University of Reading, U.K., unpublished manuscript.
Sallot, J. (1984), 'Secret Agency Keeps Data on Individual "Security Risks",' *The Globe and Mail*, 21 November.
Schiffer, M.E. (1991), 'Police Use of Paid Informers,' in: RCMP (1991b), *Board of Inquiry on the Activities of the RCMP Related to Allegations Made in the Senate of Canada: Research Studies 1991* (The Honourable René J. Marin, Chairman), Ottawa, RCMP.
Shearing, C.D., Stenning, P. (1981), 'Modern Private Security: Its Growth and Implications,' in: Tonry, M., and Morris, N., eds., *Crime and Justice; An Annual Review of Research*, 3, Chicago, University of Chicago Press.
Shearing, C.D. (1992), 'Public and Private Policing' in: Tonry, M., and Morris, N., eds., *Modern Policing, Crime and Justice; An Annual Review of Research*, 16, Chicago, University of Chicago Press.
Security Intelligence Review Committee (SIRC) (1987), *The Security and Intelligence Network in the Government of Canada; A Description*, Ottawa, S.I.R.C., Expurgated copy.

Security Intelligence Review Committee (SIRC) (1990), *Annual Report 1989–1990*, Ottawa, S.I.R.C.

Stober, M. (1991), 'The Limits of Police Provocation in Canada,' in: RCMP (1991b), *Board of Inquiry on the Activities of the RCMP Related to Allegations Made in the Senate of Canada: Research Studies 1991* (The Honourable René J. Marin, Chairman), Ottawa, RCMP.

Windsor, H. (1991), 'Tories Block Testimony in Inquiry on Mashat,' *The Globe and Mail*, 12 June.

Wool, G.L. (1986), 'Police Informants in Canada: The Law and Reality,' *Saskatchewan Law Review*, 50, 2, 249–270.

Cases Cited

– *Le Procureur Général du Canada et Claude Vermette, requérants c. La Commission des droits de la personne, intimée et Bertrand Roy et autres*, mis en cause [1977], C.S. 47–67.
– *The Queen v. Dufresne* (1988), 1 R.C.S., 1095.
– *Mack v. The Queen* (1988), 44 C.C.C. (3d) 513–565 (S.C.C.).

Peter Klerks* | Covert Policing in the Netherlands

1. INTRODUCTION: POLICING UNDER THE LEE OF PUBLIC TRUST

In Holland, as in nearly all other European countries, a shift can be observed in the ways serious crime manifests itself. More stable and enduring organizations simultaneously operating in multiple criminal markets have been established, and their vulnerability to traditional criminal justice and policing interventions appears to be limited.

The police are changing as well, partly in reaction to evolutions in crime, but also in an effort to answer society's demands for a more responsive force which reflects in its composition the multi-ethnic and emancipated community it seeks to serve.[1] Of course transformation processes in the police also resemble those

---

* Researcher, Faculty of Law, Department of Criminal Law and Criminology, Erasmus University Rotterdam, Rotterdam, the Netherlands. With thanks to Ms. A. Borsboom for her research support.
1. The Dutch police are presently going through the most far-reaching reorganization process since World War II. After a number of unsuccessful attempts over the last fifteen years, the present moderate left government has set in motion a major operation to replace the 148 local police forces (some 25,000 officers), the *Rijkspolitie* (state police for the rural areas, some 13,000 strong) and a handful of national specialized services by 25 regional forces and an integrated national service. This operation will be a significant step toward a further centralization and rationalization of the Dutch police system.

Reflecting society, the Dutch police can be described as a modern, well-equipped and liberal organization. Although rising crime rates have caused a shift away from basic policing functions with an emphasis on helping the public, toward an orientation that concentrates on law enforcement and crime fighting functions, on the whole public acceptance of the police seems to be quite high compared to other European countries. Controversial issues such as police attitudes toward minorities, the integration of women in the force and the control over police violence are the subject of public debate. Social science research on the police is intensive, and police personnel on all levels generally show responsiveness when confronted with criticism. Within the police all sorts of political views may be encountered, with Christian Democrats dominating the rank and file and Liberals, Social Democrats and Christian Democrats about equally represented in the higher ranks. It should be noted however that many police officers

in any other modern organization, tuning in to more mundane developments such as the introduction and evolution of computers, new opportunities in telecommunications and innovative management techniques. Furthermore, certain sections of the Dutch police and the responsible ministries have been quite active in stimulating and initiating applied academic research.[2]

Within the Dutch police a development can be traced since the mid-1970s (i.e. before 'organized crime' became an issue) which most visibly manifested itself in the gradual build-up of special teams and capabilities such as the highly specialized 'violence specialists' (arrest squads and anti-terrorist teams) and intelligence-gathering and processing units (covert surveillance teams, again anti-terrorist teams and infiltration sections working in the criminal milieu). The usual pattern has been to initiate the use of certain tactics and techniques in the field without much formal ado in the way of legislation or political approval. Such novelties would then only become the subject of debate after their existence was revealed in trials, through leaks or mistakes (Klerks, 1989).

In the confrontation with serious and organized crime, the police increasingly rely on methods and techniques that have been labelled 'proactive policing.' This is related to the collection and analysis of tactical and strategic intelligence. Combating organizations, networks and perilous social processes (e.g. money laundering, illegal arms trafficking) demands an approach quite different from the traditional conviction-oriented methods. In this respect one could hypothesize about a gradual merging of certain aspects of two traditions in internal security: policing and security intelligence. In this paper it is argued that there are indications that in fact a 'third service' is presently taking shape, located somewhere between the traditional police detectives and the security and intelligence services. A central characteristic of this secret or covert police is that while it largely manages to avoid the traditional controls of both regular police management and the judiciary, it is also immune from the oversight apparatus that monitors the security and intelligence services.

The Dutch police has virtually no public history of scandals, corruption or controversial political policing. This means that there is little distrust in the general public toward the police; police integrity is still more or less taken for granted, except among some lawyers and outside critics.

Fighting serious crime is to a large extent carried out beyond the view of the general public. It is a rather secluded world on which lawyers generally fail to

---

show only little interest in politics and hold rather traditional views. Membership of non-democratic or racist organizations is considered incompatible with serving in the police. In the last fifteen years the Dutch police has experienced a significant influx of academically trained cadre and professional managers, resulting in an explicitly civilian-orientated and non-militaristic atmosphere, with the possible exceptions of some special-duty branches such as the marksman units, the specialized arrest teams and the VIP teams.

2. The relatively open atmosphere enables a researcher good access to sources and functionaries. Much research is initiated by the police or the ministry of Justice, and Holland enjoys a good infrastructure of study and training centers, libraries and specialized documentation centers, most of which are open to outside visitors. There are three major police magazines one of which, the monthly *Tijdschrift voor de Politie*, features articles on new research and initiates debates.

get a handle and in which academic researchers are an unknown species. The police officers and special units usually operate in secret without any substantial oversight from outside. The only 'outsiders' in the know are some selected functionaries from the public prosecutor's office, who share many of the central interests and values with the police operatives and management. This situation – a combination of public confidence, lenient judges and a general acceptance of the seriousness of the cause by both the legislative and executive powers – results in an optimal climate for covert policing. As long as law enforcement authorities manage to avoid serious scandals in the headlines, much of what they do is accepted as a matter of course.

These circumstances somewhat resemble the state of affairs in most countries in conventional security intelligence work until the 1970s. The existence of internal security services and their operating practices were seldom questioned where they involved countering communist espionage and subversive threats. The revelations and scandals in the 1970s and 1980s and the subsequent reforms in many countries have convinced politicians, but also many practitioners of the necessity of an effective oversight system. The argument in this article is that the secretive sections of the police are now in need of a similar constructive accountability structure. Such positively motivated outside interferences will not only help to avoid corruption and overzealousness, but may indeed contribute to the quality of the work process and the value of the end product.

1.1. Introducing Secrecy inside Police Organizations

In the gradual adaption to 'big-league policing,' the Dutch police was confronted with the need to introduce a system of inner-departmental secrecy and compartmentalization to prevent leaks. This has resulted in irritations where the prevailing attitude toward secrecy in the down-to-earth Dutch police is to frown upon the pomposities usually associated with hush-hush behavior. The emergence of so-called 'embargo teams' unavoidably undermines the central availability of information on all investigative activities. In daily practice, this translates into duplicating investigations and surveillance, hunting each other's informers and other nuisances. This is all the more frustrating for those managers whose efforts in convincing many of the local forces to share information and resources finally began to bear fruit. The reluctance to accept and incorporate inner-organizational security measures seems to be a typical problem for a traditional law enforcement organization that is gradually adopting a more intelligence-centered orientation.

1.2. Research Methodology and Structure of this Chapter

The author aims to introduce the reader to some aspects of covert and proactive policing in the Netherlands that may serve to illustrate the processes described above. Although police studies flourish in Holland and the research atmosphere is relatively open, little factual information on the more concealed police practices can be found in the open literature.[3] The reasons for this are obvious, but it would seem that the subject merits at least some discussion. The researcher formally interviewed ten practitioners and other well-informed individuals.[4] In semi-structured interviews, the interviewees were asked about their experiences and knowledge of covert policing. Their opinion on the effectiveness and risks of such methods was sought, with an emphasis on the process of oversight under the rule of law.[5]

---

3. Elsewhere it has been argued that Dutch academics generally avoid researching sensitive issues, and that there is no strong tradition in investigative journalism (Punch, 1985, 6, 192; Klerks, 1989, 209–210).
4. All the practitioners approached by the researcher were quite willing to be interviewed about covert policing, although some spoke more freely than others. Still, the impression remained that it is very difficult to unveil the daily realities of covert policing by interviewing those directly involved in it. A non-spoken taboo on asking about concrete cases and problems in this sensitive area induced some form of self-censorship with the researcher. Practitioners generally avoid speaking of individual cases or persons, but referred to structures, mechanisms and regulations instead. Only the interviewed attorneys sometimes used concrete cases to illustrate their views on the matter. Several of the interviewees used the opportunity of the interview for off-the-record discussions. On the whole, the information this produced did not contradict the rest of the collected material. It did serve to illustrate the 'operating code' by which workers solve the organizational constraints and dilemmas they face (Punch, 1985, 187). As two of the interviewees observed while seeing me out of their offices, 'the real information you get over coffee, not from the files.'
5. In selecting suitable candidates for interviewing, the author tried to attain a representation of as many different views of the law enforcement process as possible. This may explain the sometimes contradictory views and explanations reproduced here. The phase of the informative or orienting pre-investigation is probably the most relevant in regard to covert policing. In Holland, the Criminal Intelligence Department (CID) is the main coordinating body here. Chief inspector Van Gestel, the head of a regional CID was therefore interviewed. The Dutch CID is dissimilar from the British Criminal Investigations Department in that it has no tactical detective role, i.e. it doesn't handle cases independently, but together with separate entities such as the observation squads and the infiltration units, it supplies the tactical criminal investigations squads with intelligence. The CID is also responsible for collecting general information on (potential) criminal individuals, groups, and activities in its operational area for strategic planning of operations and resources. Commissioner Karstens, chief of the bureau for National Coordination of Police Infiltration (ANCPI) at the national Criminal Intelligence Service (CRI) in The Hague was interviewed on infiltration operations. Mr. Kruizinga, secretary of the Algemene Christelijke Politiebond (General Christian Police Union), provided insights on the police unions' views.

In the Dutch legal system, a *'rechter-commissaris'* (RC, examining magistrate) has to give permission (warrants) for some intrusive investigate means such as telephone taps and (house) searches. In such cases, a *'gerechtelijk vooronderzoek'* (GVO, magistrate's preliminary inquiry) is opened against a known or unknown suspect. Mr. Pulles, RC at the district court in Arnhem and chairman of the national assembly of RC's, was interviewed. The *'Openbaar Ministerie'* (OM, public prosecution department) as a hierarchically organized state body has control of the detection of criminal offenses, the prosecution of perpetrators and the execution of sentences. The *'Officier van Justitie'* (OvJ, public prosecutor) is the OM's representative at the district courts. Mr. Ficq, chief public prosecutor at the district court in Den Bosch and chairman of the CID supervision commission, told of his experiences. At the next higher level, the courts of appeal, the *'Advocaat-Generaal'* (Advocate General) represents the OM. Mr. Myjer, working in The Hague, is a leading commentator on the human rights dimensions of

COVERT POLICING IN THE NETHERLANDS

Raising questions on the appropriateness of certain police methods and on civil liberties issues seems almost old-fashioned in a time where serious crime problems are evident. This author still argues that it should be an indispensable complement of any study related to crime control. It was stimulating to find several of the interviewed practitioners expressing their sincere interest in this debate, and some spoke freely about their incertitude over the problem of containing serious crime while maintaining the rule of law and protecting civil liberties.

Four elements of covert policing are examined in this chapter: the Criminal Intelligence Department, the practice of police infiltration, surveillance teams and informant handling.[6] Additionally, the problem of secrecy within the force is discussed and some conclusions are drawn.

2. THE CRIMINAL INTELLIGENCE DEPARTMENT

As intelligence is becoming a dominant factor in the policing of serious crime, the Criminal Intelligence Department (in Dutch: *Criminele Inlichtingen Dienst*, CID) plays a central role that is perhaps insufficiently recognized in current studies of the police. The CID and the information flows it controls and produces are in some domains taking over the role of the citizen reporting a crime as the main factor in initiating investigations. The following section describes the development and structure of the CID in Holland, the role of the CID in strategic planning, the concealment of CID information in court, the problem of controlling the intelligence operatives under the rule of law, and the risks of developing 'tunnel vision' in CID work.

2.1. Development and Structure of the CID

The CID has a pivotal role in the modern police that finds itself being transformed into an information-organization, i.e. an organization which is not only an information-processing system, but in which information systems replace

---

criminal law. He and his colleague Mr. Den Os, the former public prosecutor for terrorism and espionage cases, gave their views as Advocates General. Attorneys-at-law Pen, Van der Plas and Prakken supplied information on their experiences with the end products of covert policing. Apart from these formal interviews dozens of contacts with various functionaries, researchers, attorneys, former suspects and journalists have influenced or contributed to this article.

6. 'Covert policing' in this chapter is defined as all police interferences in which the police refrain from making their identity as a police officer known to those on whom their activities have an impact. While this could stretch the definition to include an off-duty police officer who happens to catch a purse snatcher (which admittedly is not intended), limiting it to only those interventions in which the undercover police officer has a personal contact with the target seems to be too narrow. The element of concealment is clearly present in covert surveillance or the use of informers, and the organizing of information-gathering and -processing in a CID-like structure to my idea should also be included in the concept. For a contrary opinion *see* Marx, 1992, 17–18.

traditional mechanisms of coordination and management (Jansen en Jägers, 1992). In policing serious crime, but also in the more secular realms of public order and petty crime, the CID with its tactical and strategic intelligence products strongly influences priority-setting and feasibility estimates, and therefore the day-to-day functioning of the police as a whole. As the coordinating office for most proactive operations, the CID is the logical starting point for a discourse on covert policing.

The practice of handling criminal intelligence in a structured way was introduced in Holland after the second World War. In the 1950s, inspired by British and U.S. experiences, several of the larger municipal police forces started operating a CID. In the mid-1980s the ministers of Justice and the Interior, in an attempt to bring some structure to the proliferation of local CID's with incompatible data structures and computer hardware, introduced the CID-regulations (CID-regeling, 1986; Broeders, 1989, 15–17; Klerks, 1989, 141). From then on CID's were only allowed to register information on 'CID subjects,' defined as:

> natural persons or legal entities of which on the basis of facts and circumstances can be assumed that they are (or as reasonably can be suspected will become) involved with crimes that – because of their seriousness or frequency or the organized mode in which they are committed – present a serious violation of the legal order (CID-regeling, 1986, Para. 1, Art. 1 under (c)).

Of such CID subjects, the following data may be registered: personal details or relevant corporate data, nationality, character traits, personal circumstances, education and professions, way of life, contacts and contact addresses, places of frequent residence, movements, means of transport, (planned) criminal activities, and *modus operandi* (CID-regeling, 1986, Para. 2, Art. 6, Subsection 1). Furthermore, the CID may register and work for a maximum of six months on 'grey field subjects,' i.e. persons or organizations who are not yet considered CID subjects.

Under the present national police reorganization regional CID's (RCID's) are being set up, varying in size from 5 to about 60 observers, crime analysts, informant runners and information researchers and suppliers (Van Gestel, interviews 1 and 2). Many of the larger cities are expected to retain their own CID's, targeted primarily at local offenders. There is even an inclination toward stimulating CID's at the precinct level. In Amsterdam, for instance (3400 police officers serving about 700,000 inhabitants plus a large number of commuters and tourists), each of the 24 precincts is supposed to have a CID officer functioning as a collator, who calls in at central CID once a week to discuss current affairs. In Rotterdam the local CID yearly receives more than 6,000 useful information reports originating from beat patrol and general surveillance. Other CID information sources are the tactical detective squads, surveillance teams, infiltration teams, informants, the central criminal registry, a wide range of public and private bodies, and various forms of documentation (media, advertisements, etcetera).

COVERT POLICING IN THE NETHERLANDS

Nationally, the *Afdeling Coördinatie Criminele Inlichtingen* (ACCI) at the CRI has a coordination function and it runs the central CID Subjects Index (CIDSI). Persistent problems with computerization processes and communication between separate CID's have so far caused many headaches (Algemene Rekenkamer, 1991, 18–19). In 1991, the ACCI reportedly processed 3,397 information reports, against 2,505 in 1990. Almost half of these concerned narcotics cases (CRI, 1992, 69).

In recent years, some new players have entered the CID field: interregional serious crime teams operating in isolation from the rest of the force for security reasons, increasingly work in a CID-like fashion with their own informants and their own surveillance and phone tapping facilities (Begeleidingscommissie CID, 1992, 22).

2.2. Role in Strategic Planning

The RCID's play a critical role in directing operations against serious and organized crime. In each of the 25 police regions, the RCID chief together with the public prosecutor responsible for serious crime and the chief of the tactical crime division, decide what groups will be investigated. Chief of RCID Brabant-West Godfried Van Gestel:

> We have in this region for example 4,000 subjects, clustered into a number of groups. We indicate their activities: robberies, car thefts ... The public prosecutor and the detectives chief bring their stats: which problems do we have? Because otherwise you get inclined to work only on narcotics cases. Then they say: give us an analysis of these ten groups, spread over the region, with different sorts of crime represented. I hand that over to the crime analysis section. (...) Next we indicate the quality of our information positions on the different groups, and advise on whether or not to go ahead. And for those groups that we can't take on, they say: 'chief, next time do your homework, so that we'll know more about them' (Van Gestel, interview 1).

Chief public prosecutor Ficq:

> In consultation with the police it is decided to come to a surface analysis, i.e. a global overview of such a group's activities. We make about 10 to 15 of such analyses a year. Then in the consultation process it is decided on the basis of priorities on which of the groups an operational analysis will be done (3 or 4 groups). With that you go deeper, looking into the options for tackling the group. This is the proactive phase. The CID-public prosecutor decides in this stage which means of investigation will be used. He has the final responsibility (Ficq, interview).

Mr. Ficq chaired the working group charged with formulating the framework within which the CID's would have to operate. This working group concluded that the chief of CID, the chief of the tactical crime division and the public prosecutor should together select so-called 'CID-targets,' i.e. CID-subjects whom it is considered desirable and feasible to remove from society for a certain period (Broeders, 1989, 17–18).

Inter-regional policy coordination is effected through regular meetings between the public prosecutors for serious crime in each of the five *'ressorts'* (jurisdiction of a court of appeal) in the Netherlands. The prerogative of the public prosecutor's office to decide what methods are fielded against a specific criminal group seems uncontested. Yet this sensitive issue appears to raise a good deal of debate. The chair of the CID supervision commission, in discussing the ethical aspects of CID work:

> has found that in the preliminary phase of any investigation there are hardly any clearly defined rules to guide the CID detective in deciding on the admissibility of certain methods of investigation. In practice the responsible prosecutor, the CID prosecutor and the chief public prosecutor confer on what in a concrete situation is admissible or not. It turns out that opinions on this can be divergent (...) (Begeleidingscommissie CID, 1992, 14).

2.3. The Concealment of CID Information in Court

Regardless of the methods used, secrecy is always a determining element of CID work. Maintaining a clear distinction from the regular tactical crime squad can be vital to ensure confidentiality of methods, personnel and informants:

> The distinction often causes problems in court. We try to maintain a strict division in responsibilities here. (...) The chief of the tactical team can be questioned about the preliminary phase, but he doesn't know much about it. For him it is harder to say 'I refuse to answer that.' To a CID-chief that's a bit easier when it comes to protecting informants, hence the strict separation. In a pseudo-purchase the tactical chief is responsible for deploying the pseudo-purchase team, the head of that team is responsible for carrying out the mission, and we are mainly responsible for the informants circuit. We refuse in principle to answer questions on each other's sections (Van Gestel, interview 1).

Most attorneys are eager to share their frustrating experiences with this compartmentalization:

> You get the *dossier*, the police report, it states something, but as an attorney you seldom manage to lay your hands on CID information. The structure of our penal system supports this to a high degree: jurisprudence agrees with CID information. Sometimes the CID has to clarify something, then the head of CID turns out, claiming the info is reliable, that they played by the rules and that all was checked. Thereupon the judge nods, and that's it. Who it is and where it comes from you'll never know. Essentially in every criminal case the proactive phase is totally shielded off (Pen, interview).

Mr. Pen illustrated his suspicions of police 'creativity':

> The CID receives reliable information that certain things are happening on a premises. They go in and *voila*, four kilos plus weapons. Presto. But how did they know? Because the German police laid it on the doorstep. A German dealer was involved, and the Germans retrieved the information in an illegal way. (...) And I can never prove it, that's true. But I want to go even further. There was this burglary in Amsterdam the other day, in which information on German addicts was stolen. I do not know who committed the burglary. Personally I'm one hundred per cent convinced that it was the German police. I have some grounds for that assumption, on the basis of later information (Pen, interview).

Ms. Prakken deems the CID to be the major problem. She claims they administer enormous amounts of information:

> Most criminal files of any importance, especially in the sphere of dope, begin with the standard phrase 'CID information indicated ...,' followed by a statement, and subsequently they take up stake-out positions to establish that what they already knew is indeed going on. That doesn't mean that the CID's are not often right, but there is no control at all on the way in which it gets in the files and where the material comes from (Prakken, interview).

She illustrates this with an example:

> A client of mine goes to fetch dope somewhere. As he enters, an observation unit is on a stake-out. They duly report: 'man enters with empty bag, leaves again with a full bag,' and my client gets busted around the corner with a pound of coke. He asks me 'how could they know? I only just got in the country.' There had been a brief telephone call to arrange a meeting. Must be a phone tap. The dossier consisted of three pages: 'CID information indicated that one Harry would be collecting dope on such a time on that place; we observed, and indeed ...' That was the dossier. I said: 'it sticks out a mile that there has been a phone tap, I want to see the logs.' Quite a battle it was, to get a hand on at least part of those tapping logs. Next I called up the head of CID as a witness. (...) He showed up at the examining magistrate's office, very correctly, to declare that 'we had on this person such and such information.' To my question as to whether that telephone conversation was part of the CID info, he said that this was not the case. He then made a phone call to his colleagues, and it transpired that this information wasn't there and that the phone hadn't been tapped. What had happened? The police had done something they weren't allowed to do, and in such cases this gets hidden under the great white-washer: CID information. At the trial the officer who made the report was called up. He declared: 'I had forgotten. That phone tap had to be shielded. We always do that by categorizing it as CID-information, so it gets filed that way.' So the police have information that is possibly illegally obtained. They turn it into CID-information themselves and then retrieve it again. The rabbit from the magician's hat. Only this time it came to light because this constable goofed. The case is still pending (Prakken, interview).

RCID chief Van Gestel is well aware of these dangers:

> It is one of the flaws of the CID-world. Here we apply the principle: the oath of office is sacred, and no single case can be important enough to commit perjury. We have to remove the mist before our eyes the moment that we get too fanatic over a certain case. You have to distance yourself from it, or you'll face your own limitations, especially in CID. We just have to be aware of the fact that it is utterly strange that I, as a policeman, can tell a judge 'my dear judge, I will not answer that. Go sort it out, I'm not telling you the name of that informant.' We may have grown accustomed to it by now, but if you consider the penal law system it is very exotic, also if you look at other countries. I happen to know a bit about the Canadian legal system, there everything has got to be unearthed, even the memo's. Very strange from our point of view. So you constantly have to be aware of your delicate position as a police officer: the judge permits you, on good grounds, to withhold certain things. There's a certain tension there, and if you mess with that, it will come back to you as a boomerang (Van Gestel, interview).

This police manager seems to be highly aware of the delicate situation of proactive operations, condoned by the judges on the basis of trust. He claims to understand the difficulties that attorneys have with the shroud of CID secrecy:

> We do try to keep things secret, but without lying about it. Sometimes it may seem like we put the judge on the wrong track, lay a mist over it. Boone (a well-known Dutch attorney, PK) has frequently reproached me: 'Mr. Van Gestel only answers me if I press the right button.' Maybe he's right. But we are positively trying to establish the limits in which we can do our work. This is mainly done through jurisprudence. We go through every single case with our own CID prosecutor. He's especially charged with CID and in principle he knows everything, except for the identity of our informants. And we would even tell him that if it became necessary. I think the role of the proper authorities, in this case the public prosecutor, is vital here, for he is the only check we can build into this system. (...) I have no secrets from a judge as such, but everything which goes to a judge an attorney has got to know of as well, and that sometimes causes problems. By the fact that you don't answer certain things, I create the impression of having something to hide (Van Gestel, interview).

2.4. Controlling the CID

Dutch investigating magistrates (RC – *'rechter-commissaris'*) appear to come in two kinds: there is an easy-going and a meticulous brand. One of the interviewed attorneys asserted that RC's ('and even the good ones') have become an extension of the police (Van der Plas, interview). This view seems to be partly supported by at least one prestigious observer, who judged the RC's investigative role in phone tapping procedures of little practical importance (Van Veen, 1984). RC Pulles is quite realistic on this:

> There are roughly two lines in the RC's. I have a colleague who says: 'I never want to have contact with a police officer, they communicate with me through the public prosecutor.' (...) That line generally doesn't want to know too much of what goes on (Pulles, interview).

This 'lenient line' seems to have the upper hand. Mr. Pulles justifies his own, inquisitive stance with an example:

> During a case I noticed that the police in their report to the court had presented an account of events that differed from what had actually transpired. It was about a cocaine deal where informants were involved. I found out by questioning witnesses. The police says: 'we got a tip, went to look, and indeed could make the busts.' I made an analysis: one witness had told the accused: if you want to sell cocaine, I know where to find a buyer. That witness was sent by the police, then Tallon (jurisprudence, PK) comes in: entrapment, etcetera. The details of that conversation suddenly became very important. The police of course refused to produce the informant, which is understandable from a point of view of protecting sources, but the accused was acquitted and got a compensation (Pulles, interview).

Mr. Pulles stresses that he doesn't want any cases with a double bottom in a trial. He sees his function as a guardian for proper procedures, and is rather worried about recent suggestions by an advisory group that the RC system is antiquated and ineffective:

> The public prosecutor pays strong attention to the interests of the investigation, I as an RC have got to establish the truth. The RC sees to it that the facts of the matter with all relevant aspects become clear. The police primarily want to find out who did it, and how this can be proved. If a crime squad chief comes to me saying 'we've got CID info that shows ...,' I ask him what the information pertains to. Who, what, where, when, why. Then they always say 'there is a source.' Is there an informant, surveillance, technical means? How does this person, this informant, know? How old is the information, how reliable the informant? The chief then says: 'I can't put that on paper.' I then have the police draw up a report containing everything that they *can* put in writing. And an oral explication follows.

Mr. Pulles emphasizes that he feels the CID makes mistakes, but that the people working there are trustworthy:

> My story may sound somewhat negative, but it's not meant that way. I realize there's a game being played, in which I have a clear role: it is the responsibility of the magistrate to question. If you don't ask anything you don't hear anything. The prosecutor really isn't in need of such a troublesome magistrate; he prefers to keep the information away from him. (...) But my somewhat negative sounding story in relation to the police doesn't emanate from a fundamental distrust. I am a guarantee, also to the CID itself. They will always make mistakes, that's what the supervision of a magistrate is needed for: I am somewhat more detached from the case (Pulles, interview).

Much 'soft' CID information about relation networks, behavior and gossip originates from 'the Big Ear.' Information extracted from telephone taps may be stored in a CID database, even when the taps are not used for prosecution and the individuals are never formally recognized as suspects. Mr. Pulles has made a deal with the local prosecutor that any material derived from 'his' taps (i.e. 'his' warrants) that goes to the CID is specially marked, so that he is consulted before the CID passes the material on to others. This arrangement is rather unique: no CID would normally think twice about the 'ownership' of such data. A prosecutor does not need an RC's warrant to hook up a printer to a telephone ('metering' or 'pen-registering'): the phone company has to provide any 'traffic information' on demand. This information too can be stored by the CID. By mid-1993, a debate can be expected on new bugging legislation that is now under preparation. Some people fear that this technique will give the police unparalleled powers to intrude into the privacy of homes and public places, especially since it would also bring more highly sensitive information for the CID. Advocate General Myjer:

> Directional microphones are totally different. You no longer need the phone company, you can just acquire a mike and start working. I fear that if this is not regulated very properly, the category of CID-information will rise immensely. Because they might bring all this kind of information under the heading 'CID-information.' I really wouldn't want that (Myjer, interview).

Mr. Myjer explains that regular telephone tapping has a 'typically Dutch' guarantee against abuse: the telephone company sends a steep bill for every phone tap which the examining magistrate has to sign for approval. Bugging operations will not include such a double-check.

Chief public prosecutor and chairman of the CID supervision commission Ficq isn't too worried about an unlimited growth of the CID files:

> We advised in an earlier report on what may and may not be stored from telephone taps: (a) you purge your files after a specified period; (b) every piece of information has an indication of reliability; (c) the police only wants to store information they can use. In the long run, you see that those CID's that initially had a very high number of registered subjects now show hardly any growth. I have the impression that there's a certain stabilization. I'm not so afraid for that. And besides, before such information gets any relevance ... it must be used in a police report. But then it becomes verifiable for a judge.

Mr. Ficq has a very positive impression of the CID's professionalism:

> I mean both their professional dealing with it and that they work in a sufficiently detached way. They ask themselves 'can we do this or not?' They are now orienting themselves on the ethical aspects of their own functioning (Ficq, interview).

2.5. He's Got the Look

There is no reason to doubt Ficq's judgment in this. Still, RCID chief Van Gestel has some disconcerting things to say on stress and other 'occupational diseases' related to CID work:

I think you shouldn't be in this business too long. It takes some three or four years before you're experienced enough to be a good runner. Then you should do it for maybe six years, but after ten years in my view you have to be out, before you get too involved in this narrow world: you develop tunnel vision. (...) Working in this environment can reinforce cynicism and misanthropy. I really wouldn't know how I could coach my people in that. I haven't seen anyone go over the edge here in that respect. But it really is a world on its own. It's a narrow world, in which you really have to rely on your colleague, you're completely dependent on that. And on the chief's support: we shield our people as much as possible. To the outer world, I am the face of this RCID; no runner of mine ever appears in court. This can lead to a situation of inbreeding. They are less open to external influences. If a case breaks down the Justice department is always to blame, and those bloody attorneys, who are really half-criminals. The whole world is against us. Of course they hear an enormous lot from their informants, at which you always have to maintain an independent position. But it can be mighty frustrating at times to have solid cases, in which you as CID know exactly how things really are, but which ultimately you can't prove. CID is always one or two steps ahead of a tactical team. And those informants, well, of course they are genuine criminals. The bigger the crook, the better the informer. Working with CID for a long span of time, and all the time maintaining contacts with such people who are very biased in this society can cause serious problems (Van Gestel, interview 1).

3. INFILTRATION

Everybody speaks of substantial buying, but that's outdated. The number of such operations has been substantially reduced (Commissioner Karstens, interview).

In this section the classic undercover method of infiltration is addressed. The recent history and gradual regulation of this method and the use of civilians for this dangerous work are discussed. The international dimension which is of growing importance and the shift from evidence-gathering to intelligence-gathering are described. This again seems to support the thesis on the changing nature of the police. The use of the infiltration method, especially when applied as an intelligence-gathering tool, involves severe risks. The lacking accountability under the rule of law, the threat of corruption and the psychological effects are examined here. Finally, the National Coordinator is asked about his views on the future of police infiltration.

3.1. Recent History and Regulation

Modern police infiltration, initially in the form of *'pseudokoop'* (Dutch for pseudo-purchase, or substantial buying) was first practised in Amsterdam in the late 1960s, although Frielink discusses a number of incidents involving infiltrators and *agents provocateur* over the last hundred years, and the very critical reactions they elicited (Van Kastel, 1989, 205; Frielink, 1990, 9–14). When the

U.S. Drug Enforcement Agency (DEA) in 1973 determined that Holland was the number one European distribution point for Asian heroin, it soon mounted its first successful undercover operations there (Posner, 1990, 189). At the same time, undercover agents (ucas) from the U.S. Military Police in Heidelberg also operated in unison with the Dutch police (Brouwer, 1988, 35). The DEA's influence in the field during this period was considerable, and the unconventional methods it introduced challenged the courts into accepting new realities (Punch, 1985, 45–46). Dutch detectives were impressed with the seemingly infinite resources their American colleagues had at their disposal. The reverse was also true: a DEA agent posted in The Hague told an American researcher in the early 1980s:

> They have no money to spend. Any drug dealer worth his weight in salt could outbid the Dutch with his spare pocket change. They don't get anyone worthwhile to talk to them. No self-respecting informant would go to the Dutch police (Posner, 1990, 185).

The Americans, convinced that Holland would be a central drugs transfer point for decades to come, provided various forms of assistance. Senior police officials were trained in the United States, and until 1983 some of the larger Dutch police forces borrowed special equipment such as their communications sets for undercover work from the DEA.

As the American ucas got ever more successful, some of them began to appear as witnesses in court. Such was the case when the American drug dealer Bruce Tallon was convicted and a Hoge Raad (Supreme Court) ruling established the Dutch infiltration doctrine that holds until the present day (Hoge Raad, 4 December 1979).

The deployment of Dutch ucas became inevitable after 1978, when most of the larger dealers became aware of the new business risks and began to avoid doing business with Americans. The pioneering Amsterdam police inspector Kees Sietsma learned the tricks of the trade from Canadian RCMP specialists, thus paving the way for 'pseudo purchasers' to be brought into action in the early 1980s by the Amsterdam municipal police, the *Rijkspolitie* and the CRI (National Criminal Information Service). Between 1976 and 1983, the Dutch police organized or supervised several hundred undercover operations (Brouwer, 1988, 32). In an attempt to attain professional standards, a working group on long-term infiltration was established in 1983. Its report *'Pseudokoop'* in 1984 led to the development of a national *pseudokoop*-course (Van Kastel, 1989, 205–229; Klerks, 1989, 143–144). In December 1985 the Minister of Justice informed parliament about his views that there was now sufficient jurisprudence to conclude that infiltration as an investigation method was permissible under certain conditions (Handelingen, 1985–1986). He formulated a.o. the following prerequisites:

– the uca is forbidden to cause the suspect to commit offenses other than those within his original intent ('Tallon-criterion'). The operation should be limited to making the suspect's original intent visible (i.e. the prosecutor has to convince the judge that the suspect has done drug deals before or that he had

voiced explicitly his intention to sell drugs before the pseudo-purchase was made);
- the infiltrator should operate after approval by the prosecutor's office, under direction of the head of the detective squad and in close consultation with the prosecutor involved;
- applying methods of infiltration should fulfil the criteria of proportionality and subsidiarity (i.e. other, less intrusive measures have been considered or tried but proved inadequate);
- using civilian infiltrators is less desired and should be limited to such special cases in which replacement by a police officer is not feasible. Operations by infiltrators not under the supervision of the police and the justice department are not acceptable, such as foreign infiltrators operating without the approval of Dutch authorities;
- the committing of crimes by the infiltrator will be accepted within certain limits.

Parliament subsequently approved these guidelines.

All three of the attorneys-at-law interviewed claimed that the above safeguards didn't amount to much in reality. According to them, the Hoge Raad is most lenient over the admissibility of evidence gathered by ucas.

> I did a case recently in which a DEA uca said 'yes, that man only dealt in hashish and I started talking about heroin.' It was only an attempt, limited to conversations. The Supreme Court confirmed the Court of Appeal's ruling that the fact that the man after a series of conversations with the uca in the end agreed to take part in a heroin transaction, proved that under circumstances he had the intention of dealing hard drugs. (...) With such a formula, the Tallon-criterion is fully eroded (Van der Plas, interview).

After the *'Bureau Nationale Coördinator Pseudokoop'* was established in 1987 the CRI stopped providing pseudo purchasers, since this contradicted its role as a non-executive support agency. As the nine infiltration teams (three teams in Amsterdam, each five strong, and six state police teams each between eight and ten strong) expanded their operations beyond pseudo purchasing, the bureau was soon renamed the *'Afdeling Nationale Coördinatie Politiële Infiltratie'* (ANCPI). Its role now lies in monitoring jurisprudence, developing new training methods and tactics, supplying props and accouterments ranging from watches and jewelry to automobiles, and coordinating operations throughout the country and beyond the national borders. The number of operations increases every year, with about 50 per cent of the capacity devoted to narcotics cases, 20 per cent to weapons and explosives cases and 10 per cent to the financial world. The total number of operations is not released (Karstens, interview; CRI, 1992, 68). A rough estimate would be about a hundred operations a year.

3.2. Civilians as Infiltrators

The problem of employing civilians for infiltration also seems to be a recurring phenomenon. The distinction between informant and infiltrator is confusing to begin with, even to police officers themselves (Brouwer, 1988, 33). It is almost unavoidable for a runner (informant's contact in the police) to influence the informant's behavior, e.g. by asking him or her to pay extra attention to certain individuals or events. The arguments to prefer police infiltrators are convincing: reliability, better accountability, safety, expertise in providing evidence, ability to organize, better options for phasing out, official secrecy (Van Kastel, 1989, 210–211; Marx, 1988). But still, several of the interviewees confirmed that assigning civilians with dangerous missions in criminal territory cannot always be avoided. National coordinator Karstens pointed to the fact that as infiltrations are increasingly targeted at more complex organizations, an education problem arises. In the future, civil servants with special knowledge such as tax specialists and economists may have to be brought in as infiltrators.

3.3. The Growing International Dimension of Infiltration

Throughout the 1980s, the newspapers write about almost a dozen incidents in which foreign UCAs appeared to be operating on Dutch soil without the permission of Dutch authorities. In early 1987, a researcher interviewed nine insiders on transborder undercover operations. In the anecdotes of frustrated police officers, attorneys and public prosecutors, over-eager German police officers receive the most criticism:

> The sense of values of the Dutch police is very different from the German police. And I put it very mildly. With them, the ends justify the means. I have very bad experiences with that, and that's the reason to keep back on certain cases. We feel then that it is really ethically insane to continue, for it's a clear case of provocation (interviewed senior police officer (Brouwer, 1988, 41).

This policeman then recounts an example of German police officers trying to set up a doubtful operation on Dutch soil, adding that such things happen 'a lot more often.'

Another incident occurred in 1988, when the regional CID in Breda, unauthorized by the public prosecutor's office, cooperated with a Canadian drugs liaison officer in an attempt to sell drugs (*NRC Handelsblad*, 21 July 1989). An inquiry of the *Rijksrecherche* (state detectives, i.e. centrally appointed detectives who investigate crimes by officials) led to a set of recommendations that seemed to have improved central control over undercover operations (Begeleidingscommissie CID, 1991, 10).

The present chief of the bureau for National Coordination of Police Infiltration at the CRI, commissioner René Karstens, affirms having had troubles in the past.

Not all the cases the Germans brought complied with our 'Tallon-criterion.' But I have to say about the German sense of values that they now also have a similar intention-clause. (...) If they want an operation, we want to have all their cards on the table. (...) They begin to perceive that it won't work any other way (Karstens, interview).

Talking about foreign operations in Holland, Karstens points out that sometimes a public prosecutor gives his permission, based on insufficient information. 'We follow up on that, asking: "do you really know what you have given permission for and that you hold formal responsibility for the operation?".' However, in recent years the level of knowledge among public prosecutors has risen considerably and mistakes have become rare indeed. Besides, an increasing number of 'CID-prosecutors' now work full-time on proactive investigations, and they operate under strict guidelines for international cases.

Mr. Karstens explains that in principle all international operations are first discussed with the national public prosecutor, who is very knowledgeable, and adds that the International Working Group on Police Undercover, the best-performing of all international working groups, is also of great help in this respect. Surprisingly, the U.S. does not participate in this International Working Group. Karstens:

> That was mainly because in the past, the philosophies on infiltration were rather divergent. Where we feel that certain limitations are needed on infiltration as a method, the Americans are inclined to let the end justify the means. With them anything goes.

In a later interview commissioner Karstens elaborates on this, explaining that the FBI's philosophy has a lot in common with the Dutch beliefs, but that reducing the mutual distrust in the relationship with the DEA requires a lot more work (Karstens, second interview). Currently about 5 per cent of the operations are run with the involvement of American counterparts, but that number is expected to increase.

3.4. The Shift from Evidence-gathering to Intelligence

Minister of Justice Ernst Hirsch Ballin first indicated a transformation of strategy when he told MPs on 25 April 1991 of a gradual change that was taking place in undercover policing. According to the minister, the short-term pseudo-buy operations of drugs and other merchandise found increasing problems because well-informed criminals became wary of any newcomer on the scene. Therefore, Hirsch Ballin called it absolutely necessary to adopt new and more risky infiltration techniques. He revealed that the six state police undercover teams together made 67 pseudo-buys in 1990 resulting in 25 arrests, but added that an increasing percentage of the undercover operations remained without pseudo-buys, their goal being primarily the collection of intelligence on the structure of criminal organizations.

The general vagueness surrounding the employment, goals and limits of the infiltration method is reflected in the professional literature and the sometimes contradictory statements of key functionaries. Although a rather extensive jurisprudence has grown over the last fifteen years, many observers and even practitioners still get confused over terminology. Chief inspector J.A.P. van Kastel when serving as National Coordinator gave the following commonly accepted definition of infiltration:

> the penetrating (by outsiders), possibly under an adopted identity, of the criminal milieu with the purpose of investigation and prosecution; outsiders being persons outside the criminal world (Van Kastel, 1989, 207).

The same author defined *'pseudokoop'* as:

> a form of infiltration, aimed at a purchase or an attempt at purchasing of goods, in order to enable prosecuting action against the seller(s) and others, who in relation to these goods have committed or will commit a punishable act. The prosecuting makes clear that the pseudo-purchase is not to be used for CID purposes (Van Kastel, 1989, 207).

Chief inspector Van Kastel often emphasized this latter point, adding that pseudo purchasing is to be considered an evidence-gathering instrument (Van Kastel, 1989, 208–209).

Mr. Van Kastel's successor as National Coordinator seems to hold different views on this. Working under the 1991 confidential guidelines that allow other forms of infiltration besides pseudo purchasing, commissioner Karstens feels that although pseudo purchasing is still being done, mainly to demonstrate trustworthiness, the primary goal of infiltration is now to acquire an 'information position' (Openbaar Ministerie, 1992, 44; CRI, 1992, 68; Karstens, interview).

Interviewees from the Public Prosecution Department seem to hold varying views on the model of operational investigations in the future. Advocate General H.J. den Os explains how the traditional investigating detective will only come into the picture after a maximum information position is acquired followed by an analysis. This can lead to a choice of operational subtargets and eventually should provide an opportunity to approach the target, i.e. the main goal of the operation. He adds:

> The traditional operational teams will be replaced increasingly by intelligence teams that try to gather the information. That's obvious, everybody feels that way (Den Os, interview).

Chief public prosecutor C.R.L.R.M. Ficq, who is chairman of the national counselling committee CID, comments:

> I see the option of infiltration in the end phase of an investigation, when it comes down to getting the evidence sought. Long-term infiltration, and infiltration as CID-method are not in my vocabulary. I consider it purely as an investigation method, not an information method. (...) The moment you

are unleashed on vague instructions in infiltration and you work more as a means of information gathering, you are in an entirely different and more insecure position. These views are held pretty widely in the Public Prosecution Department (Ficq, interview).

Commissioner Karstens's reaction:

> What is a 'means of investigation'? You try to develop investigative activities, with the dismantling of a criminal organization as the final goal. At the moment this is no longer being done through buying, or just a little, but through collecting information in a structural way. Working on a good position. In my view, that's still investigatory activities (Karstens, interview).

Mr. Karstens describes his views on the present period of new developments, and the memorandum he is writing for the top of the Public Prosecution Department on 'project-wise infiltrations.' He explains that infiltrations only take place with the public prosecutor's approval, but that they aren't necessarily part of a preliminary inquiry. Infiltration teams get involved in CID investigations, and his problem is that it is often very hard to get a tactical investigations team to follow up on such initiatives:

> There are two forms of infiltration that in the Netherlands are like a red rag to a bull. That's when you call it in-depth-infiltration and the carte blanche mandate. (...) the length is not decisive, we can be working on an operation for two years, and it's still not in-depth infiltration. We would consider three months, eight hours a day to be in-depth (Karstens, interview).

Because operations have become more complicated and take longer to unfold, the Coordinator coined the phrase 'project-wise infiltration.' Criminals become wary of newcomers, so it takes more time to work one's way into an organization. Karstens:

> We used to be introduced by informants, but I consider that less desirable, since you allow the informant to know the face of those people. We feel more for a direct approach, i.e. we hang around in the environment of the criminal target.

Mr. Karstens explains that the 'reverse sting' is still a most sensitive issue in Holland, but 'I sometimes speak of "reverse offers," i.e. that we for example offer facilities such as transport for a criminal organization.' In his view it is conceivable that in the future an operation would be organized in which drugs are being offered by police officers, but such ideas are still under discussion with the public prosecutors.

3.5. The Risks: Lacking Accountability under the Rule of Law

Most observers agree that uca operations should be accounted for in the courts. Independent judges can watch over proper procedures and guard against entrapment and overzealous crime fighters. The examining magistrate interviewed declared that he always insisted on being informed about an infiltration operation. He opts for a regulation in formal legislation, and feels that a judge should decide on the deployment of ucas (Pulles, interview).

In his juridical dissertation, P.M. Frielink also calls for a careful use of infiltration. He proposes restricting its use to those crimes punishable with at least 4 years in prison, and deems the risks of infiltrating crime syndicates too great for both the infiltrators and the integrity of the legal order (Frielink, 1990, 124–126, 171). Frielink feels that controlling infiltration through a judge is problematic because of the anonymity of the uca. The interviews left me with the impression that Frielink's views are not widely shared among practitioners.

Attorney-at-law Mrs. Van der Plas maintains that a ruling by the European Court, in which the Dutch practice of relying on anonymous witnesses for convictions was condemned, has no effect in practice. The uca has become all but invisible: often the dossier of a client just starts with there being CID-information which led to the arrests. 'The undercover remains under the table. They are fed up with all those lawyers who want to see an infiltrator, they now act completely differently' (European Court, 1989; Van der Plas, interview). In another ruling the Strasbourg Court recently decided that police infiltration does not violate Article 8 of the European Convention, but that the accused should be allowed to call up the infiltrator as a witness (European Court of Human Rights, 1992; Myjer, 1992, 812–813). The consequences for Dutch operations cannot yet be foreseen.

National Coordinator Karstens emphasizes that judicial control is real:

> If you take on an organization, then you'll have to put it on the table. I almost dare to say that close to 75 per cent of all our operations end up in court. Unless you have an operation that doesn't produce what you expected; in that case you phase it out and it never makes it to court. But every successful infiltration operation ultimately ends in court, for the goal always remains a criminal prosecution (Karstens, interview).

In a later interview commissioner Karstens added that possibly under new guidelines other than purely penal law approaches, such as applying fiscal or administrative measures, could be more effective under a diversified strategy.

3.6. The Risks: Police Corruption

Most of the interviewees agreed that infiltration can be a risky method, but noted that major scandals have thus far not been described in the scarce Dutch literature. Several insiders have warned of the risks of sudden exposure of an uca, of police corruption or 'going native,' but commissioner Karstens seems unperturbed:

> If we are talking about police corruption, then I say if there is one operation tightly under control, it surely is an infiltration operation. We take everything

down in reports, and the accompanying team is always present (Karstens, interview).

Attorney-at-law Jurjen Pen, who has defended many police officers against criminal charges, has strong views on police corruption:

> The scale on which it occurs can be indicated by two simple rules. (1) Police officers are not better or worse than other human beings; (2) the opportunity makes the thief. With that you can make your own calculations. If you confiscate things which the owner would be embarrassed to have found in his or her possession, e.g. controlled substances, they will not complain if you pinch them ... (Pen, interview).

He goes on to explain that finding some possessions that cause an excessive administrative burden unnerves every police officer who hates paperwork, and describes in detail the incredible fuss of processing 36 guilders found on a corpse.

> The hassle ... just put it in your pocket, no problem. The drunk you pick up, loaded with cash that you confiscate. He won't remember if it was 3600 or 1600 ... Creaming off, non-reporting, that's where police corruption begins. Structural police corruption, someone infiltrating, no doubt it will occur, but I don't think it has serious dimensions in Holland. But some officers taking the first step and getting the taste of it, and then taking the second and third step, yes, that you have. (...) In covert teams the damage is far more extensive, your information has greater value. Chatting for ten minutes is worth three, four hundred grand. Ergo it happens, inevitably. No system can totally eliminate it.

Mr. Pen claims his police clients frequently tell him that their superiors get away with things far worse than the mishaps they get nailed for:

> The question is, would the client benefit from wielding such information? Most often not. Occasionally someone is close to spilling the beans, but at the last moment almost all shy away from it. If you want to remain with the police, you don't do that (Pen, interview).

Pen's assertions are backed up by his clients. Amsterdam police detective Jan van Daalen published a controversial book in which he documented eleven cases of corruption among his colleagues, and the unwillingness of his superiors to do anything about it (Van Daalen, 1991). There have been a number of other corruption scandals in the Amsterdam force over the last decade, some of which have been dealt with in an unsatisfactory way, and some of Van Daalen's colleagues support his accusations (Karstens, 1991). Maurice Punch, in a thorough study on police corruption in the Amsterdam force in the late 1970s, came to the conclusion that:

> the most we can expect is a cycle of deviance, scandal, reform and repression, gradual relaxation and relapse into former patterns of deviance, followed by a new scandal (Punch, 1985, 200).

Punch observed few lasting changes in the organization: 'when the sound and fury die away, it is all too often a case of returning sooner, or later, to business as usual' (Punch, 1985, 200).

With some hesitation in his voice, commissioner Karstens asserts that no infiltrator has so far fallen. In that, he says, lies the importance of his coordinating Bureau.

> What you have to watch is that at some moment such teams will be inclined to adopt a wider interpretation of norms and values, believing that the ends will justify the means. That's where we come in, that's when you want people who are very straight, saying 'No further.' That's our monitoring function: if things come up, we say 'Hey guys, you're doing this, but we think it's not right' (Karstens, interview).

Shortly after this interview a scandal unfolded in the Amsterdam police force, in which the *Pseudokoop* department was compromised. Large amounts of money reportedly remained unaccounted for over the years, and at least one officer is under investigation for leaking information. Commanding officers allegedly were involved as well, and field operators complained about the lack of guidance and supervision they experienced as undercovers (*Het Parool*, 15 January 1993; *Volkskrant*, 16 January 1993). As a result, all infiltration operations by the Amsterdam teams were temporarily suspended. The Minister of Justice has pledged to initiate a thorough evaluation of the experiences with infiltration so far.

3.7. The Risks: Psychological Effects on the Undercover Agent

Little is publicly known about the occurrence of psychological problems among (former) ucas in Holland, and those in the know are less than forthcoming in discussing it. Commissioner Karstens thinks that the time limit is crucial:

> Infiltrators are only allowed to work for three years max, plus a year's training and a year for phasing out. And you have to protect these people from themselves: no matter how happy they feel under cover, you have to get them out after that period. We always say: a working infiltrator has no problems, but those who have stopped frequently do, or at least they acknowledge their relief to be released from the pressure. You shouldn't underestimate the consequences (Karstens, interview).

For accounts of psychological problems one has to resort to gossip or dated newspaper stories. Reportedly, in the late 1980s an Amsterdam uca had to stop prematurely because he couldn't handle the stress. A colleague developed serious drinking problems. It is said that a police officer from the pioneering years became an alcoholic and had to give up his job (Bommels, 1989, 19–20).

A journalist writing on the recent problems in the Amsterdam team, himself a former uca, mentions several incidents of ucas who developed acute paranoia, couldn't handle their sudden 'wealth,' became addicted and even stole about 200,000 dollars worth of cash after a drugs deal (Van den Heuvel, 1993). Commissioner Karstens' comment on such problems:

> We recently had a survey among the early agents. Some of them show a rise in alcohol consumption, but so far this hasn't led to any problems for the infiltrators insofar as corruption or going criminal is concerned. We have spotted almost no problems with ucas. Of course some get off, they have that freedom. We now agreed, since we did receive some signals, that we have to coach them longer, until three years after their exit. Coaching meaning that they have an interview once or twice a year. Naturally, those that need it can call on us later as well. We didn't have that at first, in fact it came down to an exit interview after four years, and then you'd lose sight of them. We now also have 'peer counseling,' former ucas helping each other.

Canadian psychologist professor Michel Girordo of Ottawa, who is a consultant to the RCMP, recently presented a study of the psychological profiling of undercover agents (*Intelligence Newsletter*, 17 December 1992, 2). In a ten-year study, Prof. Girordo has attempted to determine the psychological characteristics of ucas who give in to corruption or other criminal activities. Karstens knows him very well:

> We have very close ties with Canada, because we have adopted the Canadian model. Our selection and training program is adapted from theirs. We are presently doing a pilot project for a new selection course that they are developing. It is remarkable that the experiences of our Canadian colleagues are identical to our own.

When confronted by the interviewer with statements by Prof. Girordo that he had to help people whose attitudes had changed profoundly, Karstens claims that 'we didn't have that specifically.' He adds that he isn't sure about the time limits of the Canadians, but:

> I once asked in the U.K. 'do you guys ever have problems with ucas?' 'No, never.' That seemed pretty questionable to me, so asked over what time span they're allowed to function. 'No limits,' he said. Then I could comprehend the situation, for a working uca doesn't have problems.

3.8. Infiltration in the future

Several of the interviewees spontaneously expressed their belief that in the end even far-reaching means such as infiltration are inadequate to get at the big league criminals. This observation struck a chord with the undercover coordinator:

> I always say if you want to take on the really big boys, it means that other priorities will have to be made, also financially. I'm still pretty sceptical about that. It all takes time, and it's my job to indicate what the marginal conditions are. The possibilities are there, but we in Holland often stick to the merchant principle, we want a champagne taste on a beer budget. (...) If we want to be even more professional, then you'll have to spend a lot more money. Right now we're still often fixing things, a bit here, a little there. You have to be able to say 'Okay, we buy some property there, we're gonna set up a company structure,' for example. I put some things on paper, saying 'if that's not possible, then the limits are in sight' (Karstens, interview).

On the other hand, Karstens is quite optimistic: the Minister of Justice does a good job in international crime-fighting: he is willing to invest his energy there. Karstens believes that more decision makers now realize that fighting serious crime costs serious money. He recently proposed to his superiors the creation of a central budget with millions of guilders for undercover operations:

> A central budget would have to be created under the responsibility of the Ministry of Justice. Such special operations cannot be foreseen in a regular police budget, some flexibility is needed.
> Criminals do not respect any borders. But at the same time you have to be aware that we are prepared to handle a specific discussion, whereas the field thinks 'Jesus, is all that possible? That's no longer what we once agreed in the *"pseudokoop"* report.' The teams and us, we try to stretch our limits, try to develop ourselves. You check out the others: 'Hey, guys, how do you do an operation?' Like the Green Ice operation that the Americans did. We are on the eve of developing similar activities. But if you want to do it really, really perfect, a perfect cover, that's an immense investment (Karstens, interview).

Asked for the most important development in the field, commissioner Karstens mentions without hesitation the increasing internationalization: 'Some 60 per cent of our operations now have an international dimension.' He continues:

> One of our present problems is that we have very nice undercover operations, also internationally, but getting a tactical criminal investigations team assigned to it is sheer despair. We have operations with the British, with Dutch suspects. In England the whole gang is rolled up, but since we can't get an investigations team to work on it, the Dutch side walks. Subsequently he again makes contacts with other ucas in a second operation. That's sometimes frustrating, and I can imagine there's criticism internationally. (...) At some moment it simply gets frustrating to be operational. Especially in these international operations we have an increasing number of instances in which we operate with the prosecutor's permission, but no specific tactical team has been assigned yet. (...) We receive high praise from many other countries for our infiltration activities, and ever more requests for cooperation. If there's criticism, it's because there's no tactical follow-up.

4. SURVEILLANCE

Surveillance teams are another powerful means of information-gathering for the police, and again one which is increasingly employed as a source of intelligence for targeting decisions and to provide a background on which regular police teams get a flying start. This section briefly shows how the present, highly professional teams evolved until they were forced to rearrange their act after they themselves came under observation. We then go on to discuss how the information the surveillance teams provide is generally kept out of the court records and how formal legal arrangements have so far been avoided.

4.1. A Short History of Police Surveillance Teams

The history of police surveillance, meaning here the covert and systematic static and/or dynamic reconnaissance of persons or objects, started in the early 1950s when the Amsterdam municipal police organized its *'volgerij'* (followers), equipped with second-hand cars, and Rotterdam got its *'postploeg'* (stake-out squad). In the early 1970s, responding to an increase in more professional forms of crime such as narcotics, robberies and the hijacking of trucks and containers, as well as the emergence of political violence, several other cities and districts started their own surveillance team (*Observatieteam*, OT) (Blaauw, s.a., 877). Since 1972, team leaders met regularly in the *Landelijke Contactgroep Observatie* (National Contact Group on Surveillance), to discuss operations, procedures and equipment. Recently the CRI created the *Landelijk Informatiepunt Politiële Observatie* (LIPO) to improve coordination (CRI, 1992, 60).

At present some 20 OTs are operational in Holland, apart from the domestic security service BVD, of which the professional surveillance capacity is estimated at about 100 well-equipped officers. Also, some of the autonomous (inter)regional detective teams rely on their own surveillance capabilities. The OTs vary in size: most have two sections (a section is the smallest unit able to perform a professional surveillance, i.e. about 9–11 persons), but larger teams like the ones operating in the Amsterdam area would have 5–6 sections. Over the last years the operational capacity of police surveillance has increased considerably as a result of intensified reliance on technical surveillance equipment such as hidden videocameras connected to time-lapse recorders and remote alarm triggers. All the same, surveillance capacity remains scarce: during major cases such as the kidnappings of the 1980s, it was often impossible to get surveillance support for 'normal' cases for weeks on end. A regional detective team that targeted a major drugs gang for three years reported that the one section it was assigned was insufficient, but during this period no surveillance support at all was available for other investigations in the entire region around Eindhoven (Van den Brand et al., 1990, 44–45).

4.2. Police Surveillance Exposed and Reorganized under a New Doctrine

The police OTs managed to maintain a low profile until they were discovered on surveillance missions against political activists. This resulted in a burglary on 15 December 1985, in the offices of OT West II in Amsterdam. The outcomes of the nightly raids were published in a 260-page book (Anonymous, s.a., 1986). This unexpected investigation revealed several irregularities, such as the theft of mail from a radio station in Amsterdam. This illegal action was approved by the team's supervisor.

The activist countermeasures and the increasing professionalism among the more organized criminals led to the development of new techniques and tactics. Radio discipline became stricter and new radio sets that were more difficult to locate were acquired. More attention was paid to counter-surveillance by criminals, activists and police buffs (Blaauw, s.a., 893–896). Recently, a CRI spokesman claimed that organized criminals operated what appeared to be professional intelligence services against the police (Criminelen observeren politieteams, 1993).

Following the activist burglary, in the second half of the 1980s a new doctrine was introduced holding that the OT would no longer be primarily used as an instrument for regular investigations. Instead it became a proactive intelligence-gathering instrument. As with infiltration, there was some confusion over this among police officers and Justice Department officials. A senior official of the *Rechercheschool* (detective school) Zutphen concluded in 1989 that OTs were no longer employed as intelligence-gathering instruments (Van Keulen, 1989, 401–406). In a (then) confidential publication of the *rechercheschool*, however, two practitioners from the The Hague and Utrecht police forces expressed their preference for using the OT as an intelligence-gathering instrument rather than employing this precious tool for regular investigations (Van der Vegt, 1989, 44–45; Lith, 1989, 61–64).

4.3. Surveillance Reports Kept out of Court

In the early days, secrecy of identities and methods was maintained through the system of the '*opstapper*,' i.e. a police officer who is not part of the OT, but who participates in the surveillance operation in order to register certain observations in his report. Under the new doctrine the OT functions as the eyes of the CID, usually in the proactive phase of investigation. This means that as a rule, the reports are kept out of court. This was expressed clearly by several interviewees: 'In principle we want to screen such activities from the tactical investigation. With us the examining magistrate only comes into the picture the moment telephone taps have to be installed' Van Gestel said in referring to surveillance and similar proactive means (Van Gestel, interview 1). Attorney Prakken stressed that the only surveillance reports she now sees are from police officers watching a dope house. 'That's the occasional detective spending an afternoon on the look-out, not the real OTs. They only produce CID or PID (political intelligence) information, and you don't even find that registered as such' (Prakken, interview).

In several recent cases, surveillance team leaders have had to appear in court to testify on their activities. An incident in which a rather clumsy attempt was made to hide the use of a direction-finding transmitter in court was criticized by several of the interviewees ('When the President of the Court orders you to answer, you answer. We never commit perjury' (Van Gestel, interview 1; Kuitenbrouwer, 1988)). But in general, lawyers seldom get the chance to pry into such reconnoitring police activities, and the Hoge Raad deems the importance of protecting secrecy over surveillance tactics and methods generally higher than the interest of the suspect to use this information in his defense (Hoge Raad, 1992).

4.4. Does Police Surveillance Require a Formal Legal Arrangement?

In recent years scholars, lawyers and police officers have debated the need to formulate legal guidelines regulating police surveillance. Although the European Court has ruled that government activities that penetrate a citizen's privacy require a legal basis, the Hoge Raad (Dutch Supreme Court) has ruled that Article 28 of the Police Law (the general article which charges the police with preserving the legal order) suffices in this sense (European Convention Article 8 paragraph 2; European Court, *Klass* case 1978, *Malone* case 1984, *Leander* case 1987, *Kruslin and Huvig* case, 1990; European Commission, *Hewitt and Harman* case 1989; Hoge Raad, 1986: 1985). Opponents emphasize that the Police Law does not provide adequate guarantees against abuse, but most practitioners resist any legal initiatives, arguing that this would restrict the creativity vital to their operations (Fijnaut, 1991). Police officers interviewed claim that the present situation in which jurisprudence sets the limits is to be preferred (Van Gestel, interview 1; Karstens, interview). Police surveillance is presented as being nothing more than what the average citizen could do.

> For example, at the moment we are attacked for using video-cameras. But in the summer, half the Dutch population walks around filming, why then wouldn't the police be allowed to do just that? Everything that is for sale, that is not illegal, we should be allowed to use. The question remains whether you have to put it explicitly in the report. It is so damned difficult to take on serious organized crime, you just have to be very creative. (...) If we just have to acknowledge all those methods, we would all be writing parking tickets in two years. (...) The work of an OT comes down to nothing more than driving a car on a public road, be it with a specific purpose. In my view, that's not intruding on someone's privacy. You're not peeking into people's houses (Van Gestel, interview 1).

But from stolen surveillance logs published by activists, it is clear that police surveillance can also include observations in private homes (e.g. Anonymous, s.a., 1986, 11). Therefore, apart from the systematic nature that makes police surveillance altogether different in the first place, this harmless presentation hardly seems justified.

5. INFORMANTS

That police informants are vital for solving consensual crimes is almost a truism (Wilson, 1978, 34–35, 136).[7] Most CID investigations somehow start with a tip-off or a rumor. Besides, using informants is a cost-effective means of obtaining information (Mount, Jr, 1990, 13). A 1986 CRI study concluded that 'paying (informants) by the authorities is moving from the use in a limited number of grave criminal acts under adoption of the principles of subsidiarity and proportionality to a much wider usage, based on economic motivations' (Lang, W.T., 1986, *Het belonen bij de opsporing van strafbare feiten*, Den Haag, CRI, quoted in Roest, 1991, 277).

This section deals with the various motives that cause informants to cooperate with the police and with the risks involved in working with informants. It concludes with some second thoughts on the effectiveness of this method in the fight against organized crime.

5.1. Motivation of Informants

The scarce academic literature on informants suggests that the phenomenon has an important social function in subcultures. Swedish researcher Malin Åkerström cites 'the obsession-like quality in talking, speculating about and finding the informer' (Åkerström, 1991, 93 and 117). Searching for and identifying 'snitches' is believed to serve purposes of social integration: group norms are upheld, potential informers are daunted and a strong desire for revenge is fulfilled. 'Pursuing snitches is seen as a manifestation of the common bonds of the prisoners or of the prison community in itself' (Åkerström, 1991, 98 and 110). Yet Åkerström's research strongly suggests that most criminals snitch at one time or another (Åkerström, 1991, 123).

A range of motives brings people to sharing their secrets with the police. The Dutch police distinguishes between one-time informants, opportunity informants, professional informants, provocateurs, and civilian informants. As possible motives money, revenge, envy, love or hate, self-interest, removing competition, the personal relation with a police officer, idealism or principles, or a sense of guilt are mentioned (Van der Vegt, 1989, 50–54). American research seems to indicate that most narcotics agents believe an informant working off a beef to be the only productive one. The threat of going to jail is, in their eyes, a great inducement, whereas money seekers are unreliable 'because you have no real hold over them.' (Wilson, 1978, 66). A 1992 British Home Office study on

---

7. Not every person that furnishes information to the police is a criminal, hence the neutral term 'informant.' Noncriminal persons in legitimate occupations who provide information without any special inducement could be labeled 'confidential sources,' whereas persons with close contacts to criminals or other investigative targets and with a proven ability to supply information could be called 'informers.' The latter category provides the bulk of the useful leads for Dutch CIDs. For purposes of simplicity, and because the Dutch language only knows the word 'informant,' this catch-all term will be used here unless an 'informer' is specifically meant.

'resident informers' seems to confirm this assumption: it showed that nearly 70 per cent of police informers are recruited while in police custody or under investigation for a crime. According to the report, informers tend to be male, under 30, unemployed and with previous convictions (*Intelligence Newsletter*, 19 November 1992, 4).

In spite of these observations, Dutch law enforcement authorities are believed to rely primarily on paid informants. Informants can be paid tip-off money, varying from 500 to (in extreme cases such as PIRA and ETA bombings) 100,000 guilders per case (*Regeling tip-, toon- en voorkoopgelden*, 1985; one guilder is about half a U.S. dollar). According to information supplied to parliament, in an average year tip-off money is paid in about 200 cases (Handelingen, 1992, 11), but payments made to regular informants are probably not included here.

When MPs asked about the number of cases in which suspects or convicts were offered reduced sentences, the Justice Department said it couldn't produce the information (Handelingen, 1992, 11). The Public Prosecution Department's guideline on exceptional agreements with criminals states that such deals are only allowed as an ultimate remedy, in cases of life or death or grave threats to the safety of the state or public health. Any proposal for a deal should be presented for approval to the Procurator-General (Modelbrief, 1983). Several of the interviewees confirmed that such deals were indeed made, and one Advocate General added 'deals with criminals' to the author's list of covert policing methods (Myjer, interview). Even before the guideline was made, deals with convicted criminals were not uncommon, though not always successful. Maurice Punch cites a 1979 case in which criminals were temporarily released from jail to secure incriminating material against a police official suspected of corruption (Punch, 1985, 173–174). One of them promptly disappeared for three months and was later arrested again.

That the criterion of life or death is not always strictly applied is illustrated by another case, in which an arrested counterfeiter offered to lure two heroin dealers into a pseudo-purchase deal (*Parool*, 19 December 1989). He was offered tip-off money and was supplied with tens of thousands of guilders, with which he bought 8 kilos of heroin. Subsequently, he withdrew as a witness, so that the police had to release the dealers.

5.2. Risks Involved in Working with Informants

Writing about the inherent risks of using informants, James Q. Wilson quotes a familiar phrase among U.S. narcotics agents: 'You are always at the mercy of your informant' (Wilson, 1978, 78). He continues:

> By minimizing their disclosures, they minimize the risk to themselves, reduce the likelihood of harming a friend or close associate, and leave open the possibility of going back into business with their old connections once the heat is off. And informants have an interest in giving up not their own suppliers but rival dealers and other competitors.

Using an informant as an agent-in-place according to him is even more precarious:

> To leave an informant in place in a criminal organization over a long period of time is to deny oneself the opportunity to test the validity of his information or to lose control over him altogether (Wilson, 1978, 78).

The greatest risk exists for the police officers controlling the informants. Chief inspector Van der Vegt draws attention to the fact that there is a clear awareness among his colleagues of the risks involved in infiltration and pseudo-purchase operations:

> Strangely enough this awareness is apparently less present when regular CID work is discussed, such as 'investigating in the milieu' (Van der Vegt, 1989, 47–48).

CID detectives 'are absorbed' in the (semi-)criminal milieu, probing for information where it can be found, such as bars, martial arts schools, gambling houses, and brothels. In this process, with policemen operating partly undercover and partly as informal police contacts, social control of their moral behavior is all but impossible (Van der Vegt, 1989, 46–50).

American law enforcement has for decades been forced to face the problem of insuring that a proper relationship exists between informant and agent in order to prevent corruption. When the Bureau of Narcotics and Dangerous Drugs was being created in 1968 out of the old Federal Bureau of Narcotics, a large number of FBN agents were discovered to be engaged in illicit dealings with narcotics dealers (Wilson, 1978, 86–87). The FBI nowadays attempts to convince other U.S. police forces to establish strict procedures:

> Each department or agency should have mid-level managers directly overseeing informant operations. This is necessary because all too often, a close, symbiotic relationship develops between an informant and informant handler. This type of relationship leads to a corresponding loss of objectivity on the part of the informant handler. (...) To assist in maintaining objectivity, each department or agency should assign two investigators to each informant (Mount Jr., 1990, 16).

The Dutch police cadre seems well aware of such risks. Colleagues are advised never to meet informants on a one-to-one basis, in order to avoid being compromised (Roest, 1991, 275). The 'living conscience' of Dutch detectives, former chief commissioner Jan Blaauw, thinks that an incorrect contact with an informant begins when a social relationship develops (Blaauw, 1991, 45). RCID chief Van Gestel's runners always operate in pairs, and all contacts, activities and information are reported in writing, but he doesn't rule out the possibility that detectives in other squads are less careful or scrupulous (Van Gestel, interview 1).

No systematic evaluation of the effectiveness of using informants could be found, but hardly anyone seems to question their usefulness. Only the authors of a frank evaluation of an Eindhoven serious crime team have some reservations in this respect.

> In investigations in the realm of organized crime, the 'informants' phenomenon produces almost no results. The top people discuss their activities preferably with as few people as possible. Often only a single individual is in possession of certain information. Should the police act on that information, the source could immediately be traced. (...) The few informants that a number of police forces managed to recruit and coach with considerable pains, had to be phased out before they could have made a substantial contribution (Van den Brand *et al.*, 1990, 76).

6. SECRECY AND THE FEAR OF CORRUPTION

According to some of the interviewed police officers, there is a tendency for specialized personnel to circulate between surveillance teams, infiltration units, the CID, VIP protection, and similar (quasi-)covert teams throughout their career (Van Gestel, interview 1; Karstens, interview; Kruizinga, interview). Apparently this is not perceived as a potential problem. One could speculate about the gradual development of a closed circuit situation in which elitist and separatist attitudes could flourish, but no clear indications for such a phenomenon can be derived from the available material.

In this section the increasing need for secrecy and confidentiality is discussed together with the effects this has on the relatively open atmosphere within the police. The emergence of totally separate 'embargo teams' is noted, and in conclusion the fear of police corruption once again appears to play a central role.

6.1. Attitudes among the Police toward Secrecy

Compared to many other European countries, the Dutch police appear to be relatively open and straightforward toward outside scrutiny. Most of the interviewees expressed a down-to-earth approach to secrecy and security. Commissioner Karstens on his infiltration units:

> We have no problem at all with appearing in court: in other countries there's much more fuss over that. We even teach it in our courses: 'guys, it's perfectly normal that we testify in court.' In principle, we have nothing to hide. We provide no information on operations, but for the rest it's just my policy. We used to be a very confidential department, even within the CRI. The director almost had to give an official order to provide information. I wanted to get rid of that: I'm not saying that we should sell out completely, but in the end your department gets so secretive that nobody would notice if you would close it down (Karstens, interview).

While the more sensitive branches are undeniably insulated from excessive outside intrusions (as the previous sections have illustrated) there is at the same time a trusting openness toward colleagues inside the force. In the current battle against organized crime, however, special autonomous task forces have popped up by the dozen. Some of the interviewees spontaneously expressed their irritation over this trend:

> I'm extremely annoyed about those 'embargo teams.' In nine out of ten cases I know what they are working on. But it is really frustrating: I notice it abroad, if foreign colleagues call, 'they don't have any info, how can that be true?' I fully agree with the importance of a prudent protection of information. Only nowadays it seems like any self-respecting force must have an embargo team. It goes to such extremes that here they almost don't want to have it any more. I'm not too concerned about that. If somebody says: 'We sort of need one of your guys,' I say 'What for?' 'Well, for embargo.' Then I say 'Well, then you won't get anybody' (Karstens, interview).

RCID chief Van Gestel points to an inherent risk of excessive secrecy:

> Nowadays the Dutch police is very strong in surrounding teams with great secrecy. Embargo teams, that's the new fashion. A bit of a farce, it always makes me laugh if they start another embargo team. That's a team that operates completely separated from the normal police organization and also keeps the objectives of the investigation secret to prevent leaks. But this means that you can have two embargo teams working on the same subjects. Because they also keep it hidden from the CRI, and that's a bad development. We are still focused too much on our own empire (Van Gestel, interview 1).

An unusually frank evaluation report produced by a regional serious crime team in Eindhoven on their operations against a narcotics organization from 1986 to 1989 provides insight in both the negative effects and the necessity of a need-to-know attitude (Van den Brand *et al.*, 1990). The authors describe how securing strict confidentiality from colleagues outside the team caused many frictions, both with team members and other colleagues. It took a full year before acceptance gradually increased. The secrecy proved not to be in vain: in its external contacts, the Eindhoven team was confronted with a corrupt police officer and an unreliable tax inspector (Van den Brand *et al.*, 1990, 72–73).

6.2. A Justified Fear of Corruption?

Fear of corruption in the ranks of the police is the understandable reason for the new secrecy awareness. Several interviewees mentioned cases of corruption in police forces throughout the country that were kept out of the media. The *Rijksrecherche* (state detectives) receives ever more information on criminal activities of police officers. A part of this is CID information (Begeleidingscommissie CID, 1992, 19). Van Gestel touches upon this sensitive subject:

> We frequently receive information on the corrupt behavior of colleagues. Often these are tall stories, that is, we can't get them confirmed. In the time that I have been with CID it happened only once that we managed to get rid

of a colleague on the basis of reprehensible behavior, contacts with the wrong people, about which we had the impression that he passed on more information. But of course that shouldn't serve as evidence for it occurring or not. We are confronted with information leaks. That criminals are well-informed about the police's interests and intentions: I think it has more to do with a certain lack of discretion, with not handling information in a professional manner. I see it in my own department: if I'm for instance reading an analysis report and a question comes up, I go next door to ask my colleague about it. I come back and the cleaning-woman is standing there. A very nice woman indeed, but who knows, she might go to a party and be indiscrete with no bad intentions whatsoever. Or colleagues frequenting the inner city, having a good time, may spot this person and tell their friends a little too much. That's not corruption, that's just lack of police professionalism.

While there is some criticism on embargo teams among police officers, in circles of journalists stories about corruption in certain interregional teams abound. The author has heard some first-hand accounts from reputable journalists about intimidation and even maltreatment of those who tried to follow up on rumors of irregularities. In some cases, this has resulted in reporters dropping the case out of fear. In well-informed circles in the Public Prosecution Department, two different stories spread in the winter of 1992 of members of special teams having connections with Yugoslav killers and traffickers of women. The reliability of such stories could not be established, and they certainly shouldn't be taken at face value. But the fact that such rumors occur is most unusual in Holland, and at least it gives some indication of the exceptional position of the covert teams.

The vital importance of confidentiality in sensitive investigations is undisputed, but the risks that fully sealed-off units run of developing excessive zeal or corruptive practices should be fully recognized. There appears to be an interesting parallel here with the Dutch security service, which also experienced severe problems with semi-autonomous units whose operations continued unhindered by internal oversight or outside scrutiny long after the need for them had passed. Excessive compartmentalization invariably causes such problems, and the security service finally had to introduce a 'quality manager' function with full access to all branches and an improved reporting system to halt 'autonomous' operations. Police managers would be well-advised to learn a lesson here and attempt to maintain some degree of central control. After all, corruption is not a contagious disease spread by the inhabitants of some netherworld: it may breed among people working in isolation while exposed to an extremely seductive environment.

7. CONCLUSIONS

The fight against serious and organized crime heads the Public Prosecution Department's priority list for 1993 (Openbaar Ministerie, 1992, 33). Official statistics seem to warrant this: a 1991 analytical survey among all CID's produced a total of 599 criminal groups connected to serious or organized crime, of which some ten per cent were classified as 'highly organized' (CRI, 1992, 16–18). This figure indeed seems alarmingly high for a small country like the Netherlands. Organized crime and the wholesale narcotics trade provide the drive for the increased use of covert and intrusive police methods.

But while serious crime is undoubtedly a worrying development requiring resolute and well thought-out countermeasures, the above-mentioned survey on criminal groups has been challenged. Researchers from the Dutch Justice Department's own study center, such as Dr. Petrus van Duyne, have criticized its poor reliability and the ad-lib way in which it was assembled (VPRO radio, *Argos*, 8 January 1993). New initiatives are now under preparation for improved research which will enable a better-informed public debate with less political bias and improved judicial and policing measures.

The material presented in this article seems to indicate that in Holland a 'secret police' exists apart from the security service, although not in the traditional sense of a 'political police.'[8] The term 'covert police' would therefore be more appropriate (*cf.* Bayley, 1985, 194: 'not all secret police operatives intrude into politics.' Bayley mentions the 'strike forces' against organized crimes in the U.S. as an example).

A considerable part of policing activities directed at serious crime and similar misbehavior takes place before a formal preliminary inquiry is opened. This is generally referred to as 'proactive policing,' and all interviewed parties believed that this category will gain even more terrain in the coming years. During a preliminary inquiry, covert investigative methods are increasingly adopted.

Most interviewees as well as the current Dutch police literature show an implicit awareness that covert policing occurs under a cover of goodwill and trust on the part of the judiciary, politicians and the general public, combined with sheer ignorance about the scale and the intensity of present-day undercover work. Most knowledgeable observers realize that a few incidents over a short time span or a mid-range scandal related to undercover police operations could seriously jeopardize this atmosphere of tolerance toward covert policing. A prophecy can thus be made: if these most intrusive and precarious methods are not handled in a very prudent manner, and if the Dutch police fail to keep the spectre of corruption from the special teams and closed departments, then scandals and a subsequent reform process will be inevitable in the coming years. Also the near-total absence of any public accountability over the credit balance of covert policing, i.e. over the revenues of special teams and methods and their effects on serious crime, could lead to incidentally leaked or 'discovered' information on administrative mismanagement or other shortcomings. This would create a crisis and lessening of the public's trust. Setting up a sound system of oversight that covers all covert and proactive branches, teams and activities while bringing in independent expertise to evaluate performance and watch over corrupting influences seems imperative.

---

8. Some of the interviewees appeared to prefer the English term 'covert policing' over the Dutch translation *'heimelijke politie.' 'Heimelijk'* has the negative connotation of 'stealth, sneaky.' *'Geheime politie'* (secret police) would be unacceptable altogether, as it implies a condemnation, a reference to 'Gestapo.'

COVERT POLICING IN THE NETHERLANDS

The interviews indicate that formal accountability procedures such as parliamentary oversight and judicial control are only functioning to a limited degree with regard to covert policing. Insofar as proactive methods and operations can be kept out of the police reports and are not discussed in the courts, only those directly involved (i.e. the police officers and the public prosecutor) are aware of their precise nature. The police officers interviewed stressed the importance of professional attitudes and integrity in avoiding overzealous or even illegal conduct. The relevance of such internal control mechanisms are well-known from the literature on intelligence organizations, where operators often function in an environment with even less formal controls and sanctions (*cf.* former CIA operator Miles Copeland's discussion of the informal 'system of fuses' that avoids unauthorized operations in a secretive environment, and the solutions that subordinates employ to sabotage assignments that they consider immoral, such as 'losing the papers' (Copeland, 1975, 301–307)). Even in such environments, however, more reliable and formalized controlling procedures are aimed for, and especially in the police, entrusted as they are with considerable powers, no units should be excluded from formal and dependable accountability. Even the undoubted integrity of nearly all Dutch police officers cannot prevent a unit operating in virtual isolation from always avoiding illegal means to frame a suspect, nor can it guarantee that some less scrupulous members of the fraternity will not join forces to participate in certain practices they are supposed to confront.

REFERENCES

Åkerström, M. (1991), *Betrayal and Betrayers; The Sociology of Treachery*, New Brunswick, NJ, Transaction Publishers.
Algemene Rekenkamer (1991), 'Criminaliteitsbestrijding,' report by the Algemene Rekenkamer (General Accounting Office) of 15 October 1991, Handelingen Tweede Kamer 1991–1992, Bijlagen 22 355 nr. 2.
Almelo, A.E., Wiewel, P.G., eds. (1991), *Politiezorg in de jaren '90*, Arnhem-Antwerpen, Gouda Quint/Kluwer.
Anonymous, s.a. (1986), *Speuren bij de bespieders; politie-observatie in Nederland*, Amsterdam.
Baarle, B. van (1993), 'Rijden we wel in dezelfde richting? Bestrijding van de georganiseerde criminaliteit,' *Algemeen Politieblad*, 6 February, 4–6.
Bayley, D.H. (1983), 'Knowledge of the Police,' in: Punch, M., ed., *Control in the Police Organization*, Cambridge, MA, The MIT Press, 18–35.
Bayley, D.H. (1985), *Patterns of Policing*, New Brunswick, NJ, Rutgers University Press.
Begeleidingscommissie CID (1991), *Jaarverslag 1990*, Den Haag.
Begeleidingscommissie CID (1992), *Jaarverslag 1991*, Den Haag.
Blaauw, J.A., 'Observatie,' in: Stapel en De Koning, eds., *Leerboek voor de politie*, Lochem, Van den Brink (loose-leaf).
Blaauw, J.A. (1991), 'Een corrupte diender is de pest voor het hele korps,' *Justitiële Verkenningen*, 17, 4, 33–52.

137

Bommels, B. (1989), 'Op pad met een koffer vol bankbiljetten,' *Elsevier*, 17 June, 16–20.
Brand, W. van den et al. (1990), *De beproeving; evaluatie van een onderzoek naar een criminele organisatie*, Eindhoven, Regionaal Samenwerkende Recherche Regio Noord Brabant Oost.
Broeders, P.A.J. (1989), 'CID in Nederland,' in: de Kerf, E.L.A.M. et al., eds., *Inkijk in: criminele inlichtingendiensten, misdaadanalyse en pseudokoop*, Zutphen, Rechercheschool, 15–21.
Brouwer, H.A. (1988), *Grenzeloos vertrouwen in de infiltratie*, Amsterdam (manuscript).
CID-regeling (1986), 'CID-regeling van 29 mei 1986,' *Staatscourant* 141.
Copeland, M. (1975), *Beyond Cloak and Dagger; Inside the CIA*, New York, Pinnacle Books.
CRI (1992), *Jaarverslag 1991*, Den Haag, Centrale Recherche Informatiedienst.
Criminelen observeren politieteams (1993), 'Criminelen observeren politieteams,' *Gelderlander*, 9 March.
Daalen, J. van (1991), *Sans Rancune*, Amsterdam, De Boekerij.
Das, D.K. (1991), 'Comparative Police Studies; An Assessment,' *Police Studies*, 14, 22–35.
Doorenbos, D.R., Verweij, R.J., eds. (1991), *Hercodificatie Wetboek van Strafvordering; tijd voor een integrale herziening?*, Nijmegen, Ars Aequi Libri.
Fijnaut, C. (1991), 'Observatie en infiltratie: toe aan een wettelijke regeling,' in: Doorenbos, D.R., Verweij, R.J., eds., *Hercodificatie Wetboek van Strafvordering; tijd voor een integrale herziening?* Nijmegen, Ars Aequi Libri, 69–85.
Frielink, P.M. (1990), *Infiltratie in het strafrecht; een onderzoek naar de materieelrechtelijke en formeelrechtelijke aspecten van het opsporen van strafbare feiten door middel van infiltratie*, Arnhem-Antwerpen, Gouda Quint/Kluwer.
Handelingen (1985), *Infiltratie als opsporingstechniek*, Handelingen Tweede Kamer 1985–1986, Bijlagen 19 328 nr. 1.
Handelingen (1992), *Begroting Justitie*, Handelingen Tweede Kamer 1992–1993, Bijlagen 22 800 hoofdstuk VI, nr. 9.
Heuvel, J. van den (1993), 'Infiltrant één stap van crimineel,' *Telegraaf*, 23 January, T5.
Jansen, W., Jägers, H.P.M. (1992), 'Integratie van organisatiekunde en informatiekunde; naar een nieuw paradigma,' *Informatie en Informatiebeleid*, 10, 3, 44–53.
Karskens, A. (1992), 'Wie appelen vaart, wie appelen eet,' *Nieuwe Revu*, 1 December, 14–18.
Kastel, J.A.P. van (1989), 'Pseudokoop,' in: de Kerf, E.L.A.M. et al., eds., *Inkijk in: criminele inlichtingendiensten, misdaadanalyse en pseudokoop*, Zutphen, Rechercheschool, 205–218.
Kerf, E.L.A.M. de et al., eds. (1989), *Inkijk in: criminele inlichtingendiensten, misdaadanalyse en pseudokoop*, Zutphen, Rechercheschool.
Keulen, S. van (1989), 'Wettelijke bevoegdheid geboden bij observatie,' *Algemeen Politieblad*, 19 August, 401–406.

Klerks, P. (1989), *Terreurbestrijding in Nederland*, Amsterdam, Ravijn.
Kuitenbrouwer, F. (1988), 'Advocaat bestrijdt geniepige politiecontrole van burgers,' *NRC Handelsblad*, 4 March.
Lang, W.T. (1986), *Het belonen bij de opsporing van strafbare feiten*, Den Haag, CRI.
Lith, A. (1989), 'Observatie,' in: de Kerf, E.L.A.M. *et al.*, eds., *Inkijk in: criminele inlichtingendiensten, misdaadanalyse en pseudokoop*, Zutphen, Recherscheschool, 61–64.
Marx, G.T. (1988), *Undercover; Police Surveillance in America*, Berkeley, University of California Press.
Marx, G.T. (1992), 'Commentary,' in: Block, A., ed., *Crime, Law and Social Change*, 18, 1–2, Special Issue: *Issues and Theories on Covert Policing*, 3–34.
Modelbrief (1983), *Modelbrief van de procureurs-generaal aan de hoofdofficieren van justitie*, 1 July.
Mount, H.A. Jr (1990), 'Criminal Informants; An Administrator's Dream or Nightmare,' FBI *Law Enforcement Bulletin*, December 1990, 24–27.
Myjer, B.E.P. (1992), 'Kwaliteitscontrole op de pseudokoper,' *NJCM-Bulletin*, 17, 7, 810–814.
Openbaar Ministerie (1992), *Jaarverslag 1991*, Amsterdam.
Posner, G.L. (1990), *Warlords of Crime; Chinese Secret Societies; The New Mafia*, New York, Penguin.
Punch, M., ed. (1983), *Control in the Police Organization*, Cambridge, MA, The MIT Press.
Punch, M. (1985), *Conduct Unbecoming; The Social Construction of Police Deviance and Control*, London-New York, Tavistock Publications.
Regeling tip-, toon- en voorkoopgelden (1985), settled by the Procurator-General's meeting on 28 August 1985.
Roest, F. (1991), 'Het belonen van informanten (I),' *Tijdschrift voor de Politie*, 1991, 275–279.
Stapel en de Koning, eds., *Leerboek voor de politie*, Lochem, Van den Brink (loose-leaf).
Veen, Th.W. van (1984), Annotation to Hoge Raad 3 January 1984, NJ 1984, 440.
Vegt, M.G. van der (1989), 'Recherche in het milieu; informanten,' in: de Kerf, E.L.A.M. *et al.*, eds., *Inkijk in: criminele inlichtingendiensten, misdaadanalyse en pseudokoop*, Zutphen, Recherscheschool, 43–59.
Wilson, J.Q. (1978), *The Investigators; Managing FBI and Narcotics Agents*, New York, Basic Books.

Interviews

- Mr. C.R.L.R.M. Ficq, chief public prosecutor, district court Den Bosch, 8 December 1992.
- Mr. G. van Gestel, chief inspector, head of regional CID Brabant-West, Breda, 26 November 1992 (interview 1) and 17 December 1992 (interview 2).

- Mr. R. Karstens, Rijkspolitie-commissioner, chief of the bureau for National Coordination of Police Infiltration (ANCPI) at the national Criminal Intelligence Service (CRI) in The Hague, 21 December 1992; second interview 12 February 1993.
- Mr. H. Kruizinga, secretary of the Algemene Christelijke Politiebond (ACP, General Christian Police Union), 24 November 1992.
- Mr. B.E.P. Myjer, advocate general of the court of appeal The Hague, 24 November 1992.
- Mr. H.J. den Os, advocate general of the court of appeal The Hague, 11 December 1992.
- Mr. J. Pen, attorney-at-law, Amsterdam, 24 December 1992.
- Mrs. A. van der Plas, attorney-at-law, Amsterdam, 11 January 1993.
- Mrs. T. Prakken, attorney-at-law, Amsterdam, 15 December 1992.
- Mr. P.W.E.C. Pulles, investigating magistrate, district court Arnhem, 17 December 1992.

Cases Cited

- Hoge Raad, 4 December 1979, *Nederlandse Jurisprudentie* (NJ) 1980, 356 (*'Tallon*-arrest').
- Hoge Raad, 14 October 1986, NJ 1987, 564.
- Hoge Raad, 27 October 1992 (not published).
- European Commission of Human Rights (1989), Report of the Commission, Application No. 12175/86, *Patricia Hope Hewitt and Harriet Harman* against *the United Kingdom*, Strasbourg, Council of Europe.
- European Court of Human Rights (1979), Case of *Klass and Others*, judgment of 6 September 1978, series A, vol. 28, Köln, Carl Heymanns Verlag.
- European Court of Human Rights (1984), *Malone* Case, judgment of 2 August 1984, series A, vol. 82, Köln, Carl Heymanns Verlag.
- European Court of Human Rights (1987), *Leander* Case, judgment of 26 March 1987, series A, vol. 116, Köln, Carl Heymanns Verlag.
- European Court of Human Rights (1989), *Kostovski* Case, judgment of 20 November 1989, NJ 1990, nr. 245.
- European Court of Human Rights (1990), *Kruslin* Case and *Huvig* Case, judgment of 24 April 1990, series A, vol. 176, Köln, Carl Heymanns Verlag.
- European Court of Human Rights (1992), *Lüdi* Case, judgment of 15 June 1992, series A, vol. 238, Köln, Carl Heymanns Verlag.

Lode Van Outrive*
and Jan Cappelle**

Twenty Years of Undercover Policing in Belgium: The Regulation of a Risky Police Practice

1. THE EARLY HISTORY

Undercover work in police law enforcement is older than the Belgian state itself. Legendary for the methods of covert policing in the early history of the modern European police, is the French police chief François Eugene Vidocq.[1] He brought new energy and resources to undercover work. In 1812, this former criminal became the head of the secret police division which set out to combat organized crime in Paris. Against the will of the uniformed French police, Vidocq was assigned by Napoléon to organize the *Sûreté* (the civil intelligence). Gradually Vidocq applied his methods to matters of political intelligence. His methods 180 years ago are not unlike modern undercover tactics. The latter have often been discussed in our country since the 1970s. If we focus attention on the problem of undercover in Belgium today, the similarities between the present rhetoric on policy and the nineteenth century are striking.

Already in 1812 it was argued that stronger police methods were necessary due to the increase in crime which could no longer be controlled with ordinary means of investigation.[2] Even then voices were heard from within the traditional

---

* Professor of Criminology, Faculty of Law, Department of Criminal Law and Criminology, KU Leuven, Belgium.
** Staff member, Police Department, Ministry of Internal Affairs, Brussels, Belgium.
1. On Vidocq, see J. Savant (1950), *La vie fabuleuse et authentique de Vidocq*, Paris, Seuil; P. Stead (1953), *Vidocq: A Biography*, London, Staples Press; S. Edwards (1977), *The Vidocq Dossier: The Story of the World's First Detective*, Boston, Houghton Mifflin Company.
2. Vidocq argues as follows on the situation in the French capital in 1809: '... one murder of passion or greed was committed in the city every twenty-four hours. Robberies were commonplace, and men of standing and wealth went out unaccompanied by armed guards. Even citizens of the growing middle class hired custodians to keep watch over their houses, but the number of burglaries committed each day continued to grow ... There were more than 5,000 pickpockets in Paris in 1809 ... The time was overripe for someone wielding a stiff broom with a good aim to clean out the Augean stables ...' (S. Edwards, *op. cit.*, 32).

police force to warn against police provocations that went too far.[3] Finally, like today, police provocation was justified by reference to the criminal intent that was believed to be always present with delinquents.[4] The methods used by Vidocq in France, and which were also employed in England since the 18th century, were later introduced in the United States, for instance by the well-known American private detective Allan Pinkerton.[5] In the 19th century there was no federal police in the United States. The means of covert policing, imported from Europe, were further developed by the Pinkerton Agency, both for private and government assignments. The Agency's way of working would at the turn of the century become a model for criminal and political intelligence in the United States.[6] The irony of history therefore shows that the undercover police methods, which were exported in the seventies from the United States to Belgium and other European countries, had originally been developed in Europe.

That the way in which covert policing had meanwhile developed in the United States was not followed in Europe, is closely related to specific historical circumstances. After the decline of Napoleon's regime, from 1815 to 1830, Belgium was occupied by Holland. In 1830 Belgian revolutionary forces demanded the dismantlement of the Napoleonic police force. Not all their demands were met: the police force of the new Belgian state clearly bore the mark of the French occupation. This was not so much the case for the methods of the regular police sections. Vidocq developed his 'new' methods when Belgium was occupied by the Dutch, and they were not inherited by the new Belgian police forces assigned to criminal investigations. However, this was the case with the new Belgian state security, which was inspired by the so-called 'haute police' of Fouché. The specific option in the Belgian constitutional law of 1830 caused a cleavage between the state civil intelligence and the police services. The Belgian civil intelligence did not receive any judicial authority, so its members could not use any police means that result from such authority.

---

3. On the methods that Vidocq would employ from 1812 onwards, Napoleon's former minister of police Joseph Fouché had five years earlier written a prophetic warning: '... This type of operation cannot be approved of ... The real police is out to fight crime and not to offer opportunities for it; the police deters crime and does not provoke it. These kinds of operation exposes the public force to dangers of which it will not always be able to recover' (note to the police of Rouan, 13 June 1807, quoted in L. Madelin (1947), *Fouché (1759–1820)*, Paris, Plon, I, 490).
4. By way of illustration, consider this quote from Vidocq: 'A man is honest or he isn't. If he is honest, not any one means, however forceful, can be employed to make him commit a crime. If he is dishonest, the only thing he may be lacking is the opportunity, and is it not obvious that it will be offered to him sooner or later? To be sure, I can never be convinced that it would cause any harm to throw a cloth at a viper on which it can squirt its poison,' from Vidocq's memoires, quoted in J. Savant (1956), *Le procès de Vidocq*, Paris, Michel de Romilly, 47.
5. See F. Morn (1982), *The Eye That Never Sleeps: A History of the Pinkerton National Detective Agency*, Bloomington, Indiana University Press.
6. See F. Donner (1980), *The Age of Surveillance: The Aims and Methods of America's Political Intelligence System*, New York, Vintage Books, 30ff.; G.T. Marx, 'Police: Undercover Tactics,' in: S.H. Kadish, ed., *Encyclopedia of Crime and Justice*, New York, The Free Press, 1155.

However, since its existence the service did adopt the French tradition of undercover tactics.

Three examples illustrate this. The first head of the civil intelligence, Isidore Plaisant, provoked the Belgian revolutionary popular hero Louis de Potter.[7] In 1830, De Potter was a member of the so-called Temporary Regime (the temporary government at the time), and he assigned Plaisant, who shared a house with De Potter in Brussels, the post of head of the *Sûreté Publique* (the Belgian civil intelligence). De Potter resigned on 13 November because he favored a republic while a majority of the Temporary Regime choose a monarchy.[8] From that time on, De Potter was given a hard time by Plaisant, who accused De Potter of organizing conspiracies in favor of a republic. Plaisant, hiding in a closet, then started eavesdropping on De Potter's conversations.[9] Moreover, so De Potter reports, Plaisant organized riots against his republican movement.[10] In the end, De Potter was forced to leave the country. After this act of police provocation had become known, Plaisant was the first head of the civil intelligence to be removed under such circumstances, but not the last one. The activities of the unregulated Belgian civil intelligence have by and large remained a closed book to the public. Yet every now and then a scandal of formidable size has appeared. These are usually closely related to the undercover tactics of the service. Best known in this regard is the so-called 'Great Conspiracy' of 1887.[11] The civil intelligence had then, in agreement with Prime Minister Beernaert, infiltrated the leadership of the left-wing section of the recently established Labor Party. Infiltrators from the service provoked a cleavage in the party, took over its leadership and organized dynamite bombings. When the case came into the daylight during a supreme jury court trial in Mons, the Minister of Justice saved his skin by firing the administrative director general Gauthier de Rasse. The last head of the civil service to resign was Albert Raes. This happened in 1990. In 1983 it was discovered that a commissioner of the civil intelligence had infiltrated a neo-nazi organization and that he had been heavily manipulated by its members.[12] The case is still not completely resolved, but it turned out that some members of this extreme right-wing group were involved in serious felonies: two murders in Brussels, as well as theft and stealing of secretly decoded NATO telex messages at the transmission center of the Belgian army. The case gained considerable attention both in the media and in the political environment. For seven years, the commis-

---

7. Isidore Plaisant (1796–1836) was administrative director-general of the *Sûreté Publique* from 1 October 1830 until 1 April 1831. See the biography on him: J. de le Court (1903), *Biographie nationale*, Bruxelles, Bruylant, 706–711.
8. See the biography on Louis de Potter by: T. Juste (1876), *Biographie nationale*, Bruxelles, Bruylant, 622–629.
9. L. de Potter (1839), *Souvenirs personnels*, Bruxelles, Meline, Cans et Companie, 232–233. De Potter called Plaisant an 'agent instigator' (*idem*, 233).
10. L. de Potter, *op. cit.*, 244–251.
11. See J. Dyck (1959), 'Een politiek proces: het groot complot, rede uitgesproken voor de Vlaamse Conferentie van de Balie van Antwerpen op 17 october 1959,' *Rechtskundig Weekblad*, 369–390.
12. See R. Haquin (1984), *Des taupes dans l'extrême-droite*, Berchem, Epo.

sioner was protected by his superiors, while his exact role in the group and the people obviously protecting the neo-nazi organization were never clarified. In the end, the administrative director general had to pay for it by resigning.

These three 'incidents' in the history of the Belgian civil intelligence illustrate clearly how, contrary to the regular police force, covert policing methods have for long been employed in our country in political intelligence work. Whenever this led to some scandal, the result would be somebody getting fired. Also, sometimes the service was transferred to another department; the Civil Intelligence, for instance, was often switched between the department of Justice and the Home Office. But the tactics themselves, leading to the scandals, have not been questioned.

Although police services assigned to judicial matters have in the past occasionally resorted to provocation methods, it was not until late this century that this was done in a more organized fashion.[13] Until now, resistance to undercover operations was strong, both in the police force and among the judicial authorities. The idea of 'undercover' to them bore the image of the *agents provocateurs*, who have in Europe, ever since the French revolution, been used to discredit political groups.[14]

2. THE AMERICAN WAR ON DRUGS DURING THE NIXON ADMINISTRATION

From 1969 onwards, things changed. U.S. president Nixon accelerated the moral crusade against drugs.[15] The fight against drugs became a top priority on the American foreign policy agenda. During the Ford and Carter administrations this declined, but was taken up again during the Reagan and Bush years. The new 1969 policy was first coordinated by the Bureau of Narcotics and Dangerous Drugs (BNDD). In the same year, U.S. embassies were instructed to give the highest priority to the drugs war. In 1973 that role was assigned to the Drug Enforcement Agency (DEA).

The DEA agents, stationed in the American embassies, were operational. They would supply and pay informants, organize undercover operations, and were actively involved in the administration of the drug cases of the local police services. DEA agents were often former BNDD agents or agents of the Federal Bureau of Narcotics (FBN). Both these organizations had received training in

---

13. Traces of this can be found in Belgian jurisdiction. *See* C. de Valkeneer, 'Les nouvelles stratégies policières: aux confins des criminalisations primaire et secondaire,' in: F. Digneffe, ed. (1990), *Acteur social et délinquance; une grille de lecture du système de justice pénale*, Liège-Bruxelles, Pierre Mardaga, 311–325.
14. The same image can be traced in the American literature on the issue; *see* P. Chevigny (1972), *Cops and Rebels; A Study of Provocation*, New York, Pantheon Books, 223–276.
15. For this section we mainly used the research by Nadelmann, *see* E. Nadelmann (1987), *Cops Across Borders: Transnational Crime and International Law Enforcement*, UMI; E. Nadelmann (1990), 'The Role of the United States in the International Enforcement of Criminal Law,' *Harvard International Law Journal*, 31, 1, 37–76, and E. Nadelmann, *The DEA in Europe*, 1990 (unpublished).

undercover work. The same holds for the American military police services, Criminal Investigations Divisions (CID) at the army bases in Western Europe.

DEA 'missionaries' in Europe were expected to encourage structural changes in the local police forces, actively lobby for more severe legislation, and promote American interests to the local authorities. The national legislation and criminal justice procedures in Western Europe often did not allow covert policing, electronic surveillance, or deep-cover informants – all tactics the Americans were convinced are effective in the combat against the international drug trade. The DEA was often faced with the indifference of several Western European governments. DEA representatives, therefore, insisted on legalizing the DEA tactics and requested an efficient drug enforcement personnel in the national police services.

3. THE 'AMERICANIZATION' OF BELGIAN INVESTIGATION PROCEDURES

Thus, the DEA approach gradually found its way into the European concept of 'modern' investigation procedures. Belgium was no exception. We next analyze this influence in the different aspects of investigation procedures in Belgium.

3.1. At the Level of Police Organization

The American influence resulted, first, in the setting up of new elite units within the Belgian police. From 1971 onwards, special anti-drug squads were established for the investigation sections of all districts within the Gendarmerie, the largest police force in the country. In the same year the Minister of Justice, A. Vranckx, established a national body, the Bureau of Criminal Information (BIC).[16] This Bureau was assigned to penetrate the criminal environment using outside agents, and offer the collected criminal information to the district attorney. This 'soft' information of the BIC was mainly transferred to the Belgian judicial police working with the district attorney or solicitor ('*le parquet*'). In competition with the BIC, the Belgian Gendarmerie established its own national bureau for criminal information in 1973, the National Drug Bureau (BND), which undertook very similar assignments.

In the same year the very first DEA agent joined the American embassy in Brussels. In most countries the DEA had to adjust its activities to a national coordination body, which told the DEA which police service it had to collaborate with. In Belgium, this was not the case: the DEA was given no restrictions with regard to its collaboration with the Gendarmerie or the judicial police. In international cases, the DEA preferred working with the Gendarmerie, because of its good contacts with other European police services. In Belgian files or

---

16. Established by Royal Decree of 2 June 1971. *See* J. Stryckmans (1971), 'L'arrêté royal du 2 juin 1971 créant une administration de l'information criminelle,' *Journal des Tribunaux*, 86, 4783, 709–712.

cases that were set up internally, the DEA collaborated with the judicial police which, the DEA judged, had better means available to recruit informants and which were thought to have more expertise on undercover tactics than the Gendarmerie.[17]

3.2. At the Level of Legislation

At the level of legislation, in 1975 the Belgian parliament changed the drug law of 1921. The new law provided more severe punishment of drug delinquents. Also, and for the first time in Belgian law, whistle blowing was conceived as a ground for exemption from prosecution.[18] In this way, it was made possible to adopt the American method of 'flipping' informants. Contrary to the United States, the Belgian drug law presupposes the agreement of the prosecuting attorney.

3.3. At the Level of Police Tactics

In 1970 the Belgian police was not acquainted with the methods of covert policing as they were promoted by the Americans. Some police officers, among them the later BND head, commander François, did have occasional meetings with the U.S. Army Criminal Investigation Division, which had already carried out some undercover operations in Europe.[19] To remedy this, five top officers of the two national Belgian police services took special training at the Advanced International Drug Enforcement School in Washington. Later, the DEA also gave special courses on the new police tactics to some ten policemen of lower ranking.

Not only did the Belgian police in 1970 lack sufficient knowledge of the American techniques, they also did not have the necessary means or specific equipment. Therefore, informants, recruited in Belgium, were 'passed on' to the DEA, because the DEA, contrary to the Belgian police, had sufficient financial means to pay them.[20] The DEA representatives in Brussels also supplied the judicial police and the Gendarmerie with the equipment necessary to execute undercover operations. Moreover, the American techniques were not compatible with the Belgian criminal justice procedures. Therefore, a 'two-track' policy was adopted. On the one hand, the DEA more or less adjusted its methods to Belgian standards; on the other hand, by creating precedents, its strategy aimed

---

17. E. Nadelmann, *Cops Across Borders*, 268.
18. Art. 6 of the Law of 24 February 1921, as changed by the Law of 9 July 1975. The article states that accused who, before they are prosecuted, hand over the identity of guilty offenders, or, when the offenders are unknown, who reveal the occurrence of felonies, may be exempt from correctional punishment.
19. Statement of Mr. Goffinon, in: *Verslag parlementair onderzoek naar de wijze waarop de bestrijding van het banditisme en het terrorisme georganiseerd wordt*, Kamer van Volksvertegenwoordigers, Parlementaire Documenten, 59/9–1988, 242.
20. E. Nadelmann, *Cops Across Borders*, 274.

at provoking favorable Belgian jurisprudence. Meanwhile, lobbying could be carried out towards a more general settlement of the matter. We will note that this involved problems.

With regard to the American tactic, we in Belgium first have the so-called 'pseudo-buy.' Fundamental in the American drug enforcement is the buy-and-bust tactic, which means that the undercover agent can for instance arrest someone from whom he has just before bought drugs. In the eyes of the Belgian legislators such a deal would cause the undercover agent to be guilty of a felony himself. Therefore, the buy-and-bust strategy, as it was developed in the United States, had to be adjusted into the European version of the pseudo-buy.[21] In this case the Belgian undercover agent, a sworn policeman or a civilian, only goes as far as to the moment just before the sale. He arranges to buy drugs from a dealer. Then he meets him to inspect the goods and he shows cash money (the 'flash') which is intended for the purchase. Then the undercover agent leaves and policemen, who were hiding nearby, arrive to arrest the dealer holding the goods.

In the police files drawn up for the official 'open' case of the prosecuting attorney, the court and the representing parties, the undercover agent never existed. The operation is portrayed as if some unknown accomplice (in reality the undercover agent or civilian) could escape from the event and not be found. Next to this, the prosecuting attorney, who is in charge of judicial police assignments, also asks for an accurate account. Therefore, next to the open file just mentioned, a 'half-open' file must also be drawn up only for the prosecuting attorney. Therein the case as it really happened is portrayed. Also, before the undercover operation is started, its intent and planning are presented to the prosecuting attorney for approval.

4. POLICE PROVOCATION AND ITS LEGALIZATION

These developments are not unique to Belgium. In other European countries similar events took place. Therefore, undercover tactics have remained a topic of controversy during the seventies and eighties in countries like Germany and the Netherlands. The general trend, however, is one of increasing use of these techniques. Little by little, the courts have approved the tactics in Belgium, therein guided by the police, which together with the prosecuting attorneys created precedents.[22] All in all, Belgian jurisprudence now rules that it is acceptable to provoke somebody to commit a felony as long as the police take into account certain conditions. This is the case when the offer was made to a third party who then notified the police. Usually this is so, when after an investigation it is discovered that the felony would occur anyway before any police action was taken, and when the police then just offer the opportunity to the

---

21. *Ibidem*, 284–285.
22. In 1983, the DEA set up an international operation in which a BKA-inspector in Karachi accompanied heroin until it reached Belgium. This case led to an important advisory judge-ruling. Cassatie, 27 February 1985, *Revue de Droit Pénal et de Criminologie*, 1985, 694.

offender to commit the crime. However, the police should be offered enough freedom of movement so that any criminal activity may be stopped during the operation. With this, then, the technique of the pseudo-buy has been legally approved. The police 'tricks' may be executed, both by the police as well as by civilians.[23]

Working with 'half-open' files for the prosecuting attorney and 'open' files for the courts has been kept alive, but not without problems. Sometimes the judge would order the arrest of the 'disappeared' buyer. But most of the time the 'buyer' used a pseudonym, so that he didn't have to worry. Sometimes the real name of the undercover infiltrator was used. In this case, the police was forced to alert the informer who could then get out of the country.[24] It is more problematic when the defense party brings evidence in court which suggests police provocation, or when it manages to identify the pseudo-buyer, as was the case during a trial in 1988.[25] Occasionally during trials fabricated police reports have entered the court minutes and police agents have given perjured statements to the court. Jurisprudence has responded to this by stating that, when the defense statements claiming police provocation are solidly grounded, the prosecuting attorney then has the obligation to prove that this is not the case.[26] In any case, such procedures seem far-off from the fair trial mentioned in Article 6 of the European Convention on Human Rights, and there does not seem to be any 'minimum right to examine the witness against him.' Therefore, in 1983 and not without reason, colleague Fijnaut has proposed to make the justifications for an undercover operation explicitly known to the courts. He writes: 'The scenario with the "accidently" escaped pseudo-buyer has to disappear from the stage as soon as possible.'[27]

To this end, a commissioner of the Brussels judicial police, after agreement with the district attorney, posed as a pseudo-buyer himself. The media then said that this was intended to 'force a fitting jurisprudence.' The man was, just like the accused, questioned and, for the first time, a report on his activities appeared in the 'open' file. This was done with the intention of meeting the

---

23. For a review of recent Belgian jurisprudence, *see* F. Hutsebaut (1991), 'Het onrechtmatig verkregen bewijs en zijn gevolgen,' in: L. Dupont and B. Spriet, eds., *Strafrecht voor rechtspractici IV*, Leuven, Acco, 47–94.
24. An example in this is officer SXQ750001, an informer who worked in undercover operations in Holland for five years in the late seventies, both for the Dutch CRI and the American DEA. In 1982 he had to escape to our country because his name had appeared in a court case. He has remained in Belgium since then. *See Algemeen Dagblad*, 7 & 10 July 1990; *De Volkskrant*, 14 July 1990.
25. In the case of *A.G.* v. *O.M.* in Leuven, two Dutchmen were caught by the judicial police with 3 kilos of cocaine. In court on 28 March 1988, it turned out that the defense party had managed, having hired a private detective, to identify the 'disappeared' buyer, locate him and reconstruct his career as an undercover agent for the DEA, the BIC, the BND and the BKA (unpublished account).
26. Court of Appeal, Brussels 3 March 1987, *R.W.*, 1987–1988, 640 with a note by A. de Nauw, 'Definitie en bewijs van provocatie door overheidsagenten.'
27. C. Fijnaut, *De zaak-François: beschouwingen naar aanleiding van het vonnis*, Antwerpen, Kluwer, 1983, 146.

increasing critique of the method of open and half-open files.[28] Still, it was not until 1990 that undercover operations were executed with fully open files. The initiative for this came from the prosecuting attorney general of the city of Gent. He established a working group on police infiltration, consisting of representatives of the magistrate and the police services, in September 1988. Their goal was to draw up a coordinated policy on the issue. The working group drew up its final report on 31 May 1989, and handed it over to the Minister of Justice. The minister then arranged a series of policy directives in 1990 for applying covert police methods.[29]

5. THE NEW POLICY DIRECTIVES

In the directives of the Minister of Justice, the principles which had been worked out in the jurisprudence were adopted. Furthermore, covert policing techniques are bound to the principles of proportionality and subsidiarity. As to the former principle, covert means can only be employed to combat serious and organized crime. As to the latter principle, covert means can only be used to the extent that proof cannot be gathered by other, more traditional investigation methods. Every undercover operation should first have the consent of the prosecuting attorney's office, or, if the case is already part of some ongoing investigation, the consent of the judge.

The operations can in principle only be undertaken by specially trained Belgian police officers or foreign colleagues, under false identity. The use of private civilians in this type of work can only be allowed under exceptional circumstances. Long-term and deep-cover operations are out of the question; but techniques like the pseudo-buy, the test-buy, accompanied shipment, short-term infiltration and privacy-destructive observations are allowed.

The anonymity of informants is assured: reports or police minutes, which are handed over to the judicial authorities, can refer to their existence, but they cannot mention their name or any other clue leading to their identification. Jurisprudence assumes that a police officer may conceal the name of the informer from the courts, in the interest of the fight against crime or in view of the protection of the informant.[30] This possibility eliminates open and half-open files. The new directives, therefore, offer the possibility that the police in court will be forthcoming on the ways that information on the accused has been gathered. The only exception to this, as mentioned before, is the identification of the informer. In this way, the anonymity of the policeman-pseudo-buyer or

---

28. *La Dernière Heure*, 15 April 1990; *De Standaard*, 16 April 1986.
29. The directives are: 'Concerning the special investigation procedures to combat severe and organized crime,' 24 April 1990; 'Concerning the use of funding from the Minister of Justice for the benefit of the police services,' 6 April 1990; 'Concerning the appointment of a national magistrate – assignments and powers,' 25 April 1990 (all unpublished).
30. Cassatie, 26 February 1986, *Journal des Tribunaux*, 1986, 328.

informer is assured. The name, can, when requested, be given to the prosecuting attorney.[31]

6. COVERT POLICING AND THE FAILURE OF BELGIAN POLICE SERVICES

We have already discussed the most important consequences of the Americanization of investigation methods in Belgian police organization: the establishment of the BIC in 1971 and the NDB section of the Gendarmerie in 1973. After several scandals, which we cannot dwell on in detail here (the most important one is the *François* case), the National Drug Brigade and later the BIC were done away with.[32] Frank Eaton, a DEA representative, had to leave the country in late 1981, shortly before the trial on the *François* case was opened. He was one of the most important of those accused in the case, and he was to be tried in 1982 before the Brussels court. However, because of his diplomatic immunity, he managed to escape from the court ruling.

In the mid 1980s, the Gendarmerie undertook a modest attempt at establishing new covert policing units. This was done in 1986, when local investigation units (BOB) of the major Belgian cities – like Gent, Antwerp, Brussels and Liège –, the so-called 'criminal information sections' (CIS), were created. The members of these sections had to collect information in the criminal milieu, just like the members of the BIC. On the basis of their information reports, plans were drawn up which had to be converted by colleagues into judicial operations. Prosecuting attorneys, it later turned out, were often ignorant of the existence of the CIS information reports. In late 1989 these sections were abolished, after the activities of two sections had been disapproved by courts and prosecuting attorneys.

In March 1990, a scandal broke out involving the judicial police. This police had, contrary to the Gendarmerie and the BIC, remained relatively unspoken of for twenty years since 1970. This changed when in 1990, F. Reyniers, the commissioner of the judicial police section of Brussels, was suspended by the Minister of Justice. There was evidence to suggest that he was involved in unacceptable conflict of interests with regard to his informants. Strikingly, informants had been used by the commissioner for years in undercover operations. At this moment his case is being tried by the Brussels court of appeal.

A glance at twenty years of experimenting with covert policing methods by the Belgian police services clearly shows many problems. Some of the reasons are evident, others aren't. We will not go into this in detail, but some hypotheses can be selected for testing in light of the new Belgian judicial policy.

---

31. This obligation caused some trouble in September 1990 in the investigation unit of the Brussels Gendarmerie. Some of its members refused to hand over the names of their informants to the prosecuting attorney. Some investigations have been stopped or not even started, because the district attorney, lacking the informants' names, refused to protect the operations. See *De Standaard*, 13–14 October 1990.
32. On the rise and fall of these services, *see* C. Fijnaut, *op. cit.*

1. It is striking that both the sentenced top members of the BIC, commander François of the National Drug Brigade of the Gendarmerie as well as commissioner Reyniers of the judicial police, were among the elite of police officers who had received training in undercover techniques in Washington some twenty years ago. The American model of proactive investigation procedures appears to have left a great impression on them. We assume that the international cooperation with the DEA influenced their standards to such an extent that this led to the scandals we have known in our country in the last twenty years. Top priority was given to the need to incorporate new techniques into the Belgian system of law enforcement. Concern with due process and democratic judicial control and sensitivity to European continental values were of secondary importance.
2. In such circumstances, they were blind to the snake in the grass. Indeed, it is evident that the programs for the international fight against crime, like the one against drugs under the Nixon administration, but also the one against terrorism in the Reagean years, are believed to be functional for the national interests of the United States. These national interests are not confined to keeping international crime outside the United States territory. The option is also embedded in and influenced by the whole of the American foreign policy. The history of the DEA offers several interesting illustrations of this. We will not go into detail on them.[33] Those who, like some Belgian police representatives, get too carried away with American programs of international law enforcement may without realizing it become a part of the machine of American foreign policy. The unique position of the DEA, with its world-wide information network, reinforces this. This is for instance the case for important international drug traffic that can only be controlled on the basis of DEA information. That the interests of the American bodies in the fight against crime are not always congruent and can even sometimes be contrary to the needs of Belgian law enforcement, is evident. It is striking, for instance, to note that the DEA in later years was mainly concerned with cocaine traffic from South America, while, out of political motivations (the support for anti-communist resistance movements in Afghanistan) it hardly paid any attention to heroin traffic from Pakistan and Afghanistan. As a result the recent large confiscations of hard drugs by Belgian police services all concerned cocaine, while, as far as can be concluded from information provided by health care centers, the Belgian problem of addiction is almost exclusively centered around heroin. In this way, Belgian police services may conflict with the evident requirements of internal security and public health.
3. Another related problem is the fit between the needs of covert methods of policing and the leading principles of fundamental legal justice. This fit

---

33. *See* the fascinating examples in J. Kruger (1976), *The Great Heroin Coup; Drugs, Intelligence and International Fascism*, Boston, South End Press; A. Langguth (1978), *Hidden Terrors; The Truth About U.S. Police Operations in Latin America*, New York, Panteon Books; M. Klare, C. Amson (1981), *Supplying Repression: U.S. Support for Authoritarian Regimes Abroad*, Washington, Institute for Policy Studies; and A. McCoy (1972), *The Politics of Heroin in Southeast Asia*, New York, Harper & Row.

came about, and not just in Belgium, with great difficulty over the past twenty years. Moreover, recent cases at the European Court in Strasbourg show that this fit fails with regard to the important Article 8 of the European Convention on Human Rights. This article protects the privacy of the European citizen. It is clear that Belgian police representatives have not respected this matter in the last twenty years. It is also evident that the present situation is far from perfect.

7. EVALUATION OF THE CURRENT SITUATION

It is striking that the new settlement of proactive policing came about under conditions of secrecy (the directives are confidential) and were created outside any public, democratic way of reaching solutions. People involved in making the directives don't deny the fact that the current rules would never have been approved by the parliament. Many members of the parliament, especially the lawyers and legal specialists, would never approve of the proposed procedures. Such a way of handling things is completely contrary to Article 8 of the European Convention which demands that with regard to citizens' privacy 'there shall be no interference by a public authority with the exercise of this right except such as is in accordance with a *law*.'

Difficulties are also to be expected because the directives are not part of any law and cannot be upheld against third parties. Policemen, for instance, who execute the directives cannot justify their doings in court. Neither the parties in a trial nor the judges have any knowledge of them. Therefore, the position of the policeman is delicate. One can think of circumstances in which he justly follows the directives, later to be accused thereof in court.

Central to the complete system is the anonymity of the informer and/or witness. It is based on doubtful jurisprudence, which can at any time be changed on the basis of the principles on the rights of defense, such as that on the contradictory nature of judicial inquiry. If this happens, then the anonymity disappears and the efficiency of the system too will fall to pieces.

Some crucial difficulties of covert policing are hardly, or not at all, dealt with in the new directives. Three of them are obvious:

1. What happens when a police infiltrator, if he is to succeed in his operation, has to commit a crime? If committing a crime is to be foreseen, so the directives state, then he can bring the problem to the attention of the prosecuting attorney. The judge, however, is unaware of this, and he could be in disagreement with it. Therefore, the undercover policeman remains liable for judicial prosecution. The position of the undercover agent is even more problematic if he has to commit a crime during the operation which he could not foresee. In this case, so the directives state, he has to judge the situation for himself: he has to bring his actions in agreement with the principle of proportionality. In other words, he has to decide on the spot whether the crime he is forced to commit is sufficiently linked to the severity of the crimes he has to investigate. What the policeman in such

case is allowed or not allowed to do, the directives don't say. For him and for us it is unclear.
2. A second problem that regularly occurs in undercover operations is related to the situation of the private civilian informer or infiltrator. To what degree can the policeman witness ongoing crimes without interference? The directives don't discuss this. Yet it is precisely on this matter that several police representatives in Belgium have faced problems in recent years.
3. Finally, there are problems with regard to the way in which and the moment at which the prosecuting attorney has to be informed. In the directives, terms like 'arrest' and 'information report' are juggled, implying that the prosecuting attorney will not add the information report to the judicial files. In this way, those who drew up the directives hoped to avoid anything that could lead to the identification of the undercover section from getting into the judicial files. We emphasize 'hope,' because, as far as we know, every prosecuting attorney is bound to add every document appearing during a judicial inquiry to the files. Again the directives are unclear.

Finally, problems are related to the police force. To put the directive into operation, special police squads are established in two police forces. Both in the judicial police and in the Gendarmerie teams of undercover agents have been set up (in total 30 agents). Technically both teams are professionalized on the basis of experiences in Canada and the Netherlands. This experience will, by the way, later be passed on to the French police services. We are pleased to see that the American model seems to have been left aside, and that countries more closely related to our system of jurisdiction have been called in. We are also pleased to notice that the investigation units themselves and the units of pseudo-buyers have been separated. The teams of pseudo-buyers and the service that protects them only come in for assistance, without taking part in the actual investigation. But we are not at all pleased to see that training, equipment and maintenance of the professional teams is extremely expensive. The equipment alone of one pseudo-buyer is estimated at 3 million Belgian franks (some 70,000 U.S. dollars) a year. Whether this financial burden is justified in relation to the rest of the police budget has not been considered.

Louise Shelley* | Soviet Undercover Work

1. INTRODUCTION

The Soviet police inherited a long tradition of undercover work by both the regular and the secret police apparatus that dated back to the Tsarist period. As Russia changed from one authoritarian tradition to another, it maintained its reliance on covert policing to both control crime and secure political conformity. The Soviet Union in both the Stalinist and the post-Stalinist period relied on undercover work more than democratic societies. The legacy of the heavy dependence on undercover work is providing the post-Soviet states with significant difficulties in making the transition to more democratic societies.

The functions of undercover work have changed with the structure of the state but in all periods of Russian and Soviet history the purpose of this operational work has been not only to detect crime but also to uphold the political order. During the Tsarist period, undercover work helped maintain the dominance of the absolute monarchy long after most European countries had moved away from such authoritarian government. In the post-revolutionary period, undercover work helped establish and subsequently maintain the hegemony of the Communist Party. In the post-Soviet period, undercover work has not been eliminated as a major aspect of police work. It remains an important tool to combat crime commission but also a weapon that is used against political opponents.

Soviet undercover work differed from that conducted in democratic societies. In democratic societies, 'it is a necessary evil' (Marx, 1988) that is an important but not a primary means of combatting crime. Societies based on the rule of law are expected to closely scrutinize undercover work to ensure that citizens are provided adequate protection against arbitrary police authority.

In a non-democratic society like the USSR, undercover work was not perceived as a necessary evil but as a fundamental means of pursuing both ordinary

---

* Professor in the Department of Justice, Law and Society and in the School of International Service, American University, Washington, D.C., United States.

criminals and individuals who might prove a political threat to the regime. In their society, the word undercover does not exist. Rather the practices discussed in this paper are part of what Soviet law enforcement officials consider militia (the regular police) intelligence work. They believe that these practices constitute the best of investigative work. By considering covert policing to be so valuable and so central to social control, the state made duplicity a central feature of the state-citizen relationship. Thereby, they denied the concept of citizenship which has been so crucial to the development of European democracy in the period since the French revolution.

In many societies, discussions of undercover work focus on both the technological means and on the informers. In the former Soviet Union and in other socialist countries, the use of individual informants overshadowed the reliance on technological means. There was a degree of citizen mobilization in police undercover work unknown in democratic societies.

The Soviet state waited little time after the revolution to initiate its undercover activity; the recruitment of citizens began almost immediately after the Bolshevik seizure of power. A decade and a half later, during the Stalinist period, Communist Party records reveal that a full ten per cent of the Soviet population were recruited as full-time police informers.[1] Although the level of citizen participation in police undercover work declined after the Stalinist period, Soviet commentators in the *perestroika* period and since the end of the Soviet Union suggest that thirty per cent of the population was forced to cooperate in the undercover work of the secret police and that figure might have been as high as sixty per cent (Albats, 1992, 9). The high percentage of the population compromised by their involvement in police undercover work was not confined to the former Soviet Union but was a phenomenon present in all the socialist countries of Eastern Europe. The former socialist states that are seeking to democratize are confronted with the legacy of citizen complicity with the security police. Their ability to confront this element of their past is a crucial test of their ability to democratize. Russia and most of the successor states to the former Soviet Union have been much less successful in confronting this legacy than many of the countries of Eastern Europe.

Undercover policing assumed such a pivotal role in Soviet police operations because the state placed such primacy on order. Furthermore, individual interests were subordinated to the needs and the desires of the state. The premium placed on political and social order meant that no operational technique or undercover work that controlled crime was subject to close scrutiny. The legal system was weighted on the side of the state rather than the citizenry. There were no legal safeguards during the Soviet period on the use of undercover techniques. During the final years of the Soviet period, there was significant discussion of the need to adopt controls on undercover work (Savitsky, 1990, 38; Feofanov, 1990, 3), but little was achieved in this direction despite

---

1. This information was found in the Smolensk Communist Party archives seized during the German invasion of the Soviet Union. The records were acquired by the Americans from the Germans. For an analysis of these archives and their revelations on undercover work *see* Fainsod, 1958, 12.

efforts by the Supreme Soviet, the legislature, to establish guidelines for the use of listening devices. In the post-Soviet period, the new legislation adopted on the police and the secret police by many of the newly independent countries does little to limit or regulate the undercover activities of the police forces.

1.1. A Comparative Framework

This paper examines Soviet undercover work in an implicitly comparative context. Soviet policing provided the model for law enforcement in all the socialist states of Eastern Europe and even other socialist countries in many parts of the world. By analyzing Soviet undercover work, it is possible to see that there existed a distinct approach to socialist policing. An approach that differed from such well-known models of policing as the continental, democratic or the traditional authoritarian. Examining undercover policing in the USSR challenges some of the basic theories we have about the police and social control.

An authoritarian state can be perpetuated without the use of much force if the individual has already been denied his autonomy. While the Stalinist period was characterized by great violence by the state against the citizen, this was not the case in the post-Stalin period. As the rapid collapse of the Soviet Union reveals, state intervention in daily life could postpone the dissolution of the successor state to the Russian empire. But even this degree of social control and state intervention could not prevent the inevitable fate of empires in the twentieth century. The forces of nationalism proved greater than the state infiltration of daily life.

Marxist analyses of policing have strongly challenged the orthodox view of police as neutral bodies that prevented and controlled crime. Instead, Marxist critics have posited that the police are a fundamental institution for the maintenance of power by the ruling class. This class analysis of policing has been applied insightfully to both democratic and authoritarian societies. It is, however, more difficult to apply Marxist analysis to Soviet policing, particularly in its initial period, because the post-revolutionary militia were explicitly established as agents of communist ideology. In accordance with Marxist theory, they were to shape the state to the desired class structure. Worker and peasant interests were to be defended and all other classes were to be repressed. Police, drawn from the worker and peasant classes, were crucial actors in the molding of the society to the state ideology.

Soviet history reveals that the state acted in opposition to its ideology. By the 1930s millions of peasants died in the campaign for forced collectivization and workers were subordinated to the state's drive for rapid industrialization. The police became tools of the Party rather than the classes whose interests they were to defend. Yet the state never officially renounced its ideology. Therefore, the militia, in accordance with its ideological mandate, maintained the right to intervene in daily life to a degree unknown in most democratic or even authoritarian societies.

The classic Weberian analysis of police as part of a state bureaucracy helps explain the implementation of some police undercover work. But the Soviet political context was quite different from the state structures which Weber analyzed. Soviet policing existed not only within a state bureaucracy but within a governmental structure subservient to a single political party. The actions of the police were explained not only by the bureaucracy but by the Party which subordinated the state structure to its will.

The Enlightenment changed the nature of Continental policing by introducing the concept of the rule of law. The ideas of the Enlightenment were, however, never integrated into the Russian or the Soviet context. Therefore, while the law enforcers of western Europe lived under the highly centralized, hierarchical continental model, their police became increasingly accountable to legal norms. Consequently, much of their behavior could be explained by Weber's highly rationalized model of bureaucracy. A model that was not applicable to the Soviet experience.

In many authoritarian states, the police use much force against the population to achieve their objectives. This was not the case in the USSR. The security police in the Stalin years had participated in such extensive repression of the population, that there was little need for the regular police, the militia, to employ much violence. The thorough infiltration of daily life, by means of extensive undercover activity, ensured that there was limited activity outside the scope of state regulation. Therefore, the reenforcing controls of the state and the community in the post-Stalin period eliminated the need for much police use of deadly force.

The heavy reliance on unregulated intelligence work by the police differentiated the Soviet police from their counterparts in democratic societies. There was no legislative oversight, no controls by the courts or independent bodies over the undercover activities of the police.

The analysis of the role of undercover work in the Soviet context reveals that the socialist model of policing, epitomized by the Soviet law enforcers, lies outside many of the theories of police and social control. The following discussion of undercover work by both the militia and security police in the USSR is a prerequisite to the development of alternative social control theories that analyze a bureaucracy subordinated to an ideology that mandated control of economic, political life as well as civil society.

1.2. Sources

This chapter is based on a great variety of sources. It draws on interview data, published and unpublished works, as well as legislative sources. Interviews were held with former police personnel in Israel and the United States. With the greater openness of the final years of the Soviet period, interviews were conducted with high level police personnel. Publications of the Soviet Ministry of the Interior (MVD) and other legal materials were used. Published and unpublished legislation was reviewed to gain an understanding of the scope of police activity. The Smolensk Party archives, seized by the Germans in World War II, were examined for their reports on police activity. *Samizdat* (unofficial writings illegally circulated in the Soviet Union) were used to analyze undercover activity directed against dissidents.

The Soviet police became a topic of central concern in the final years of the USSR when reformers sought to address the fundamental institutions of state control. Extensive use was made of late Soviet and post-Soviet publications in order to understand the dimensions and impact of police covert intelligence work. The heavy reliance on Soviet materials has been necessary as there has been neither Western research in the field nor the site access that might accompany such a study in a more open society. Even the collapse of the Soviet state has not resulted in the opening up of the archives of the security police. Furthermore, many important records were destroyed in the final period of the Soviet state. Therefore, even if the reformers succeed in securing public access to the archives of the security police there will be many questions that will remain unanswered.

1.3. Objectives

This paper examines undercover work by both the militia (the regular police) and the security police. The absence of a legal framework to regulate this activity combined with the socialist ideology which justified state intervention in daily life resulted in the penetration of undercover activity in all sectors of society – political and economic life, educational institutions and daily familial life. The techniques which were used to penetrate the society so completely, the citizen complicity in this state intervention and the long-term consequences of this intrusion are the subjects of this paper.

2. UNDERCOVER WORK AND THE LEGAL FRAMEWORK

Undercover activity was one of the basic tools used by the regular police in the Soviet Union and other former socialist countries to both prevent and detect crime. In comparison with many other societies, there was less emphasis on actual detective work and more on the penetration of the criminal world. This enabled the police to operate more effectively than the absence of technical resources, equipment and the presence of outmoded technology might suggest.

Undercover work acquired such primacy for several reasons. First, the state was not based on the rule of law and the observance of law was subordinated to the needs of the state. The concept of a socialist rule-of-law state was introduced as a state objective only during the Gorbachev period. Second, the laws that were enacted were not intended to protect individual rights but to ensure the promotion of the interests of the state. Third, there was not a concept of privacy as exists in the Anglo-American context. As one Hungarian commentator on socialist police explained, 'the state had a right to intervene in any life relationship, and it executed this with the state apparatus' devoted to security ... 'the omnipotence of the government and public administration was the character of the police state' (Szamel, 1992, 18). Fourth, there was no concept of police accountability either to the state or to the citizenry. There was, however, accountability to the Communist Party which promised the citizenry a greater degree of order than in western societies. This order was acquired at significant cost to the individual rights of the citizen.

During the Soviet period, the Constitution was not a fundamental document of Soviet law. Even though the Constitution promised its citizens various rights, these rights were not unequivocal. In exchange for the social safety net, the citizen had numerous obligations to the state. Individual rights did not exist if they contravened the interests of the state and the Communist Party. Furthermore, according to Article 6 of the Constitution, the Party was the leading and guiding force of Soviet society. Because there was no mechanism to ensure compliance with the Constitution, there was no need for any of the laws to protect the rights granted citizens in the Constitution (Biscaretti di Ruffia et al., 1979).

The Code of Criminal Procedure, the basis of much of Soviet police work, authorized investigators to take necessary operational steps. There were no constitutional or other legal limits to this mandate (Kolganova, 1991, 48). Furthermore, there were a significant number of secret laws that governed police activities (Shelley, 1991, 140–155). These were not merely secret operational manuals or guidelines that exist for federal prosecutors in the United State but classified laws that were not known and inaccessible to the population. They provided a legal framework for the regulators that had no benefits for the citizenry. This was legality which served the state rather than the citizenry. Consequently, significant areas of police operational work remained outside of any kind of public legal regulation. Furthermore, there was no system of protection that would assist the citizen subject to intrusive or even illegal undercover work.

Soviet judges because of Communist Party pressure were forced to convict in 99.8 per cent of criminal cases. Even illegally collected evidence was used in the courtroom because prosecutors and judges, although legally required to exclude such evidence, were not permitted by the Party except in exceptional circumstances to drop or dismiss cases. Once an individual entered the criminal justice system, there was little possibility of exiting without a conviction. Therefore, the major control over undercover work which exists in the United States, the exclusion of evidence, did not exist in the USSR (Marx, 1988, 188). Therefore neither constitutional guarantees, legislative restrictions nor procedural safeguards restrained Soviet undercover work.

Americans value privacy and autonomy. Police techniques that contravene these values are viewed with particular suspicion (Marx, 1988, 148–152). In the USSR, there was not a legal or a social concept of privacy. There was no demarcation between the lives of citizens and the right of the *militsiia* (the regular police) to learn about and monitor their daily existence. Autonomy was an alien value in a state that expected state intervention into daily life. Undercover work did not, therefore, challenge central societal values. Listening devices, surveillance and hidden cameras were almost taken for granted by the citizenry.[2] It was not until 1989 that the newly elected legislators of the

---

2. Police, however, were not allowed to tape-record conversations in their patrol cars.

Supreme Soviet rejected their Stalinist past, and prohibited police wire-taps.[3] But there was no enforcement mechanism to ensure that the law enforcement apparatus abided by the legislative decision and the law was subsequently changed in 1990.

3. THE MILITIA AND UNDERCOVER WORK

The Soviet reliance on undercover work to detect crime continues even during the post-Soviet period. As a high official of the criminal investigative branch of the Ministry of Interior (MVD) recently acknowledged, 'Nearly 50 per cent of all crimes are exposed with the help of secret operational contacts of our professional agents' (FBIS, 15 May 1992, 39). Even though Soviet officials during the reform period of *perestroika* acknowledged that undercover methods such as wire-tapping violated the constitutional rights of citizens, they were justified in terms of their efforts to improve the struggle against crime (FBIS, 1990).

Reliance on undercover work that is in many ways easier, more effective and often no more costly (FBIS, 1990), than overt policing techniques, prevented the development of open police detection techniques. This observation contradicts the popular wisdom that overt and covert methods develop in tandem. While overt techniques improved in the post-Stalin period, they did not develop to a sufficient degree to address the serious crime problems of the late Soviet period.

The imbalance in the control apparatus proved destructive to the state. Covert policing eclipsed many aspects of overt policing because so many individuals were at the disposition of the government and the Party. The limits on this co-optation were evident both to the citizens and to the law enforcers. Individuals could be subordinated to the authoritarian states of previous centuries or even to the fascism of the mid-twentieth century. But it is difficult for a highly educated population to remain tools of an industrialized state for an extended period. The citizenry suffered as did the law enforcers who became increasingly corrupted.

3.1. Developing Informants

Throughout the Soviet period, a very well elaborated system existed to develop informants for both regular as well as secret police operations. They were recruited from different pools, with different inducements and for different objectives. The KGB (the secret police) could use more positive inducements than the regular police because it had more resources at its disposal. It recruited more respectable citizens to promote its objectives – enforcing political conformity among all strata of society and maintaining Soviet power. In contrast, the MVD drew more of its informants from a more limited sphere – the criminal world, the trade sector and employees of houses, dormitories and hotels. The

---

3. The discussions of the Supreme Soviet were heated. One of the decisive speeches in this debate concerned the Stalinist past and how the society must move away from this legacy.

one feature they had in common was that usually the police had compromising material on the individuals they recruited (Albats, 1992, 9). Many of the informants recruited by the regular police were members of the criminal population who faced criminal prosecution. Charges could be dropped in exchange for future services or reinstated for a failure to comply. Moreover, many individuals who might be considered law-abiding citizens in other societies found themselves in compromising positions in the former Soviet Union because the scope of the criminal law was so great and so much of individual behavior was subject to state regulation and control.

The skill of developing informants was one of the basic qualifications for criminal investigative work in both the KGB and the militia. Their role in law enforcement was more reminiscent of the police in 18th and 19th century Continental societies than in the police forces of contemporary Western countries. Two kinds of informants existed – recruited and ordinary. In the ordinary category fell many whose job responsibilities included cooperation with the militia – building commandants, doormen (*dvornik*), and watchmen (*storozh*) (Shelud'ko, 1982, 27–28). Their services complemented those of the more removed community committees and those at apartment complexes. The close cooperation between doormen and the police was not a Soviet innovation; doormen were major informants for the Tsarist police (Weissman, 1985, 49), as in many other societies. The unique Russian and Soviet twist was that this collaboration was required by legislation.

In less settled rural areas where this established infrastructure did not exist, militia personnel had to rely more on individual informants. The informant system, however, worked better in the anonymous urban environment than it did in close-knit rural communities where individuals perpetrating a Tsarist tradition often preferred to rely on community justice. In certain Moslem republics, a similar situation existed and Islamic justice operated in some rural communities.

A key element of the training period in the criminal investigative unit, explained one former officer, was learning how to turn ordinary citizens and criminals into informants and provocateurs. A manual existed to help them (Albats, 1992, 9). Investigators might be assisted by the local district inspector who would detain, on a pretext, individuals who might be sought as informants. By finding a suitable individual in a compromising situation – or by using individuals with checkered pasts and uncertain presents – militia personnel might escape paying for their information. Rarely were informants placed on the militia payroll. A generally law-abiding citizen found drunk and disrupting public order might be convinced to serve as an informant rather than be penalized for his misconduct. If the subject hesitated, the individual might be confined for a period of two or three weeks until he consented. But, as one militia officer explained, there were some stalwarts who resisted despite the threat of prosecution.

Officers in the criminal investigative unit typically developed six to twelve regular informants. Employees of the branch devoted to investigating economic crime relied more heavily on informants than other categories of investigators. Investigating embezzlement and corruption in many different state enterprises, they tried to develop several reliable informants in diverse branches of each organization. Their identities were hidden not only from associates but usually from other *militsiia* personnel as well.

Certain categories of individuals were not considered appropriate candidates for informant work. Juveniles were rarely employed because they often proved unreliable, but occasionally they were enlisted to provide information on youth gangs. Although some militia personnel used prostitutes, others found them unsuitable because many suffered from serious alcohol and drug problems, limiting their reliability. Party and Komsomol members could not be recruited by the militia without special permission. Because the authorization was so difficult to obtain, Party members were rarely enlisted as informants.

The militia did recruit successfully among youth and school drop-outs attracted by the romanticism of police work. Furthermore, ex-offenders who lost the right to reside in a major city after receiving a five-year labor camp sentence could be persuaded to inform by granting them the much coveted registration permit that would allow them to return to their home community. A member of the criminal underworld who became an informant might subsequently commit certain criminal acts with impunity. Getting an individual to serve sometimes required tricks as well as money. Although militia personnel routinely paid 10 to 25 rubles for useful information, like police everywhere they preferred to obtain information for free.

The recruitment of informants was formalized. Before recruitment, an officer filled out a form that was submitted to his division chief. In a five to ten-day period, the officer received a response concerning the suitability of the proposed individual. Contractual agreements, drawn between militia and recruited agents, were not a recent development. The Smolensk Party archives reveal that the conditions of service as an OGPU-NKVD (the supervisory organization for the militia and security police) informant were adopted in 1927. These contracts, like those more recently concluded with militia informants, stipulated that the signatory could not give away state secrets under threat of prosecution (Fainsod, 1958, 162). With a signed agreement, a militia informant might be given a code name and sent to a briefing session.

3.2. Deployment of Informants

In the early Brezhnev period in the mid-1960s, informant work was routinized and several categories were established including: prophylactic; surveillance; operational and observational. Prophylactic work was used primarily among juveniles to redirect behavior or to provide grounds to arrest or isolate troublemakers. The surveillance method was used to keep track of recently released prison inmates and those suspected of significant criminal involvement. Ex-offenders who were on militia records as potential dangers to the community could, through the agent system, be quickly returned to labor camps. Operational informants were used to obtain information under various different guises. For example, informants might pose as electrical employees or utility personnel to enter apartments and elicit information from neighbors. Observational informants might not be conscious of the service they were performing for the police. For example, recidivists, thinking they were being granted their liberty, were in fact only used as decoys for their fellow gang members. The police would observe the contacts they made in the community and then they would be returned to prison along with their former gang members.

The informants' reports focused primarily on crime. Surveillance existed not only in the political and criminal arena but also in the sphere of daily life. Informants residing in buildings might report on domestic violence, alcohol abuse or violations of passport regulations. Housing personnel, a backbone of the maintenance of order, were rarely compensated for their tips by the police. There was often much to report because a complex system of passport registration existed which prevented the migration of citizens into many major cities which were closed to new residents. Much of police work was concerned with detecting violations of passport regulations. But the informant system was far from fully effective in this area. Approximately one million citizens managed to reside in Moscow illegally without being expelled by the police. This was possible because citizens illegally residing in an apartment complex would routinely bribe the superintendent or guard personnel to prevent them from informing on their unauthorized residence.

The informants reported exclusively to one officer, either by telephone or at appointed times at one of the special apartments maintained by the militia for these encounters. Informants who could not be met in an apartment might be met in corridors or movie houses, stadiums and other populated areas where such meetings would not be easily detected. Officers tried to avoid using the same apartment consistently. Several safe apartments were located in ordinary residential buildings in every large urban area. Every effort was made to mask the functions of these safe apartments from neighbors. Often, one officer pretended to reside there, always dressed in civilian clothes.

Safe houses also existed for the KGB scattered throughout the city. In the final years of the Soviet period, when corruption became pervasive even in this body, some safe houses were let to foreigners and the rental money was pocketed by the agents responsible for these apartments (Radio Liberty, 1992).

Informants also existed in prison investigation cells. This special class of informant had a name (*nasedki*). The cell informants also were used to extract confessions during detention or to obtain information for the investigators. These informants often spent much of their day performing this task but their professional identity was often known only to the police investigatory division and not to the police assigned to their immediate neighborhoods. Illustrative of this was a case in which a man was brought up by his local police authorities on parasitism charges (a crime defined as the failure to work). The judge was not forewarned about the defendant's identity and routinely asked the defendant 'What do you do?' The man replied that he worked for the militia. The perplexed judge replied, 'In what capacity?' The accused man's response was greeted by general laughter: 'I sit in jail all day and then recount all.'

3.3. Employing Informant Information

The use of informants could prove problematic for the police in some western societies because the courtroom testimony of criminals is sometimes not considered reliable evidence. The militia, however, did not generally face this problem with informants. Even during *perestroika*, Soviet procurators showed no reluctance in using informants' testimony to complete investigations. Judges did not hesitate to accept this evidence. The 98 per cent conviction rate in criminal cases even during the late 1980s showed that the courtroom favored the prosecution. In contrast, in the final years of the Soviet period there was a greater likelihood to drop cases before trial in which evidence had been obtained covertly without proper authorization.

In some former socialist countries such as Hungary the existing informant system, imported along with the police system from the USSR, was destroyed after the collapse of communism. In contrast, critics within the Soviet police system wanted to establish legislation regulating undercover work rather than abolishing this operational method needed to apprehend criminals (Kolganova, 1991, 49).

3.4. Anonymous Tips and Denunciations

The militia detected some of its crime through another undercover technique – anonymous tips. All these methods disclosed crime and undesirable conduct not routinely reported by citizens. Citizens, especially in the Stalin era, were urged to denounce their compatriots for their misconduct, but this practice did not disappear entirely following Stalin's death. Kievan residents in 1981, according to Ukrainian *samizdat* (unofficially published and disseminated literature), received postcards requesting that they report anonymously to the Council of the Public Order points (a neighborhood body) the names of parasites, alcoholics, problem families and adolescent drop-outs (Solchanyk, 1981). With the growing awareness of democratic values that preceded *perestroika*, this approach raised concern among some governmental officials in Moscow. Early in the following year an article in *Izvestiia* appeared, criticizing the Kiev request for anonymous denunciations (Parkhomovskii, 1982, 3). Yet the furor over the anonymous denunciations to the militia did not disappear; it only became more apparent with *glasnost* (Grafova, 1988, 13).[4]

In fact, denunciations grew rather than diminished in the late 1980s. The Procuracy (a very powerful prosecutor's office with responsibility for the enforcement of legality in all sectors of Soviet life) and the MVD defended their necessity (*Joint Publication Research Report*, 1988, 6), stating that the 25 per cent of serious undisclosed crime would remain undetected without their continued use. But anonymous tips did not bear the fruits law enforcement personnel suggested. Fifty per cent of the inspections made by the personnel responsible for economic crime, consuming 30 per cent of their time, were based on such sources. But only one to two per cent of them panned out. Critics contended that their value was oversold, while they unnecessarily encroached on individual rights (*Joint Publication Research Report*, 1988, 13).

---

4. *See* also a negative view of this phenomenon expressed by the distinguished director of the Institute of State and Law, V.N. Kudriavstev, 1988, B/5.

The increasing technology available to law enforcement personnel in developed societies makes undercover work threatening to the citizenry in a way never known previously (Marx, 1988). This problem was especially problematic in modern authoritarian societies like the USSR where the citizens did not enjoy legal safeguards and the law enforcers did not have a legal consciousness. The 1990 adoption of a law authorizing investigators to use videos, films and tape recordings by the Soviet Union legislature was an effort to regulate behavior that was previously outside the reach of the law. This legislation stipulated that taping could be carried out only in cases where 'proceedings have been instituted and only on the prosecutor's approval or on the court's decision' (FBIS, 19 October 1990). This legislation did not resolve many of the problems of undercover policing because no means were instituted to ensure compliance with the law.

4. UNDERCOVER WORK OF THE SECURITY POLICE

For most of the Soviet period, the undercover work of the secret police was directed at actual or what were believed to be potential enemies of the state. Particularly in the Stalinist period, a vast network of informers existed throughout the country that helped to fuel the extra-legal criminal processes which sent millions of individuals to their death or to labor camps. Although approximately one out of ten individuals were acknowledged informers, most of the population was compromised in some way through their cooperation with the secret police.

The depth of citizen cooperation in the undercover work of the secret police in the former Soviet Union will never be fully known because in the period immediately after the failed coup of August 1991, millions of documents were destroyed within the KGB headquarters which might have implicated individuals as police collaborators. Furthermore, the Russians have not as yet engaged in a thorough house cleaning of their domestic intelligence apparatus as has been the case in Czechoslovakia or the former East Germany. The end of 1991 marked the dissolution of the Soviet state, the successor to the Russian empire, but not the complete dismantling of the Communist system. In contrast to the situation in many countries in Eastern Europe, Communist era officials continued to hold key positions in the bureaucracies of most post-Soviet states.

The legal systems of Eastern Europe were based closely on the Soviet model and close contact was maintained between their secret polices and that of the Soviet Union. The efforts to deal with the problem of citizen complicity with the secret police in the socialist period has been a major problem for the democratic transition of these societies.

4.1. Technology and the Security Police

In the Stalin period listening devices were used, but they became more common when technology expanded. Technology was used to listen in on conversations and to observe the contacts of individuals who were under suspicion. Foreign technology was imported to improve surveillance that was not available to the ordinary police. While the regular police might lack vehicles to get to the scene of the crime, the secret police was able to import sophisticated listening devices to install in cars that would be stationed outside the home of dissidents for months on end. The technology was used to monitor every international telephone conversation and to listen in on the conversations of individuals whose behavior had aroused suspicion among security personnel. Numerous employees were at the disposal of the secret police to perform this function. Conversations were terminated if they proved objectionable to the state. Instructions for eavesdropping by the secret police were maintained within the 12th department of the KGB that was devoted to government communications (FBIS, 31 July 1992b).

Political dissidents had their phones tapped but secret police scrutiny was not limited to these people. Testimony at the Russian Constitutional Court case of 1992 on the status of the Communist Party revealed that monitoring of the democratic reformers was also undertaken by the KGB. At the Court hearings, the chief of Russia's former Federal Security Agency revealed that the Soviet KGB since 1989 had monitored Boris Yeltsin's phone conversations as well as those of his relatives. This was done with such sophistication that it could be done in such odd places as the tennis court and the locker room frequented by Yeltsin (FBIS, 1992c). Furthermore, the phones of parliament members of the Inter-Regional Deputy Group, a group of democratically minded legislators were also bugged.

Wire-tapping was focused, but a pervasive informant apparatus existed to monitor the population in their homes, workplaces, and in their personal relationships. The undercover activity of the security police was much more pervasive than that of the militia and involved individuals in all different sectors of the society. There were different levels of collaborators with the KGB who ranged from full-time employees to individuals who would occasionally provide information. At every workplace, the personnel department was reporting to the secret police apparatus.

4.2. Recruitment of Informants

Many citizens were coerced into cooperating. The extent of this cooperation is not known as in the East German context where the exposed records of its secret police, the Stasi, reveal that even husbands and wives would inform the secret police of the conduct of their spouses. Individuals were compelled to provide information on those closest to them as well as on friends and acquaintances. In every delegation that went abroad there was at least one individual who would inform on his colleagues and everyone on the trip had to write a report that discussed their contacts while they were abroad. A Prime Minister of post-independence Lithuania, Prunskiene, was ousted from her position after disclosure of her collaboration with the KGB during foreign travel as an economist during the Soviet period.

One former KGB captain suggested that there were four main reasons why individuals started collaborating with the secret police: 'career considerations, compromising materials, fear of the KGB, and the victim's belief that the KGB never gives up' (Albats, 1992, 9). The pay-offs for such cooperation were clear. There were trips abroad, promotion at work, the possibility of better housing. For individuals who refused to cooperate, the consequences could be quite severe and might include loss of work, failure to travel abroad or even criminal punishments. The encompassing nature of the criminal law and the constant shortage of consumer goods made most citizens vulnerable to prosecution on some charge. The conditions of confinement in Soviet prisons and labor camps were so severe that many would do almost anything to escape confinement.

In December of 1991, the deputy chief of Russia's Security Ministry told a commission of the Russian parliament that there were no more undercover agents. But this was really a question of terminology rather than an actual change in policy because the collaborators with the security apparatus were renamed as 'attached personnel' (Albats, 1992, 9).

During the Soviet period there were three main categories of undercover personnel used by the Soviet secret police. The first were the so-called 'professionals.' These were KGB career personnel who worked under cover in departments concerned with relations with foreigners, as deputy directors at research institutes, as translators, hotel personnel, telephone engineers and journalists. They received the pay for their position as well as extras for their rank and service (Albats, 1992, 9).

'Trusted persons' were the second largest category and consisted of individuals who were not in the direct employ of the secret police apparatus. These individuals might be enterprise managers, organizers of Communist Party cells in the workplace, telegraph operators, academics. Their responsibility was to report popular feeling in professional circles. Rewards for their collaboration were often trips abroad.

The third largest group consisted of observers, consultants, agents of influence and residents. Many of these had to report on the popular mood and the opinions of specific personnel. Approximately ten per cent of these secret agents of the KGB were agents of influence. An example of such a person was the doctor of Andrei Sakharov who tried to talk the famous dissident out of making public speeches on the grounds of his poor health.

The recruitment of KGB personnel was explained in a manual. Assistance was provided by the Technical Service of the KGB which monitored the private correspondence of individuals. The KGB could easily locate individuals in a compromising position because it opened foreign correspondence and routinely eavesdropped on international conversations (Yasmann, 1990, 8). Those who were recruited had to be between 18 and 60 years of age. Most of the more elderly recruits were used to maintain safe houses (Albats, 1992, 9).

Before the coup attempt in August 1991, KGB personnel were under a quota system to recruit two new agents a year. Those who failed to meet their quota suffered a thirty per cent reduction in their bonuses. Some recruited five and received bonuses while others were reprimanded for not recruiting more (Albats, 1992).

4.3. Surveillance Methods

The surveillance methods used by the secret police in its undercover work were formalized but secret. In late 1992, former KGB officers disillusioned with the chaos of their former organization released an instructional manual to a right-wing nationalist newspaper in the hope that these methods could be used to combat pro-Western forces in Russian society (Yasmann, 1992 and Tainy Gospozhi NN, 1992a). The first method is tailing an individual by car, public transport or in public places such as stores and movies. The purpose of this kind of surveillance was to gather information, to obtain a one-time result or to construct a psychological profile. The personnel of stores they frequented, the banks they used and the post office where they collected their mail might be interviewed. Also undercover agents might go to cafes or beer halls to engage the person under surveillance in conversation. After months of such surveillance, the normal walk or manner of behavior was determined. Therefore, any unusual step or gesture would be discernable by agents who constantly monitored their conduct. This kind of surveillance technique was deemed particularly useful in pursuing racketeers (a function of the secret police) and pursuing other forms of criminal conspiracies (Tainy Gospozhi NN, 1992a).

A classification system was established for the type of surveillance that was maintained over an individual. These included: accompanying, meeting, parallel, combined and demonstrated. The first required close monitoring of the individual under surveillance to ensure that he was never let out of sight. The meeting method was often used when a person suspected he might be under surveillance and he had an established route to his activities. Two agents would stay in front of the person and one would stay much farther along the established route than the other. When the person under surveillance advanced to the location of the agent, he would move ahead of the agent farther down the route. Parallel surveillance required that several individuals observe from the other side of the street. Someone always needed to be in reserve so that the individual under surveillance was not lost. The combined technique used all the above methods ensuring surveillance both on the street and in vehicular transport. Demonstrated surveillance ensured that the individual was aware that he was being followed at his every step. If he stopped to read a newspaper, then the agent was required to stand beside him (Tainy Gospozhi NN, 1992b). This demonstrated surveillance helped perform one of the vital functions of undercover activity: 'To be a major hindrance to the smooth functioning of a criminal operation' (Brodeur, 1992, 123).

A vast range of technical equipment could be used to assist in the surveillance operation. This included a variety of listening devices, mini-cameras, disguised vehicles in which to follow an individual (Brodeur, 1992, 123).

Undercover agents were expected to be subtle in their activities so that they would not be visible to the person under surveillance or to others in the community. Highly visible surveillance was considered the work of amateurs. It was important, for example, in a supermarket or shopping area to take a moment to pretend to be looking at the windows. In an apartment building, it was important to go up two or three floors and then descend to the floor where one needed to go. On a trolley bus, it was preferable to stand near a door so that one could descend rapidly if necessary. In the subway, undercover personnel were instructed not to run to the escalators. When travelling by car, agents were advised to know the area where they would be travelling. One of the most effective techniques was for agents to converge on the same location from different starting points if they knew the intended destination of the person under surveillance. The purpose of this complex maneuver was to control the area of the person under surveillance (Tainy Gospozhi NN, 1992c).

Instructions were given to agents concerning the response of individuals once they realized that they were under surveillance. Further behavior by the agents had to be decided, depending on whether the criminal group changed their conduct in response to the monitoring of their conduct. With visible surveillance, if the individual became nervous or inhibited his activity, it could be advisable to curtail the surveillance temporarily (Tainy Gospozhi NN, 1992c).

Some criminal groups also engaged in surveillance prior to commission of their crimes. For undercover agents, it was important to determine what sites or individuals were the targets of the criminals' reconnaissance. In some cases, it was useful for agents to engage in visible surveillance to deter this activity. Special precautions, however, were expected to be taken in these cases (Tainy Gospozhi NN, 1992d).

The lengthy manual on surveillance techniques made it apparent that a very large number of personnel could be deployed in this surveillance activity. Even though the personnel employed for this role by the KGB were paid considerably more than full-time militia personnel or even many highly paid professionals, there was no indication that human resources needed to be conserved. Rather large numbers of personnel were deployed to deter crimes perceived as a threat to national security either for their political significance or their severity. Technical means supplemented rather than supplanted the extensive undercover work performed by individuals. This was labor-intensive undercover work unlike that in many western societies where technical means are given priority over the full-time work of police agents.

5. POST-SOVIET DEVELOPMENTS

The collapse of the Soviet Union has not led to the dismantling of the security apparatus or policing based on extensive citizen collaboration. The acute examination of past policing techniques that has occurred in Hungary, Germany, Poland and Czechoslovakia has not transpired in the countries to emerge from the former Soviet Union. In the major countries of Eastern Europe, the societies have scrutinized the practices of the former secret police apparatus and have analyzed the dependence of the regular police on citizen collaborators. Poland, in an effort to combat this problem, has replaced most of its regular police, West Germany had made the former East German police respond to West German police techniques and the Hungarians abolished the network of informants that was the basis of their undercover work. In many of these countries, much thought has been given to the conditions needed to create a more democratic police force.

In the former Soviet Union, with the exception of the Baltic States, there has been limited transformation of the police forces or their methods of operation. In fact, the police in some of the countries which have emerged from the former Soviet Union have used their new-found independence to enhance their powers at the expense of citizen rights. For example, in Kazakhstan new statutes on the militia and the secret police institutionalize powers which infringe on citizens' rights granted in international conventions. There are no limitations on police undercover activity and the police have the right to commandeer a citizen's car if needed for their operations without concern for compensation for the citizenry.

In Russia two laws were passed in 1992 that had significant bearing on police undercover work. They were the law on the operational activity of the police and the law on private detectives. But the police mandate for operational work remains large and the legal safeguards which have been instituted are weak, particularly in a society without a real division of powers or a well-developed legal consciousness. According to the legislation on operational activity, the police have the right to engage in surveillance activity, to monitor mail, to eavesdrop on telephone conversations and other forms of communication. Technical devices that are not life-threatening can be used to monitor citizen behavior. The circumstances under which police personnel can initiate such undercover activities are delineated and the methods may not be employed without the sanction of the courts or the procuracy. This element of the law appears to be a formal significant advance over previous conditions (Law of the Russian Federation, 1992, 1222–1223).

The section on the use of informants, however, reveals a highly systematized procedure for securing the services of informants but with no concern reflected in the legislation for the protection of the rights of the citizen subject to their scrutiny. The section on informants reveals that contracts can be made with adults without regard to their citizenship, nationality or sex, social or financial position or religious or political convictions. In other words, there should be no discrimination in the selection of informants. But certain groups are excluded by the legislative mandate from being recruited including legislators, procurators, defense attorneys, judges, priests and other representatives of officially recognized religious bodies. The legislation does not mention doctors or the press which are included in American legislation. The reason for this difference is that doctors and journalists were considered arms of the state.

Informants are entitled to protection, if necessary, as well as pension benefits for their term of service. The latter condition reflects the establishment of long-term police-citizen relationships in undercover work (Law of the Russian Federation, 1992, 1226–1227).

Several forms of protection are offered from police undercover work. First, the citizen, if he feels that his rights or liberties are being encroached on by the undercover activity, has the right to appeal to the courts. Several institutional mechanisms are delineated to maintain control over police undercover work. A parliamentary committee is assigned the oversight function over police undercover activity. The procuracy is to ensure the observance of legality in undercover operations. Individuals in organizations engaged in undercover activity have personal responsibility for the observance of legality in undercover measures (Law of the Russian Federation, 1992, 1228).

These institutional guarantees of legality are not sufficient to protect individual rights. First, in the absence of a democratically elected and autonomous parliament, a legislative committee cannot provide citizens protection against the abuse of police power. The procuracy has the function of both authorizing and overseeing police operational work. This is an inherent contradiction. Third, the establishment of individual responsibility for the violation of undercover work personalizes responsibility rather than ensuring institutional accountability.

6. CONCLUSION

In some European countries such as France 'informers are irretrievably linked to the idea of policing and they have been systematically used since at least the 17th century. Yet civil liberties are still very much alive in countries like France' (Brodeur, 1992, 122). Russia, which unlike France did not incorporate the legal ideals of the Enlightenment, never established a legal framework to control or regulate its agent network. Civil liberties were not alive because they were never allowed to develop by the pervasive undercover activities of the regular and secret police.

The citizenry was well controlled by police undercover activities that coopted or compromised the majority of the population. This vulnerable status enhanced state control over the citizenry. It helped ensure a high degree of political control and social conformity. Crime rates were lower and many overt acts of political resistance against the state were deterred by means of the state penetration of private life.

The state intervention in individual life and the extent of state co-optation of the citizenry quashed civil society. There was no area of cultural, personal or economic life that was outside the surveillance of the state. Increasing technology did not result in the substitution of technical means for human ones. Instead, it merely enhanced the surveillance capacities of the state. Corruption and inefficiency, with the absence of legal guarantees for the citizenry, remained the only protections for the citizenry from the tactics of the surveillance state.

The heavy reliance on undercover activity and the co-optation of the citizen by the state denied the concept of citizenship which was at the basis of the Enlightenment. While the concept of citizen rights developed throughout western Europe and many parts of the Anglo-Saxon world, in the socialist states individuals remained tools of the state rather than autonomous individuals. The penetration of undercover activity into life was the most visible evidence of this state denial of citizen rights. The movements of 1989 in Eastern Europe which asserted individual rights over the citizen toppled those societies and in many cases led immediately to the storming of their security police and the destruction of the undercover activity in both security and regular militia activity.

The political revolution of Eastern Europe had its repercussions in the former Soviet Union. But the destruction of the Communist system was not so great. The Russian state and many other newly independent states failed to exploit the impetus for change that followed the unsuccessful coup attempt or the break-up of the Soviet Union. While the statue of Dzerzhinsky, the founder of the security police, was removed from its pedestal in front of the KGB headquarters, the reformers were more successful at removing the symbol of state coercion rather than in attacking the institutions of state control. Insufficient steps were taken to dismantle the secret police apparatus or its system of informants. Furthermore, little was done to reconceptualize policing along a more democratic model as was done in several countries of Eastern Europe and the Baltics. Infiltration of the state into the lives of the citizens by both the security and militia apparati remains a fact in most of the post-Soviet states. The crucial question remains: to what extent will these states eliminate this penetration into their society and create the conditions necessary for citizenship? Only if they do this can they provide the basis for more democratic societies.

REFERENCES

Albats, Y. (1992), 'Shadowy Figures,' *Moscow News*, 5–12 April, 9.
Biscaretti di Ruffia, P., Crespi Reghizzi, G. (1979), *La Costituzione Sovietica del 1977*, Milano, Fott. A Giuffrè – Editore.
Brodeur, J-P. (1992), 'Undercover Policing in Canada: Wanting What Is Wrong,' *Crime, Law and Social Change* 18, 105–123.
Fainsod, M. (1958), *Smolensk under Soviet Rule*, Cambridge, Harvard University Press.
Feofanov, Y. (1990), 'Minister of Interior Vadim Bakatin: "What the Militia Can or Cannot Do",' *Izvestiia*, 5 August, 3.
FBIS (1990), 'Plan for Phone Taps in Criminal Cases Outlined,' *Foreign Broadcast Information Service (henceforth FBIS) Daily Report*, 19 October, 46.
FBIS (1992a), '"Secret Helpers" Importance Noted,' *FBIS Daily Report*, 15 May, 39.
FBIS (1992b), 'Ivanenko on Surveillance Techniques,' *FBIS Daily Report, Supplement Central Eurasia Constitutional Court on CPSU Legality*, 31 July, 13.
FBIS (1992c), 'KGB Monitoring of Yeltsin Since 1989 Noted,' *FBIS Daily Report, Supplement Central Eurasia Constitutional Court on CPSU Legality*, 31 July, 13.
Grafova, L. (1988), 'Neuzhto bez anonimki,' *Literaturnaia Gazeta*, 10 February, 13.
Joint Publication Research Service Report (1988), 'Interior Minister Interviewed by Yugoslav Journal,' 1 July, 6.
Kolganova, T. (1991), 'Nuzhna Li Nam Agentura?,' *Sovetskaia Militsiia*, 1, 48.
Kudriavtsev, V.N. (1988), 'The Presumption of Innocence No Longer A "Bourgeois Invention",' *News Service of the BBC*, SU/0149, 12 May, B/5.
Law of the Russian Federation No. 892 (1992), 'Ob operativno-rozysknoi deiatel'nosti v Rossiiskoi Federatsii,' *Vedomosti s'ezda narodnykh deputatov Rossiiskoi Federatsii i Verkhovnogo Soveta Rossiiskoi Federatsii* 17, 23 April 1992, 1222–1223.

Marx, G.T. (1988), *Undercover; Police Surveillance in America*, Berkeley, University of California Press.
Parkhomovskii, E. (1982), 'Ne zvonite anonimno,' *Izvestiia* 16 January, 3.
Radio Liberty Broadcast Based on New Soviet Reports (1992), 3 June.
Savitsky, V. (1990), 'And Yet – Trial by Jury?,' *New Times*, 22, 38.
Shelley, L. (1991), 'Soviet Criminal Law and Justice: Are There or Were There Secrets?,' in: Buxbaum, R.M., Hendley, K., eds., *The Soviet Sobranie of Laws: Problems of Codification and Non-Publication*, Berkeley, University of California at Berkeley (Research Series, 78), 140–155.
Shelud'ko, G.P. (1982), *Sovetskaia Militsiia na Strazhe Obshchestvennogo Poriadka*, Kiev, Vishcha Shkola.
Solchanyk, R. (1981), 'Kiev Authorities Seek Informers to Assist Police in Combatting Crime,' *Radio Liberty Research* 488, 8 December.
Szamel, L. (1992), 'Constitutional State and Security,' in: *Selections from the Former Articles of the Security Review Budapest*, Security Bureau of the Home Office.
'Tainy Gospozhi NN' (1992a), *Den'* 37.
'Tainy Gospozhi NN' (1992b), *Den'* 38.
'Tainy Gospozhi NN' (1992c), *Den'* 39.
'Tainy Gospozhi NN' (1992d), *Den'* 42.
Weissman, N. (1985), 'Regular Police in Tsarist Russia, 1900–1914,' *Russian Review*, 45–68.
Yasmann, V. (1990), 'Ending KGB Eavesdropping,' *Radio Free Europe/ Radio Liberty Daily Report*, 16 July, 8.
Yasmann, V. (1992), 'KGB External Surveillance Code Made Public,' *Radio Free Europe/Radio Liberty Daily Report,* 2 October, 3.

Gary Armstrong*
and Dick Hobbs** | **High Tackles and Professional Fouls: The Policing of Soccer Hooliganism**

1. INTRODUCTION

Soccer-related violence has been with us for many years, and its various manifestations continue to pose serious problems for the sports administrators, police and public alike. While football hooliganism is a problem, it is our contention that police, media and politicians have generated a moral panic on a par with that detailed by Hall *et al.* (1978). Soccer-related disorder both in and around grounds has caused death and injuries. The first football hooligan-related death occurred in August 1974. One writer (Smith, 1983) found 'several more' in the 1975 and 1976 seasons, six murders between 1979 and 1982, and dozens of injuries through slashings. Yet, we would argue that casualties from football hooliganism compare favorably with, for instance, fatalities on the roads as a result of drunk driving. which in 1989 totalled over 800. It is our contention that the police response is disproportionate to the problem, and that covert policing has been developed as the primary tool of a police force seeking to promote and extend both the tactics and ideology of a pervasive and intrusive surveillance culture.

Until the introduction of the Public Order Act 1986, football hooligans were invariably dealt with by the legal process, by use of minor charges contained in the Public Order Act 1936 (Coalter, 1984; Cook, 1978; Trivizas, 1980, 1981). The first use of serious public order charges against football fans was, we believe, in November 1973 in London. Three fans were charged with affray after attacking a fifteen-year-old rival. The Metropolitan Police were quoted as saying that this new measure would be used in future (*The Sheffield Star*, 16 November 1973). The situation became more grave, so that the very serious charge of riot was served upon a Chelsea fan in 1985, normally meriting a maximum sentence of ten years. However, Judge Argyle sentenced the fan to life imprisonment. The facts of the case were that outside the grounds on which

---

* Research Fellow, Department of Criminology, University of Hull, United Kingdom.
** Reader, Department of Sociology, University of Durham, United Kingdom.

the youth was arrested, and on the evidence of one police officer was charged, his actual actions were that of attempting to kick a rival fan. His attempt failed and there were no injuries. Although welcomed by various MPs and police representatives, in the Court of Appeal in May 1986, the life sentence was reduced to three years.

This early prosecution gave a taste of things to come. The response of the criminal justice system to soccer hooliganism from 1986 onwards rested largely upon the utility of conspiracy charges. In total, 36 football fans in London were charged with 'conspiracy to cause an affray' in 1987. This is significant because as Kettle and Hodges (1982, 20, 187–188) have written, 'The conspiracy theory is just about the oldest card in the authority's pack,' being the same as that used against the emerging labor movement in the 19th century and in the 1960s against political activists. The authors chronicle the period from the 1780 Gordon Riots to the 1981 inner-city riots, and show how both media and police have consistently sought to uncover plots and ringleaders. Further, as Bunyan (1977) notes, charges of incitement and conspiracy do not require proof that any crime was actually committed.[1]

2. THE INHERITANCE OF COVERT POLICING

The infiltration of groups of travelling supporters travelling abroad was originally requested by the English games governing body, the Football Association in 1981. The FA also asked the Foreign Office for names and addresses of England supporters arrested at a match in Switzerland in order to blacklist them. The FO refused, arguing it would be an infringement of liberty (Croker, 1987). On a domestic level the FA recommended that plainclothes police be used in the mid-1960s and again in the early 1980s. Requests for the co-ordination of information pertaining to football hooligans was repeatedly made by football authorities, but refused by the Home Office (*The Times*, 11 May 1983).

Covert policing can be a powerful device in presenting criminal behavior as being especially problematic. Brought to the attention of the public, it serves to stress the seriousness of the threat and the danger to which the officers are exposed. The boring, routine, essentially administrative, nature of everyday detective work (Manning, 1980) is ignored in favor of the low-life glamor of the policeman who temporarily goes over to the other side. The selective presentation of covert policing is especially effective in the constant competition for resources that takes place both inside and outside of the police; it is also a potent political tool for the dramatization of the fight against crime, particularly in the fight against violent, seemingly narcissistic, crime. For, as in the case of football hooliganism, both votes and resources can be acquired from being seen to do something about such apparent evil. During the 1980s, this tactic which

---

1. Further, he specifies that the first time conspiracy was used in connection with a public order offense was in Britain in 1973. An Anti-Internment League march marking the anniversary of Bloody Sunday in Derry turned violent, and four marchers were charged with 'conspiracy to cause threatening and riotous behavior' (Bunyan, 1977, 35–51).

had previously been associated with attempts to apprehend armed robbers and terrorists was applied to football supporters. It had become in Marx's (1988, 1) terms 'a cutting edge tactic.'

Historically, British society has a highly ambiguous relationship with covert policing, and has traditionally avoided presenting any form of police work other than the uniform patrol as its primary rhetorical device. The dynamism for this selectivity can be located within the socio-economic climate that prevailed in the era immediately before state policing was introduced in Britain.

Localized, pre-industrial precedents for latter-day policing agencies conformed to a community ethos with a strong emphasis on an overt accessible presence (Critchley, 1978). By the Middle Ages, the preservation of the King's Peace was firmly established as the primary function of the police, establishing via statute 'a direct link between the authority of the constable and the power of the monarchy' (Hobbs, 1988, 17).

Formal social control in Britain became bonded to the maintenance of the prevailing social order. This principle was reinforced by the Statute of Winchester in 1285 which introduced three measures; the watch, indicating the involvement of the citizenry in routine patrol and order maintenance; the practice of hue and cry that forced all citizens to participate in the apprehension of criminals; and the requirement for all men to keep weapons in their homes in support of hue and cry (Critchley, 1978, 6). Social control was localized, overt and, via the majesty of the law, it retained powerful links with the highest authority in the land (Styles, 1987, 21).

By the time that the government was forced by increased disorder to consider a unified state-funded police force in London, the role of the police had been taken up by many disparate professional, semi-professional and amateur organizations (Armitage, 1937; Ascoli, 1979; Critchley, 1978; Dilnot, 1929; Radzinowicz, 1956). These organizations were funded from a variety of state, local government and private sources, but they all shared an essentially preventative function. Resistance to reorganizing these various constables, watchmen and runners into one coherent structure was vehement and leant heavily upon the belief that policing and republicanism went hand in hand. While musket volleys and sabre charges were regarded as appropriate ways of dealing with provincial unrest (Silver, 1967), such bloody behavior on the streets of London, where a sedate rationally ordered commercial world was rapidly emerging, was hardly good for business (Miller, 1977; Reith, 1956, 157).

Consequently, a form of identifiable civil control was needed, one that did not embody the republican threat of the insidious French informer and *agent provocateur*, yet was essentially non-militaristic in its practice. The model that Parliament eventually bought in 1829 was the preventative, uniformed 'impartial socio-legal-sanitary inspector' (Miller, 1977). The emphasis on prevention in the political rhetoric that preceded the 1829 Police Act is especially crucial. The Police Act was sold to Parliament as creating 'a vigorous preventative police consistent with the free principles of our free constitution' (Robert Peel, quoted in Radzinowicz, 1956, 362). Consequently,

> the early police presence was far from the threatening, insidious, unseen spy from the French system and, in forming a fully professional force of paid

constables, visually accessible to all, the clientele were also easily distinguished, and the internal binding of the organisation assured. (Hobbs, 1988, 34; *see* also Manning, 1977, 128–129).

The political and organizational tone for British policing was therefore set, and there was apparently no room for covert operations. Yet it rapidly became apparent that a detective function in some form was necessary. Initially this took the form of a small, low-key 'Detective Branch' which came into being in 1842, and which was severely restricted by organizational rules from indulging in any practice that so much as hinted at covert activity. For instance, its officers were forbidden to mix with criminals (Critchley, 1978, 60; Hobbs, 1988, 40–41).

By the time the CID was formed in 1877, the overt nature of British detective work was firmly established and even subsequent corruption tended to be the result of administrative or licensing discrepancies (*see* Ascoli, 1979, 210; Sherman, 1974, 98). Any hint of undercover work was met with outrage, and the fear of 'foreign' or 'continental' policing inspired the tag of *agent provocateur* being applied to such un-British activity (Prothero, 1931, 100). Indeed the British detective was expected to display qualities that were not only unsuited to covert operations but also remarkably similar to the attributes that one might require of any member of the 'lower orders.' As Clarkson and Hall-Richardson (1889, 266) explain:

> Englishmen possess pre-eminently qualities which are essential to good detective work such as dogged pertinacity in watching, thoroughness of purpose, an absence of imagination and downright sterling honesty.

Covert policing remains an essentially 'un-British' enterprise, as an officer who infiltrated a gang of armed robbers explained to us:

> I had been in the field for over a month, was on the edge of a real result. So I go to a final briefing before we nick 'em, there's two of us and as we walk down this corridor in the (Scotland) Yard a uniform governor sees us, calls us back and tells us get a shave and put a tie on (Fieldnotes).

3. LEADERS OF MEN

There is a long history of media-induced belief that public disorder is manipulated by sinister and highly organized forces; collective activity, particularly that of the lower orders, is normally presented in terms of malevolent masterminds controlling a naive but impressionable majority of lumpen followers. The process has been neatly summarized by Chibnall (1977, 28).

The professional imperative of personalization encourages their identification and isolation as objects for the projection of negative popular fantasies. A whole social demonology is established and the genre of exposé journalism is enriched by stories of the form, 'we name the men behind the …'

Further, Northam (1989, 32) notes that the British urban riots of 1981 were blamed on left-wing groups who organized the mob: 'social explanation is exhausted with the discovery of a villain.'

The first presentation of the 'organization' and 'leadership' at the heart of soccer hooliganism emerged at the trial of the 'Cambridge casuals.' In May 1985 the British public discovered through massive media coverage the 'new' way football hooligans operated, basically of how fights now took place in city centers and around public houses, and how the participants now wore clothes which did not conform to the stereotypical image of the football fan.

In February 1984, an incident involving Cambridge fans and Chelsea visitors resulted in enormous publicity over a year later when those arrested in the incident stood trial. The outcome of this lunchtime fight was a Chelsea fan receiving a bad wound to the neck after being hit by a bottle. Another sustained a broken jaw, and one policeman sustained damaged vertebrae. Others required hospital treatment for minor injuries. Twenty-four fans were jailed for their involvement, 23 receiving between 15 months and four years. Most were aged in their twenties, quite a few were married, some with children. Several others had no previous convictions and were considered 'good' characters in their work (one, much to media fascination, in his local church).

The Cambridge fans were portrayed by the mass media as a militaristic, highly organized unit which caused havoc throughout the country. Nobody was safe from their rampaging excesses, and one man ('the general') was behind it all. 'General' Muranyi was a 25-year-old window cleaner, he had been barred from Cambridge United's ground by the club in 1983, and had served a six-month prison sentence for 'unlawful assembly.' His other offenses included 'possessing an offensive weapon' and 'assaulting police.' After the incident involving Chelsea fans he was charged with and pleaded guilty to 'riot.' Sentencing him to five years imprisonment, Justice Millard said,

> You are the General, the Colonel and Majors are not before the court. You know who they are and so do they ... By your actions you have ruined the lives of several of your co-defendants. Some of them weaker characters than you and lads of good character ... This was organized, planned violence which endangered life (*The Times*, 22 May 1985).

And so it began, led by a general, organized on military lines; their uniform was described in *The Times* (*ibid.*) as 'Pringle label sweaters, jeans and Nike training shoes – so they could easily identify their comrades during disorders.' 'Look-outs' were posted to seek out and divert rival fans to the pubs wherein they would run out in a 'pincer movement.' *The Times* claimed that their violence was immense, 'they caused havoc in football towns and cities throughout the country,' and, because they 'made every match day a problem,' a special team of detectives was used against them.

4. TACTICAL PERSUASIONS

Pioneered by Scotland Yard's Public Order branch, undercover operations aimed at soccer hooligans began in 1985. In some cases officers were given new identities and told to live the life of hooligans. Unfortunately some did this only too well, and in two cases which were never publicized two undercover police officers who had apparently infiltrated hooligan groups were arrested by uniformed officers (Armstrong, 1995).

The mass arrests of suspected football hooligans in dawn raids involving dozens, sometimes hundreds of police officers began in March 1986. The format was similar wherever the 'dawn swoop' was carried out – the hooligans had been 'kept under surveillance' and 'infiltrated' over varying lengths of time. Dossiers were written on various individuals regarded by police as ringleaders, many of whom initially were charged with conspiracy either to cause an affray or to commit violence. The charge was significant, showing there was no hard evidence to link individuals with any particular acts of violence.

The process of vilification and the establishment of the prisoners as the embodiment of evil could then commence. Officers on dawn raids would remove various artifacts from the accused's houses, and these would then be displayed to a compliant media who had accompanied the police. Those arrested were revealed as the generals or the notorious core hooligans.

Between them, the police and media had written the template for a script which merely required changing the name of the accused, in order that after each raid the public could be informed that the arrested had the following characteristics in common:

1. They had led at least part of a vicious gang that had caused havoc throughout Britain for months/years.
2. They had a name for their hooligan gangs, were highly organized, and organized and plotted their attacks in great detail.
3. They used calling cards (always exhibited) which they pinned on victims of their violence.
4. They used a terrifying array of weapons (always exhibited) which included not only items such as a chain-mace, shotguns, bows and arrows, but also pool cues, bread knives, carpet knives and other articles found in nearly every household in Britain.
5. They often possessed literature linking them to politically extreme-right organizations. When this could not be found and displayed, a Union Jack flag or the Cross of St. George was sufficient. With these would be displayed any photographs fans may have had of one another and scrapbooks of press cuttings related to hooligans. On one occasion, even a bottle of toilet cleaner and Leicester University's book *Hooligans Abroad* were shown to the media as incriminating proof of the owner's dangerousness.

We have chronicled elsewhere in some detail major police operations against football hooliganism (Armstrong and Hobbs, 1994). Further, it is our contention that they constitute a stunning magnification of an issue that at a time when serious criminality, for instance, in the form of the drugs and arms trades at one end of the spectrum, and the humdrum coerciveness of petty crime, vandalism and everyday incivilities at the other currently make massive demands upon police manpower and ingenuity.

5. TRYING TIMES

In May 1988, three months into the trial of 11 West Ham fans at Snaresbrook Crown Court, the Judge stopped proceedings and ordered the Jury to clear all the defendants on the charge of conspiracy to cause an affray. The charges covered a two year period from 1986–1988 formulated in part from documentary evidence seized from the fans' homes and in part from a four month undercover operation involving seven officers. The 60 hours of video evidence was of little utility. Evidence given orally contradicted the written evidence and two of the officers involved were under suspension at the time of the trial due to allegations against them regarding a pub assault. The defense brought in a retired forensic scientist who stated that pages in police log books had not been written at the same time. What was written was either untrue or inaccurate. The Judge's correction came after the prosecution offered no evidence. One of the accused, 'Cassie,' claimed afterwards that the police had 'set criminals to catch criminals, and got found out.' A week later charges were dropped against eight Chelsea fans when the defense discovered that eight pages of a police log book had been tampered with. Three of the officers involved had been part of the 'Own Goal' operation the previous year. However, the media remained impressed, 'at no time were they recognized when they infiltrated the fans again' (*Evening Standard*, 19 May 1988). This was untrue as there is some doubt about whether the police did in fact 'infiltrate' the group and, secondly, Chelsea fans knew the police officers' identities precisely, having watched court proceedings a year earlier (Fieldnotes).

In court, one youth accused of various violent offenses was rightly found not guilty. In fact the man who was really guilty had, in the early part of the trial, listened to the evidence from the public gallery, realized it was his activities that were being discussed and fled the country, only returning when the trial was over. His name differed from that of the accused by a single vowel (Fieldnotes).

After an 18-week trial which had cost over £2 million, four Chelsea fans, variously leaders of the 'Chelsea Mob' or the 'Headhunters,' were convicted of conspiracy to cause affray between January 1980 and March 1986. They were found guilty of orchestrating violence by meticulous planning, their roles being described as 'Field Marshals' who would leave the scene when the fighting began. The group were accused of using code-named travel arrangements to avoid police, as well as starting 'mock' fight decoys to draw police from an area when they would subsequently attack rival fans. The group would ambush rival fans and would leave upon their victims calling cards which stated 'You have just been nominated and dealt with by the "Chelsea Headhunters".' One of the accused was jailed for ten years along with other Chelsea fans. Justice Schofield stated: 'You were strutting about like a little tin-pot leader whose vanity and arrogance has no bounds,' and remarked that he was undoubtedly the ringleader acknowledged as such by the Chelsea mob. The *Daily Mirror* (9 May 1988) called him the 'Field Commander' who 'waged a six-year campaign of terror against other fans and innocent bystanders.'

In June 1989, in Manchester, sentence was passed on 21 men aged between 15 and 27, the charges against them varied from theft and impersonating a police officer to wounding the match referee and conspiracy to riot. Five admitted conspiracy to cause violent disorder when all charges of conspiracy to riot were dropped by the prosecution; only one had all charges against him dropped (interestingly, he was a 26-year-old probation officer). One largely unreported but important aspect of this trial was the fact that the four undercover police officers all gave evidence in Crown Court behind a screen in order to disguise their identity.

A similar trial took place in Manchester against 19 Manchester United fans. In April 1992 the High Court ruled that the prosecution could not appeal against the judge's refusal to allow undercover police to give evidence behind screens. The fans were to face charges ranging from conspiracy to riot to violent disorder. The prosecution had argued that the lives of officers would be at risk because criminals and drug dealers could sit in the courts and recognize them. In the end, however, all charges were dropped.

Those subjected to the first 'dawn swoops' were released from prison in November 1989. Three men jailed for a total of 27 years were freed when the Appeal Court ruled that the undercover police officers did not write their evidence when they claimed they had. Chief Justice Lane said their statements were falsified and unreliable and 'the creditworthiness of the officers involved in making them has been destroyed.' None of the six officers behind Own Goal were prosecuted, although the Commissioner of the Metropolitan Police, Peter Imbert, said he could 'brook no part with officers who do this.' An internal investigation by Scotland Yard did not bring about charges. The failure of the operation was blamed on 'administrative inadequacies, lack of experience and in some cases unacceptably low levels of supervision.' An article in the *Evening Standard* (17 November 1989) claimed the young officers chosen had no proper CID training, and whilst they could 'blend unobtrusively with the dangerous and vicious thugs,' they 'did not understand the vital importance of the paperwork' for a successful prosecution. The article goes on to explain how, whilst eavesdropping in noisy pubs, they could only scribble details in toilets on scraps of paper. Instead of logging this later in the station 'after working long hours in isolation they went home to their wives and families and left the notes until morning.' Details left out were later put in and their logbooks accordingly altered. To the great credit of the Met, Scotland Yard's own forensic scientists decided to check the evidence and discovered the discrepancies which caused the collapse. However, this was not all that was wrong with the police case. Photographic evidence contradicted written statements and oral evidence contradicted that written. A commander explained the unreliability of the police infiltrators' evidence by claiming they drank heavily with the group because they were unable to turn down drinks (Graef, 1989, 165–166). This was stretching credulity too far as an excuse for incorrect notebooks; after all, wasn't the police claim originally that such hooligans stayed sober to co-ordinate the troops?

One interesting account emerged which had hitherto been ignored by the media – how and what did the police infiltrators do? One of the defendants in the Operation Full-Time trial told a journalist that the plainclothes policemen who stood with them at matches urged them to 'organize bigger groups to cause violence' and added, 'They were worse than the hooligans. They wanted trouble' (*The Independent*, 28 June 1988).

One undercover operation which was relatively successful was in Leeds, West Yorkshire. Operation Wild Boar did involve the successful infiltration by police of Leeds fans: undercover officers going into pubs, to matches, and even staying the night in a flat of two of those arrested on the morning of the dawn raid. On the morning of the raid, both officers were sleeping in one of the accused's flat. In the court, the defense solicitors were suspicious of the police evidence and were particularly interested in the fact that one of the undercover officers had been arrested in the course of his work at Bradford railway station by a uniformed officer stationed locally. The arrest was genuine, with the detective taken away in a van, having a charge sheet made out and being put in a cell, until a phone call between Bradford and Leeds police stations sorted the matter out. He was not charged with any offense, although the charge sheet stated he was arrested for 'threatening behavior.' The uniformed officer, when in the dock, claimed that he arrested the detective for not having a train ticket. The defense solicitors thought this story nonsense and questioned the arresting officers at length about what the detective was really doing to merit arrest. The uniformed officer, though, stuck to his story and the truth did not come out. Later, when talking to the Leeds supporters, all were angry that the operation had been carried out against them. They maintained the undercover officers had constantly encouraged them to break away from police escorts on the way to various matches and to fight, even trying to arrange fights themselves. In court the two officers were accused by one defendant of urging violence against blacks (*The Guardian*, 20 May 1988).

The one trial that produced a large number of convictions was Operation Gamma. The result was proclaimed as one which had resulted in close liaison between carefully trained undercover officers and lawyers for the prosecution. The seven month operation put officers under 'immense personal and psychological pressure' and they had reconstructed identities which included false names, addresses and numbers in the telephone directory. Their observations were handed over to senior officers immediately after they had been written and then examined by lawyers.

6. PAYING FOR ADMISSION

The policing of football supporters is a political issue which has seen the normalization of surveillance and control without protest. When these tactics are applied to other citizens, voices are raised. During the Miners' Strike the liberal left questioned certain procedures which, when used against football supporters, produced silence. Consequently, in May 1984, the Home Office announced that the police had a right to photograph those who were detained in custody without their consent, provided they did not use force to do so. The Home Office explained that the pictures were only to establish who was arrested, where and when, and were automatically destroyed if no charges were brought. When charges were preferred, photos were destroyed after the case if requested (*The Guardian*, 21 May 1984). The collection of photographs and their circulation as 'potential troublemakers' precedes that of 1980's policing tactics for industrial disputes. In fact, police collecting 'mug shots' of suspected football hooligans for a 'rogue's gallery' was an idea not totally new to the 1980s. In the *Daily Mirror* (4 May 1973) a report told of how at two grounds in the country, Coventry and Ipswich, police were keeping photograph albums of such fans and passing them on to other police forces.

Despite Home Office safeguards, photographs of convicted and suspected hooligans are kept in police stations throughout the country. With these snapshots, usually taken secretly from a distance, are various dossiers on the individuals which are often the product of hearsay brought to the police and collated by uniformed Football Intelligence officers (Armstrong, 1995). To assist in the control of hooligans, the police have acquired a considerable array of new technology. Elements of the media went into rapture when the 'Hoolivan,' a specially equipped vehicle, was unveiled to assist crowd control outside football grounds in August 1985. In *The Sunday Times* (August 1985) an article by Roger Ratcliff described how the new surveillance could 'identify hooligans from a distance of 150 yards' (how, he did not say) and that it contained a rogue's gallery of known offenders, and pictures of 'those wanted for questioning about previous incidents'; in other words, in contravention of the 1984 commitment, photographs of those not convicted are held on police files. The article tells how the idea was developed in 1983 and tested at Chelsea in 1984 without publicity. The technological capabilities allowed the vehicle to be plugged into the closed circuit TV of football grounds and be in constant radio contact with officers inside and outside grounds.

We need note also how other surveillance was a product of private donations to the police. From the mid-1980s, various businesses financed the creation of a new morality around football. Thus banks, supermarkets, and newspapers promoted via publications and prize money the better behavior of fans. The most notable of all was the Football Trust, which gave the police millions of pounds to assist in surveillance and the building of dossiers on people. Following the closed circuit TV monitors they installed in all English Premier and First Division grounds came their financing of mobile video-recorder cameras which police used both inside and outside grounds. Thus, thousands of people are now held on police files thanks to the generosity of the 'Spot the Ball' competition companies that constitute the Trust.

Another form of surveillance is of course the deployment of plainclothes police at football grounds. Initially termed 'spotters,' these officers would travel to away games and point out 'their' hooligans to local police. This process was extended to an international context when police plainclothes 'spotters' were sent to West Germany for the 1988 European Championships to assist in the control of English hooligans. Previously they had been used for an International in Yugoslavia, funded by the Football Association.

This is of particular significance in the context of the use of both covert policing and associated surveillance tactics in other situations: Northern Ireland (Brewer & Magee, 1991; Ryder, 1989), during the Inner City riots of the early 1980s (Kettle & Hodges, 1982), and as strategic devices during the 1984–1985 Miners' Strike (Geary, 1985; Green, 1991; Samuel et al., 1986). These examples of the extension of covert policing were carried out quietly with no attempt to stress the change in emphasis of police tactics. For a while, certainly in public order operations, uniformed officers remained at the leading edge of police activity; this activity was increasingly being informed by intelligence-gathering techniques that were the antithesis of the original preventative-focused police mandate. However, the 'new police undercover work' (Marx, 1988) had yet to be sold to the general public as integral to good police practice. Sectarian strife, the eruption of urban populations and the most divisive industrial dispute of the 20th century all involved massive conflicts. Their very complex natures have led to unresolved debates, and most importantly to the role of the police being fundamentally questioned.

Football hooliganism however is a relatively non-contentious target for covert policing and it has been argued that the key to selling covert police practice as 'good' practice, thereby normalizing the concept, is the creation of the undercover cop as cultural hero (Marx, 1988, 33). The hero must face peril, and we contend that this is why covert work with organized groups of hooligans is trumpeted publicly as essentially dangerous, even while routine covert work, which is carried out quietly on less contentious targets, goes on without acclaim despite very real dangers faced by officers and even the occasional death (see Cater & Tullet, 1990, 274–285).

The success of the aforementioned covert operations against football hooligans has been varied, with many of the early covert efforts ending in stunning and embarrassing failure. The success of the more recent operations is due to the selection of charges, for it can be seen that charges of conspiracy tended to be unsuccessful in gaining a conviction, while less substantive charges got 'results.' As Marx has noted, 'the law's requirements shape police means,' and the difficulty of obtaining convictions for conspiracy led the police to turn to other legalistic means in order to gain what even politicians were regarding as a good result. As Reiner (1985, 88) has noted, 'police officers experience external pressure for "results" more or less so at different times according to particular moral panics or trends in crime statistics.' Certainly during the 1980s, with crime rising at an unprecedented rate, any political party staking claim to a law and order mandate had to be seen to be tough on crime (Crook, 1993; Downes & Ward, 1986). This was exemplified by Colin Moynihan, Minister for Sport, who stated in 1988: 'Football hooligans are worse than animals, a cancer in an otherwise healthy body.'

7. HOOLIGAN CONSPIRACIES: PLAYING AWAY

Established following the 1988 European Championships in Germany, the National Football Intelligence Unit became fully operational in March 1990. The unit consisted of six full-time police officers with a civilian employee led by a superintendent seconded from the Greater Manchester Police, a force well to the fore in anti-hooligan operations, having executed three dawn raids on local fans. The unit was given a budget of £500,000 and a job description which sought to gather hooligan and 'hooligan-related' intelligence. The information collated came from a variety of sources, primarily the local police Football Intelligence officers that follow nearly all professional football clubs. These officers were able to inform the NFIU of how the local hooligans operated and what they did. Other information came from overheard gossip and informers. All information was computerized and coded as to how reliable the unit considered the intelligence. By 1992, 6,000 names and mug-shots were held on the computer files.

The Unit was well grounded in the ideology of hierarchical conspiracy. Prior to the 1990 World Cup Finals, Superintendent Appleby, head of the Unit, told of the following impending atrocities:

> One thousand have pre-arranged a series of clashes ... two years liaising with each other ... culmination of two years planning ... apex of their hooligan careers ... arrangements are in hand to effect meetings in Sardinia ... Our intelligence is that planned violence is in the pipeline between the Dutch and English ... Terribly violent people who get a lot of pleasure out of inflicting harm on other people ... potential is pretty staggering (*ITN News*, 13 March 1990).

However, the equivalent police officer in Holland, with whom Appleby had liaised for the previous six months, knew nothing about this and was furious over this claim (Armstrong, 1994). Contacted the following day by dozens of reporters, he had to confess to knowing nothing about either the conspiracy or the announcement. Diplomatically, Chief Inspector Peter Van Essen gave the following reply in an interview with G.A.:

> We, the Dutch and English, visited each other's grounds very recently. We don't have information that the fans are having a conspiracy to create public disorder in Italy. We would like to make clear that whenever the Dutch played abroad in the last three years they behaved well and that includes games against England in West Germany and at Wembley. The British press for both games were predicting massive disorder, but nothing happened. We are trying to assist the British police to prevent anything happening. If we had knowledge about such a conspiracy it would have been used to prevent the incident happening. If I was so sure of it I would ensure I was in a position to use the information to prevent it. It should not be a matter for the media. The Dutch are convinced that information on conspiracy can only come from them and they deny all knowledge of a conspiracy. We cannot imagine what provoked the British police into saying what they did. In my opinion they have no justification. I am reluctant to link it to self-interest (Fieldnotes).

In the meantime the media caught the spirit of the day. *The Sun* in an exclusive back-page article headlined 'We'll Bomb England World Cup Fans,' added '31 days to go and the aggro has started.' Journalist Brian Woollnough told of

British police having urgent talks with the Sardinian police to prevent a 'total bloodbath' and quoted a spokesman of the Dutch Supporters Association telling of a build-up of tear gas and bombs to throw at the English in revenge for having the reputation as Europe's most fearsome fans. In response, the article told of 150 highly trained officers with machine guns from Holland going to the grounds. However, in an interview with the Dutch police we found that they had no knowledge that their officers were to attend in such large numbers or so well-armed. In fact, six unarmed officers attended the tournament (Fieldnotes).

Meanwhile the Home Secretary sent to the Italian authorities the names and photographs of 100 'hard men' English hooligans supplied by the NFIU. The Italian authorities could then decide whether to exclude those named or not. Soon after, on the night of 30 May, Superintendent Appleby announced the 'Hooligan Hotline' launched by the Home Office on British TV, manned by his Intelligence Unit and open 24 hours. Home Office Minister, Earl Ferrers, whose responsibility covered the seven-officer strong unit was quoted in *The Guardian* saying, 'I would ask anyone with information, no matter how minor or seemingly unimportant, to ring.' Callers were allowed to give information and names whilst remaining anonymous about movements, intentions and persons they knew who were attending the Finals. This was not the first time such a ploy was used. The West Midlands police had operated a similar 'hotline' in 1988 and two clubs, Manchester United and Leeds, had telephone facilities for people to ring in with knowledge of both hooligans and people who used bad language in the ground.

By coincidence, in the same issue of *The Guardian* in which the hotline was advertised (with phone numbers), the letters page contained one titled 'Safeguard for Every Citizen,' written by 12 members of 'Charter 88,' various peers, professors, solicitors and journalists (all members of the Labour Party), which sought a written Bill of Rights in which liberties would be coded in law, which arose out of, in their words, 'our faith in social justice and individual freedom; our belief in the right of the citizen against power, public or private.' This admirable quest for safeguarding liberties contrasted with their silence concerning the plight of football fans.

Meanwhile, the unit was given further publicity when the Assistant Chief Constable of Manchester, Mr. Malcolm George, Secretary of the Chief Constables Committee on Football Hooliganism was quoted as saying, 'We have a lot of good intelligence in this country about plans being made that will involve the Dutch – plans for hooligan activity' (*The Independent*, 31 May). Over 1,000 names and photos held on the unit's dossier were to be made available to the French and Italian police and to seaport and airport officials. Some of the 100 'hard men' listed were deported, even those with no criminal record. Meanwhile, as fans gathered, Superintendent Appleby told *The Sunday Times* (20 June 1990) they were now 'awaiting leadership.'

The planned showdown with the Dutch came to nothing. The claims of Superintendent Appleby were not resurrected by the media as the match passed without incident between the two sets of fans, although incidents before the game between England fans and the Italian military were ugly and regrettable (*see* Buford, 1991). The final match against the Egyptians was peaceful; the fans prepared for the next match against Belgium in Bologna.

It was before this game that the most significant incident involving England fans occurred, albeit miles away from any of the tournament's venues and days before a match. England fans staying in the resort of Rimini before their match against Belgium in Bologna were involved in skirmishes with Italian youths. Riot police moved in to tear-gas a crowded bar, beat those who ran out seeking refuge and then arrested and deported any Englishman they could find. The Rimini deportations brought both praise and condemnation and became, to an extent, a party-political issue. The Shadow Sports Minister, Denis Howell, protested that 'we should not convict by mass libel of this sort people who claim they are innocent and haven't been given the opportunity to prove it.' The reply of Sports Minister Moynihan was that Howell 'has echoed the plea of the louts who comprise the football effluent tendency.' Innocent people were arrested and deported, their crime that of being English, in bars or streets two miles away from where the incident took place. They were deported without being allowed to pick up luggage and, in some cases, passports. On arrival at Gatwick Airport, they were photographed without their consent by police officers of the NFIU and the photographs and personal details were placed on the police computer. The information was then sent by police to local newspapers in the areas where the fans had given their address so further condemnation and shame could be written without proof of guilt. None were charged with any crime but all were subject to deportation orders which banned them from returning to Italy. One month later, the Italian authorities rescinded the orders. There was no evidence to suggest that any of these events was a product of organized violence and hierarchical leadership.

That this deportation was calculated by the Italian and British police was almost certainly proven when the defense committee for the deported fans found that the plane that brought them to England had been chartered in advance and was detained in Rimini until sufficient fans to fill its seats had been arrested. As a result, while some were detained overnight, 25 more were arrested in hotels the next morning to achieve a total of 237 – exactly the number of seats available on the plane. Mr Howell stated bluntly, 'I think Scotland Yard police, under the orders of the Government in the shape of Colin Moynihan, had organized it with the Italian police' (*Footie Magazine*, August 1990). Confusion reigned. A total of 60 English fans had been arrested in Italy and over 300 deported. But less than one month later, Mr. Johanssen, President of UEFA, said after an Executive Committee meeting which allowed English clubs back into European competition, 'I think isolation is not a good thing ... English fans are no worse than others.'

The police have persisted with their model of hierarchical hooliganism and continued also the pursuit of the conspiracy theory. In November 1990, police revealed to a committee of MP's a 'Mafia-style command system running football violence in Britain.' This is very significant because it illustrates how, despite the collapse of the show trials and the absence of any evidence to support their script, the police can still sing the same song without being questioned. Every submission to the Committee from various police representatives had elements of the organized/hierarchical gang construct. The NFIU submission was more extreme, telling of hooligan 'status' being gained by attacking rivals and police, acting boisterously in motorway cafes, urinating on food in pubs, and pulling up or down women's clothing. As for organizations, such gangs had various 'post-holders,' including intelligence officers, photographers, armor and transport managers, all in a 'dedicated and highly disciplined central command.'

Away from football such people commit offenses to finance their football activities. Interestingly, details of the NFIU's computer information were revealed. With over 6,000 names of 'hooligans' it is interesting to note that the offenses that brought them to the attention of the unit are just over 1,500 for violence, yet over 4,000 for non-violent offenses including drugs (470), fraud (446), auto-crime (497) and others (747). What the latter four offenses have to do with football hooliganism is a mystery. Not a scrap of evidence was produced to substantiate these claims. Yet the document *Policing Football Hooliganism* produced by the Home Affairs Committee is now the latest word on the subject. The British police in this document recommend to European police readers that they learn by example how to deal with the problem.

In January 1991 a conference audience in London were addressed by two members of the NFIU about the hooligans' domestic and international activities. Superintendent Appleby reiterated his unit's knowledge of hooligans in 'organized, dedicated teams of violence' who carry Stanley knives which are 'used all the time' and told of the 'new weapons' in their arsenal which included cattle prods which give a high voltage electric shock. Where and when this latter, potentially lethal weapon had ever been used he did not say (Fieldnotes).

Expanding on the conspiracy between the Dutch and English supporters, Mr. Appleby told the conference that there were four hooligan conferences – two in Walsall, one in Victoria, London, the other in Tenerife. The first, in Walsall, involved hooligans from twelve clubs with two representatives each. All stayed one night in a hotel and took in a local match as part of the discussions. In both cases he claimed to have officers on the spot who knew what was being planned. Later there was a meeting in Victoria, London between 'twelve hooligans of Utrecht and London thugs,' but then 'so paranoid about secrecy were the hooligans that as a result the next meeting was in Tenerife.' However he did not say if this involved the Dutch; in fact there were no details at all about this meeting.

The Superintendent continued, 'I deliberately went public, and took a chance and told them what was going on. It worked. Once they knew I knew they changed their plans.' We were never told what the plans were (*see* also HAC, 1990, 26, 32 & 46, 36). It has been impossible for us to verify the existence of either these meetings or the consequences. We did learn however that Tenerife was brought to the notice of the police at Christmas 1989 when twelve fans who had met over the years following England went away for a week's holiday. As part of their fun they sent a postcard to the police (Fieldnotes).

More was to follow in August 1992. A national, 24 hour 'Hooligan Hotline' was established by the unit, which was now incorporated into the new National Criminal Intelligence Service. We can only speculate on whether this was a response to a 21 per cent rise in football-related offenses in the 1991–1992 season, the first rise in four years. Later still, the unit found a new *raison d'être*, in December 1992. It established what one journalist called a 'Special Task Force' to curtail the new Nazi hooliganism in Britain, and examine their links with European counterparts (*The Mail on Sunday*, 13 December 1992). We soon learned that the hooligan had turned his attention to rape and armed robbery (*Sunday Times*, 27 December 1992). We await with interest evidence to emerge to support these claims. When it does emerge we will have to deal with the problem of whether to define these criminals as organized rapists or organized football hooligans.

8. CONCLUSION

Via football hooliganism the British police have been able to introduce and normalize covert tactics and strategies of surveillance, which in other settings would have inspired widespread condemnation. Despite the traditional antipathy to covert policing in Britain, the creation of a moral panic around the phenomenon of soccer-related disorder served to market a solution that, as we have indicated above, has symbolic rather than pragmatic utility (Manning, 1977). Whilst this is accepted and is not a political issue when imposed upon football supporters, when applied to other sections of society moral indignation sets in.[2]

The British police were sent reeling in the 1980s and early 1990s by a series of highly publicized miscarriages of justice. Morale has been affected and public confidence damaged. By locating and vigorously concentrating their efforts on relatively soft targets as football hooligans, a few safe results can be gained. But only at massive cost in terms of time, money and resources. The police as an institution have status, and the manner in which they define a situation is taken as authoritative by many politicians and news editors. As Douglas (1987, 92) explains, organizations 'channel our perceptions into forms compatible with the situations they authorize,' 'endowed with a rightness' and 'narcissistic self-contemplation,' offering solutions based only on the 'limited range of their own experiences' which in the case of the policing of our national sport means more control, greater power, and more surveillance. The form of policing that we have described consequently serves more than merely symbolic functions.

Discipline, to borrow from Foucault (1977), can be imposed by three principal methods: hierarchical observation, normalizing judgement, and examination. With the introduction of hoolivans, CCTV and hand-held cameras, heralded as a 'good thing' and a 'cure' and financed by private pressure groups, surveillance has been normalized. The population at large has welcomed the movement because, obviously, if you are doing nothing wrong you have nothing to fear. But when the 'Hoolivans' and the videos are used on other groups in society, will it be too late to ask questions concerning civil liberties, and the

---

2. In December 1990, plainclothes police officers were sent to stand incognito in pubs in Humberside. Three other forces, Bedford, Dorset and Dumfries and Galloway publicized freephone telephone lines along which observers would inform on law breakers. The issue in question was drunk driving, an extension of tactics of covert policing to a more serious but more widely committed offense. Despite drunk driving killing 800 people annually in Britain an editorial of *The Independent* found the tactics troubling, and called it an unnecessary, big brother, police state activity.

privatization of law and order? The use of surveillance and computer-held intelligence should be of concern to everyone. Yet the policing of football leads us to question what actually constitutes 'intelligence.'

'Intelligence,' as Campbell (1980, 87) noted, can be nothing more than gossip (*see* also Ackroyd *et al.*, 1977, 151–196; Bunyan, 1976, 74–101; Mainwaring-White, 1984). When profiles of individuals are held by the NFIU because the person is 'known to keep the company of hooligans,' we have entered a danger zone that threatens to affect societal groups other than the terrible, tattooed, effluent tendency.

The motivation for targeting hooligans relates to their position as a sub-group of society who, unlike for instance black youth or strident trade unions, would be unlikely to gather sympathy from any source. For instance, the Football Supporters Act 1991 introduced three offenses specific to football grounds – throwing missiles, racist chanting and running onto the pitch. All three of these offenses were more than adequately dealt with by existing legislation (Public Order Act 1985, Sections 1–5). Police officers had utilized this legislation at soccer matches with no specific problems in gaining convictions. The law, therefore, is used in this context as a symbolic device for indicating the strategic intent of government to locate and isolate a societal group already marginalized by their behavior. The pragmatic reality of promulgating a law that has no actual effect in terms of prevention, arrest or conviction, is of secondary consideration to the public relations benefits gained from talking tough about crime.

Aided by electronic evidence (Marx, 1988, 134–135), computerized predictive profiles (often based on non-criminal data), the use of private resources (provision of electronic equipment and funding police officers for overseas trips), a moral order is created based on an a-historical notion of post-traditional leisure pursuits (*see* F.A. Blueprint for Football, 1991).

As Marx (1988, 57) has noted, the new surveillance is highly supportive of 'stage management and scripted scenarios' and the dramatized context of soccer matches is difficult to ignore. It constitutes in many ways a Hollywood-type film set for the performance of both hooliganism and covert policing. Complete with cameras, microphones, monitoring screens, playback facilities, producers, directors and the full galaxy of major and minor actors, from extras (uniformed police, non-violent spectators) to stars (undercover police and 'top' hooligans). This is real method acting with a backdrop as purpose-built as any film set, a cast of thousands and the occasional corpse to provide narrative focus.

REFERENCES

Ackroyd, C., Margolis, J., Rosenhead, J., Shallice, T. (1977), *The Technology of Police Control*, Harmondsworth, Penguin.

Armitage, G. (1937), *The History of the Bow Street Runner 1729–1829*, London, Wishart.

Armstrong, G. (1995), *Fists and Style; An Ethnography of Football Hooligans*, University College London, Department of Anthropology, unpublished PhD thesis.

Armstrong, G., Hobbs, D. (1994), 'Tackled from Behind,' in: Guilianotti, R., Bonney, N., Hepworth, M., eds., *Football Violence*, London, Routledge.
Ascoli, D. (1979), *The Queen's Peace*, London, Hamilton.
Blueprint for Football, London, Football Association.
Bordua, D. (1967), *The Police; Six Sociological Essays*, New York, NY, Wiley.
Brewer, J.D., Magee, K. (1990), *Inside the RUC*, Oxford, Oxford University Press.
Buford, B. (1991), *Among the Thugs*, London, Secker and Warburg.
Bunyan, T. (1977), *The History and Practice of the Political Police in Britain*, London, Quartet.
Bunyan, T. (1977), *The Political Police in Britain*, London, Julian Friedman.
Campbell, D. (1980), 'Society Under Surveillance,' in: Hain, P., ed., *Policing the Police*, London, Calder, vol. 2.
Cater, F., Tullet, T. (1990), *The Sharp End*, London, Grafton.
Chibnall, S. (1977), *Law and Order News*, London, Tavistock.
Clarkson, C.T., Hall-Richardson, J. (1889), *The Police*, London, Leadenhall Press.
Coalter, F. (1984), *Crowd Behaviour at Football Matches; A Study in Scotland*, Edinburgh, Centre for Leisure Research.
Cook, B. (1978), 'Football Crazy?,' *New Society*, 15 June.
Critchley, T. (1978), *A History of Police in England and Wales 1900–1966*, London, Constable (1st edition).
Croker, T. (1987), *The First Voice You Will Hear Is ...*, London, Collins Willow.
Crook, F. (1993), 'One brutal exception does not prove the rule,' *The Independent*, 23 February.
Dandeker, S. (1989), *Surveillance, Power and Modernity*, London, Polity.
Dilnot, G. (1929), *Scotland Yard*, London, Geoffrey Bles.
Douglas, M. (1987), *How Institutions Think*, London, Routledge.
Downes, D., Ward, T. (1986), *Democratic Policing*, London, Labour Campaign for Criminal Justice.
Foucault, M. (1977), *Discipline and Punish; The Birth of the Prison*, New York, Pantheon.
Geary, R. (1985), *Policing Industrial Disputes*, Cambridge, Cambridge University Press.
Graef, R. (1989), *Talking Blues; The Police in Their Own Words*, London, Fontana.
Green, P. (1991), *The Enemy Without; Policing and Class Consciousness in the Miners' Strike*, Milton Keynes, Open University Press.
Hall, S., Clarke, J., Critcher, C., Jefferson, T., Roberts, B. (1978), *Policing the Crisis*, London, Macmillan.
Hillyard, P. (1981), 'From Belfast to Britain,' in: *Politics and Power 4: Law, Politics and Justice*, London, Routledge.
Hobbs, D. (1988), *Doing the Business*, Clarendon Press, Oxford.
Home Affairs Committee (1991), *Policing Football Hooliganism*, London, HMSO.
Lettle, M., Hodges, L. (1982), *Uprising*, London, Pan.
Manning, P. (1980), *The Narcs' Game*, Cambridge Mass., MIT.

Manning, P. (1977), *Police Work*, Cambridge Mass., MIT.
Manwaring-White, S. (1984), *The Policing Revolution*, Brighton, Harvester.
Marx, G.T. (1988), *Undercover; Police Surveillance in America*, Berkeley, California, University of California Press.
Miller, W. (1977), *Cops and Bobbies*, Chicago, Ill., Cambridge University Press.
Notham, G. (1988), *Shooting in the Dark*, London, Faber.
Prothero, M. (1931), *The History of the Criminal Investigation Department at Scotland Yard*, London, Herbert Jenkins.
Radzinowicz, L. (1956), *A History of the English Criminal Law and its Administration*, London, Stevens, vol. 3.
Reiner, R. (1978), *The Politics of the Police*, Brighton, Wheatsheaf Books.
Reith, Ch. (1956), *A New Study of Police History*, London, Oliver & Boyd.
Ryder, C. (1989), *A Force Under Fire*, London, Methuen.
Samuel, R., Bloomfield, B., Boanas, G. (1986), *The Enemy Within*, London, Routledge.
Sherman, L.W., ed. (1974), *Police Corruption*, New York, NY, Anchor.
Silver, A. (1967), 'The Demand for Order in Civil Society,' in: Bordua, D. (1967).
Smith, M. (1986), *Violence in Sport*, Toronto, Butterworth.
Smith, M. (1975), 'Sport and collective violence,' in: Ball, D.W., Loy, J.W., eds., *Sport and Social Order; Contributions to the Sociology of Sport*.
Styles, J. (1987), 'The Emergence of the Police – Explaining Police Reform in Eighteenth and Nineteenth Century England,' *British Journal of Criminology*, 27, 1, 15–22.
Trivizas, E. (1980), 'Offences and Offenders in Football Crowd Disorders,' *British Journal of Criminology*, 276–288.
Trivizas, E. (1981), 'Sentencing and the Football Hooligan,' *British Journal of Criminology*, 342–349.

Michael Levi*

Covert Policing and the Investigation of 'Organized Fraud': The English Experience in International Context

1. INTRODUCTION

In this article, I will try to confront what I see as a paradox: the U.K. has liberal *law* relating to undercover work, yet outside the drugs arena and intelligence-gathering, little undercover work occurs. I will start by discussing the legal framework, and then go on to discuss the background to what in many respects is a non-topic in U.K. practice: the use of covert operations in U.K. white-collar crime investigations. However, what is meant by 'covert policing'? Do we mean the active deception in which 'the crooks' unknowingly have contact with 'the goodies' or their representatives (e.g. sting operations, or deep cover ones)? Or does it include the passive deception (without direct offender/police contact) involved in surveillance, including telephone tapping, and the obtaining of information about suspects' financial dealings without their knowledge, for example by accessing bank accounts (*see* Levi, 1991, 1993)? To include in the definition of 'covert policing' *all* 'tricks' by the police – for example their pretense that they know things they do not – would be too wide for all but the most earnest civil libertarians, for it would include almost all 'competent' policing.

2. ENGLISH LAW AND UNDERCOVER WORK

It would be fetishistic in the extreme to regard the analysis of 'black-letter' rules as an index of police practice. Nevertheless, most sociology of law (e.g. Cotterrell, 1992) now recognizes that practice is shaped by, as well as shapes, law. This article shares the view of Marx (1988) that the law of entrapment is one of the principal issues that undercover operations confront, since given the

---

* Professor of Criminology, University of Wales College of Cardiff, Cardiff, Wales, United Kingdom. The author wishes to thank Mike Maguire and Al Reiss for their comments on an earlier version of this paper.

expense of undercover operations, it is only if the evidence they obtain will be (i) legally *admissible*, and (ii) legally *acceptable*, that such operations will be mounted (there are exceptions to this, where information may be collected by police officers or by private detectives for intelligence, for blackmail or simply to inconvenience and/or discredit).

2.1. Provocation and Entrapment

In the English context, though there does not appear to be any legal definition, an *agent provocateur* is 'a person who entices another to commit an express breach of the law which he would not otherwise have committed and then proceeds or informs against him in respect of such offences' (Royal Commission on Police Powers and Procedure, 1929). However, this begs the key question of what counts as provocation. In *Brannan* v. *Peek* [1948] 1 KB 68, the Lord Chief Justice stated that 'the court observes with concern and with strong disapproval that the police authority at Derby apparently thought it right ... to send a police officer into a public house for the purpose of committing an offence [of offering a bet to a bookmaker] in that house,' and continued with a strong declaration of opposition to such practices without specific Parliamentary provision.

Two cases in 1974 held that although provocation was salient to sentence (as mitigation), it did not affect guilt or innocence (in law). However, its relevance to the admissibility of evidence is more open. In *R.* v. *Burnett and Lee* [1973] Crim.L.R. 748, one of the defendants charged with conspiracy to utter forged banknotes gave evidence that a police informer named Edith had persistently urged him for some two months to obtain forged U.S. dollar bills which eventually led to his obtaining them from his co-defendant. Edith had not given evidence for the prosecution and did not give evidence in rebuttal. The trial judge directed an acquittal on the general ground of unfairness. English law clearly states, however, that there is no general defense of entrapment, and the English Law Commission (1977, 47) recommended that there *ought not* to be any such defense: 'a defence of entrapment where the inducement alleged is solely that of the police or informers corresponds with no moral distinction in his behaviour.' This is consistent with the general reluctance of English lawyers to use the exclusionary rule as a way of disciplining police behavior (*see* e.g. the Royal Commission on Criminal Procedure, 1981, and its eventual translation into the Police and Criminal Evidence Act 1984 for further illustration of this). The Law Commission noted that administrative circulars by the Home Office – though producing a risk of disciplinary action against officers – were unlikely to be effective, not least because they did not apply to informants (it might have added non-police agencies such as H.M. Customs & Excise or the Inland Revenue to the list of the unaffected).

Entrappers can themselves be prosecuted as accomplices, and the residual right of private prosecution exists in the Prosecution of Offences Act 1985, in case the entrapped wish to prosecute them. However, the Law Commission (1977, 50) asserted that:

however undesirable the methods used in particular instances of entrapment may be, we cannot think it right that a trapper who, for example, succeeds in entrapping drug pushers should lay himself open to a penalty of fourteen years in prison, since his activities are, after all, aimed at stultifying the offence.

Note here the reference to drug trafficking – the commonly agreed serious offense – to justify the line taken. The Law Commission went on to recommend the creation of an offense of entrapment, which 'would penalise anyone who takes the initiative in instigating or persuading another person to commit an offence, even though he intends that that person should be prevented from successfully carrying it out' (p. 52).

Typically, no legislation has followed the Law Commission report. However, the House of Lords ruled in *Sang* (1979) 69 Cr.App.R. 282: 'whatever be the ambit of the judicial discretion to exclude admissible evidence, it does not extend to excluding evidence of a crime because the crime was instigated by an agent provocateur.' In that case, the accused was charged with conspiracy to utter forged banknotes. His argument – which was rejected – was that evidence against him had been obtained by an *agent provocateur* and that this should be excluded: had this been accepted, it would almost certainly have resulted in his acquittal. However subsequently, the Police and Criminal Evidence Act 1984 regulated more closely interviews by the police, and widened the scope of the judicial discretion to exclude evidence improperly obtained (Zander, 1991). In *Edwards* [1991] Crim.L.R. 45, the Court held that section 78 was not applicable to evidence obtained by an undercover agent precisely *because* he was *not* an *agent provocateur*, since the continuing conspiracy to supply drugs was already being committed when he intervened. In *Bainbridge* [1991] Crim.L.R. 535, the Court of Appeal upheld the conviction of a man for soliciting the murder of his wife. There, an undercover agent posed as a contract killer, after the man – who had no previous convictions – let it be known to an acquaintance that he was seeking to have his wife killed. He then asked the undercover officer to murder his wife.

The most intriguing case in recent years has been a British sting operation called Operation Herring, *Christou and Wright* [1992] 3 WLR 228. There, the Court of Appeal in 1992 rejected the defense claim that the establishment in 1990 of a false jewellery shop which netted over 40 burglars and robbers in a high-crime division of North London was an improper means of obtaining evidence and constituted entrapment. Previously, the British police had adopted a very conservative approach to sting operations, being concerned that they would be viewed by the courts as unfair (or even 'unBritish'!). However, concerned about the high level of street robberies and burglaries in some ethnically 'sensitive' parts of North London, the Metropolitan Police (in consultation with the local Crown Prosecution Service) decided to set up a three-month experiment in which they rented a jewellery shop – staffed by one Jewish and one Asian police officer who were trained by jewellers prior to the operation – and bought a home opposite from which videotaping and surveillance could take place. They did not advertise formally but simply opened up for business and, at the end of the operation, arrested over 40 people – those against whom they had the most clear-cut evidence of 'guilty knowledge' that they were selling the proceeds of crime – for burglary, robbery, and handling stolen goods. After the test case, most have pleaded guilty.

Lord Chief Justice Taylor set out the parameters of acceptable practice (at least in this sort of operation) as follows:

> The police were clearly engaged in a trick or deceit. However, they did not themselves participate in the commission of any offence; nor did they act as 'agents provocateurs' or incite crime. The offences charged had already been committed before the appellants entered the shop and the police, so far from having any dishonest intent, were concerned to return the property to its rightful owners and bring offenders to justice. The police referred daily to the current price of gold announced by Johnson Matthey and pitched the prices they offered appropriately to the form of dealing in which they purported to be engaged. So, no market was provided which would not have been available elsewhere ... It is not every trick producing evidence against an accused which results in unfairness ... In [other cases where convictions were quashed] the defendant was in police custody at a police station. Officers lied to both the defendant and his solicitor ... We agree that the operation should be treated as a whole (p. 232).

The Court concluded that the rules requiring a caution to be administered before suspects are questioned about an offense did not apply to this sting. There was no pressure by the undercover agents on the accused, nor did the officers really ask questions about the offenses, except insofar as the officers asked what areas should be avoided in reselling the goods (to maintain their cover and enable the goods to be returned to their owners). It dismissed the argument that the shop was contrary to public policy by enabling the offenders to continue offending until the time when the 'front' was disbanded, observing (p. 238):

> Clearly, it must be a matter for policy and operational decision by the police as to how they reconcile and balance the need on the one hand to bring an individual offender swiftly to book and deter crime, and on the other, the desirability of apprehending a larger number of offenders and recovering property.

In short, there remains general judicial disapproval of entrapment, but there is a very fudged line about what 'entrapment' constitutes! The line appears to be drawn at the point when individual accused might have been provoked to commit acts which otherwise they would not have done: that is partly a predictive position in relation to which the psychological propensities of the individuals involved appears irrelevant.

Subsequent to *Christou and Wright*, the Court of Appeal quashed the conviction in *R. v. P. Bryce* [1992] Crim.L.R. 728 of a man who had bought a supposedly stolen car stereo from an undercover officer. The latter had called him on his portable phone and – unrecorded – claimed that the appellant had deactivated the alarm and removed the coded stereo from the car; had refused to answer questions on tape at the police station; but after the tape had been switched off, had made admissions. The man was convicted after the trial judge refused to exclude the evidence. The Court held that the conversations were a blatant attempt to circumvent the Code of Practice on police interrogations, and since there was no corroboration (as there had been in the taped sting), the evidence should have been excluded. So long as the undercover agent confines himself to negotiating a new transaction, s/he is on the right side of the law. However, once the officer begins to ask questions about the transaction of which evidence is sought, legal difficulties begin unless – as in the jewellery sting – the court concludes that the questions were necessary to the undercover operation. It is also legally easier if the criminals come to the undercover agents rather than the other way around. In cases that involve less active deception by undercover agents – for example leaving open the backs of trucks and then arresting those who steal from them – the courts have recently shown considerable tolerance: enticing is clearly different from entrapment!

Although the *Burnett and Lee* forgery case referred to earlier is the only *white-collar* entrapment one that I have found on appeal – and it is more blue-collar than elite crime – judicial tolerance is susceptible to shifts in judicial attitude to crime seriousness. Judicial views about money laundering and white-collar crime have hardened considerably over the past decade (Levi, 1987, 1991), and though this might not lead judges actually to *approve* of entrapment, it might make them more tolerant of it. On the other hand, if judges begin to perceive that the police are abusing their powers, this could lead to a reining in, especially in the white-collar arena (*see* the overview of law and practice in serious fraud investigations by Levi, 1993).

2.2. Disclosure Rules

The other major strand of the law of evidence that is relevant to the issue of covert policing is the question of disclosure to the defense of information relevant to their work. This is a major area of controversy which has been considered by the Royal Commission on Criminal Justice (forthcoming). There are essentially two disclosure obligations on the prosecution at common law: the duty to ensure that the defense is supplied with material relevant to the credibility of a prosecution witness; and the duty to provide to the defense particulars of potential witnesses whose evidence might be material to the defense case. In the light of concern during the 1990s about police misconduct, these rules have been interpreted with increasing rigor. Thus in *Edwards* (1991) 93 Cr. App. R. 48, the Court of Appeal held that the defense was entitled to cross-examine prosecution witnesses (who were police officers) not only about disciplinary findings made against them but also about any earlier trial in which a jury had rejected their evidence in circumstances indicating that they were not believed. In that case the defendant alleged that his 'confession' had been fabricated.

As for people who were not prosecution witnesses, *Bryant and Dickson* (1946) 31 Cr. App. R. 146 held that it was 'the duty of the prosecution ... to make available to the defence a witness whom the prosecution know can, if he is called, give material evidence,' but this left to the judgment of the prosecution the question of whether a witness could give material evidence. However, this was criticized as being too discretionary, and in 1981 the Attorney-General published *Guidelines for the disclosure of 'unused material' to the defence in cases to be tried on indictment* [1982] 1 All ER 734, which are still in force. In the first fraud trial relating to the takeover of Distillers by Guinness, Mr. Justice Henry ruled that not only signed final statements but also all previous draft statements made by witnesses and suspects (on tape, computer or handwritten) and investigators' notes had to be disclosed to the defense, and that any failure to observe those rules would count as a material irregularity which 'would be capable of being the basis for a successful appeal against conviction.' The effect of this was to make it potentially riskier for the police to hide the source of any information covertly obtained. For in *Bolton Justices ex parte Scally* (1991) 2 All ER 619, the Divisional Court held that 'the prosecution' included the police. Similarly, the final judgment of the Court of Appeal in the 'IRA bombing' case involving 'the Maguire Seven' [1992] 2 All ER 433 regarded the prosecution's duty of disclosure to extend to the notes of forensic scientists: by this logic, the notes of accountants employed by the investigation agency should become available to the defense. It is now Home Office policy that the defense should be told the previous disciplinary records of police officers giving evidence.

It is agreed that only the defense can tell whether information is relevant to the defense, but the prosecutor (and, indirectly, the police) still has the responsibility to decide whether unused documents are 'capable of having an impact on the evidence of the case.' One reason why the police are particularly concerned about this issue is that disclosure is a method by which the defense can excavate their investigation and discover what information was in their possession and whether there were any informants in the case. Since informants are an important source of clearing up serious crimes for gain and are viewed very protectively by detectives – to the extent of their not calling them but rather providing some false (or no) explanation as to how they came to suspect the accused persons – disclosure rules open up Pandora's Box. From the defense viewpoint, such tactics can legitimately be a method of uncovering potential participating informants and *agents provocateurs*: one powerful illustration was in a prosecution of an alleged heroin dealer in 1993, where the defense convinced the jury (who were unanimous) that a former mercenary and convicted blackmailer, John Banks, had 'set up' the accused, persuading him that he was working with Customs as part of an official sting operation against others while in fact he was being placed in criminal jeopardy (*The Observer*, 11 April 1993). Without independent evidence of what was said or not said, professional participating informants may implicate the innocent in this way.[1]

---

1. Home Office guidelines state: 'No public informant should counsel, incite or procure the commission of a crime. When an informant gives the police information about the intention of others to commit a crime in which they intend he shall play a part, his participation should be allowed to continue only where (i) he does not actively engage in planning and committing the crime; (ii) he is intended to play only a minor role; and (iii) his participation is essential to enable the police to frustrate the principal criminals and to arrest them ... [T]he police must never commit themselves to a course which, whether to protect an informant or otherwise, will constrain them to mislead a court in any subsequent proceedings.'

Disclosures can also be used to put pressure on the prosecution to drop a case rather than reveal the fact that informants were involved (the mere fact that defendants know that an informant is involved can point to whom it was, leading the police sometimes to produce an artificial reason for collapsing the case).

3. THE CONTEXTS OF POLICE UNDERCOVER WORK

Marx (1988, 62) observes that there are a number of types of police undercover work:

(1) Intelligence operations, in which agents are relatively passive, though they may need to participate in crime in order to gain credibility. Such operations can be *after* or *before* a particular crime. The Internal Revenue Service (IRS) gained access to a taxpayer's books by posing as a potential buyer of his business. When asked to justify this, he said: 'We are not inducing anybody to break the law. The tax returns have already been filed, and the crime has already been committed long before we've come around.' But such *ex post* investigations are relatively rare: *anticipatory* undercover operations are much more common. This can involve the creation of false fronts, in the classic sting operation mode (though it is arguable that apparent 'equal justice' legitimates capitalism, those who might suspect that white-collar stings could be used as a method of legitimising the tactic to penetrate poor neighborhoods should note that historically, the process was the other way around: U.S. investigators adapted to white-collar crime the method first used on the poor).
(2) Such operations can also be used to *prevent* crimes from taking place, or for educational purposes: the U.S. Postal Inspection Service (p. 65) placed via an alias enticing advertisements offering an easy way to earn money or to lose weight. People who responded received politely worded letters advising them that they ought to be more careful about offers that sound too good to be true, and containing stamps for the postage expended and a booklet on mail fraud schemes.
(3) Facilitative operations, in which the agent is either victim or co-conspirator. In the white-collar arena, the classic examples of this are in money-laundering investigations or cases such as those in which a professional confidence trickster allegedly involved former General Motors executive John De Lorean – who was suspected, *inter alia*, of defrauding the Northern Ireland Development Agency of millions of pounds[2] – in a purchase of large amounts of cocaine to pay off his debts. De Lorean was acquitted.

---

2. During 1992, a senior executive of De Lorean, Fred Bushell, was imprisoned after pleading guilty to his part in this massive fraud. The statute of limitations means that De Lorean himself cannot be tried in relation to these allegations, but the civil litigation continues.

4. COVERT INVESTIGATIONS OF WHITE-COLLAR CRIME IN AMERICA

Before Watergate, the American approach to investigating white-collar crime was not unlike that of the U.K. It had a very low priority in police terms. Undercover investigations – except against 'political subversives' – were greatly deprecated by Hoover, though Nixon allegedly used the Internal Revenue Service to investigate his political opponents and turn a blind eye to his political and financial friends (Block, 1990). However, post-Watergate, the FBI started to take white-collar crime very seriously and though most investigations remained reactive, it decided in 1978 to tackle political corruption by planting an undercover agent as an Arab head of Abdul Enterprises, and spread the word that the 'sheikh' needed help on immigration. A professional confidence trickster of some notoriety was employed on the government payroll as undercover agent, to look for legislators who would help the sheikh with work permits. This led to successful prosecutions of 6 Congressmen and one Senator, and a lot of publicity. In 1973, the FBI mounted 53 undercover investigations; in 1980, there were 300, mainly in 'kickback' cases involving the underworld, but some 'upmarket' white-collar cases too. As always, there were problems: in Operation Corkscrew, an undercover con man gave $100,000 of FBI money in bribes to someone posing as a 'judge,' who was actually a friend of his, and ran off with the money.

Technological improvements in audio- and video-recording encouraged the development of this methodology, which was used in Operation Greylord to try to crack the corrupt state level judiciary and public officials in Cook County, Illinois. By 1983, this operation had netted only nine people – three judges, three lawyers, and three 'bagmen' – but the FBI and prosecutors hailed it as a major breakthrough nonetheless. However, through the same process observed in later insider dealing cases, those charged in the first round plea bargained with their colleagues' liberty in the next round, and altogether, nine judges, 37 lawyers, and 19 police and clerks were convicted in Greylord (there have been more convictions subsequently, and trials are still going on).

In 1984, a major commodities producer with a grievance against the Chicago Board of Trade was referred by the Chicago Futures Trade Commission to the FBI. The moral entrepreneurial ambience for criminal investigation was right. As one investigator expressed it (Greising and Morse, 1991, 183):

> We were being told that if you were an honest man in the pits, you couldn't make it because nobody would deal with you ... Nobody believed me, until this guy showed up.

The FBI then set up a meeting with the U.S. Attorney for approval to organize an undercover operation in the commodities exchange (by the time the case came to trial in 1989, the same U.S. Attorney was defense lawyer to the first person to plead guilty in the prosecution, and advised the Chicago Board of Trade on its defense to racketeering charges). The operation required a major financial investment by the FBI: a $300,000 seat on the Exchange, a Mercedes, subscription to a fashionable exercise club, and even a Rolex! The project went through a local undercover review board, the Agent in Charge, a national undercover panel, and finally was signed by the FBI Director. Unlike the usual white-collar sting operations, this did not have the problem of disreputable prosecution witnesses that bedevilled a number of trials (Marx, 1988). It was only a slight complicating factor that the commodities producer, ADM, was fined $50,000 (reduced on appeal to $25,000) for refusing to give evidence in a disciplinary hearing for manipulating the soyabean-oil market (the charges that gave rise to the refusal were dismissed later for lack of evidence).

The agents were chosen from a pool of 8,000 who volunteered for undercover assignments. But the FBI decided that to avoid charges of favoritism on behalf of the Chicago Mercantile Exchange, which had just as bad a reputation, it would have to mount a parallel sting there also. They found a sponsor for their FBI agents in a disillusioned older broker there. The agents had a six-week general undercover training course, but for the specific area of work, they had just three afternoons of classroom instruction on the futures business. The 1987 stock market crash led one agent to lose $30,000 in trading, plus the general costs of dealing.

One trader frisked the FBI people for hidden recorders but found nothing, since the whole room was bugged. After a lengthy enquiry, which was terminated when information began to leak, the FBI issued 500 subpoenas, conducted well over 500 interviews, and reviewed more than a million documents. 1,275 pages of charges and 608 counts were issued against 46 defendants. However, no major exchange names were indicted, and the amounts of money involved in the alleged frauds – some of which were as low as $12.50 – were not aggregated, assisting the defense claims that the prosecutors were scraping the bottom of the barrel in order to justify themselves. Those unlucky enough to have traded with the agents found themselves indicted, some with as many as 96 counts: it is not only the English Serious Fraud Office which is accused of over-charging (Levi, 1993)!

When the indictments were issued, some went for plea bargains and co-operated with the government; others fought. In the trials, however, which started nine months after the indictments, things became less clear-cut. Audiotapes turned out to be far more ambiguous and inaudible than the FBI believed – there were sometimes significant disparities in defense and prosecution versions – and agents' discretion in when to turn them on was used by the defense to allege selective bias, which argument found favor with some jurors (similar issues arose in other unsuccessful prosecutions using professional confidence tricksters as undercover informants).

Covert tape-recording by participating informants was also used in the series of insider trading investigations (Levine, 1992; Stewart, 1992), and the interview transcripts make it clear that the questions asked by people such as Boesky were aimed to get their business colleagues to implicate themselves. These occurred in the context of criminal conspiracies already known (in general terms) to the Department of Justice, where the informants were seeking to obtain credit for use in sentencing proceedings.

MICHAEL LEVI

5. COVERT POLICING OF WHITE-COLLAR CRIME IN BRITAIN

In many countries, the amount of police attention to white-collar crimes, whether *by* or *against* corporations, is very low (Levi, 1987). In spite of their surprisingly high seriousness ratings, crimes involving organizations rank low in the priorities of populist law and order. Under these conditions, an uneasy friendship develops between public and private sector organizations, since the private police come in to fill the regulatory gap. On the one hand, the police see the private sector as a future employer for their services and as a method of reducing the police input into a 'cleared up' case; on the other hand, they are resentful of them for reasons that are obscure, but relate probably to some regulatory megalomania. Corporations would prefer to see much more public police attention than they get (Levi & Pithouse, forthcoming), largely because they do not wish to *pay* for their policing except where they want control over investigations (e.g. against their own staff).

Additionally, in the U.K., there are semi-public investigation agencies, such as the Post Office Investigation Department, which unlike the U.S., is licensed by the government but is expected to make a profit on its operations. The POID has a staff of some 300 ex-detectives to review thefts from the postal service, mainly by employees (Levi *et al.*, 1991). In addition to the normal range of *reactive* investigations, they infiltrate post office sorting offices to observe activities of postal workers, often in stealing cheque and credit cards: in 1990, about 160,000 credit cards did not reach the person to whom they were sent, though there is dispute about whether these were stolen from sorting offices, by postal delivery staff, or by persons taking letters from the public areas in office or housing blocks where post is often delivered (partly due to the POID operations, and partly due to changes in secure delivery methods, the number of cards not received which were used fraudulently has dropped markedly).

In the cases above, the existence of specific crimes is known. In other cases, however, investigations can be aimed at getting 'dirt' on target *people* who are giving aggravation on political or commercial grounds. In the U.K., there have been several complaints of political interference in white-collar investigations, but these have not included allegations of *covert* police activity, unless in 'covert' one wishes to include deceptions about the purposes for which information is being obtained. In the case of Manchester businessman Kevin Taylor, the police had a strong interest in finding out about his business dealings during the 1980s because he was a friend of Deputy Chief Constable John Stalker, whom they allegedly wished to see removed from his overzealous investigation of the 'shoot-to-kill' policy in Northern Ireland (Taylor, 1990). In order to get access to his bank accounts without arresting him, the Crown Prosecution Service applied for an order to search for evidence, telling the judge that they had grounds for suspecting Taylor's involvement in drugs trafficking (in fact, the police probably had no need to show the prosecutors their information and could have applied for the warrant themselves). When, at the subsequent trial of Taylor on fraud charges, the judge found that there was no drugs connection, he was furious and dismissed all the charges against Taylor, who is currently (1995) suing the police for millions of pounds over lost business and collateral damages (his co-accused has already accepted large sums in settlement).

COVERT POLICING AND ORGANIZED FRAUD: THE ENGLISH EXPERIENCE

Covert white-collar crime operations have mainly been in the private sector, such as the notorious Dixons/Woolworths takeover battle, and the Guinness/Bells one, during the 1980s, where private detectives allegedly rummaged through people's dustbins, tapped their telephones, and interviewed all persons having prior contact, etc., in the hope of generating some personal 'dirt' on company directors. One might describe this as a form of private sector Extra Positive Vetting. There are a number of private detectives who carry out surveillance operations, sometimes long-term ones, on business rivals: the long-running conflict between the Fayed brothers, who purchased the House of Fraser chain (including Harrods), and 'Tiny' Rowland, chief executive of Lonrho, has provided a rich seam of finance for such activities. Finally, there are random tests in the attempt to find out whether violations are occurring: test purchasing with marked notes, for example (in addition, there is surveillance of private sector activity, such as the – generally non-secret – recording of all financial services telephone conversations by the firms themselves, principally to provide an objective test of disputes about the nature of oral contracts to buy and sell products, but consequentially to provide an audit trail for those dishonest practices which are conducted from the business premises). During 1993, former SAS officers and a director of National Car Parks were acquitted of all criminal charges, though they admitted an operation in which they planted an undercover agent in their rivals Europarks, whom they suspected of having inside information about National Car Parks! They also admitted searching waste material from Europarks for clues. British Airways has also been accused of misusing its computerized bookings systems to 'poach' business class customers from Virgin Airways in the US.

To place this in context, most white-collar crimes are investigated *reactively*, and – other than the taking of witness statements and the obtaining of documents and bank records unknown to defendants, which would be a curious interpretation of 'covert policing' – covert activity is restricted mainly to the informal obtaining of financial information or, again depending on the definition of 'covert,' the official obtaining of information about suspected bank accounts without the knowledge of the account-holder. For example, without judicial oversight and without prior notice to the suspect unless s/he is the holder of the information wanted, the Director of the Serious Fraud Office may issue a notice under s. 2 of the Criminal Justice Act 1987 to a banker or anyone else to disclose information relevant to a serious fraud investigation: this was done on 657 occasions during 1993–1994 for documentary evidence (in drugs and terrorism cases, where court orders *are* required for banking information, bankers risk prosecution if they inform customers either before or after the court order). However, there are some *proactive* police fraud investigations, particularly in London, where informants – some of whom are regulars – tip off the police that a 'scam' is being mounted and they are given permission (on strict guidelines) to act as 'participating informants.' There, unless police officers are used as undercover 'plants' (which is extremely rare), the problem arises that the police cannot readily know the extent to which their informant actually acted as an *agent provocateur*. The financial rewards (from the police, banks, or insurers) can be lucrative and could induce high levels of activism on the part of informants. Given the disclosure rulings discussed earlier, the police would then have the dilemma of whether to inform prosecutors (and risk them disclosing to the defense or dropping the case), or whether to keep the information to themselves and risk embarrassing questions in court about how they came to suspect that a fraud was in operation, given that they broke it up in the course of its commission. The police generally adopt the line that unless their informant is willing to give evidence in court, they would rather let the case collapse than reveal their identity.

One of the areas examined by Marx relates to whether the undercover work takes place in natural or artificial environments. Agents may work in a setting that is already there: in the U.K., Automobile Association, Consumer's Association, and (municipal) trading standards officials regularly test for fraud by garages in 'identifying' nonexistent motor ailments. As in the U.S., a considerable amount of computerized market surveillance is carried out on securities transactions to attempt to detect insider trading. These monitor patterns of unusual transactions, particularly price changes in advance of the release of company results or takeovers, and serve as a heuristic to guide the detailed audit of who acted as principals and nominees in the deals (whether anything further happens depends on the competence and number of investigators, and on the opacity of the nominees and/or their bankers under the law of the country in which they were incorporated. In some jurisdictions such as England, shares can be frozen until the beneficial owners are revealed. However, sustaining a loss may be better than being prosecuted). Similar heuristics based on developed mathematical risk analysis are used by tax authorities, particularly in America and Australia, to test the integrity of tax returns: the U.K. can expect this when it moves over to greater self-assessment system during the mid-1990s.

However, unlike in the U.S., there are no examples in the U.K. of strategic testing of nursing home fraud by undercover work, though with rising health care costs this may happen in the future. Then there are operations started by the police to function in a 'normal' criminal environment, for example classic stings involving fencing and money laundering. Here, too, the U.K. lags behind the U.S. in refusing normally to contemplate many such stings apart from drug busts (for which, *see* Dorn *et al.*, 1991).

Finally, there are more problematical areas in which police come into a *milieu* which is *not* known to be criminal. This can come out of an obsession with uncovering 'hidden areas of criminality,' but it can easily degenerate into a Dr. Strangelove-like psychosis, neatly combined with self-interest in sustaining operations (however, this is so only in a fairly cost-uncontrolled environment in which resources are not a major problem: i.e. not the U.K., where overtime payments have to be justified very specifically). It may be – as in Operation Herring – that covert operations lead to a greater chance of guilty pleas, thus saving enormous court costs: lawyers are paid more than police. However, the police and legal budgets are separate, and the problem of cost in policing operations is a very real one: surveillance operations in white-collar crime – which are only sometimes tied in with 'undercover' ones – are greatly discouraged because of budgetary problems in the financial environment of the 1990s. Even in a short-term operation, at least ten people are needed for surveillance, and the cars and personnel are not normally available for continuous coverage over a long period of time. They can be available where reliable informants are involved – which, partly for economy reasons, are viewed as preferable to 'police undercover' plants or to longer-term, untargetted surveillance – and the main trend is towards this sort of covert operation in Regional Crime Squads or the National Criminal Intelligence Service (established in 1992). There, sometimes in collaboration with overseas agencies, operations may be mounted to discover counterfeiting, narcotics trafficking, or money-laundering organizations, though long-term operations are discouraged on grounds of cost-ineffectiveness.

Sometimes, as in the case of actions against collusive traders who pass transactions through their books using credit card numbers obtained from insiders in hotels or on the phone (telemarketing), whether by simply typing in the numbers or making up crude counterfeit embossed cards ('whitecarding'), the police may co-operate with private sector organizations such as credit card companies. Indeed, there is some potential for sting operations by setting up traders who will be approached by credit card fraudsters to co-operate in this way (in Italy, many traders are made 'an offer they cannot refuse' to accept stolen cards). But except where they are suspected of involvement in terrorism or drugs trafficking (both of which can involve the use of businesses as 'fronts'), covert operations have never to my knowledge been used by the U.K. police against members of 'the elite' (however problematic that is to define). Surveillance operations by HM Customs & Excise in relation to Value-Added Tax fraud are probably the closest analogy to what happens in U.S., but even they are passively covert (e.g. simple surveillance of, say, meetings between already suspected conspirators) or are involved with test purchases or sales: they seldom use long-term dummy companies.

6. JUSTIFYING WHITE-COLLAR UNDERCOVER WORK

Marx (1988) discusses how we might justify undercover work:

1. Citizens as part of the social contract grant to government the right to use exceptional means, such as coercion and deception, in order to be protected (p. 91). This Hobbesian view of the world – that we surrender our rights to the Sovereign, Leviathan – may be too extreme for many: we want to balance the harms of deception against the harms of the particular sort of crime, rather than just 'crime' itself (in fact, this is what those who have to allocate scarce undercover resources have to do).
2. Without undercover work, there would *de facto* be no equal enforcement of law. Some crimes are easier to deal with 'upfront,' while others – white-collar crimes, narcotics trafficking – can be investigated to the same level only by using undercover tactics, particularly where high-status professionals or crime syndicate members are involved.
3. Undercover work work provides best possible evidence, avoiding problems of mistaken identity, confessions (coerced or not), and intimidated witnesses. U.K. jewellery store sting operation Herring, discussed earlier, was an example of a policing strategy which was far less intrusive than stop-and-search tactics normally used in poor neighborhoods. On the other

hand, as the De Lorean case demonstrated, problems can be caused where the undercover person is not a police officer and has a disreputable past (though this designation of disreputability can be applied to some police officers individually or collectively, as was allegedly widespread in the West Midlands Serious Crimes Squad during the late 1980s, against whom in 1992 the Director of Public Prosecutions decided that there was insufficient evidence to prosecute).
4. Undercover work is ethical where there are already grounds for suspicion and where the organization is accountable. This raises particular issues of accountability to whom for what. In the case of *public* sector policing, sufficient critiques have been made of the accountability process to raise doubts as to its salience, though this has been within the context of judicial compliance with police-rule violations. However, the judicial dislike of *agent provocateur*-type operations leads almost all police – at least on the British mainland, excluding Northern Ireland where it may be viewed as a necessary expedient to combat terrorism – to *expect* that superiors will *disapprove* of them, unless they arise in very serious crimes such as murder or sale of arms to unfriendly nations. This is reflected in my discussions with them about why they do not seek to mount sting-type operations: they cannot account for the high cost and they might face rejection from the courts (though the latter objection has been diminished by Operation Herring, the court approval may not extend to white-collar crimes in which the fraudster obtains the money which does not have to be converted in the same way that stolen jewellery does).

In the case of *private* sector sting operations, the major area has been in product counterfeiting, where there has been some limited alliance with police. In credit card fraud investigations, there is some undercover work in relation to merchants who collude in fraud, but the main successes have resulted from sophisticated crime pattern analysis which yields information about levels of acceptance of fraudulent cheques and credit card vouchers. Accountability of private sector personnel, however, is mainly to their employers, though if they seek to prosecute, they normally must present a case through the police to the Crown Prosecution Service.

Undercover work is a slippery slope of morality. Is it ethical to offer temptations to those who otherwise would be unlikely to encounter them? Or to present very attractive terms for stolen goods that might tempt *non*professional criminals or even noncriminals into crime by providing a ready outlet? This is one area where the decision as to who shall be a target is critical, as it can degenerate into a method of trying to eliminate political opponents or – where a decision is made *not* to target – of protecting political friends. This, in turn, may depend upon the political autonomy of the police or non-police agency. It is reasonable to argue that the British police – outside London, particularly – are fairly autonomous of governmental operational control. But what about the Inland Revenue? Or the Department of Trade and Industry? Are there political or financial corruption factors that influence whether some business organizations are investigated thoroughly while others are investigated much more modestly, or that influence whether 'insufficient evidence' is 'found' to justify their prosecution? The exploration of this 'non-decision making process' is important, but it is fertile ground also for paranoid political conspiracy theorists. The history of the Bank of Credit and Commerce International, which allegedly was allowed to run for years *because* police and intelligence agency informants could keep track of criminal operations which used it to launder money (Kerry, 1992), is instructive but atypical.

6.1. Intended Consequences of Undercover Work

Evaluating the success of operations depends on what they are. If the target is known, then evaluation is easy. Where it is hard is when there is a more general possible supply of criminals whose size and frequency of criminality is unknown. Some investigations mushroom from defined ones into racketeering. In the middle are property stings and anticrime decoys. White-collar crimes rank high among the 'unknown' areas, since 'dark figure' estimates of 'its' prevalence are not feasible (though it *is* possible to find out more about levels of 'detected but unreported' fraud against corporations: *see* Levi & Pithouse, forthcoming).

However, one thing that is not considered in the *critiques* of undercover work is the saving in court time that is generated by evidence that is indisputable. In fraud cases, this may represent a major saving: for instance, my earlier work showed that the average cost of fraud trials at the Old Bailey was over £100,000, a large multiple of policing costs (Levi, 1987). This has accelerated subsequently (Levi, 1993). Yet although there are 'passive covert' surveillance squads who work for the Fraud Squad, their impact in most cases is limited because many of the frauds processed come to the attention of the police only when all the money has gone and the company is in or near liquidation. Consequently, except for asset-tracing, there is little surveillance potential, which can be maximized only where there is direct police involvement. Moreover, unless there are inside informants, the frauds carry on for a long time and may require very substantial surveillance outlay. Infiltration is sometimes used as a tactic, e.g. secretaries in bankruptcy frauds, but again, this largely depends on following 'target suspects' who may have moved upmarket into white-collar crime.

6.2. Unintended Consequences of Undercover Work

One difficulty with using confidence tricksters as inside people in undercover investigations is that they find it hard to resist opportunities. The question of how far can you go is difficult. Should the police be allowed to pose as reporters to gain interviews, as doctors, lawyers, or clergymen (taped confessionals for the IRA?) The FBI are allowed to, but only after high-level approval. The IRS can, too, but only when posing as investors, not to get confidential information associated with their fake professional role. The Los Angeles Police Department prohibits police use of press passes. Again, in the U.K., none of these deceptions are permitted by police or non-police managers in public sector white-collar cases.

Worst of all from the viewpoint of police managers, there is the detective who becomes marooned morally and goes native, or part-native, whether corruptly or just sympathetically/romantically. 'Deep cover' undercover work is practised most heavily in Northern Ireland, but much of the controversy in mainland Britain relates to drug trafficking.

One final unintended (or perhaps, in some cases intended) consequence of covert policing is that it tends to expand the size of specialist crime squads or, in the case of the U.S., of the federal police forces. This expansionism (or, in privatizing times, defensiveness against cuts) is particularly true of the rise of narcotics agencies such as the U.S. Drugs Enforcement Agency, and is part of the background to the 'turf war' between the police and HM Customs and Excise and, in 1994–1995, MI5 over responsibility for combating drugs trafficking: but it might also happen if white-collar covert operations were to expand significantly.

7. CONCLUSION

This short article on the involvement of covert policing in U.K. white-collar crime investigations has revealed that hitherto, it has played an insubstantial role. The reasons for this are (1) cultural, in terms of unimaginative, conservative attitudes to detective work combined with opposition to 'foreign' ideas; (2) cost, since given finite resources which can be employed on known, reactive work which does not have to be specifically authorized by senior officers and whose effects are not particularly visible, covert policing is relatively risky and expensive – though unlike the police, Customs & Excise officers have unsocial hours work built into their salaries – and cost savings from guilty pleas instead of long trials cannot be transferred from prosecution/Legal Aid to police budgets; and (3) legal, in terms of uncertainty about the admissibility of evidence and, more probably, explicit statements of judicial disapproval of their tactics, which can harm their *personal* career prospects as well as the reputation of what senior police managers would now have us regard as the 'service' rather than the 'force.' Despite the enormous growth in the requirements on financial institutions to supply information about 'suspicious transactions' proactively, on their own initiative (Levi, 1991), preliminary indications are that in no country are resources available to process much of this information rapidly enough to mount covert operations. There is a high degree of overlap between suspicions of drugs, terrorism, and tax and non-tax fraud – to the banker, 'suspect money' is simply money – but it is hard to foresee a great expansion in the use of covert policing in white-collar crime.

Unless there is a relaxation of the Attorney-General's Guidelines on disclosure to the defense of police logs and the involvement of informants, the *proactive* supply of information to the police from insiders will dry up (at least prior to the plea bargaining process). As for FBI-style white-collar stings, unless drug or terrorism funds were involved as well, it is unlikely that senior police managers would be brave enough to risk criticism by politicians and the media that they were acting as *agents provocateurs*: whatever the crisis in perceptions of the police and courts, public confidence in the integrity and legitimacy of key British social and financial institutions has not been undermined sufficiently hitherto to enable stings to take place there without raising fears within 'the Establishment' about what the opening of Pandora's Box might lead to, given the relative autonomy of the British police forces from direct political control. It is ironic that those methods that give the 'best evidence,' at least in principle uncontaminated by the problems of reliability in *ex post facto* interviews with witnesses-who-might-be-offenders and with suspects-who-ought-only-to-be-witnesses, should be neglected in favor of traditional policing methods which consistently do give rise to suspicions of, if not actual, miscarriages of justice.

REFERENCES

Block, A. (1990), *Masters of Paradise; Organized Crime and the Internal Revenue Service in the Bahamas*, London, Transaction Books.
Cotterrell, R. (1992), *The Sociology of Law; An Introduction*, 2nd ed., London, Butterworths.
Dorn, N., Murji, K., South, N. (1992), *Traffickers; Drug Markets and Law Enforcement*, London, Routledge.
Greising, D., Morse, L. (1991), *Brokers, Bagmen, and Moles*, New York, John Wiley.
Kerry (1992), *The BCCI Affair; A Report to the Senate Committee on Foreign Relations*, Washington, Govt. Printing Office.
Law Commission (1977), *Criminal Law Report on Defences of General Application*, London, HMSO, Report no. 83.
Levi, M. (1987), *Regulating Fraud: White-Collar Crime and the Criminal Process*, London, Routledge.
Levi, M. (1991), *Customer Confidentiality, Money-Laundering, and Police-Bank Relationships: English Law in a Global Environment*, London, Police Foundation.
Levi, M., Bissell, P., Richardson, T. (1991), *The Prevention of Cheque and Credit Card Fraud*, London, Home Office, Crime Prevention Unit, Paper 26.
Levi, M. (1993), *The Investigation, Prosecution, and Trial of Serious Fraud*, London, HMSO, Royal Commission on Criminal Justice Research Study no. 14.
Levi, M., Pithouse, A. (forthcoming), *The Victims of Fraud*, Oxford, Oxford University Press.
Levine, D. (1992), *Inside Out*, London, Century Books.
Marx, G.T. (1988), *Undercover; Police Surveillance in the United States*, Berkeley, University of California Press.
Royal Commission on Police Powers and Procedures (1929), *Report*, London, House of Commons.
Royal Commission on Criminal Justice (1993), *Report*, London, HMSO.
Royal Commission on Criminal Procedure (1981), *Report*, London, HMSO.
Stewart, D. (1991), *Den of Thieves*, New York, Simon and Schuster.
Taylor, K. (1990), *The Poisoned Tree*, London, Sidgwick and Jackson.

Zander, M. (1991), *The Police and Criminal Evidence Act 1984*, 2nd ed., London, Sweet & Maxwell.

Gary T. Marx*

When the Guards Guard Themselves: Undercover Tactics Turned Inward

> You must first enable the government to control the governed; and in the next place, oblige it to control itself (James Madison).

Covert means in the United States have recently become much more important as criminal justice tools – whether directed externally or internally. For example consider the following:

- In Los Angeles nine officers from an elite narcotics unit were arrested for the large-scale theft of seized funds. The Los Angeles Sheriff's Department and the FBI staged a phoney drug operation and videotaped the deputies stealing money (*L.A. Times*, 2 September 1989).
- In Cleveland FBI undercover agents set up and ran two gambling operations as part of a two year sting directed at local police. Thirty officers were arrested as a result and charged with extortion, obstruction of justice and narcotics and gambling violations (*Law Enforcement News*, 15 June 1990).
- A New York prosecutor was arrested after taking money for arranging the dismissal of gun charges against a person he thought was an organized crime figure, but who was actually a federal agent (Blecker, 1984).
- As part of an FBI undercover operation, a Federal district judge in Florida was arrested on charges of obstructing justice and conspiring to collect bribes from a defendant posing as a racketeer (*N.Y. Times*, 29 November 1987).
- In 1986 the New York City Corrections Department began placing undercover corrections officers in the city's jails to investigate drug offenses, excessive use of force and theft of weapons. (*N.Y. Times*, 6 November 1986).

These efforts at internal control are illustrative of a broader problem faced by any complex society: controlling those with the authority to control others. In the first century A.D. the Roman poet asked '*quis custodiet ipsos custodes*' –

---

* Professor of Sociology, University of Colorado, Boulder, United States. A longer version of this paper appeared in *Policing and Society*, 1992, vol. 2, no. 3, 151–172.

'who guards the guards?' There are few questions of greater practical or theoretical import. All organizations of course must devote some attention to matters of internal control (Katz, 1977). But the issue has special poignancy and symbolism when it involves organizations whose primary goal is creating, interpreting or enforcing law.

The answer to Juvenal's question for despotic regimes may be 'no one.' The guards are a law unto themselves, and with respect to the public are relatively uncontrolled.[1] But in the United States with its pluralistic system, the executive, legislative and judicial bodies watch and constrain each other. Outside institutions such as the mass media and professional associations (American Bar Association and International Association of Chiefs of Police) and public interest groups concerned with democracy and civil liberties also play a role.

However, the guards are also expected to guard themselves. Self-regulation is a central tenet of professionalization. In the case of law enforcement, by careful selection, training, policy, and supervision the guards are expected to keep their own house in order. Day-to-day responsibility lies with self-control on the part of individual agents and bureaucratically defined supervisory roles, internal affairs units and inspectors general.

This paper focuses on one means of self-regulation which has recently become much more important: undercover tactics.[2] The topic of undercover work is rich in complexity and paradox. If we wish to see the guards guarded using these means how is this best done? What are the risks and costs to other important values? If an undercover policy works and is legal, is it therefore necessarily good public policy? Should those in positions of authority be subject to greater restrictions on their liberty because of the greater temptations they face? Can we be sure that the evidence discovered is not itself simply an artifact of the investigation? How should we balance the access to evidence that may be otherwise unavailable, with the invasions of privacy and other unintended consequences that may be present? Will the internal use of covert means lower morale and productivity and mean less risk-taking and innovation? With multiple agencies with overlapping jurisdictions, can authorities avoid ensnaring each other in their traps? Is it appropriate to do good by doing bad? When the state uses deception does it set a bad example, modelling and legitimating the use of deception for its citizens? Given the power of the tactic to tempt and entrap, can political targeting be avoided? These issues run throughout the examples we consider and are discussed in the concluding section.

---

1. Ironically, corrupt regimes often have very strong means of internal control, since the ruler's power rests so clearly on the guards whose loyalty is essential. However, the goal is not to see that the rule of law is enforced, but to look for disloyalty and even the failure to share ill-gotten gains.
2. Of course in a strict sense it is self-regulation only if done within the same organizational structure. However, law enforcement is a relatively homogeneous world in which feelings of solidarity commonly transcend organizational boundaries and operational interdependence often occurs.

1. THE EXPANSION OF COVERT POLICING

Changes in crime patterns, public attitudes and law enforcement priorities, in conjunction with organizational, legislative, judicial and technical changes, have supported the general expansion of the undercover technique. But brief mention can be made of several judicial, legislative, and resource factors that are particularly relevant to the increased internal use of the tactic.

The civil rights movement helped call attention to the inequality in law enforcement that exists when government focuses only on the violations of the poor, while ignoring those of the rich and powerful. In addition, public indignation over the Watergate scandal involving former President Nixon and related abuses both reflected and contributed to the declining tolerance for white collar violations. The struggle against the corruption of authority is one strand of that. The diffuse, often victimless quality of corruption lends itself well to discovery via covert means.

Federal legislation such as The Hobbs Act and the 1961 Travel Act have come to be applied to anyone who obstructs interstate commerce – including those who offer bribes, and this has been applied to local and state officials and not just to federal officials. Interstate commerce can be obstructed because of a threat of violence and direct extortion, or merely by obtaining government benefits passively 'under color of official right.' This 'federalization' of local offenses has reduced the burden of proof for prosecutors and helped open the way to the vast increase in federal corruption prosecutions at the local and state level.

The 1970 RICO Act (Racketeer Influence and Corrupt Organizations Act) permits convictions on the basis of a 'pattern' of activities comprising a criminal enterprise. Such a pattern of 'racketeering' is very broadly interpreted to include a variety of offenses – as long as they are repeated several times. In a 1981 decision the Supreme Court held that prosecution need not be restricted to criminal organizations that infiltrate or take over legitimate business, but instead could be applied to any group which demonstrated a pattern of racketeering activity. This law and subsequent interpretations vastly increased white collar prosecutions of those not usually thought of as involved in organized crime.[3]

New federal resources such as a public integrity unit in the Justice Department, the Federal Witness Relocation Program, the Federal Law Enforcement Training Center and the creation of offices of Inspectors General made internal investigations easier. In 1976 the Justice Department created a public integrity section within its criminal division. This now has more than 25 attorneys who specialize in the supervision and oversight of undercover operations for serious corruption cases. This unit offers training, seminars, lectures, and consultation to prosecutors and investigators for the prosecution of corruption cases.

This paper focuses on an area where the changes in covert means are particularly clear and dramatic – the use of undercover means by government against itself. The vast expansion of drug enforcement has greatly increased

---

3. *U.S.* v. *Turkette*, 101 S. CT. 2524 (1981).

corruption temptations. Among those arrested in recent police stings have been Drug Enforcement Agency and FBI agents, as well as many local police. Concern over drugs and violence has sent still other agents to prison – although posing as prisoners – in a trick used by Vidocq (Stead, 1953 and Gerson, 1977). It is no longer uncommon to hear of police, legislators and even judges and prosecutors as the targets of undercover investigations.

Let us move from consideration of the broad expansion of undercover tactics in the last two decades (of which uses within government is one strand), to some of the difficulties involved in seeking to control those with the authority to control others.

2. THE PROBLEM OF GUARDING THE GUARDS

If there are forces operating to expand the internal use of covert means there are also powerful forces opposing this. To the social analyst, as against the social reformer, what might seem remarkable is that there is as much internal social control among law enforcement agencies and government as there is, rather than how far from ideal the situation is. As with dancing bears, the point may be not that they dance badly, but that they dance at all.

Many factors work against the guards guarding themselves as aggressively as they guard others. The separation of powers doctrine may inhibit enforcement agencies from actively investigating judicial and legislative bodies. Judges control the issuance of warrants and may be hesitant to judge their peers. The rule-making, budgetary, and approval power of the legislature over executive and administrative agencies may subtly (or not so subtly) inhibit the latter's enforcement actions.[4] Judges may owe their appointments to the very politicians they could be asked to judge.

Within the same enforcement organization simple self-interest and reciprocity work against aggressive action. Those within the same organization have a strong interest in getting along. Reaching organizational goals requires cooperation, and loyalty is valued. Boat rockers and whistle blowers are not usually rewarded. Violations may be tolerated as resources and rewards. There may even be a kind of implied blackmail in which those with the power to sanction rarely use it in order to keep the peace and assure the organization's functioning.

---

4. An impetus to the creation of the FBI was congressional anger over a Justice Department investigation of corruption in Congress. In an effort to prevent such investigations the Congress prohibited the Justice Department (which had no agents of its own at the turn of the century) from borrowing agents from other federal agencies. That led the Justice Department to create its own detective force – the FBI – against the wishes of Congress (Cummings and McFarland, 1937, Whitehead, 1956, Ungar, 1975). Following Abscam there were congressional calls for restricting the FBI. One FBI agent believes that 'the congressional probes which followed Abscam were aimed more at the investigators than at the corrupt officials under investigation, and the guidelines which resulted really amount to an implicit OFF button' (Welch and Marston, 1984, 278).

American police, lacking the lateral entry of European police are thought to have a higher degree of inner solidarity and weakened supervision. Since leaders rise from the ranks, they may find it more difficult to act decisively. Also unlike the situation in Europe, being a prosecutor or a local judge is rarely a life-long career insulated from political pressures, or assessments of future career moves. Rather, such positions are often stepping stones to other public offices or jobs in the private sector (e.g. as defense attorneys). This may mean lesser professionalism and greater receptivity to political pressures.

District attorneys for example are usually elected and very much a part of their communities. They are generally not inclined to make cases against the political establishment that nurtures them and is likely to hold the key to their futures. Federal or state agents are freer to do this; on the other hand they may not know the local scene as well, and they must often work together with local officials on other matters.

Local prosecutors who wish actively to enforce corruption laws need to obtain a critical mass of evidence, such that an investigation creates its own momentum and can proceed in spite of the political pressures that may be brought against it.

As a result of the above factors, the ecology of internal enforcement generally flows downward from federal to state and local levels (and from state to local) rather than the reverse. As noted, for political reasons it is often easier for outsiders to act. The federal government of course also has greater resources, and broader laws and jurisdiction.[5]

A related issue arises from the special skills of control agents. Even when the will is present, it is more difficult to catch those in criminal justice because of their knowledge of the system and contacts within it. They are likely to know how to protect themselves and to identify investigative efforts.

Given resource inequality within organizations, internal enforcement, when present, is more likely to be directed at those lower in the organizational hierarchy. Those higher up usually have more information and are in a better position to defuse an investigation, or to retaliate, not to mention their formal and informal control over those carrying out an investigation. They are likely to have legitimate discretion which permits starting or stopping an investigation, this may mask cover ups. The issue of when (in the words of one agent) 'to pull out the plug' as against when 'to run out the string' is rarely formally reviewed. The folklore of some police and radicals is in agreement that investigations are likely to be stopped before they get to the really big fish in government.

Maurice Nadjari for example was appointed Special Prosecutor with responsibility for investigating corruption throughout the criminal justice system by Governor Rockefeller in 1972 (Nadjari, 1977). He successfully prosecuted

---

5. In general it is easier for federal prosecutors to make such cases. Federal laws and evidentiary rules have greatly aided this. Prosecutors can gather evidence from grand jury witnesses without granting them total immunity, as local prosecutors are required to do. Indictments and convictions can be obtained on conspiracy charges with less proof than is required in state court. The witness protection program which permits federal informants to begin a new life elsewhere is also a factor, as is the broad geographical and social network federal investigators have.

police and minor public officials; however, his major cases involving high-level politicians and the judiciary were dismissed (as was Nadjari).

Investigations may be subtly derailed in many ways and sometimes with competing moral justifications. The damage caused by letting an investigation continue once evidence against a corrupt official has been gathered may not be balanced by the lure of getting higher-ups. For example, in a controversial action at the end of his term, Mayor Ed Koch of New York refused to reappoint a corrupt city official as a way of continuing an investigation. Koch viewed the reappointment of a known corrupt official as very damaging to the workings of government. The moral ambiguity is clear. Should a corrupt official be allowed to continue to profit from his position and to do harm, in the hope of building the strongest possible case and widening the net of those charged?

But among other less noble factors that may lead to the premature closing of an investigation of elites are fear of reprisals, the richness of the reward or favor that may be forthcoming as a result of cessation or a subtle warning, and concern over damaging legitimacy. The complexity of many such investigations and the fact that they may be of lengthy duration also increases the chance of leaks or accidental discovery. Also because of the sensitive circumstances a stronger predicate may be required to begin an investigation than is the case for those not in government.

Aggressive actions are more likely to be taken by outsiders – whether organizationally or socially. To be effective internal authority must to some degree be insulated from the pressures that would corrupt it. In New York City once an officer works in Internal Affairs he or she can rarely go elsewhere in the department. The building is isolated and so are its members (even to the point of having to be promoted in secret so other members of the department won't know their identity). The absence of camaraderie from, and rejection by one's colleagues and their view of you as a rat, may take an enormous stress toll on those assigned to such units. This is compounded by a sense that higher authorities, regardless of their public pronouncements, are ambivalent about your activities.

Cultural and psychological factors may work against the active pursuit of official rule breaking. As an embodiment of a society's values, leaders may be held in reverence and surrounded by an aura of the sacred (although this may be less true for the United States than for more traditional societies). There may be psychologically rooted inhibitions about challenging those in authority and suspecting ill of them; although that may be more true of Europe where there is a tradition of the strong state and greater fear of what would happen if it is weakened.

There is probably a cultural tilt toward wanting to believe that officials are good. If not 100 per cent pure, they are seen to have a very hard job to do and to need all the support they can get. Everett Hughes (1962) in an important article on 'good people and dirty work' develops this argument. Some official violations are seen to be 'necessary,' or at least unavoidable in the pursuit of important social goals. The expression 'it's a tough job, but somebody's got to do it' captures this. Moderate rule breaking and rule bending can also be seen as rewards or perks for those in high status positions.

WHEN THE GUARDS GUARD THEMSELVES

Even when the above factors are absent, the collusive nature of many official violations operates against discovery and prosecution. For example, with political corruption there is usually no complainant and the damage is diffused. Such cases tend to lack a 'smoking gun.'

With respect to bribes three important situations can be identified. The first and most common ('back-scratching') involves a willing, even joyful exchange among a bribe offerer and receiver. Both wear black hats (although given the official power of the person in government, a hint of extortion hangs over many such relationships).[6] In return for compensation, the bribed person agrees to deliver a contract, provide inside information, withhold information, fix a case, introduce legislation, vote a particular way, or otherwise act to advance the payee's interests. While the public may be victimized, both parties get what they want and neither is likely to come forward to complain. This is the quintessential economic relationship, it just happens that the currency is corruption. This serves the interests of the involved parties, but has costs for the public at large.

The symmetry in the above contrasts with the asymmetry in situations where a bribe is requested or offered. In the latter ('citizens bearing gifts') bribes are offered to those with authority. They may accept for obvious reasons. Again the mutually enriched parties enter into a conspiracy of silence.

But even when the bribe is refused, the appropriate authorities are unlikely to be informed. The bribe refuser may conclude that since the offer was rejected, no real harm was done. Norms of reciprocity also work against reporting such crimes (i.e. turning in someone who offers you a gift and who defines it as a token of appreciation, 'here's a little something for you, a show of good faith and support').

In the third form, 'the coercive power of office,' the source is a demand for payment from the office-holder, rather than a citizen-initiated offer. Yet this too, is usually unreported. The target of the briber or extortionist may be offended, but nonetheless go along because the latter's cooperation is needed, or out of intimidation. Even if the individual refuses to pay, the fear of retaliation may be great enough to prevent reporting. A further constraint on reporting is that many of those victimized by this type of corruption are themselves involved in illegal and/or morally discrediting activities. They do not want to call attention to themselves and, with their potentially impugnable reputations are unlikely to be believed, relative to the claims of a government official.

Finally, even rejected asymmetrical corrupt proposals may not be reported for some of the same reasons that other violations are under reported – a belief that reporting will do no good, fear of retaliation, and a desire to avoid unwanted publicity and entanglements.

Yet as we noted, there are also factors encouraging efforts at internal control. Organizations differ in the amount and kind of resources they devote to internal control. However lacking government may be in some ideal sense, it appears

---

6. As a Boston prosecutor put it, 'if the person taking the money is wearing a uniform and carrying a gun, I am unwilling to believe that doesn't influence the state of mind of the person paying the money – you have a built-in element of extortion.'

to devote relatively greater resources to internal control when compared to many other institutions (e.g., universities). More abstractly we can hypothesize that the extent of resources devoted to inner control is dependent on factors such as:

1. the internal and external costs of rule violation;
2. the extent of opportunities for rule violation;
3. the visibility of the violation after-the-fact;
4. the extent to which organizational goals can be obtained by following the rules;
5. the degree of professionalization;
6. the relative size and power of external organizations charged with enforcement with respect to the organization;
7. the relative heterogeneity and extent of stratification within the organization;
8. the type of organization.

However, precisely because of the hidden quality of such violations and the incentives and fears of the involved parties, if police are actively to enforce anti-corruption laws other means such as informers, infiltration, undercover traps and wire-taps are used. As Special Prosecutor Nadjari (1977) notes, 'the prosecutor who waits for clearly defined [corruption] cases to be brought before him will spend long days in mental repose.' Let us consider the diversity of uses in recent cases within government.

3. SOME EXAMPLES

The secrecy associated with undercover investigations means that they can ensnare unlikely persons. Serendipity sometimes means that police (along with judges, legislators and college professors), unaware of who and what they are dealing with, are swept up in stings. Thus, in New York a police officer was arrested in a fake insurance scheme when he paid to have his car stolen and an Atlantic City policeman was arrested when he sold his badge and motorcycle to a property sting run by the New Jersey State Police (Marx, 1988). But our concern here is with undercover means directed against those in criminal justice.

There is an important distinction between using covert means in a targeted fashion in response to intelligence (predicated use), which suggests that a crime is occurring, and routinely using them absent specific suspicions (open-ended use). Predicated uses are a traditional tactic, even if police are often reluctant to apply them internally. What is new is the willingness of some departments to now use undercover tactics as a routine part of the inspection process.

Targeted uses are common during the periodic reform periods that police departments experience. Thus O.W. Wilson in Chicago, in response to claims that police were stealing welfare checks and shaking down motorists, had internal affairs agents secretly watch suspects, and his agents posed as motorists to see if they would be shaken down. William Parker, the reform chief in Los Angeles, came to his position after serving as head of internal affairs. It was widely believed that he used his information from secret investigations as a way to have informal and formal leverage over the department (Woods, 1973).

The Knapp Commission and Patrick Murphy in New York City also made effective use of the tactic (The Knapp Commission, 1972). The Knapp Commission was appointed in 1970 to investigate police corruption. Officers facing corruption charges agreed to work undercover against their former colleagues. Police corruption was found to be systematic and widespread. The Commission rejected the 'bad apple' theory of corruption in which the problem is seen to be one of a few bad individuals who somehow managed to slip through, in favor of an approach which looked at police organization and culture as factors which supported corruption.

In response, under Police Commissioner Patrick Murphy the department instituted a variety of reforms aimed at *preventing,* as well as investigating corruption. The extraordinary enforcement challenge posed by police who are criminals was seen to require innovative approaches. The department routinized complex sting operations. An undercover capability (previously available only to narcotics and organized-crime units) was added to the Internal Affairs Division. 'Field internal affairs units' within borough headquarters subjecting officers to random integrity tests were created. A 'field associates' program, designed to break the 'code of silence' was also set up in which hundreds of officers assigned to regular duty secretly agree to report on corruption among their colleagues. The goal is prevention, as well as general intelligence to assess a problem. Integrity tests are used absent specific suspicions. Police are warned they may be subjected to various tests at any time. The warning is intended to deter violations by creating fear that any corrupt offer might be other than what it appears to be. The tests carried out by members of internal affairs may take a number of forms – an interracial couple asking a police officer for information, a person turning over cash they claim they found, or a confused drunk with a fat wallet.

The largest New York City corruption investigation since the Knapp Commission in the early 1970s (Commission, 1972) was in 1986 in Brooklyn's 77th Precinct. Thirteen officers were suspended following an investigation. The officers are alleged to have taken cash and drugs from addicts and dealers. A drug dealer who complained was wired and he gathered evidence against two officers. In the 'domino' process common to undercover investigations, under threat of prison the two officers were then wired and gathered evidence against their colleagues (McAlary, 1988).

In Los Angeles a tip from an FBI informer passed on to the police department led to the setting of a trap that caught two members of a special burglary unit.[7] After an initial investigation, a fake burglary situation was created and the suspects took the bait and were arrested. The arrested officers had an ideal situation for continually committing crime. They were part of a special burglar alarm response unit. After responding to the alarms, the officers would then

---

7. This investigation was carried out by the Los Angeles Police Department. In other cases, partly as a result of a lack of faith in a department's ability to investigate itself, the FBI may choose not to pass on a tip and carry out the investigation itself.

pilfer the store themselves. They were believed to trip the alarms of stores specializing in expensive electronic equipment and then respond to the alarms. Investigators turned the tables and set off an alarm at one such store. They then watched as the two officers made several trips carrying out cash and expensive goods which had been treated to leave an indelible, invisible mark on anyone who touched them. In later searches of their homes and those of several other suspects, authorities seized almost a truckload worth of electronic equipment.

Some departments use stings as part of a procedural audit to be sure that rules are being followed. The idea is to create a secret test to see if policies are correctly carried out. Thus after civil rights groups complained that Long Beach, California police supervisors were ignoring complaints of police misconduct which were phoned in, agents secretly called in complaints, and monitored their treatment. The rationale is clearly expressed by police commander Billy Thomas, 'it did get the attention of the personnel here, in that they never know who is on the other end of the phone' (*Law Enforcement News*, 15 June 1990).

The potential for corruption is particularly rich in agencies charged with licensing, inspection and regulation. A significant amount of discretion, a heavy workload, lack of resources for full enforcement and lack of public visibility are conducive to influence purchasing and peddling and compromised enforcement. The value of discretion to the corrupt official is greatly enhanced when delays can cost vast sums, as with construction. Bribes may be used to obtain expedited treatment. They may also of course be used to more directly hurt the public.

New York City's Commission of Investigation has pioneered in using covert techniques in this area. In its 'Operation Ampscam,' for example, more than half of the 26 employees of the New York City Bureau of Electrical Control, the agency that inspects electrical installations, were arrested after a 14-month investigation (*N.Y. Times*, 8 June 1984). Two bogus electrical companies were set up and investigators pretended to have done work at buildings supposedly being rehabilitated, yet the buildings had dangling wires, water deposits, and lack of grounding. Payoffs were accepted in return for licenses. In another part of the operation, agents posed as inspectors and arrested contractors who paid bribes.

In 'Operation Undertow' eight undercover investigators – six pretending to be car owners who owed unpaid fines and two posing as employees – gathered evidence that workers at a New York City car pound solicited and accepted cash from persons who wished to retrieve their vehicles without paying outstanding traffic tickets (*N.Y. Times*, 15 March 1985).

In an audit example an investigator filed a fraudulent disability claim which demonstrated how easy it was to cheat the city's pension fund. He faked a back injury and used the X-rays of another person with an actual injury. He was then filmed lifting heavy boxes and playing paddle ball. Doctors on the pension medical board were told about the films, but they nonetheless granted the disability claim. A report based on this case did not charge the doctors with wrongdoing and noted that they did not have time to adequately review the many cases they handled at their weekly meetings. The report recommended a number of policy changes (*Boston Globe*, 15 April 1982).

A related topic is citizens' and private groups' use of covert means against police. Publicity around the tactic and the availability of powerful, easily hidden audio and video recording devices evens up the odds in a sense. They can offer evidence of official misconduct that might not be believed were it just the citizen's word against an official. In this sense there is a democratization of surveillance.

In a controversial Long Beach, California case a black police sergeant, Don Jackson, in conjunction with the Los Angeles Police Misconduct Lawyers Referral Service, ran a private sting which was videotaped and nationally televised. In the incident he and a colleague were stopped by two white officers, unaware of his identity. One of the officers used profanity when the sergeant at first refused an order to raise his hands above his head. After he finally did so, the officer rammed his head through a store front window. In their police report the officers said that the sergeant cursed at them and made threatening gestures. After the video tape was shown, one of the officers acknowledged that the report contained inaccuracies. Charges were dismissed, to the dismay of the Long Beach Police Department who felt that they were set up. The arresting officers were themselves arrested. The sergeant hopes to 'export [his] activities nationwide' and he reports he will consult 'with various civil rights leaders as to which are the worst areas and I'm going to set these things up anywhere and everywhere I can' (*Law Enforcement News*, 14 February 1989).

The Grand Jury system offers a powerful tool for conviction, although not always for the initial offense of interest. Thus Paul Rao, a Chief Judge of the Federal Customs Court in New York, was indicted for perjury in a simulated robbery case. An acquaintance, acting in an undercover capacity, asked him to help the son of a friend who was supposedly in trouble. The judge suggested that the agent see 'a lawyer [who] knew the judge.' He recommended his own son as the lawyer. Rao was called before a grand jury a year later and denied making that statement. A special grand jury indicted him for perjury (Marx, 1988 and Gershman, 1981).

Operation Corkscrew, an investigation into alleged municipal judicial corruption in Cleveland, is a classic example of how not to carry out an investigation (Report of the Subcommittee, 1984). The story is one of incompetence and exploitation by an unwitting and then a witting informer. Marvin Bray, a court bailiff, did not know that two men hanging around the court who expressed an interest in bribing judges to fix cases were really FBI agents. Bray bragged that he had two judges in his pocket and agreed to set up payoff meetings. Over an 8-month period he held a series of tape-recorded meetings between the two 'judges' and the agents. The FBI paid out $85,000. The 'judges' did not know that the fixers were really FBI agents and the FBI agents did not know that the judges were really impostors. Bray had persuaded two friends to pose as judges. They were told that they were part of an undercover investigation to protect the judges and to combat corruption. One of the impostors, a man in his thirties, impersonated a judge who was 68.

Once Bray realized that they had been dealing with government agents he fled. The FBI located him and he convinced them that there really was corruption in the court and that he could help them gather evidence by directly approaching judges. He did not document any corruption, but the case demonstrates how a tape can be misused to make it appear that a target has committed a crime. With the hidden tape recorder on, Marvin Bray asked a judge to revoke an arrest order for a friend who had missed a scheduled court appearance. The judge agreed to this routine request. Bray then left the judge's quarters and later said into the tape: 'that envelope on the table is for you, judge.' He then presented the tape as evidence that the judge had accepted a bribe in return for revoking the order. The investigation was closed. Bray was indicted but no judges were, although they were stigmatized by the publicity the case received.

Operation Greylord in Chicago, which targeted judges and lawyers in Cook County's judicial system, was a much more professional investigation (*N.Y. Times*, 12 August 1983 and Tuohy and Warden, 1987). Greylord is a reference to the wigs used by British judges. FBI agents posed as arrested criminals and as lawyers, and a state judge cooperated by wearing a tape recorder hidden in his cowboy boot. The investigation focused on payoffs between lawyers, police officers and judges suspected of having fixed cases in the past.

Finally, let us briefly consider two undercover corruption investigations outside the criminal justice system, which raise some common issues. We will compare the use of undercover tactics against elected officials in the Abscam (Abdullah Scam) and CorCom (Corrupt Commissioners) investigations. Abscam involved FBI agent Anthony Amoroso posing as a sheik with immigration problems who sought to purchase political influence (Select Committee, 1983).

Abscam began on Long Island in 1978 and went on for two years. It began as an inquiry into stolen art and securities and ended as an investigation of political corruption. When a subject spoke of his ability to influence politicians, the focus of the investigation changed. As a Senate Committee of inquiry observed: 'Abscam was virtually unlimited in geographic scope, persons to be investigated and criminal activity to be investigated ... it was, in practical effect, a license for several agents to assume false identities, to create a false business front, and to see what criminal activities could be detected or developed throughout the country' (Select Committee, 1983).

Abscam stands out because it was not in response to allegations about particular individuals, or in response to known offenses. It used Mel Weinberg, who had been involved in the use of stolen credit cards, income tax evasion and fraud, as the principle informant. It also made extensive use of unwitting informers who had a strong financial incentive to draw in subjects who there was no prior reason to suspect were corrupt. This contrasts with prior corruption investigations that usually involved either a person from whom a bribe is demanded, playing along under police supervision, or a 'tamed' suspect who agrees to cooperate. The subjects attended secretly videotaped meetings believing they were coming to discuss campaign contributions. A script was followed in which in return for help with his problems the sheik would make various 'gifts.'

There were a number of Abscam cases and these raised somewhat different issues. One involves how persistent agents should be after a subject initially refuses. In the case of Senator Harrison Williams, agents persisted until he finally accepted money, after twice rejecting their suggestions. He was led to believe that he would not have to take any illegal action. The main informant coached him in what to say, practically putting words in his mouth: 'you gotta tell him how important you are, and you gotta tell him in no uncertain terms without me, there is no deal. I'm the man who's gonna open the doors. I'm the man who's gonna do this and use my influence, and I guarantee this.' The senator was then assured that nothing wrong was happening: 'it goes no further. It's all talk, all bullshit. It's a walk-through. You gotta just play and blow your horn.'

In the case of two city councilmen in Philadelphia, George Schwartz and Harry Jannotti, the bribe was presented as necessary to a much broader plan to help rebuild their financially troubled city. They were told that in accordance with the 'Arab mind' and 'Arab way of doing business' that they had to convince the investors that they had friends in high places. In order to do this, money had to be accepted from the investors. The defendants were not asked to offer any commitments or to do anything improper, contingent on accepting the payment. The situation was structured so that acceptance of the money would be seen as payment for consulting services. Neither of the defendants asked for money, and both indicated that no payment was necessary. They were simply told that the project would not come to the city if they did not accept the sheik's 'gift.' While in Abscam all those arrested were convinced other standards must be considered beyond strict legality.

In contrast, CorCom, which resulted in guilty findings against more than 200 county commissioners in Oklahoma in 1981 for taking kickbacks, was more focused. A lumber-mill owner agreed to cooperate and secretly recorded 110 taped conversations with vendor colleagues, many of who admitted their complicity. A building materials salesman who testified that he had made 8,400 payoffs worth over $1 million to county officials secretly videotaped his dealings with commissioners in an Oklahoma City hotel room. In contrast to Abscam, a U.S. attorney observes, 'we simply had Moore do business like he had for 28 years' (*Newsweek*, 21 September 1981). There was a clear predicate for the corrupt temptations presented to targets – they were known to have previously had corrupt dealings. It would be difficult to claim that the crime was an artifact of the investigation or that the corrupt nature was not clear. The investigation was carried out in a 'natural' environment rather than an artificially created one.

4. SOME CONSEQUENCES, COSTS AND CHOICES

In this section we consider the difficulty of evaluating the use of covert means in corruption cases, some preventive measures that would lessen the need to rely on them, and some broad policy issues faced by a democratic society in its efforts to guard the guards.

There have been no efforts to systematically evaluate the government's use of undercover tactics against itself.[8] Unlike a fencing sting which involves many roughly similar cases over a period of time and for which before, during

---

8. For a useful typology based on an analysis of cases prosecuted under the Federal Ethics Act that identifies variables likely relevant to different outcomes *see* Harriger (1989).

and after measures of reported crime are available, the corruption cases vary greatly among themselves. Since corruption is rarely reported, there are no easy measures of deterrence or prevention.

Evaluation measures for corruption cases have a type of face-validity. If clear evidence of serious wrongdoing is found and guilty verdicts are returned, then they are presumed to have worked (assuming the violations are not simply an artifact of the investigation). This of course does not tell us whether they are more effective than some other measures, or have a deterrent impact. The impact may be significant at first and later diminish. The 'wise' may learn to negate the controls – through special tests and language, indirect payments, payments abroad, or when an official retires, etc. Knowledge that undercover tactics are in use may keep some from breaking the law, but it may simply make others more clever and careful. There is likely significant variation in outcomes. For example, most observers agree that following the reforms and publicity of the Knapp Commission systematic widespread corruption in New York City stopped, even though pockets resurfaced. In contrast in Philadelphia reforms seem to have had less impact. There is a clear need for research here.

Even if the tactic 'works' in a particular case in the sense that offenders are identified and prosecuted, such control can be seen as merely a bandaid or tourniquet, stopping the bleeding by external pressure, but having no impact on the source of the problem. Apprehension of an offender whether through undercover or other means suggests a failure of social control – the damage has likely already been done. In most of the cases considered here government is simply picking up the pieces after-the-fact.

The U.S. attorney in the CorCom cases observes, 'we can win all these cases, but if the system isn't changed, we've lost the war. It would be business as usual unless the legislature adopted new laws' (*N.Y. Times*, 12 October 1981). Actions taken to lessen the likelihood of corruption include: limits on campaign contributions and spending; public financing of election campaigns; disclosure laws; restrictions on political party leaders, legislators, and former officials going into a related private business immediately upon leaving government; higher salaries; stricter rules for competitive bidding; centralized purchasing; better accounting and audit procedures; a requirement that bribe offers be reported; and independent ethics committees with enforcement powers.

One way to overcome the difficulty in discovering violations is to have laws or internal policies requiring that bribe offers be reported. Disclosure rules are important because they may deter, or if not followed, offer a means for pursuing an investigation. In cases where prosecutors have other grounds for suspicion, but are unable to prove a bribe, they may still pursue a suspect for not disclosing questionable contributions or sources of income.

On the other hand such rules can create a new resource to threaten people with claiming a bribe offer was made when it wasn't. Such a requirement might create perjury on the part of the agent who ignores a bribe offer and later, if challenged, defends himself by denying the offer was ever made. Such requirements can also result in integrity tests being taken to a new extreme: targets may face double testing – initially to see if they will accept a corrupt offer and, then to see if they will report the offer. Individuals may become the targets of an undercover trap not because they are suspected of wrongdoing, but to see if bribes are reported and other procedural rules are followed. This may offer a means to get rid of an employee whose performance is satisfactory, but who is disliked by a supervisor.

With respect to police, among anti-corruption measures are: careful selection, adequate pay, anti-corruption training, more intensive field supervision, having sergeants present when arrests are made, and a *de facto* policy of non-enforcement for minor offenses likely to give rise to problems; and a policy of requiring two people to be present during situations that are most likely to give rise to allegations of corruption (meetings with an informant, counting money, male-female encounters). Paper audit trails, audio and video recording, polygraphs and drug-tests are also used. Some departments have a rule which requires employees to immediately report any misconduct they are personally aware of, or any allegations of misconduct that they hear of. Failure to make such notification constitutes misconduct.

More effective prosecution (and less need for it) might follow from local equivalents of the federal Special Prosecutor, appointed by legislatures or attorney generals and from the establishment of inspector general's offices at the municipal and state levels. Tougher criminal and civil penalties, increased provision, protection and rewards for whistle-blowers and informers might have some preventive effect. The law might be changed to make it easier to offer proof of corruption. If public officials were prohibited from taking anything of value from those they have regulatory jurisdiction over, it would be unnecessary to prove the often elusive concept of 'corrupt motive' for purposes of prosecution. Specific legal presumptions could be written into the criminal law to indicate *prima facie* evidence of corrupt intent, e.g., any transaction of public business in a covert fashion, as with Abscam. A well-publicized policy of prosecuting citizens who pay bribes, or fail to report such requests rather than only officials who demand them, might have preventive impact. Laws that made it easy for citizens to recover damages from officials whose false reports or perjurious testimony contributes to detention, imprisonment, or prosecution could be adopted.

Given the special issues that are present, should investigations of official rule breaking, whether in the criminal justice system or among elected officials, involve a different standard than for investigations of citizens? If so, should the standard be more or less restrictive than is the case for general investigations?

Should the special advantages, powers and temptations that come with official positions subject their occupants to a voluntary waiving of privacy expectations? As a condition of office and a form of *noblesse oblige,* should they agree to things such as periodic random integrity tests and public filing of income tax statements?[9] Boxers' fists are considered to be lethal weapons and

---

9. Sherman (1983) for example advocates random testing under controlled circumstances. Even if the principle of randomness is accepted, its use might depend on an assessment of how widespread the problem is believed to be and the specific information available. Randomness (as a tactic for apprehension) would make the most sense if it is believed that corruption is rampant, but there are no specific suspects. In contrast, if the problem is thought to be focused and there are suspects it makes less sense. Other than for a vague faith in its deterrent power, it makes the least sense when there are no reasons to suspect corruption and no specific suspects.

lobbyists must register and report certain actions. Should there also be restrictions and special conditions on those in government, such as elected officials and judges?

On the other hand, one might argue that because the risks of misuse are greater, undercover policy should go in the other direction when it is used in government (or against certain persons such as judges or elected officials). More stringent standards involving special internal review and a warrant could be required before undercover means are used against those in government.[10]

5. SOME ADDITIONAL CONSEQUENCES

Apart from direct impact, using covert tactics internally may have other mixed and paradoxical consequences. Just because a policy may work and is legal, it does not follow that it is a wise policy. Covert anticipatory means have a price tag not found with conventional overt tactics, such as interviews and forensic analysis carried out after a violation has occurred.

Undercover tactics, regardless of the context in which they are used, raise troubling issues such as the possible creation of crimes that are an artifact of the investigation, the direction of resources from known to possible offenses, police becoming criminals, the tangled web of interaction that can follow deception, the setting of bad examples by the state, the invasion of privacy and the creation of climates of suspicion and fear. When the state uses the tactic against itself the danger of political targeting is clear and there may be unintended threats to legitimacy.

The undercover tactic offers a resource which the unscrupulous can use against their rivals and, taken to an extreme, can involve a kind of civil war between the branches of government.[11] Secrecy and the ability to tempt and manipulate may make it possible to present evidence of seeming violation. Even when there are fair grounds for an investigation, political issues may arise with respect to the timing of the inquiry and arrests. If done too close to an election, charges of partisanship may arise.[12]

---

10. Wilson (1980) suggests such a warrant procedure. Yet introducing a restrictive standard such as probable cause means that the investigation must follow the contours of what authorities can obtain probable cause for. There is no reason to think that the probable cause available to authorities will conform to the degree of social harm from an offense, nor that it will contain less biases than those found with the traditional system of mobilizing the law in a reactive fashion. This defeats one of the main advantages of undercover means which is to find out if wrongdoing is going on, in order to justify obtaining a warrant for searches or electronic eavesdropping.
11. This contrasts with a checks and balances view, in which the prospect of occasional secret investigations by other branches or units is thought to create honesty. It can prevent cover-ups, oversights and laziness. Italy with rival national police forces is cited as an example of the guards keeping each other honest, if at the price of some overlap of function and increased expense. The same argument holds for competition among federal and local prosecutors.
12. It is interesting to note that some Congressmen have even been elected after having been arrested and found guilty.

Relative to offenses such as theft and homicide, corruption is not only harder to discover, it is also generally harder to define, and easier to justify. The norms of a free enterprise, democratic society encourage 'wheeling and dealing' and give and take. They support negotiation and persuasion. This can mean some persons back into committing technical violations without the intent to commit a crime. It can also mean greater ease in manipulating an individual into committing an offense than is the case for most other violations. For elected officials, the line between political contributions and buying favors and extortion can be thin. It is often not clear just what money buys – access or influence. This of course also offers protection for those wishing to commit crimes under color of serving constituents and responsive leadership. The language used may mask the essence of the transaction. It also makes it easier to justify. The accused often testify that they gave money as a gift, or a political contribution, not as a bribe and sometimes they are telling the truth. Yet those in office must be sensitive to the appearance of misconduct, as well as the reality.

The routine discretion in the enforcement role, the breadth of criminal laws such as conspiracy and the legitimate imperative to follow up on suggestions of illegality (which can be secretly contrived by agents wishing to carry out an injury) can mask the political motivation that may lie behind an investigation.

The case of Washington D.C. Mayor Marion Barry nicely illustrates some of the above issues (*N.Y. Times*, 27 June 1990 and Marx, 1991). Barry was lured to a police-arranged meeting with a former girl friend. After he purchased and used drugs she provided, he was arrested on a misdemeanor possession charge.

Barry was widely believed to be a user of illegal drugs, and many of those close to him had been indicted on corruption charges. Yet some observers saw this as an example of a discriminatory pattern in which scarce federal resources have been disproportionately focused on minority government officials. The Barry case appeared to some observers to be a witch hunt in which the government went to great lengths to find evidence against Barry. It was unable to find sufficient evidence to obtain a warrant or to indict. It then turned to the undercover tactic, for which there is no legal requirement, and it further traded in, what is to some observers, the cheap currency of intimate relations.

The prosecutor who directed the case announced the highly publicized arrest three days before he himself announced that he was running for office. It also appears that the criminal law was being used not for prosecution, but as a resource to negotiate a political end. The prosecutor hinted he would exchange leniency in return for the Mayor's resignation.

Some questions apply regardless of whether or not the target is in government: is it wise to focus scarce resources on occasional users rather than dealers? Shouldn't authorities try to prevent crime rather than to facilitate it? Or if the latter, shouldn't they seek to minimize it (in this case intervening after cocaine was purchased, but before it was used)? If a case for indictment cannot be made before a grand jury, or before a judge for permission to search, wiretap or bug, is it appropriate to move to an undercover temptation for which there is no legal minimum threshold, particularly when a political figure from a minority group is involved?

Of course an official who is thought to flagrantly violate the standards he is charged with enforcing communicates cynicism and hypocrisy. The behavior of leaders is not only instrumental, it is also educational and symbolic. Were law enforcement authorities to apply a more restrictive standard before a political figure became the target of an undercover investigation, they might be accused of favoritism and corruption themselves. It would be wrong for authorities not to pursue allegations of wrongdoing, regardless of whom they implicate. The issue is in how those are pursued.

Some of the dangers of undercover means can be minimized by appropriate policies for targeting and carrying out an investigation. The FBI for example requires a special high-level review of all 'sensitive' cases, a category which includes any investigation of an important political figure. There are restrictions on how tempting an offer can be (it shouldn't exceed what would be found in the real world) and on how many times a target can be approached. Some investigations can be structured so that those drawn in self-select, rather than their being directly targeted.

Even absent political targeting, the expanded use of the tactic to deal with corruption has led to unintended consequences and conflict among agencies with similar goals. The tables may get turned and the original police targets seek to arrest those trying to arrest them. For example in a case in Bridgeport, Connecticut, as part of an FBI corruption investigation, an informer offered a $5,000 bribe to the superintendent of police, who at first pretended to be interested. However as the bribe was to be passed, the superintendent rejected it and arrested the informer. He later sought to have the FBI agents involved arrested for bribery. The FBI in turn threatened to have him arrested on obstruction-of-justice charges. The FBI demanded its money and bugging equipment back, while Bridgeport officials wanted to give the $5,000 to charity (*N.Y. Times*, 21 August 1981).

In what the sheriff of Galveston County, Texas, called 'the sting that got stung,' a man approached sheriff's deputies with an offer to 'buy protection' for a cocaine smuggling operation. He offered to pay $75,000 in bribes to three county officials. The sheriff s department in response set up its own undercover operation for what it thought was a major drug-smuggling operation. After several meetings, the bearer of the bribe was arrested and spent the night in jail. The sheriff's department sought to prosecute the agent, but the district attorney was unwilling. County officials gave the FBI a $7,000 bill for expenses incurred in their part of the investigation (Marx, 1988). Such keystone cop fiascos generate bad publicity and may harm cooperation between agencies. There is also the risk that competing agencies will make illegitimate use of covert means as part of interagency struggles. Even if it doesn't come to that, inter-organizational strains may be created and cooperation among agencies that need each other may be reduced.

Do such investigations help or hurt legitimacy? Law enforcement leaders publicly proclaim that internal investigations show that the agency is vigilant and can control itself. Aggressive internal uses can send a message to the public that the agency is honest and will not tolerate abuses. As such they may increase confidence in government and law-abiding behavior.

Public images of the honesty of social control agents is likely to affect the public's behavior. Internal enforcement has symbolic communications consequences. It may increase public confidence in government. Elected officials, judges and police are role models and parental figures. When they are viewed as moral exemplars and beyond reproach, there is probably less violation of the rules they are charged with enforcing and public cooperation is greater. There are both moral and practical reasons for this.

Practically, citizens may not report violations if police are seen as corrupt. They may believe that to do so would do no good, or that they would be subject to retaliation. That belief may encourage law breaking. Morally, the belief that authority is corrupt can be a powerful 'neutralization technique.' Sykes and Matza (1957) note that cultural restraints against violations are weakened by beliefs such as 'everyone is doing it' – when that belief extends to authorities, it becomes even easier to justify rule breaking. How serious could the rule be, if even those charged with enforcing it don't honor it? While dynamic and democratic societies need a degree of skepticism and cynicism, they don't need that kind.

Yet corruption patterns are complex. They reflect citizen attitudes and expectations, as well as those of police. There are likely limits on what administrative reforms can accomplish in the short run, when public attitudes are indifferent to or supportive of traditional corruption. Without an aroused citizenry exerting pressure on political leaders and unwilling to tolerate corruption, change will be modest.

Ironically, corruption investigations may serve to decrease legitimacy as well. This involves the mythology around the sacred. Some citizens may conclude that if a few in government are revealed as corrupt, that many more are as well. They may see an investigation as only the visible part of the iceberg and see the revealed evidence as a sign of how bad things really are. Those arrested may be viewed as scapegoats and the investigation as a kind of periodic window dressing. Anything that creates negative publicity for the regime may be seen to harm the public. The example of the government using devious means can also serve to legitimate and stimulate lying among the public.

With respect to internal morale, the tactic is again likely to have contradictory consequences. For the honest it may be welcomed as a way to clean up a problem and to improve the image of the department or institution. Knowledge that undercover investigations are common could help keep people honest and can help them resist peer pressure to participate.

On the other hand it can also lower internal morale, if targeting is done on a basis perceived to be unfair (e.g., directed against political opponents or those a supervisor doesn't like, rather than the worst offenders). It can further the gap between employees and management. The view that 'they are out to get us and they don't trust, appreciate or understand us' is not conducive to the best performance. Aggressive efforts at internal control may even create challenges in which employees in effect say 'if by your actions you imply that you don't trust me and treat me like a potential criminal when I work hard and risk my life, then I'll show you.' An expression found in some police departments is 'you got the name, play the game.' Given the complexity of the law enforcement situation and pressures on police to produce, some internal enforcement efforts may seem from the police perspective (as put by a Los Angeles sheriff's deputy) to be 'like hiring a guy to be a mechanic, and then they don't want you to be greasy.' Police unions have attacked field associate programs as being 'unAmerican.'

Even police leaders of unimpeachable personal integrity often tend to prefer to approach such problems piecemeal and to see corrupt officers simply dismissed, rather than to have extensive investigations and drawn-out trials. The desire to avoid bad publicity is one factor and the protection of higher level colleagues is another. An experienced undercover officer in New York who spent his career investigating his colleagues eventually concludes 'I wasn't a cop hunter; I was a public relations man.' He states 'we would never come close to eliminating police corruption unless we busted through two walls. The Blue Wall that surrounded the entire department was formidable enough, but there was a much stronger Brass Wall protecting the inner enclave, guarding the reputations and careers and pensions of the members of a very exclusive club' (Murano, 1990, 239).

It is an American truism that effective government requires free and open exchange. Yet diplomacy and secrecy have a place as well, particularly in the early stages of policy. These would be damaged if undercover tactics were used on a much wider and more indiscriminate scale. When individuals believe that they are constantly being watched and may be tested at any point, conformity may increase as candor, spontaneity, innovation, and risk-taking decline. Organizations need to encourage flexibility and a confident encountering of their environment. But the fear that any colleague might be an informer, that any conversation recorded, or that secret integrity tests are rampant may encourage a pulling inward and passivity. While it is understandable, the sentiment expressed by former Special Prosecutor Maurice Nadjari: 'if we cannot have absolutely honest public officials, then let's have frightened public officials' must give one pause.[13]

REFERENCES

Cummings, H. McFarland, C. (1937), *Federal Justice*, New York, Macmillan.
Gerson, N. (1977), *The Vidocq Dossier,* Boston, Houghton Miffin.
Gershman, B. (1981), 'The Perjury Trap,' *University of Pennsylvania Law Review,* 129, 624–700.
Hughes, E. (1962), 'Good People and Dirty Work,' *Social Problems,* 10, 3–10.
Commission to Investigate Allegations of Police Corruption and the City's Anti-Corruption Procedures, (1972), *The Knapp Commission Report on Police Corruption,* New York, G. Braziller.
Lardner, J. (1977), 'How Prosecutors Are Nabbed,' *New Republic,* 29 January, 22–25.
Law Enforcement News, 15 June 1990.
Marx, G.T. (1988), *Undercover; Police Surveillance in America,* Berkeley, California, University of California Press.
McAlary, M. (1988), *Buddy Boys,* New York, Charter Books.

---

13. In *Olmstead* v. *U.S.*, 277 U.S. 438 (1928).

Murano, V. (1990), *Cop Hunter,* New York, Pocket Books.
Nadjari, M. (1977), 'I have No Regrets,' *New York Times Magazine,* 27 March.
President's Commission on Law Enforcement and Administration of Justice (1967), *The Challenge of Crime in a Free Society,* Washington D.C., GPO.
President's National Advisory Commission on Civil Disorders (1968), *Report of the National Advisory Commission on Civil Disorders,* Washington D.C., GPO.
Purvis, M. (1936), *American Agent,* New York, Garden City Publishing.
Report of the Subcommittee on Civil and Constitutional Rights (1984), *FBI Undercover Operations,* Washington D.C., GPO.
Riley, W. (1982), 'Confessions of a Harvard Trained G-Man,' *Harvard Business School Bulletin,* October.
Select Committee to Study Law Enforcement Undercover Activities of Components of the Department of Justice (1983), *Hearings, Law Enforcement Undercover Activities,* Washington D.C., GPO.
Sherman, L. (1983), 'From Whodunit to Who Does It; Fairness and Target Selection in Deceptive Investigations,' in: Caplan, G., ed., *Abscam Ethics,* Cambridge, Ma., Ballinger.
Stead, P. (1953), *Vidocq: Picaron of Crime,* London, Staples.
Sykes, G., Matza, D. (1957), 'Techniques of Neutralization; A Theory of Delinquency,' *American Sociological Review,* 22, 664–670.
Ungar, S. (1975), *The FBI,* Boston, Little, Brown.
Welch, N., Marston, D.W. (1984), *Inside Hoover's FBI,* Garden City, N.Y., Doubleday.
Whitehead, D. (1956), *The FBI Story,* New York, Random House.
Wilson, J. (1980), 'The Changing FBI – The Road to Abscam,' *The Public Interest,* Spring, 3–14.
Woods, J. (1973), *The Progressives and the Police; Urban Reform and the Professionalization of the Los Angeles Police,* University of California at Los Angeles (Ph.D. diss.).

Helgi Gunnlaugsson*
and
John F. Galliher* | # The Secret Drug Police of Iceland

1. SECRET POLICING AROUND THE WORLD

Totalitarian regimes of all political stripes on the political right and the left are well-known for reliance on controls applied by highly sophisticated domestic covert policing. One need look no further than former Soviet bloc nations such as East Germany or the crypto-fascist military dictatorships once found in Chile or Argentina to see that this is true. What is more surprising and disturbing is that Marx (1988) found a dramatic level of undercover policing in the United States. One argument available to justify such policing in the U.S. is that the high levels of violent crime, as well as organized drug trafficking, require such extreme measures even in a democratic nation.

However, even in Western democracies with relatively low levels of crime undercover policing has been flourishing in recent years. It has been repeatedly demonstrated that in relatively small and homogeneous nations one can expect low crime rates (Adler, 1983). It is well-known, for example, that Nordic countries such as Norway and Finland have relatively little crime when compared with the United States or even with other European nations. Yet as a consequence of a moral panic in Scandinavia involving drugs, undercover policing has in recent years developed into a sizeable enterprise (Stangeland, 1987) even while drug use in Norway, Sweden, Denmark and Finland has actually been steadily decreasing since the early 1970s (Hauge, 1987). Oslo has a narcotics squad of 100 officers. Helsinki has 40 narcotics officers, even though almost all Finnish drug arrests involve nothing more than hashish (Stangeland, 1987).

---

* Assistant Professor of Sociology, University of Iceland, Reykjavik, Iceland.
** Professor of Sociology, University of Missouri, Columbia, Missouri, United States.

2. CRIME IN ICELAND

In studies of crime patterns in Nordic countries Iceland is typically ignored, perhaps because it has such a small amount of crime, even when compared to other Nordic countries (Table 1), in recent years leading to approximately 100 prisoners, the national prison capacity.

Table 1. Number of Prisoners per 100,000 Population among Countries of the European Council, 1988

Northern Ireland	125.2	Spain	69.2
Scotland	106.2	Denmark	69.0
Luxembourg	103.7	Italy	62.0
England	96.6	Sweden	61.0
Austria	96.0	Ireland	56.0
France	92.0	Norway	47.0
Turkey	90.2	Greece	42.9
West Germany	86.7	Cyprus	42.0
Portugal	84.0	Iceland	41.3
Switzerland	77.6	Holland	36.0
Belgium	70.5	Malta	19.7

Source: *Prison Information Bulletin*, No. 11, June 1988.

Denmark, it has been reported, had twice the Icelandic per capita murder rate and Sweden had five times the Icelandic rate of homicide (Archer and Gartner, 1984). Both had even higher rates of other crime. By the 1990s Iceland had only one recorded case of bank robbery (van den Hoonaard, 1991). Additional research documented 45 murders in Iceland between 1900 and 1979, or just over one every other year (Petursson and Gudjonsson, 1981). Prior to 1970 government records included only 12 cases of murder and 24 from 1970–1989 (Hardardottir, 1991). A recent study (Skinner, 1986, 287) found very little drug use among Icelandic adolescents, with over 92 per cent reporting they had never used any illegal drug, and no evidence of a 'drug culture' there.

It is not surprising that Iceland has so little crime for it is a nation with no marked poverty and relatively little social and economic stratification (Gunnlaugsson and Galliher, 1986). As Tomasson (1980, 195) has noted: 'There are few things Icelanders believe more about themselves than that theirs is a country where there is equality among interacting individuals and equality of opportunity.' Iceland has one of the highest standards of living in the world, with 100 per cent literacy and an unemployment rate hovering around one per cent (Tomasson, 1980), even though during the 1990s unemployment has been increasing. It is arguable that this egalitarian ideology and actual lack of deprivation is a consequence of the fact that Iceland is one of very few European nations never to have had a system of nobility. A constitutional representative form of government was established in A.D. 930 making it the oldest parliament in the world (U.S. Department of State, 1984).

In addition, this small nation of approximately 260,000 people, about the size of Kentucky, is ethnically homogeneous and isolated by over 500 miles of the

North Atlantic ocean from its nearest European neighbor. The low Icelandic crime rate may not only be a consequence of its geographic isolation, but also of low immigration from foreign nations. This in turn is a product not only of government policy but the probable lack of appeal to foreigners of this isolated island near the North Pole, covered primarily by glaciers, lava fields, mountains and volcanos.

Perhaps because there was little other crime to concern itself with for over 70 years Iceland attempted to use the penal law to prohibit one alcoholic substance, beer, while allowing all others (Gunnlaugsson and Galliher, 1986). Indeed, between 1929 and 1938 half of the prison population was serving time for alcohol offenses such as illegal brewing of various alcoholic beverages (Heiddal, 1957). In spite of its low crime rate we will demonstrate that a moral panic has in recent years descended upon Iceland that has resulted in the abrogation of its constitutional law, providing an important object lesson for other nations.

3. EVIDENCE OF AN ICELANDIC MORAL PANIC

Legislation dealing with narcotics dates back to 1923 when an international convention, of which Iceland was a member, passed a resolution banning importation, exportation, and production of raw opium (Parliament Law 14/1923; see also Bruun et al., 1975). There is no evidence of this law being enforced, but by the late 1960s with international concern about drug use among the young increasing, Iceland's narcotics laws were revised and extended to make cannabis and LSD illegal. In 1969 the Icelandic police first seized a controlled substance. In 1971 a specific unit was established within the Reykjavik police force solely to investigate drug cases. In 1973 a separate drug court was established (Parliament Law, no. 52/1973). In 1974 new drug laws were passed which were intended to replace the old opium law of the 1920s and impose more severe penalties on major drug violators because according to the law's preamble (no. 65, 1974): 'use of drugs is becoming a serious problem.' This new type of crime continued to grow until the 1980s when prison statistics from 1985–1990 demonstrate that property and traffic offenders are the most common charges against prison inmates followed by drug offenses (Table 2).

Table 2. Cause of Incarceration, 1985–1990

Type of Offense	1985	1986	1987	1988	1989	1990
Property Crimes	137	161	150	146	180	166
Traffic	52	66	65	57	82	101
Drug Violations	16	33	30	32	25	23
Homicide	12	11	12	11	14	16
Sex Crimes	10	7	6	12	12	21
Other	22	25	24	37	21	14

Press reports taken at five year intervals from 1969 through 1984 from the *Morgunbladid,* the largest circulation daily newspaper (circulation over 50,000) reflect the development of this concern. The paper is read by virtually the entire nation and takes pride in being the nation's newspaper with an objective approach to newsworthy events. In 1969 of 239 crime-related articles only 16, or seven per cent, dealt with drugs. Reporting on drug use among Icelanders began to heat up in the fall. A headline sounded the alarm: 'Rumors that Adolescents use Hashish' (*Morgunbladid*, 1969a). However, the article's text admitted: 'though such substances have never been found among passengers to Iceland ... Customs officials have increased their control to suspend all doubts.' Soon the suspicion of drug use among adolescents was confirmed (*Morgunbladid*, 1969b): 'Adolescents found using drugs.' This incident involved two fourteen-year-old girls and a fifteen-year-old boy. On 18 November a story with the headline 'Arrested with Hard Drugs' (*Morgunbladid*, 1969c) involved five Icelanders (18–20 years old) arrested at a Reykjavik party. To emphasize how serious these events were seen to be, an editorial which appeared on 16 December (*Morgunbladid*, 1969d) observed that 'this has not been a problem here in Iceland which is why there is no legislation concerning drugs. The parliament needs to pass a law where stiff penalties are adopted.'

In 1974 there were only 17 drug-related crime stories (6 per cent of the total), and most involved cannabis. One story involved LSD. Several involved foreigners, especially soldiers stationed at the NATO base in Keflavik. But by 1979 out of a total of 277 crime stories, 68 or 24 per cent dealt with drugs. On 14 December (*Morgunbladid*, 1979b) a full page was devoted to a lengthy interview with the deputy director of Iceland's new drug policing agency in which he stated that the drug problem in Iceland due to the growth of heroin trafficking and indoor marihuana growing in his view 'has escalated in recent years and more police manpower and education about drugs is needed to combat this problem.'

In 1984, 40 or 18 per cent of crime-related press articles dealt with drugs. Seven of these articles report on conferences for the public on the dreaded effects of drugs, one of which was organized by an Icelandic political party. Wire-tapping was used in drug cases, for 'by law a judge can permit wire-tapping when the security of the state permits it or when there are major criminal cases' (*Morgunbladid*, 1984b). The paper agreed that these drug offenses were major criminal cases, stating its position strongly in one of two anti-drug editorials that year: 'penalties should be stiffened as this is such serious and condemnable behavior that it is not possible to justify a soft approach. [And] four tons of hashish are believed to be used in Iceland per year' (*Morgunbladid*, 1984a). A member of parliament was so outraged that he proclaimed (*Morgunbladid*, 1984c): 'We need more than anything else to exterminate this disgrace, find those bastards who are behind the smuggling of drugs for monetary reasons, changing children to wretches in a relatively short period of time.' Two drug cases received particular attention. The first involved a drug seizure by the police on an Icelandic ship. Four people were arrested and accused of having smuggled 700 grams of amphetamines and 400 grams of hashish oil (*Morgunbladid*, 1984e). The other case involved the smuggling of 226 doses of LSD and 100 grams of amphetamines and cocaine: 'The largest case involving LSD ever' (*Morgunbladid*, 1984g).

Finally, in 1989, 52 or 20 per cent of crime-related articles dealt with drugs. An investigator assigned to the police was interviewed by the press (*Morgun-*

bladid, 1989a) about the drug situation in Iceland. He claimed that his agency had information indicating that the methods of smuggling drugs into Iceland were becoming much more sophisticated and that the use of hard drugs was becoming much more widespread, but he admitted that the exact dimensions of these problems 'had not been mapped out.'

A phone survey was conducted in June 1989 by Helgi Gunnlaugsson, with the assistance of the University of Iceland's Social Science Research Institute. A sample of one thousand individuals were selected. The response rate was approximately 73 per cent and a satisfactory congruence between the sample and the nation by sex, age and residence was achieved. Of these, 68 per cent responded that crime in Iceland was either a 'great' (12 per cent) or 'rather great' problem (56 per cent). In addition, 90 per cent felt crime was a growing problem in Iceland. Seventy-three per cent felt that punishments were too lenient. Forty per cent of respondents indicated that drug use was the most serious single type of crime in Iceland – nearly twice the next most frequently mentioned type. Moreover, 55 per cent said that substance abuse is the 'most likely explanation' of why Icelanders become involved in crime – more than doubling the next most frequently mentioned reason given. Finally, respondents were asked if they or anyone in their household had been the victim of a violent crime during the preceding 6 months. At approximately two per cent, the level of violent crime victimization is lower than in other Scandinavian countries (Aromaa, 1974). Yet Icelanders see crime as a serious problem that is getting worse. This is true even though few have been personally victimized, and fewer than is true in other Nordic countries. They also see drug offenses as the most serious crime problem, and also see most crime as caused by substance abuse. The fear of crime absent the experience of crime is not unlike the fear of witches reported by Erikson in the Massachusetts Bay Colony (Erikson, 1966).

4. HISTORY OF POLICING IN ICELAND

The first evidence of police officers in this nation has been traced to the late 18th century in Reykjavik which would later become the capital city. The first officers were paid by local trading companies to watch for fires at night. After Reykjavik was granted the official status of a municipality in 1786 two officers were hired by the city. By 1918 the city had ten officers to police a city of 1,703 (Jonsson, 1938). As of 1990 the city had 260 police officers serving a population of approximately 120,000. One unit in this department has the specific responsibility of narcotics control and has become its largest specialized division. Policing grew more slowly in the sparsely populated regions of the nation, but by 1990 (including customs officials) there were over 300 officers stationed outside the capital city. Sixty-five of these are assigned to the national airport area and 42 to the State Criminal Investigative Police (SCIP). The SCIP was established by law in 1976 (no. 108). This marked a major step in the direction of separating policing from the courts in the nation's movement away from an inquisitional system to an accusatory system as required by law (Law no. 27, 1951; Thormundsson, 1979, 58).

5. SECRET POLICING IN ICELAND

In contradiction to 1951 legislation separating the police and the courts, in 1973 the parliament (Law no. 52) established a separate drug police unit to be supervised by a separate drug court (Thormundsson, 1980, 12). Creating a separate apparatus, contrary to the emerging accusatory law, reflects the deep concern many Icelanders felt about this new and frightening problem. The drug police were sent to the United States for training on American methods of narcotics law enforcement. In a recent interview in a popular magazine the head of the drug police stated: 'Our officers do participate in seminars held by the U.S. federal police division in charge of drugs, the DEA [Drug Enforcement Administration]' (*Mannlif*, 1992). A continuing legal problem with these American-trained agents is that in two occasions, 1989 and 1990, the Supreme Court disqualified the head judge of the drug court due to the close ties between the court and the drug police. These decisions would lead in 1992 to the disbanding of the separate drug court, but the drug police still operate as a separate unit. Earlier the narcotics officers had been critical of the idea of joining forces with other police and customs agencies (*Morgunbladid*, 1984d), but the chief of the SCIP noted that from the beginning of his agency drug cases were to be investigated by the SCIP, but not as a separate narcotics police organization and not under court authority (*Morgunbladid*, 1984f).

What triggered this change was a surprisingly minor case which took place in Akureyri, a town of approximately 15,000 in northern Iceland (*Morgunbladid*, 1991). The story began in 1985 when a man was charged with failing to observe a stop sign. The driver was issued a citation by the local sheriff and then, with the sheriff acting also as the local judge, the driver was found guilty and fined. The driver was, however, convinced of his innocence and appealed to the Icelandic Supreme Court. When the court dismissed his appeal he then appealed directly to the European Human Rights Council and here his appeal was sustained, but the parliament and the Justice Ministry had already decided to adopt accusatory legal procedures throughout the nation.

Given the very close ties with the drug police, acquittals in the drug court were understandably almost nonexistent. The drug court records of case dispositions indicated no cases that resulted in not guilty findings (*see* Table 3).

Table 3. Legal Outcome in Drug Court Cases, 1985–1990

	1985	1986	1987	1988	1989	1990
Guilty Plea (Reconciliation)	271	227	301	299	276	297
Indictment	39	34	29	18	34	15
House Search Warrant	0	65	120	73	79	70

However, another source (Kristmundsson, 1985) indicates that approximately one per cent of drug cases have ended in acquittal. In any case, once the court and the police have worked up a case together and brought it into court there is little further prosecution work to be done to guarantee a conviction. Compared to charges of rape, for example, the differences are dramatic. The SCIP reports that from 1 July 1977 to 31 December 1983 of 126 cases of rape allegations handled by the police only 30 resulted in rape convictions.

Not only are acquittals in the drug court nonexistent, but predictably in such a legal environment appeals are very rare as well. The drug court judge observed:

> In fact they are very few, but they seem to come up with many cases pending at the same time. One year, for instance, we had a total of 16 cases being appealed and it looks like this is being done to make processing these cases more difficult and cumbersome. They are, I am sure, merely buying themselves some time.

This judge obviously sees appeals as unessential for a modern democratic legal system. Correspondingly, two people were arrested for attempting to smuggle in one kilo of cocaine from the United States (*Morgunbladid,* 1989b). The principal offender was sentenced to 7 months of solitary confinement. The severity was due to his steadfast refusal to admit his guilt despite the testimony of others to the contrary.

According to one of the Drug Bureau's investigators the precise number of narcotics officers is a state secret, but another source in the Reykjavik police department reported it to be around 14 by 1990. As seen in Table 4 the drug police annual reports indicate they have arrested approximately 400 suspects per year between 1986 and 1990 and over 75 per cent of these cases involved drugs for private use as opposed to sales. In addition, it should be noted that over 90 per cent of the grams of drugs seized by the drug police have involved cannabis seeds or plants, hashish or hashish oil and marihuana (Table 5). Narcotics police understandably spend some time at the international airport in Keflavik in cooperation with customs and airline officials. They especially look for suspicious travellers, like those with a prior drug conviction. This is one of the few routes into Iceland, making drug smuggling more difficult and easier to control.

Table 4. Number of Suspects Known by the Icelandic Drug Police, 1986–1990

	1986	1987	1988	1989	1990
Private Use	304	366	388	306	344
Sale	57	85	80	71	53
Importation	35	39	53	30	47

Table 5. Type and Amount of Substances Seized by the Icelandic Drug Police, 1985–1990 (expressed in grams, except LSD in doses)

	1985	1986	1987	1988	1989	1990
Hashish	8906	10383	14916	1917	9321	6759
Hashish Oil	0.2	0	962	105	4	0
Marihuana	573	272	235	55	47	73
Cannabis Seeds	0	0	0	6	1014	43
Cannabis Plants	27	0	16	31	13	15
Amphetamines	970	1698	365	639	198	199
Cocaine	24	7	534	100	746	205
Heroin	0	0	0	0.1	0	0
LSD	2223	2	0	6	694	58

In addition, to give some insight into the ages of those charged, the 1986 annual report of the drug police indicates that 55 per cent of those charged were between the ages of 21–30, and 18 per cent under 20.

One relatively frequent method the drug police uses involves the search of private homes. The drug court judge:

> This year [as of August 1991] I have already issued 60 search warrants and the most the court has issued in one year is a total of 120 search warrants, which is much more common than in other criminal cases. This is in fact a good method and it keeps drug trafficking under some control, deters customers and dealers from major drug dealing.

In 1984 the *Morgunbladid* (1984d) printed an open letter from six narcotics officers critical of a recommendation from parliament that all law enforcement agencies join the fight against drugs, including the SCIP and customs officials. The officers said: 'We believe that investigation of drug cases has to be held in only one hand instead of splitting up the work between different agencies ... the separate drug police is the most practical thing.'

When a principal investigator of the drug bureau was asked about the nature of the nation's drug market he said:

> We first got in touch with drugs in Iceland around 1970, during the hippie era, when people got together and pitched in money to send someone abroad to purchase drugs for their own private consumption. Now, the pattern is different and is becoming more business-like with a specialized division of labor. One person comes up with the money, another takes care of the importation, and the third distributes the drug here in Iceland. And these people do not necessarily use drugs themselves, they are only doing this for high financial returns. This is actually very similar to methods employed abroad.

If it can be argued that the crime problems in Iceland largely mirror those in other nations, then foreign methods of law enforcement become reasonable. According to this investigator, the official policy of the drug bureau is not to give information about their search and seizure procedures, but stated that their top priority was:

> to control importation, then distribution and finally consumption of controlled substances. Most of our cases come out of prior investigation inquiries and only a few out of random search at airports and landing docks. This is what makes our activities different from other police work, we investigate cases before the actual crime is committed.

That is, the Icelandic drug police are largely engaged in what Marx (1988) has referred to as facilitative law enforcement, which is facilitative in the sense of attempting to create some crime that might otherwise not take place.

THE SECRET DRUG POLICE OF ICELAND

6. EXAMPLES OF COVERT POLICING PRACTICES

In arresting two men in 1979 an investigator with the Keflavik police department secretly

> had two females put a bag with two bottles of vodka on which taxes had not been paid and a case of [illegal] beer in their trunk. Then he asked the females to have the two persons drive them to a specific location. The police investigator then sent other officers to this location to arrest the two men for the goods in the trunk of their car (*Morgunbladid*, 1979a).

It seemed that one of the suspects, a taxi driver, had been suspected of illegal activities for some time but the police had never been able to make a case against him. The officer who planned this event was sentenced to 9 months in prison, a deputy judge, another police officer and the women received lesser sentences. Thus, the courts sent a clear message that such practices would not be tolerated.

In spite of this clear precedent the director of the drug police made a confidential agreement with an ex-convict to work as an *agent provocateur* for him to attempt to purchase 1.2 kilos of cocaine from an acquaintance whom he had met in prison the preceding year. The acquaintance was reportedly not at all interested in selling drugs in Iceland and instead planned on transporting the cocaine in his possession to Denmark (*Prosecution* v. *Magnusson*, 1992). But the informant was persistent and finally his acquaintance grudgingly decided to sell most of it, even though he had originally not planned to sell it in Iceland, and had in fact attempted earlier to market the drugs in Denmark.

The director and several of his officers, none of whom were told the full story, then gathered to make a major drug arrest. There was a car chase in which one officer was seriously injured. This case created an uproar in Iceland, where among other things, the legality of the police operation was questioned, as well as the secret nature of the director's agreement. This was seen by some in Iceland as an illustration of an FBI/CIA mentality where the ends justify the means. A newspaper article noted:

> Drug police officers had been keeping an eye on a male person and gave him a signal to stop his car around midnight last night but he failed to do so and sped away ... his speeding car hit a police car parked on the highway to block his way, and a fire broke out.

The article's headline told it all: 'Police Officer's Life in Danger' (*Morgunbladid*, 1992a). The leaders of the Reykjavik police force publicly defended this chase as being in accordance with 'proper regulations' (*Morgunbladid*, 1992b).

On the other hand the head physician of Iceland's drug rehabilitation unit dismissed the danger of this individual and the significance of the charges (*Morgunbladid*, 1992c). He said: 'I don't have the slightest idea of how 1.2 kilos of cocaine can be marketed here' because there were only 5–10 heavy users of cocaine diagnosed in the nation each year. And an Icelandic Law School textbook argues that such practices are:

hardly within legal limits ... [and] may not be used if only to make someone do something he otherwise would not have done ... it is by all means better that a police officer should be an agent rather than an ordinary citizen ... [and it is] not feasible to use convicts (Thormundsson, 1980, 139–141).

An attorney who has often defended those arrested in drug cases argued in an interview that: 'I think it is very doubtful that this police conduct was legal ... they could have avoided the car chase and seized the drugs without it.' Yet most recently the Supreme Court confirmed the seven year sentence against the suspect even though the court recognized that the director of the drug police:

did not consult sufficiently with the Reykjavik police ... [and] it is especially important in this case because the *agent provocateur* was an ex-convict awaiting a new conviction for a drug violation ... [But] despite the lack of consultation it is not sufficient to grant acquittal or reduction of the penalty (*Morgunbladid*, 1993).

Marx (1988) discussed similar 'facilitative operations' in American drug cases. 'In a ... Florida case, a female undercover officer offered sexual favors to a suspect if he would sell her marihuana' (Marx, 1988, 131). In another case 'a man purchased heroin from a government informant; the latter then put the suspect in contact with two other government agents to whom the heroin was sold' (Marx, 1988, 64). Yet the closest parallel involving injury to law enforcement agents was where 'Police pretending to be drug dealers may be attacked by vigilantes playing an undercover role. This apparently happened in the Los Angeles case ... when a narcotics agent was shot while trying to purchase heroin' (Marx, 1988, 178).

7. MORAL AND GEOGRAPHICAL BOUNDARY MAINTENANCE

Icelanders have long had a deep concern with substance abuse, especially involving youth, as reflected in their long-lasting prohibition of beer. The beer prohibition was for many years justified primarily as a means of protecting young people (Gunnlaugsson and Galliher, 1986). Consistent with this cultural aversion to mind-altering substances is that in the Icelandic language the term for drugs, *eiturlyf*, translates literally as 'poison medicine.' In addition, in Iceland the rate of traffic offenses involving alcohol is considerably higher than in other Nordic countries. Criminal court cases involving drunk driving and smuggling accounted for a third of all criminal court cases for the period 1966–1971 (Tomasson, 1980). Further evidence of this concern is that a poll in 1990 found that eighty per cent of Icelanders believed that it is never justifiable to use cannabis, and 74 per cent claimed that they did not want drug users as neighbors (Social Sciences Research Institute, 1991). This concern in turn was traditionally based on beliefs about Icelander's special vulnerability due to their Icelandic heritage. For example, one M.P. noted: 'Icelanders are not able to use alcohol as civilized persons, their nature is still too much of the Viking kind, they get too excited and brutal with alcohol usage. The parliament should be like a father to a child' (Gunnlaugsson and Galliher, 1986, 341). But a reflection of the relatively minor nature of Iceland's drug problem is that a study found that during 1987–1988 less than four per cent of all emergencies involving intoxication involved illegal drugs, a significantly lower percentage than found in other western nations (*Journal of Medical Doctors,* 1991). A report in 1985 could verify not a single death from drug overdose in the nation's history (Kristmundsson, 1985). In 1983 approximately 25 per cent of Icelandic respondents ages 16–36 had used cannabis at least once (Kristmundsson, 1985), compared to 54 per cent of American high school seniors in 1985 who had done so (Bachman *et al.*, 1986).

Iceland is changing both due to external pressures and the internal dynamics of the nation. There is more international travel routed through Iceland and also the nation is becoming increasingly urban (Gunnlaugsson and Galliher, 1986). Since Iceland has a very short growing season, drugs are generally imported, and are therefore perceived as being a foreign threat, making them ideal for boundary maintenance. In his description of the Massachusetts Bay Colony, Erikson (1966) argued that crime was required to maintain the collective meaning or moral boundaries within a group irrespective of the local stratification system. Thus in a small, isolated society such as the Massachusetts Bay Colony, in the midst of a largely unsettled wilderness, with little traditional crime, crime was invented and thoughts became crimes. Iceland is somewhat similar to the Massachusetts Bay Colony in that it is a relatively small society with little crime, and isolated by the North Atlantic from its nearest European neighbor. In the final analysis, the Icelandic case demonstrates that in any society, whatever the most serious offenses are, they will be considered serious offenses. This being the case, there is always the likelihood of law enforcement overreaction even in nations with the longest traditions of democratic governance.

REFERENCES

Adler, F. (1983), *Nations Not Obsessed with Crime*, Littleton, Co., Fred B. Rothman and Company.

Archer, D., Gartner, R. (1984), *Violence and Crime in Cross-National Perspective*, New Haven, Yale University Press.

Aromaa, K. (1974), 'Our Violence,' *Scandinavian Studies in Criminology*, 5, London, Martin Robertson, Ltd., 35–46.

Bachman, J.G., Johnston, L.D., O'Malley, P.M., Humphrey, R.H. (1986), *Changes in Marihuana Use Linked to Changes in Perceived Risks and Disapproval. Monitoring the Future*, Ann Arbor, University of Michigan, Institute for Social Research (Occasional Paper no. 19).

Bruun, K., Pan, P., Rexed, I. (1975), *The Gentleman's Club; International Control of Drugs and Alcohol*, Chicago, University of Chicago Press.

Erikson, K.T. (1966), *Wayward Puritans; A Study in the Sociology of Deviance*, New York, John Wiley and Sons, Inc.

Gunnlaugsson, H., Galliher, J.F. (1986), 'Prohibition of Beer in Iceland: An International Test of Symbolic Politics,' *Law and Society Review*, 20, 335–353.
Hardardottir, R. (1991), 'On Violation of Article 211 of the General Penal Code,' *Journal of Law School Students*, 1st issue.
Hauge, R. (1987), 'The Controversy between Self-Reported Studies and Crime Statistics on Drug Use,' *Scandinavian Studies in Criminology*, 8, Oslo, Norwegian University Press, 22–23.
Heiddal, S. (1957), *Destiny at Litla Hrauni Prison*, Reykjavik, Idunn.
Jonsson, G. (1938), *The Police in Reykjavik*, Reykjavik.
Journal of Medical Doctors (1991), 'Research on Intoxication at Borgarspitali Hospital 1987–1988,' 10 December.
Kristmundsson, O.H. (1985), *Illegal Drugs in Iceland*, The Justice and Church Ministry of Iceland.
Mannif (1992), 'The War Against the Dealers of Death,' November, 6–15.
Marx, G.T. (1988), '*Undercover; Police Surveillance in America*, Berkeley, University of California Press.
Morgunbladid (1969a), 'Rumors that Adolescents Use Hashish,' 9 October, 28.
Morgunbladid (1969b), 'Adolescents Found Using Drugs,' 25 October, 32.
Morgunbladid (1969c), 'Arrested with Hard Drugs,' 18 November, 32.
Morgunbladid (1969d) [Editorial], 'All Drugs Are Dangerous', 16 December, 16.
Morgunbladid (1979a), 'Sentenced to Nine Months in Prison for an Illegal Arrest,' 1 June, 32.
Morgunbladid (1979b), 'The Drug Problem in Iceland is Becoming More Serious,' 14 December, 17, 32.
Morgunbladid (1984a) [Editorial], 'National Force Against Drugs,' 7 January, 20.
Morgunbladid (1984b), 'Drug Police: Telephones Tapped in 10 Cases in the Past Two Years,' 10 January, 2.
Morgunbladid (1984c), 'Emergency Center for Young Drug Users,' 4 March, 38–39.
Morgunbladid (1984d), 'Strange Propositions on Actions in Drug Cases,' 27 March, 13.
Morgunbladid (1984e), 'Police Seize 700 Grams of Amphetamines and 400 Grams of Hashish Oil,' 30 May, 48.
Morgunbladid (1984f) 'Comment from Chief of SCIP, Drug Police and the Drug Court May Be Improved,' 5 July, 2.
Morgunbladid (1984), 'Biggest LSD Case in Iceland Ever, 6 in Custody,' 25 November, 2.
Morgunbladid (1989a), 'Methods of Smuggling Become More Sophisticated: Use of Hard Drugs Not Mapped Out, Outside the Group of Reprobates,' 12 February, 2.
Morgunbladid (1989b), 'Released after Seven Months in Custody,' 8 December, 2.
Morgunbladid (1991), 'Farewell to the Legacy of Monarchy,' 6 October, 25–27.
Morgunbladid (1992a), 'Police Officer's Life in Danger,' 18 August, 52.
Morgunbladid (1992b), 'The Car Chase Was in Accordance with Proper Police Conduct and Regulations,' 19 August, 21.

Morgunbladid (1992c), '5–10 Heavy Users of Cocaine Diagnosed Each Year at Vog Detox,' 20 August, 20–21.
Morgunbladid (1993), 'Investigative Methods within Reasonable Limits,' 22 May, 25.
Parliament Laws: 1923, no. 14; 1951, no. 27; 1973, no. 52; 1974, no. 65; 1976, no. 108.
Petursson, H., Gudjonsson, G.H. (1981), 'Psychiatric Aspects of Homicide,' *Acta Psychiatry Scand.*, 64, 336–372.
Prison Information Bulletin (1988), no. 11, June, The European Council.
Prosecution v. *Steinn Armann Magnusson*, no. S–105/1992, 4 December.
Skinner, W.F. (1986), 'Delinquency, Crime, and Development; A Case Study of Iceland,' *Journal of Research in Crime and Delinquency*, 23, 268–294.
Stangeland, P. (1987), 'Introduction,' *Scandinavian Studies in Criminology*, 8, Oslo, Norwegian University Press, 7–11.
Social Sciences Research Institute (SSRI) (1991), Olafsson, S., Jonsson, F.H., *Values in Modern Societies*, Reykjavik.
Thormundsson, J. (1979), *Court Procedure*, vol. 1, Reykjavik.
Thormundsson, J. (1980), *Court Procedure*, vol. 2, 2nd edition, Reykjavik.
Tomasson, R.F. (1980), *Iceland; The First New Society*, Minneapolis, University of Minnesota Press.
United States Department of State (1984), *Bureau of Public Affairs; Background Notes*, July.
Van den Hoonaard, W.C. (1991), 'A Nation's Innocence: Myth and Reality of Crime in Iceland,' *Scandinavian-Canadian Studies*, 4, 97–114.

Dennis Töllborg* | Undercover in Sweden: The Swedish Security Police and Their Modi Operandi

1. DIRECTION AND DATA SOURCES

This essay addresses what in Sweden are called 'unconventional methods.'[1] Following a description of the organizational structure and tasks of the security police I describe their operations as this relates to registers, searches, wire-tapping, bugging, and informers and crime provocation. Finally, I offer some conclusions reflecting my perspective as a legal scholar.

'Unconventional police methods' are used primarily by the Security Police. My main references are the Swedish Government Official Reports (SOU). The most important SOU in this essay are the investigations by the so-called *SÄPO-kommittén*, which actually are three more or less connected committees which between 1987 and 1990 have been investigating the Swedish Security Police and the practice of the Swedish Personnel Control Ordinance, a system for positive vetting. Their reports number SOU 1988:16, 1989:18 and 1990:51. Another important source for this essay is the extensive preliminary investigation records from Stockholm Prosecution District (C6–1–004–88) and the Customs Criminal Section of the Helsingborg Police District (R 189–88) in the so-called bugging and smuggling trials.

The 'bugging-case' involved some of the highest ranked police chiefs in Sweden for illegal bugging of some Kurds after the Palme assassination. In December 1990, the former head of the Security Police and leader of the Palme investigation, Hans Holmér and P-G. Näss, deputy commissioner of the Security Police, and Christer Ekberg, head of the operations bureau, were fined for illegal listening in.

---

* A.i. Professor, Department of Law, School of Economics and Law, University of Gothenburg, Göteborg, Sweden.
1. This is a shortened version of the report *Covert Policing in Sweden; The Swedish Security Police* (1991). The full version, which contains footnotes and references to quoted material and sources, can be ordered from Dennis Töllborg, Department of Law, Viktoriagatan 13, S-411 25 Göteborg, Sweden.

The smuggling trial (the so-called Ebbe Carlsson affair) involved an unsuccessful attempt at smuggling bugging equipment into the country. Ebbe Carlsson began a secret investigation, sanctioned by his friend the Minister of Justice regarding the murder of Olof Palme. To do that he needed bugging equipment, not available in Sweden. Since bugging equipment may not be used in Sweden, it needed to be smuggled in. Help for this was received from the French security service. Using external financing and sham invoices they hoped that the equipment could not be traced to the Security Police. The subordinate policeman commissioned to enter the goods into the country on 1 June 1988 was arrested by the Customs Criminal Section. The whole story was then presented in the mass media. The Minister of Justice was later forced to resign, and Ebbe Carlsson and some of the involved policemen were convicted for illegal smuggling.

2. THE SWEDISH SECURITY POLICE (SÄKERHETSPOLISEN): ITS ORGANIZATIONAL STRUCTURE AND TASKS IN THE NINETIES

The Swedish police was nationalized on 1 January 1965, organized as a national police board headed by the Department of Justice. The National Police Board was placed under the leadership of the National Police Commissioner, appointed by the government, and a board of directors. The local community police are organizationally and financially steered by the National Police Board. The main political parties are represented in the local community police boards as well as in the national police board, but neither these police boards nor the Minister of Justice are to make decisions about police operations.

The Security Police are organized as a separate division (division D) of the National Police Board. Since 1 October 1989, the Security Police is centrally organized into four main units: an administrative unit, a coordinating unit, a counter-espionage unit and a protection unit. 'At the administrative unit there is a personnel section, a financial section and a computer section. The coordinating unit is divided into an organization and planning section, an investigation section, a registry section, a defense section and a coordinating secretariat. The unit for counterespionage includes an analysis unit and sections for counterespionage and counter-subversion. The protection unit has a staff, a security protection section and sections for personal protection and counter-terrorism. Questions concerning co-operation with foreign security services are handled by the staff' (SOU 1990: 51, 45 and 50f). Around fifteen police superintendents work as heads of the sections. The sections are divided into squads and groups, normally under the leadership of an inspector. Outside Stockholm, there is a field organization which administratively is subordinate to the coordinating unit, although the operative command is exercised directly by the protection unit and the unit for counter-espionage. However, virtually every part of the field organization has its own operational activities and for this work they have the same access to the computer terminals at the central registers as the central unit in Stockholm. At least the major regions of Malmö and Gothenburg carry out wire-tapping. The official budget for 1993 is some US$ 52,293,666.

The Security Police report directly to the National Police Commissioner and the board of the National Police Board. In the Ordinance (1989: 773) with instructions for the National Police Board, the tasks of the Security Police are described as follows:

> *4 §* The National Police Board lead the police activity to prevent and disclose crime against the security of the nation. The National Police Board are also involved in:
> 1. fighting terrorism,
> 2. guarding and security work concerning the central leadership of the state, or in connection with state visits and similar events, and
> 3. other personal protection, to an extent decided by the board.
> Within the National Police Board, the police work mentioned above is carried out by the Security Police.
>
> *5 §* The Security Police shall also:
> 1. carry out the work incumbent on the National Police Board to perform in accordance with the Personnel Control Ordinance (1969: 446), the Ordinance (1981: 421) on Security Protection of State Authorities, and the Ordinance of Purchasing (1986: 336),
> 2. account for the preparedness planning which the National Police Board has to carry out, and
> 3. give technical assistance to the police to an extent appropriate in regard to the nature of the activity.

The special investigator of the work of the Security Police, the former Paris ambassador Carl Lidbom, speaks plain language in his report on how the Security Police follow the instructions: 'Within the Security Police they have learned to live in a grey zone and retract from the insight of the government and the supervising authorities when the lawfulness or the justifiability of the activities can be questioned.[2] No minutes with legally dubious decisions shimmer in the eyes of the Attorney-General or the Parliamentary Ombudsman when they undertake an inspection of the Security Police. Naturally, it is then only by close observation that the inspector will discover disparities that it is his task to deal with. Through the knowledge I've gained during my investigations of the Security Police's way of working, I'm not the least surprised that neither the supervising authorities, parliamentarian members of the board of the National Police Board, nor especially appointed commissions like the Edenman-Commission have discovered any dubious or illegal decisions or procedures of the kinds I have touched upon, by listening to reports from officers at the Security Police or by going through their documents. In order not to do the Security Police an injustice, I want to add that among jurists whose task it is

---

2. *Cf*. P-G. Näss, at the time a leader of the Security Police, interrogated in the bugging case; *I:* 'Do you mean to say that you don't want to disclose the fact that people within the Security Police have committed crimes?' *Näss:* 'Yes.' *I:* 'Is that your basic attitude?' *Näss:* 'Yes, if you mean it is a question of crime ...' *I:* 'Yes.' *Näss:* 'I'm not willing to discuss names.' (Stockholm Prosecution District, db. nr. C6–1–004–88, preliminary investigation record [later quoted SPD] nr. 17, p. 62).

to investigate the legality of the decisions or moves of the Security Police, I have sometimes come across the attitude; "It is probably better if we don t know so much." When it comes to an activity that ultimately is concerned with the security of the nation, it might not always be possible to maintain normal standards' (SOU 1988: 18, 30).

At present, Swedish law gives no opportunity to appeal decisions from the Security Police on registration or handing out information. In matters of personnel control, the controlled person as a rule may not know what information has been handed out about him.[3] In this situation, when the registers of the Security Police play an active part in the everyday life of individual citizens, it is thus impossible to determine the correctness and relevance of the information that is provided.

3. MODI OPERANDI

The official goal of the Security Police is to try to disclose and prevent crimes against the security of the nation by systematically processing information about events and people. The ultimate symbol of this systematizing is the various police registers, all of them gathered under search registers. Because the fundamental method is the processing of systematized information, the activity has to a large extent become centralized.

The main working method of the Security Police is thus analyzing and processing information retrieved from registers. In such a system the outer limit for the kind of methods the Security Police legally have a right to use will essentially be built on the rules on what kind of information the Security Police have the right to register. In the Police Registry Act (*Polisregisterlagen*) and the Personnel Control Ordinance (*Personalkontrollkungörelsen*), the limits the police are supposed to stay within are stated. The two statutes allow both the Security Police and all other police to note in a register all information they find necessary in order to prevent or disclose crime, as well as information needed to carry out their work in general. Notes in the registry of the Security Police may, according to the words of the regulation, never *be founded* solely on the fact that the registered person is a member of a certain organization or has expressed a certain political opinion. The government has, however, in official directions for application, in general terms stated that belonging to a certain organization, or expressed sympathies with them, *shall* result in registra-

---

3. However, a foreign citizen applying for Swedish citizenship may, whenever applicable, acquaint himself with, and answer to, the facts stated by the Security Police for why he should not be given Swedish nationality. This information is based on the same classified register as the personnel control. After major criticism, 1 October 1993, the law was revised, giving the controlled person the right to comment upon information handed out 'as far as his interest of being given this opportunity is more important than the governmental interest of keeping the information secret.' It is an empirical question if the Security Police will follow the new law – history tells us that they so far consistently ignored earlier issued rules with the same content (*see* European Court of Justice, 8 July 1987, Series A, No. 116).

tion. The government in secret directions for application has specified the organizations in question.

The registry of the Security Police is built upon three different modules involving objects, activities and events. The information in the register is, in code, available on line for the county divisions of the Security Police. Among information registered about people are things such as that the individual is responsible for stencil copying, is manager of a book-cafe, or has appeared on the election papers of a certain political party. Other types of available data include information on membership of different Swedish or foreign political organizations, participation in demonstrations or political meetings, relations between different communist parties, solidarity work for foreign liberation organizations (e.g. FRELIMO), as well as information about travel, restaurant visits, financial situation, kinship and social life (*see* Töllborg, *Personalkontroll; En ideologikritisk studie kring den svenska personalkontrollkungörelsen*, Stockholm-Lund, 1986, 219ff, esp. 245). Furthermore, information is noted down on marital and name changes, and co-habitation. In the former cases it appears that this happens automatically, since the original notification from the registered himself to; for example, the Postal Administration when moving, is forwarded to the Security Police. Many of the notes in the registers seem 'to be the results of an almost routinely carried out surveillance of certain political groupings' (SOU 1990: 51, 256). The extensive registration is built on the notion that certain personal circumstances *'based on experience* (can) be a gateway for a person developing into a security risk. This includes alcohol, economic, work, and domestic problems. Also a long stay abroad, friendship with foreigners or sympathy with extremist political parties can be conditions of importance in this respect' (SOU 1988: 16, 205). Hence, the empirical evidence suggests that the Security Police consider note-taking on membership in suspect organizations as a very important factor in identifying presumptive security risks. Neither the Security Police, the central leadership of the police, the government nor the Standing Committee on the Administration of Justice (*Justitieutskottet*) is of the opinion that this violates the law, which otherwise is said to express a ban on registration based on opinion.

3.1. Search

In a security context a condition for efficient search is often that the identity and intentions of the searching person are kept secret from the subject. For this reason, it often happens that the searcher is dressed as a civilian, and sometimes even has no observable contact with the police. Such unconventional methods are quite common in traditional police work and are normally brought to use in criminal investigations, i.e. in cases when a crime has been committed and the police have one or several suspects whom they are trying to secure evidence against. This kind of work is not particularly controversial and is hardly in opposition to Swedish law. It is also legal in operations work for a policeman in civilian clothes, or an independent agent, equipped with a microphone to secretly tape a conversation the policeman or agent participates in.

On the other hand it is legally questionable when the policeman himself takes no active part in the conversation, but is present at the observation place as a 'microphone bearer,' e.g. dressed as a tradesman. Listening to a conversation between outsiders with the help of technical equipment is prohibited. However, whether permissible or not, the method is in use. So are tracking devices, beacons, or beepers as they sometimes are called, i.e. radio transmitters that periodically send out signals.

An important source of information, apart from reports from the public or defectors from political movements, is people in charge of security at Swedish companies. Also, information that surfaces at the so-called in-depth investigations carried out for appointment to special security classified positions, are registered and processed. At this type of investigation the controlled person himself reports on his personal situation. At the same time the Security Police may contact relatives, neighbours, lovers, etc. Information from the Swedish girlfriends of immigrants and refugees may also be sought. For example, after the Palme murder, raid-like interrogations among Kurds living in Sweden were carried out, as well as extensive wire-tapping and bugging. A strikingly large part of these interrogations and conversations included questions with no connection to the murder whatsoever, questions intended to gain knowledge of the organization PKK and its branches in the country. Just as with the nation-wide raids against communists in 1940, threats can be used as an excuse for unrelated forms of investigating persons. Thus the Palme murder resulted in investigations of several persons, peripheral to the murder suspicion. This offered a chance to obtain information about other events unrelated to the original investigation.

A special kind of search is the so-called 'signal intelligence.' This refers to a search involving radio transmissions within or outside the country. In Sweden this activity is carried out by FRA (*Försvarets Radioanstalt*), a division in the National Defense, which carries on certain forms of co-operation with the Security Police. The defensive part of the search, which is said to be very successful, and also of great value to the activities of the Security Police as a whole, 'is aimed at identifying the transmissions so that they can be grouped together in different patterns, so-called radio-plans, which are assumed to be different for different agents' (SOU 1991: 51, 92). Even if the transmissions are coded, they can give information about the level of activity of foreign operations in Sweden and about who may be behind the operation. Sometimes the search has, together with other information, contributed to apprehension and sentencing of spies. According to Dagens Eko – the Swedish national broadcasting news – FRA taps all radio traffic, including wireless telephoning. The first analysis is made by computers, which respond to the use of certain key words. The technique has radically reduced the costs for bugging and telephone tapping, which otherwise demands high manpower.

3.2. Wire-tapping and Letter Control

Traditional wire-tapping is technically performed by the Telecom Administration on directions from the police. The administration connects the listening device of the police with the phone network. The listening and taping is done by the police.

All police wire-tapping, including that of the CID, is managed by the Security Police. The work up is carried out according to a priority system decided by the handler and the leadership of the section. If the Swedish language dominates, the tape is first examined by a Swedish-speaking person and then by an interpreter, whereas it is done in the opposite way if the conversation is primarily in a foreign tongue. After the tapes have been listened to and their contents noted down, the examiners write a summary of the most interesting parts and present this to the handler. After that, a discussion can take place between the handler and the interpreter/examiner regarding the correct interpretation of what has been said. The notes that are considered of no importance are then destroyed together with the tapes. If there are doubts about the value of the contents of the tapes, both the tape and the notes are kept. 'In cases when the notes are estimated as having value as evidence, a clean copy is made of the first transcript and this is given to the prosecutor at the following month's request for prolonged use of the invasive measure. In these cases the tapes are always kept. A copy of the edited tape shall be stored at the Security Police' (SPD 19, 76f); 'During the whole time a continuous follow-up of the gathered material takes place, as well as personal identifications and updatings in the work registers.'

Wire-tapping is such an intervention into the protected private sphere of the citizen that, according to the Constitution, it can only be carried out when it is supported by law. Phone calls carried fully or partly without a cable, via radio, are not included in the limitations mentioned here. These cases are included in the Radio Act (*Radiolagen*, 1966: 755), and this statute contains no rules that prohibits the listening to radio messages. The statute does, however, prohibit the receiver of the radio message from forwarding information of the contents to someone else. The police have the legal right to perform wire-tapping for the purpose of disclosing and preventing crime. The basic regulations regarding wire-tapping, as one of many invasive measures, are to be found in the Code of Judicial Procedure (*Rättegångsbalken*). The rules in the Code permit using such measures, including wire-tapping, in the preliminary investigation of the police. These rules aim at investigating already committed crimes, to secure evidence. The rules of the Code of Judicial Procedure involve several protections against undue use of wire-tapping: the measure shall be decided upon by a court of law, it can only be used against a person suspected on reasonable grounds for certain serious crimes, permission can only be given for a month at a time and must only refer to the phone of the suspect himself or a phone that on reasonable grounds is believed to be used by this person. Additional information must be destroyed. Similar legal security rules exist for the surveillance of mail. A milder variant is the so-called secret tele-surveillance, a newly established invasive measure, in which the Telecom Administration can be asked to give information about calls to or from a certain telephone. This measure, which is not as invasive as wire-tapping, does not have to be based on crimes as serious as for wire-tapping, but the suspicion must still be reasonable and the measure decided on by a court of law.

The basis of the rules of the Code of Judicial Procedure is the belief that the integrity of the citizen is a concern superior to the concern of disclosing crime. Measures violating personal integrity may be carried out for the purpose of a search only in exceptional cases and must then always be decided upon by a court of law and be targeted against those of whom there is reasonable suspicion that a crime has already been committed. The only allowed purpose is to take legal action against a crime, i.e. secure evidence, and not to disclose or prevent crime. Therefore, the rules of the Code of Judicial Procedure regarding intrusive measures are insufficient for those in the Security and Narcotics police whose main activity is to disclose and prevent crime. The surplus wire-tap information that has to be destroyed according to the Code is the very type of information that the wire-tapping in these cases is directed towards!

The aim of the wire-tapping in most cases is to gather in an unprejudiced way information about a person, an organization or a civic occurrence in order to lay the foundation for a decision on how further searches shall be carried out. Naturally, the wire-tapping is also a complement to the rest of the search work. But even in these cases wire-tapping is not primarily a means of evidence collection, but for mapping out. Its value, even in this limited sense, has however in recent times been questioned by the Security Police's own staff. For example 'A.Ö.,' one of the policemen at the terrorist section of the Security Police, is of the opinion that 'the telephone control can be thrown on the dump because it is of no value nowadays ... You might get to know whether the person in question is at home or not. You never get anything more. Those who are up to something never talk on the phone' (SPD 12, 151f). Hans Holmér, the former chief of the Security Police, is of the same opinion: 'This kind of telephone control never gave us anything of value ... What we got to know was the usual. We got the pattern of intercourse so to speak, which can be quite useful, and some strange calls we would like to know the background of' (SPD 15, 22f). P-G. Näss, another former leader of the Security Police, explains that telephone control is necessary when investigating a suspect 'in order to get a grip on travels, plans and the like' (SPD 17, 257).

The contradiction between the aim of wire-tapping according to the Code of Judicial Procedure, namely to catch the offender, and the usefulness of it as an investigative measure when preventing crime, has led to tactics such as that described by P-G. Näss: 'We had incoming material. It wasn't really all that good, *but it was good enough for telephone control'* (italics added). In this case the prosecutor refused to ask for an extension because two security policemen at their own responsibility had failed to present all the material since they 'had come to the conclusion that for tactical reasons it would be better to keep the information for a month.' The tactics aimed, as far as I know, to extend wire-tapping as far as possible, regarding the weak material already gathered. When the material given so far by the wire-tapping later is presented, at the request for continued telephone control, the deciding authorities are given, 'small parts of telephone control that covers the hypothesis' (SPD 17, 258).

Apart from the rules of the Code of Judicial Procedure concerning coercive measures, wire-tapping is authorized in another four statutes; the Institutional Correction Act (*Lagen om kriminalvård i anstalt*, 1974: 303), the Act on Treatment of Arrested and Detained Persons (*Lagen om behandling av häktade och anhållna,* 1976: 371), the Terrorist Act (*Terroristlagen,* 1989: 530), and the Act on Special Rules for Coercive Measures in certain Criminal Cases (*Lagen med särskilda bestämmelser om tvångsmedel i vissa brottmål,* 1952: 98). In contrast to the Code of Judicial Procedure, these statutes radically extend the possibilities for police wire-tapping.

Wire-tapping of an inmate at an institution as a rule may only be performed in protecting the security of the institution. The inmate shall be informed that wire-tapping will be carried out. Calls between the inmate and his counsel may not be tapped. According to the Institutional Correction Act, § 31, the government can by a special decision authorize extended permission for wire-tapping of an inmate at a criminal correctional institution. The cause of such a decision shall be a consideration of the security of the nation, or a risk of an inmate participating in a terrorist act. The Terrorist Act (1989: 530) gives, when particular reasons exist, the right to wire-tap, as well as to examine post and telegraph messages, even without specific suspicion of crime, if such wire-tapping can be considered of importance to find out whether a certain organization or group is planning acts of terrorism. The decision shall be taken by the District Court in Stockholm and may only be aimed at aliens who would have been rejected or deported with the support of the Terrorist Act, had this not been prevented by the risk that the execution of such a decision could lead to corporal or capital punishment, torture or other persecution – *see* the Aliens Act (*Utlänningslagen,* 1989: 529) 8, 1–4. The decision can only be valid for a maximum of a month at a time, and surplus information, if any, must be destroyed.

This would apply primarily to cases where expulsion has been replaced by so-called municipal arrest, for the reasons stated above. For example, during a period of approximately six years nine Kurds with Turkish citizenship had been placed under such municipal arrest. Several of them were subjected to both legal wire-tapping and illegal bugging. During the fiscal year 1989–1990, one expulsion was carried out under the Terrorist Act.

Up to 1989–1990, 33 expulsion decisions on the basis of the Terrorist Act have been taken. Eighteen of these expulsions could not be carried out and were therefore replaced by limitations and conditions for continued stay in Sweden.

The statute of most importance for the Security Police regarding the right to wire-tap is the Act on Special Rules for Coercive Measures in Certain Criminal Cases (1952: 98). The statute, originally time-limited, emanates from the days of the Cold War and is sometimes called the Enbom Act, after a well-known espionage case at the time. The statute also extends the possibilities of detention and gives a broadened right to carry out wire-tapping and letter control. According to the statute these can be carried out without any special requirements regarding the seriousness of the crime. However, as far as I know, the same formal requirements exist about reasonable suspicion towards the person to be wire-tapped. Attempts, preparations or conspiracy of crime, are independent of whether a more lenient punishment than two years imprisonment is prescribed for the crime in question. It might be that all these circumstances added together could make the courts seems to almost always think the requirement of a reasonable suspicion is fulfilled in these cases. Awaiting the decision of the court, the prosecutor and the investigator can decide on the intrusive measure. All matters are handled by the same judge at the District Court in Stockholm. 'It rarely or never happens that a request for using wire-tapping is rejected by the court' (SOU 1989: 18, 64). The law is only applicable when there is a suspicion of crime, or attempt, preparations or conspiracy of crimes such as high treason and crimes against the security of the nation, as well as generally dangerous crimes, like arson and sabotage. On the other hand, there is no expressed regulation in this statute that surplus information must be destroyed. The surplus information is also kept to the extent considered necessary. 'Since the investigations can go on for several years, it can be difficult to know at an early stage which material one can get rid of' (JK, db. nr. 1570–82–25).

According to an investigation made by the Attorney-General from the mid-eighties, the Security Police use approximately 25,000 tapes for wire-tapping. The corresponding figure for the CID, where wire-tapping essentially is used when investigating suspicion of narcotics crime, is only about 5,000 tapes. Each tape is normally used only one hour at a time, depending on how much of the conversation is carried on in a foreign language. The tapes are written out, and if they are in a foreign tongue they are first translated. Between 75 and 100 tapes per day are distributed among interpreters for transcription, in addition to the tapes where the conversation is held in Swedish. 'The number of recorded tapes can sometimes be so big that it is hard to find the time for translation and transcription' (SOU 1990: 51, 89). The parts of the conversations that add something to the investigation and perhaps even are considered to have value as evidence are recorded on a tape for the archives. Afterwards, the original tape is demagnetized and re-used.

3.3. Bugging

Bugging means the surreptitious technical interception of oral communication carried out in another way than over the phone. It is a criminal offense to bug in Sweden: Penal Code (*Brottsbalken*), 4: 9a. There is no exception for the Security Police. The crime is called illegal listening and is punishable with a fine or imprisonment up to two years.

Technical developments have led to increasingly advanced bugging devices at increasingly lower prices. The traditional bugging device – a pin-sized microphone connected to a tape-recorder with a cable – is today complemented with sophisticated wireless listening devices. An advanced variant is to let the windows in the bugged room act as a kind of microphone, a membrane, whose vibrations are transmitted by laser and translated into words from a listening point. Available technical home equipment can also be used, for example the telephone, in which a microphone is installed beside the existing one or, more advanced, a printed circuit card which can activate the existing microphone from outside for bugging the room even when the phone is not being used.

According to P-G. Näss, the latter is the most common way of performing bugging. In this case the Security Police modify the printed circuit card and replace the ordinary one at the Telecom Administration. This card is necessary if the microphone is to receive sound even when the phone is not being used. The cost is moderate. A decisive advantage with this type of bugging is that one can let the recording be done in the px, i.e. the special recording studio of the police for wire-tapping. Connected to a vocally driven Revox machine, supervision of the locality is no longer necessary, nor is it necessary to find an observation place (with all the risks and problems that this can involve). The most decisive drawback of this type of bugging, is that it can only be used against unprofessional antagonists who do not check for bugs. A variation of this theme, developed by PK Electronics, is a simple door-warner. The door-warner consists of a magnet relay that is fit by the door and a small bar magnet fit on the door itself. When the door is opened or closed, a signal is transmitted that operates the turn-on and turn-off of the tape-recorder, to which in turn the separate microphones (possibly wireless) are connected. The most advanced variant of this system I have heard of is when the microphone of the telephone from outside is activated with no interventions in the existing tele-equipment. The technique, known as radio frequency flooding, has been used in Sweden as well in Northern Ireland, mainland U.K. and elsewhere.

At some of the Kurd buggings that took place after the Palme murder, two of the microphones were installed in a bed and a sofa. These transmitters ran on batteries of a type that could be activated from outside with the help of a radio signal. The batteries had a lifetime of up to 1,000 hours, and could be used more than two years after installation.

The technicians of the Security Police normally build their own equipment.[4] An, as far as I know, ordinary type of cable bugging device is described as follows by a technical expert of the Security Police: 'If we start with the microphone at the tip, it is of the size 5 x 4 mm – a so-called electret microphone. Electret microphone means that it shall be fed with voltage and electric current from a unit to function. This microphone is then fastened at the end of a thin cable, a few metres long – required number of metres. At the other end of this cable there is a contact that can be connected to an amplifying box. From this amplifying box, the microphone is fed with 5 volts, if I remember correctly, and later you get the signal back from the microphone by the same cable. Hence, the received conversation in this case goes back into the amplifying box which is run on a 9 volt battery. The signal is amplified in two stages in the amplifier. And between these two stages there is a built-in limiter which, briefly expressed, keeps the outgoing signal in check so that you get an even out-going level, independent of whether the people talk quietly or laugh or shout. It is thus no problem to adjust the level in this tape recorder, since the tape recorder has an automatic level control. If we continue from the output of

---

4. In the so-called Ebbe Carlsson-affair the equipment was bought from PK Electronics. Among this equipment was a number of vocal microphones and telechips, 'run with the existing voltage of the telephone and (where) the transmitter is activated when the receiver is lifted. Conversations can thus be overheard even when the dial has not been used. The reach is estimated to be 600–800 metres under favourable conditions. Transmitters marked A operate on the frequencies 139 and 600 MHz, those marked B on 140 and 800 MHz, whereas those marked C operate on 140 and 1,000 MHz.' The microphone type is called FET, an abbreviation of Field Energy Transmitters, and have the advantage that they, since they get their voltage from the voltage field of the ordinary telephone, are difficult to localize through bugging detection.

the amplifier, a long cable is needed to the tape recorder in use. In these places we have used various kinds of tape recorders. We have used these expensive and exclusive Nagra tape recorders for reel-to-reel tapes and in some cases we have worked shortly with simpler models. We have used a double-track tape recorder and in those cases on one track taped the time to make it easier for the interpreter to know which date the recording was done, what time, etc. So basically, one track contains information on time and other data, and the other track contains spoken information' (SPD 9, 54f).

It is, in this case as in all others, easy to be blinded by the apparent efficiency that seem to be associated with the use of the various wonders of technology. Against the value of gathering information in a relatively risk-free, technically and practically uncomplicated way, must be weighed the fact that the amount of information can be so overwhelming that there are simply not enough resources to actively process the information. This kind of operations 'require enormous resources' (SPD 12, 170), e.g. interpreters to translate material and secretaries to write it out. It has been discovered through the so-called bugging trial that the police had big problems in translating the material, not only in regard to the workload but also – and perhaps most important – in finding reliable and discerning interpreters.

Folke Axman, today retired after 28 years with the Security Police, goes so far as to state that almost all interpreters are unreliable and that you can never be sure whether the interpreter is a double agent or at least gives away secrets. Another policeman opines that sometimes there are reasons 'in some cases to question the neutrality of the interpreters regarding their way of handling the material' (Helsingborg Police District, Customs Criminal Section, preliminary investigation, Record R 189–88 [later quoted HPD], 2041). According to P-G. Näss, a special problem when bugging the Kurds was a concern that several of the interpreters 'possibly worked for the Turkish regime' (SPD 2, 38). This is of course a very serious problem since it can affect the chances of getting a correct analysis, especially of the surplus information. The interpreters do not just translate the tapes, they also make a first judgement of which information shall be translated. At worst this can be a question of pure misinformation. As an efficient means in crime prevention work, bugging works best in combination with other means. First, when you know what kind of information you are after, for example time and place for a terrorist act, or a contact between an agent and his new contact, bugging can be an efficient alternative to infiltration and crime provocation. As far as I know, it is also in such cases that bugging, according to foreign experiences referred to in the Swedish debate, has been shown to be efficient. Since bugging, unlike infiltration, normally is bound to a certain place, it is reasonable to believe that the ordinary informer, as well as skilfully performed infiltration, are superior as methods for disclosing and preventing crime, even considering the difficulties and risks of these methods.

This discussion really ought to be irrelevant for the Swedish police. Bugging is prohibited, even for the Security Police. It is, however, not prohibited to import, make or possess a bugging device. Consequently, the Security Police have, by referring to educational purposes, purchased such equipment. With the floating boundaries between the permissible and non-permissible in this area, it is not surprising that the equipment, for a well-meaning purpose of course, is used in operational work as well. 'The prohibition against electronic bugging devices is at this time rather undermined. The morale in this area seems gradually to have loosened up within the police' (SOU 1989: 18, 85f).

Bugging as a method has been used by the Swedish Security Police – and possibly foremost the Swedish Intelligence – at least since the end of the sixties and the beginning of the seventies. Already in the spring of 1970, microphones were installed in the headquarters of the communist group KFML in Gothenburg. At approximately the same time, similar installations were made in the home of at least one person, a stateless woman residing in a suburb of Stockholm. Several housebreakings are said to have taken place at the same time in the embassies of Egypt, Iraq and Algeria. It is likely that bugging devices were installed in those places as well. In recent times it was revealed that for a long time suspected representatives of the Kurdish resistance movement PKK were subject to bugging.

In June 1990, a parliamentary committee (*SÄPO-kommittén*) presented its final report and proposed that bugging should be legalized for the Security Police. After a decision in a court of law (valid for two weeks only), bugging would be permitted, according to the proposal, if the measure is of significant importance for the investigation. Bugging may then be aimed at not just the residence and work place of the suspect, but also every locality, space or place where the suspected person can be assumed to stay. To install the bugging device, the Security Police shall be permitted to encroach on otherwise protected areas, for example someone's residence, without the consent of the owner of the premises, or its user. The suggestions of the committee have not yet given rise to a Government Bill in the matter.

Secret TV-surveillance may, according to the Act on TV-Surveillance (*Lag 1990: 484 om övervakningskameror m m*), be used for surveilling plants and areas which have been declared restricted. For a limited period (maximum of 14 days) the police are authorized to, without special permission, use secret TV surveillance when strictly necessary to preserve peace and order. Otherwise permission is needed for using a TV for surveillance and signs should announce that the area is being watched with TV cameras. In June 1990, the parliamentary committee in connection with the suggestion of allowing bugging, proposed that even secret TV surveillance be permitted with the approval of a court. Such a license would be valid for a certain time and place, and for no longer than a month at a time. However, there has not yet been a Government Bill in the matter.

3.4. Enlisting and Crime Provocation

Successful police work is based on good contacts with people who have insight into the environments and the groups where illegal activities occur or may be assumed to develop. *Informers*, or sources as they sometimes are called by the police, are together with confessions, the most important channels of information when disclosing or preventing crime for the CID, as well as the Security Police. The information is sometimes given for pecuniary reasons, and is sometimes in return for something else. As far as I know most of this information is received free of charge, and if it is a question only of pecuniary reward, the sum is often relatively modest.[5] Only rarely have the Swedish police offered public rewards. For example, for such information on the Palme murder that would lead to the arrest of the murderer, the police in co-operation with the government posted a large reward.

It is up to each official within the Security Police to recruit informers. 'The source is personal and the identity is not revealed to any superiors until the information from the source has to be included in preliminary investigation material' (HPD, 1856).

These sources are kept strictly secret, even for colleagues at the Security Police. The internal regulations of the Security Police instruct the staff not to try to find out who the source is. 'The one who ... recruits a source keeps him and his identity for himself. Only valuable information is handed over to superiors and only if it is found necessary to let the information be included in a preliminary investigation is the name of the source given to the superior' (HPD, 267). Even the head of the operative unit at the time, Christer Ekberg, explains that he 'has to' trust the information from his staff about the credibility of the sources. The staff of the Security Police is dependent on the judgement of the reliability of the source that the individual policeman offers. There is a special danger in that the more interesting and important information the source presents, the more important and central the policeman becomes. The source can sometimes, like a scoop for a journalist, be the winning lottery ticket on which the policeman's professional future can be built. In such a situation it is likely that the source is not scrutinized critically enough. A policeman in the pursuit of the Palme murderer even used a woman who claimed to be clairvoyant as a source. Great efforts were made in pursuit of this trail, until the value of the source became evident. Jan Barrling, one of the policemen who has most ardently pursued the Kurds, reports that one sometimes has to deal with sources whose reliability cannot be estimated. One simply has to hope that accounts are correct. In the pursuit of the Palme murderer, there are even examples of how the Security Police, in order to give credibility to a hypothesis, considered transferring information to the military intelligence to get it in circulation so that it would come back to the Security Police.

It should be emphasized that when information in the registers of the Secret Police refers to a certain 'source,' it does not have to be a source in the real meaning of the word. Information produced from illegal bugging is said to spring from a certain 'source.'

The ordinary informant is spontaneous and is not built on any ongoing information about a certain group or environment. If the information is given more regularly from someone outside the police the term used is *enlistment*. This could be defectors who themselves contact the Security Police to give information on a certain group or event. It can also be a question of active enlistment where the Security Police 'convert' an agent or terrorist, so that he then informs about the group and their activities. The Swedish Security Police

---

5. Lately, the CID seems to have been more positive about buying information from criminals, partly financing this from contributions from private insurance companies.

are proud of their successes with this method. Now and then they let different people announce in the evening press how they were enlisted by the Security Police as double agents after the KGB had tried to get them to spy. The various stories have in common the fact that the Security Police, after they say they learned that the KGB and the GRU tried to lure innocent Swedes into giving secret information to the Russian intelligence, contacted the Swede to warn him about what he was about to get himself mixed up in. They talk the person in question into joining the game in order to reveal the Russian contact. The most controversial of all known enlistments is 'source A.' Source A was a defected terrorist with a criminal record from whom the Security Police hoped to get important information about the PKK's suspected involvement in the Palme murder. This enlistment was very dubious since no one knew whether he was a real defector, or only tried to use the Security Police to be able to plan and carry through new attempts. As far as it is known, the enlistment had neither impact.

The drawback of enlistment, apart from the risk of being discovered when approaching the double-agent, is that one can never know for sure whose side the agent is really on. Seen from this angle, it is safer to *infiltrate* the organization with your own agents. The risks for the agent are not likely to be greater than for an enlisted person, but it can be difficult to produce an agent who in a convincing way becomes a part of the organization. It is not clear to what extent the Security Police use this method today. It has been said that it is not acceptable to plant a police agent into an organization or a specific environment only for the purpose of continually gathering general information, but that the method is acceptable if its aim is to investigate a more specific suspicion of crime. This way of reasoning is double-edged. Considering the values of freedom of opinion and the right to organize it is, of course, imperative that infiltration only be accepted for the purpose of securing evidence of a suspected crime or to prevent the crime from taking place. On the other hand, such requirements can lead to the police agent himself being provoked – and sometimes in the name of the organization carry through – the criminal acts needed to legitimize his own contribution and thus also the police's decision to infiltrate the movement.

Among the public in Sweden, the most well-known case of infiltration is 'the hospital spy' (*Sjukhusspionen*). A young Social Democrat by the name of Jan Lindqvist was given a cover employment by the Medical Administration in Gothenburg. Formally, Lindqvist was hired to work on one of the ongoing projects of the administration. Lindqvist's main task seems to have been to try to map out and identify members of various supposed secret groupings within the Medical Administration, groups said to have connections primarily with the Marxist-Leninist party KPML(r). This party had for a long time had good contacts with the PFLP and many of its members had done medical volunteer service in the Palestinian refugee camps. It is not clear whether Lindqvist's mission was carried out for the Security Police, the military intelligence or for the Social Democratic Party and LO (the head organization of the trade union) which are said to have their own Security Police with close connections to the military intelligence. The only thing that is clear is that Lindqvist was discovered almost immediately and that the Security Police, probably on unjust grounds, was blamed for the unsuccessful operation.

A more successful infiltration was carried out by Gunnar Ekberg. Ekberg worked for the Swedish military intelligence, which in the beginning of the seventies was called *Informationsbyrån* (the Information Bureau), IB. According to the IB, Ekberg on his own initiative penetrated into Palestine solidarity groups, the student organization SDS, the communist group KFML, and the DFFG (the united organizations for the support of the FNL), after which he offered his information to the IB. In turn, the Security Police bought the information Ekberg gave to the IB for between SEK 1,800 and 2,400 for a six-month period. Ekberg managed to photograph member lists, receipts of payments and other internal documents. 'Through the reports from Ekberg, the IB received information on Swedish citizens who went to the Middle East, for example to the Palestinian training camps, or to Israel' (JO 1975–1976, 164). To some extent, this information later was forwarded to the Israeli Security Police.

One purpose of infiltration may be to try to prevent, or at least make more difficult, criminal activity, by systematically feeding the group misleading information. The aim can be to create anxiety and antagonism within the organization and to provoke carelessness. *Misinformation* for that purpose has, at least if it is aimed at reaching a specifically limited target (e.g., to protect an infiltrator or another source and not just to generally destabilize), been accepted by Swedish justice.

The use of *agent provocateurs* is a controversial question. More passive crime provocation, such as buying drugs, is regarded as permissible in Sweden, whereas more active crime provocation, like selling drugs, is not allowed. Recently, two policemen were sentenced for the careless exercise of authority after they provoked others to commit narcotics crime. The sentence, which was set aside by the Supreme Court for process reasons has, however, been met with strong criticism. The Attorney-General has also accepted the shipping of amphetamines, whose content had been partly substituted with another substance, to secure evidence against the person suspected of the crime. The infiltration of a Palestinian solidarity group in Gothenburg, carried out by Ekberg, was initially defended by arguing that through this infiltration information was received about 'various far-reaching terrorist activities, and more or less advanced sabotage plans against ports and ships in Gothenburg.' It later turned out that the only specific terrorist activity, or preparation of it, that could be pointed out were bomb threats of the airports in Frankfurt and Copenhagen. These bomb threats were carried out on Ekberg's own initiative, without the knowledge of the Palestinian group, but were later used both by the Security Police and the government as 'evidence' that they were dealing with cunning and dangerous criminals. Claiming that this was the case, the police were able to argue that an efficient crime fight required the use of conspiratorial countermeasures, surveillance, tailing, and the enlistment of secret informers.

4. CONCLUSIONS

The boundaries between the permissible and non-permissible in this area are not very clear. Wire-tapping, for example, is not allowed without special legal approval, whereas tapping a phone call one participates in, even if the aim is to ensnare the other in a way resembling crime provocation, is permitted. Furthermore, to secretly listen to other people's conversations, with the help of technical equipment is prohibited, but to secretly overhear other people's conversation if it can be done without technical equipment is permissible. In the same way, it is not criminal for a policeman to record a conversation he himself participates in with the help of a microphone hidden on his body, whereas it is considered illegal if he, with the help of the same technique, records a conversation he has no part in, despite the fact that the purpose in both cases has been to secure evidence of crime on tape.

In my opinion, it is very peculiar that the ban is based on the use of technical aids and not whether the operation, with or without aids, takes place in secret. For the policeman convinced that he is dealing with a cunning criminal, the difference mentioned here must appear to have been constructed by confused jurists with no connections to real life. This can in turn not only have a disastrous effect on respect for the law, but when there is a risk of an illegal measure being revealed, exaggerate and sometimes even corrupt information achieved from secret operations. This must be especially disastrous for young, new policemen who are sent into this type of work and have neither the courage, nor the energy, to oppose illegal orders they may be given.

In a classical sense the police symbolize something good, and the thief something bad. Truth is associated with the Good, whereas lies are associated with the Bad. Consequently, if you tell the truth you have nothing to hide, and can therefore act in the open. It has thus been a part of the very ideology that the police act openly, whereas those who have something to hide act secretly. The use of unconventional methods has also, the few times it has been discussed openly, been justified by the argument that conspiracies must be met with conspirational counter-measures. James Bond has a license to kill, but he only kills 'the bad guys.' It is on this ideology that the increased use of undercover activities is built, and it is on this ideology that the leadership of the police and politicians build their arguments for the use of bugging, crime provocation and misinformation as morally acceptable police methods. Another way of expressing this is that the end justifies the means.

However, the western constitutional state, and what we call humanism and a civilized society, are built on the principle that the end must never justify the means – every legal security guarantee is therefore by nature less than maximally efficient. Legal protections slow down the judicial process. One expression of this is the principle that the uncertain judge should rather acquit than convict, a principle that naturally is frustrating for the one who claims to 'know' that the suspect is guilty. But that is the price the civilized society has to pay for the right to call itself civilized!

It is, however, inevitable that undercover activities have a number of attractive characteristics to *those in law enforcement.* They are believed to be more efficient than the traditional criminal investigation, at least as measured in the number of convictions, and they are undoubtedly more exciting for both the hunter and the hunted, and give both of them higher status. The traditional local policemen of Peel, in their uniformed naivety, culturally come off badly in comparison with the plain-clothed James Bond, alias 007.

Since unconventional methods may threaten integrity and involve morally reprehensible behaviors (e.g. pretended love for the suspect), the need to make sure that the methods are not used against an innocent person is strong. The converse effect of this legitimacy requisite is an increasing risk that the police, prosecutors and courts tend to presume that the suspect is guilty, all in order to avoid any criticism of violating *innocent* citizens' integrity. All forms of integrity-violating measures towards *guilty* individuals seems to be easily accepted – no forms of encroachment are accepted on innocent people, at least not innocent people who otherwise appear to be irreproachable citizens. Hence, the need to produce evidence may be reduced due to the fact that there is a perceived need for the public to respect the judicial authorities in a specific case which outweighs the importance of not punishing an innocent person. Therefore, as Gary Marx argues in *Undercover*, unconventional methods can be doubly dangerous – they affect the integrity of those involved while also increasing the risk of an innocent person being punished.[6]

The legitimacy of undercover activities is built on the fact that they are successful – all parties involved are playing with high stakes, stakes that rise with the importance of the suspect's civil position. This is the rule both generally and in individual cases, and leads to several dubious consequences.

Firstly, the work will primarily be aimed at already marginalized groups, which for the Security Police denotes immigrant groups and shadowy political groups with low social legitimacy. A failure in measures against these groups has a relatively low price, partly since the majority of citizens are never exposed to risk, partly since a claim of crime committed by the former groups is presumed to be true. The other side of the matter is that it is extremely rare that resources are used towards groups in society where criminal violations have very serious consequences, for example among top military officers, politicians and policemen. The price of failure for the investigators in such a case is so high that it is not worth the risk – at least not for their superiors. Individual, often young, policemen are therefore forced to risk a price twice as high should they wish to proceed with such cases. To carry through in these cases is likely to require that they ignore their superiors. The superiors will deny all knowledge of the measures in case of a failure, but take all the honor if the operation is successful. The phenomenon, named 'deniability' when applied to politicians, is especially widespread in the work of the Security Police, but appears on all levels.

Secondly, the use of these methods tends to *lead to* a self-fulfilling prophecy. Crime provocation is an institutionalized example of this – the use of an *agent provocateur is* considered a legitimate method. But the use of informers can in at least two ways work in the same direction. The informer and the policeman

---

6. G.T. Marx, *Undercover; Police Surveillance in America*, Berkeley, Cal., University of California Press, 1988.

have, like the infiltrator, a personal interest in seeing that the suspect is convicted. If the suspect is sentenced for the alleged crime it is a feather in their caps, and proves to themselves as well as to others that they are important and skilful in their work. On the other hand, an acquittal leads not only to revealing the identity of the infiltrator and informer, but also to questioning the judgement of the policeman. Hence, the policeman who for example plants drugs in the suspect's home, to later arrest him on suspicion of narcotics crime, is not necessarily a thoroughly evil policeman. For the policeman the suspect simply seems extra cunning if, in spite of considerable investigational efforts, he can not be caught committing a crime with the usual methods. Undercover operations – especially those involving crime provocation, infiltration and misinformation – may therefore give rise to the very criminality they are supposed to prevent, either deliberately as was the case with Gunnar Ekberg in the early seventies, or not deliberately, as with the PKK in the late eighties.

In police activities directed towards subversion, terrorism, and counter-espionage, the effects become especially obvious. Groups which have been defined as extremist have therefore, within the 'democratic society's right to self-defense,' to be tracked down, watched over, registered, and prevented from obtaining jobs that require 'civic reliability.' Some – especially young people – will be enticed by this, whereas most people will be frightened: the unknown is suspicious and perhaps dangerous and devious. And if the suspected political opinion can be connected to an alien, seemingly strange cultural and religious pattern, the attribute is already clear – the Security Police register and watch over these groups because they *are* dangerous.

This can give rise to a vicious circle; the most likely principal reason why political dissidents in different countries choose to discuss political matters in secret is that by experience they know that a public expression may lead to reprisals from those in power. But at the same time it is activities carried out in secret that scare those in power the most. A system of registration and various forms of reprisals, that fundamentally originate in deviating political opinions and culture, give rise to this vicious circle. In order to gain access to and control over the activities, the Security Police feel they must resort to undercover activities. The use of these methods gives rise to fear and hatred within the group. The Security Police and their creators are seen as undemocratic. The registration forces the deviating groups to go underground. The very fact that they consider themselves forced to work secretly is then used as a justification for the belief that their activities are of an especially dangerous character. The use of uncertain information, based on infiltration and other kinds of undercover activities, can cause persons to be denied citizenship, lose their jobs or be pilloried in the press as suspected terrorists. This confirms for these marginalized groups that their fear was justified and can give rise to counter-measures, or at least verbal threats. The presence of a flowery language full of invective, can be used as a 'proof' by the state and the police that the groups really are dangerous, and so on. In the end this leads to the system itself contributing to the security problems it was established to remove – this puts democracy at risk of committing suicide for fear of death.

Ethan A. Nadelmann* | The DEA in Europe

1. 'AMERICANIZATION' OF EUROPEAN DRUG ENFORCEMENT

My objective in this chapter is to analyze the relationship between the objectives and tasks of U.S. law enforcers and the foreign environments in which they have operated.** The fact of operating extraterritorially dramatically transforms the nature of the DEA agent's work, which is why the task of an agent stationed in Frankfurt has more in common with that of an agent stationed in Lima or Bangkok than one located in Detroit or Los Angeles. Within the United States, the DEA agent is lawfully authorized to arrest those whom he believes have violated federal drug laws. He is often expected to coordinate his efforts with state and municipal drug enforcement agents, but it is not a legal condition of his work. By contrast, the agent abroad retains no powers of arrest and the requirement that he coordinate his efforts with local agents is ignored only rarely and at some risk. In many foreign countries, DEA agents are forbidden to carry firearms, and in some they are legally precluded from even conducting interviews and other investigatory inquiries on their own.

The relationship between the DEA agent abroad and host police agencies is thus one of substantial dependence. If the latter close their doors to him, there is relatively little he can accomplish. On the other hand, the resourceful agent is typically successful at creating a relationship of mutual dependence based upon his own access to intelligence, funds, and expertise desired by his hosts.

Like a private corporation that retains most of its operations within the United States but earns a disproportionate share of its profits from its overseas activities, the U.S. Drug Enforcement Agency has always retained a strong international orientation despite the small proportion of its personnel stationed abroad. Among all other federal law enforcement agencies, only U.S. Customs has shared a comparable perspective. Driven by both the international nature of

---

* Director of the Lindesmith Center, Open Society Institute, New York, United States.
** This draws from Chapter Four of E.A. Nadelmann (1993), *Cops Across Borders*, University Park, The Pennsylvania State University Press; reprinted with permission from the publisher.

drug trafficking and the strong international orientation of its first chief administrator, the Federal Bureau of Narcotics (FBN), and thereafter the Bureau of Narcotics and Dangerous Drugs (BNDD) and the Drug Enforcement Administration (DEA), always emphasized the inherently international nature of the task delegated to them. But while the central objective of the DEA in 1990 differed in no substantial way from that of the FBN in 1930, the ways in which the contemporary agency has pursued its objectives, as well as the consequences of its activities for foreign law enforcement systems, have differed substantially from those associated with the original drug enforcement agency. If we say that the FBN's international activities are similar to those of a fairly small corporation with modest but highly profitable sales overseas, we can fairly say that the DEA's international operations can be analogized to those of leading multinational corporations such as IBM, General Motors and McDonalds. By and lare, smaller organizations extract what they require without changing in any subsantial way the environments in which they operate. By contrast, major multinational organizations powerfully influence both the foreign environments in which they operate and the ways in which comparable institutions pursue comparable objectives. That influence stems not just from the pressures they exert but also from the models they provide, the examples they suggest and the concessions they expect as the costs of doing business together.

Between the late 1960s and the late 1980s, the central objective of the U.S. Drug Enforcement Agency remained constant, as did most of the limitations on its agents' actions imposed by considerations of national sovereignty. By the mid-1970s, the agency's personnel in Europe had also reached the level it would more or less maintain thereafter. As for their quarry, the people who were doing the drug trafficking changed over time, as did many of their routes, their evasive tactics, and to a certain extent the drugs in which they trafficked, but the basic contours of their activities remained much the same. What did change, however, were the criminal justice environments in which the American drug enforcement agents pursued their objectives.

These changes were of three types. One was institutional. Until well into the 1960s, relatively few European police agencies possessed specialized drug enforcement squads, and virtually no prosecutors specialized in drug trafficking cases. By the late 1980s, most European police agencies, be they national, state, cantonal, or municipal, claimed such units and quite a few worked closely with specialized prosecutors.

A second change was operational. When U.S. drug enforcement agents arrived in Europe, they brought with them a variety of investigative techniques – including 'buy and bust' tactics and more extensive undercover operations, 'controlled delivery' of illicit drug consignments, various forms of non-telephonic electronic surveillance, and offers of reduced charges or immunity from prosecution to known drug dealers to 'flip' them into becoming informants – that had been practiced in the United States for decades, and approved by U.S. courts during Prohibition if not before.[1] Throughout most of continental

---

1. K.M. Murchison (1982), 'Prohibition and the Fourth Amendment: A New Look at Some Old Cases,' *Journal of Criminal Law and Criminology*, 73, 471–532.

Europe, however, virtually all of these techniques were viewed, even by police officials, as unnecessary, unacceptable, and often illegal.[2] Only the internal security agencies in certain countries resorted to such techniques with any frequency, and their activities were rarely subjected to any sort of judicial oversight. Nonetheless, during the following two decades most of these investigative tactics were adopted by European drug enforcement units, albeit at strikingly different rates and to very different degrees.

A third change was legal. Even as European drug enforcement agents adopted DEA-style techniques during the 1970s and 1980s, their legality remained highly questionable. Judges, and even prosecutors, were often kept in the dark as to the exact nature of the agents' investigations, and all sorts of charades were concocted in order to obscure the true nature of many of the drug enforcement operations. By the late 1980s, however, many of the DEA-style methods had been not only adopted by the local police but also authorized, and hence legalized, by local courts and legislatures.

All of these changes can be viewed as part and parcel of the harmonization of drug enforcement both within Europe and in relation to the United States. But how one evaluates these changes depends in good part upon one's perspective. From the perspective of the DEA, and more generally of the U.S. government, all of these changes were of consequence less in and of themselves than for what they contributed to the accomplishment of the DEA's central objective. This is not to say that the changes occurred only as incidental by-products of the DEA's efforts, or to suggest that the urge to proselytize or the satisfaction derived from seeing one's own approaches adopted by others were entirely absent. Quite the contrary, DEA agents consciously advocated and lobbied for the reforms and felt a sense of vindication when they were adopted by their hosts. Their principal motivation, however, was to improve the capacity of the DEA, and by extension European police agencies, to immobilize drug traffickers and seize illicit drugs destined for American markets. Underlying this motivation was the realization that the DEA's success abroad depended less upon its own freedom of action in foreign territories than upon its capacity to generate effective vicarious drug enforcement capabilities within foreign police agencies.

From the Europeans' perspective, however, the changes wrought in part by the efforts of the DEA were of significant consequence in and of themselves. This was particularly true of the changes in the laws, which occurred in many countries only after substantial political, legal and professional debate about the nature of policing and the proper reaches and methods of the state. As in the United States, but in a far more compressed period of time, judicial, legislative and executive authorities in Europe were obliged to address difficult legal issues regarding the distinction between legitimate undercover techniques and entrapment, the degree to which undercover agents could participate in criminal activities, the credibility of informants who had been offered financial or

---

2. References to Europe hereafter refer only to the western and central European nations on the continent, all of which adhere to the civil law tradition. The common law nations of Great Britain and Ireland as well as the previously socialist law nations of eastern Europe are excluded from the discussion.

judicial compensation for their services, the need to shield informants' identities in court, and the proper limits on electronic surveillance. But unlike their American counterparts, European judges, administrators and legislators also had to address more basic obstacles to the 'Americanization' of their drug enforcement, including a deeply felt, and historically rooted, antipathy toward the notion of *agent provocateurs* and even undercover agents generally, the absence of any clear legal authority for police undercover operations, and the powerful influence of the 'legality principle,' or 'rule of compulsory prosecution' – all of which greatly hindered the acceptance of undercover operations and controlled deliveries as well as the ability of criminal justice agents to recruit informants from among those arrested for illicit drug dealing or any other crime.

It is fair, I believe, to speak of the 'Americanization' of European drug enforcement provided the term is understood broadly and the substantial differences within Europe are acknowledged at the outset. The notion of 'Americanization' applies most accurately to the changes demanded and incited by the Americans. With respect to some, evidence of the DEA's active hand is readily apparent and openly acknowledged by the Europeans: the creation of specialized drug enforcement units in major police agencies; the initial adoption of DEA-style undercover tactics and the subsequent training of European police in a variety of DEA-style techniques; the notion of 'flipping' informants; and the enactment of legislation authorizing the forfeiture of drug traffickers' assets. But the notion of 'Americanization' can also be understood more passively as including changes in European drug enforcement caused not only by American pressures, incitements, and training but also those shaped by the experience gained in working with U.S. drug enforcement agents, by the models and examples suggested by the DEA's own history and *modus operandi*, and by the popularization through fiction and non-fiction media of the American approach to drug enforcement.

There is, of course, an even more passive sense in which one can speak of the 'Americanization' of European drug enforcement, one that suggests only an element of chronology, not one of causality. Many of the changes in European drug enforcement may well have had nothing whatsoever to do with the influences or examples of the Americans; rather, they may have reflected the simple lack of effective alternatives for dealing with the spread of illicit drug trafficking. That those changes appeared as an 'Americanization' of European drug enforcement was simply a consequence of the Americans' chronological 'advantage' both in confronting a drug trafficking boom some years before the Europeans, and in having first addressed many of the same difficult legal issues raised by drug enforcement tactics decades earlier during Prohibition – an experience in alcohol control eschewed by most European nations south of Scandinavia. On the other hand, the fact that some European countries, notably Germany, Austria, and Belgium, have followed closely in the footsteps of the Americans while others, such as France and Italy, have proven more resistant, suggests that the DEA's approach to drug enforcement was not the only option for dealing with the common problem of illicit drug trafficking.

The process of 'Americanization' described in this chapter can well be contrasted with the very different 'Americanization' of criminal justice and other governmental domains that preceded it.[3] Many of the curbs on police powers that have so frustrated DEA agents were initially imposed by U.S. occupying forces in the aftermath of World War II. U.S. policy makers initially regarded the centralization of police and other governmental power associated with the defeated fascist regimes as an evil to be avoided in the post-war era. But the onset of the Cold War, rising concern with Soviet espionage and communist agitation, and the growing threat of terrorism all provided incentives for U.S. policy makers to reverse stride and encourage the expansion of police powers in Europe as in America. Criminal justice norms and institutions were among the first to be shaped by the 'national security state' mentality that emerged in tandem with the Cold War.

The evolution of European drug enforcement since the late 1960s has also been shaped by other influences.[4] Many of the tactics and laws initially devised to investigate and suppress terrorist groups such as the Red Brigades in Italy and the Baader-Meinhof group in Germany provided the initial experience, legal authority, and practical models for subsequent responses to illicit drug trafficking and organized crime.[5] National approaches to drug enforcement within Europe have also been influenced by the initiatives taken by individual countries as well as by multilateral initiatives. The German BKA (*Bundeskriminalamt*), for instance, has promoted itself as a model for other European police agencies and assumed a leading role in inter-European police affairs. Multilateral law enforcement conventions, as well as multilateral arrangements such as Interpol, TREVI, the Council of Europe, and the Pompidou Group have played an increasingly important role.[6] The European Court of Human Rights has exercised some influence by virtue of its decisions in a number of cases involving the use of informants and of electronic surveillance.[7] Regional arrangements, such as those among the Scandinavian and the Benelux nations respectively, have shaped the domestic law enforcement policies of the member countries. And more generally the prospects of open borders in 1992 created pressures for greater conformity among European criminal justice systems.[8]

My focus on the adoption of U.S.-style methods in Europe should not obscure the extent to which European police have been able to take advantage

---

3. I am indebted to Walter Murphy for this point.
4. *See* Ethan A. Nadelmann, *Criminalization and Crime Control in International Society*, New York, Oxford University Press, forthcoming; and H-J. Albrecht and A. van Kalmthout, eds. (1989), *Drug Policies in Western Europe*, Freiburg, Germany, Max-Planck-Institut für Ausländisches und Internationales Strafrecht, 41.
5. *See*, e.g., L. Weinberg and W.L. Eubank (1987), *The Rise and Fall of Italian Terrorism*, Boulder, Colo., Westview Press, 125–133.
6. C. Fijnaut (1987), 'The Internationalization of Criminal Investigation in Western Europe,' in: C.J.C.F. Fijnaut and R.H. Hermans, eds., *Police Cooperation in Europe*, Lochem, Van den Brink, 32–56; P. Wilkinson (1985), 'European Police Cooperation,' in: J. Roach and J. Thomaneck, eds., *Police and Public Order in Europe*, London, Croom Helm.
7. Note (1981), 'Secret Surveillance and the European Convention on Human Rights,' *Stanford Law Review*, 33, 1113.
8. C. Haberman (1989), 'Europeans Fear '92 Economic Unity May Benefit Mafia,' *New York Times*, 23 July, 1.

of police powers that do not exist in the United States. In many European countries (but not all), police and prosecutors can legally detain criminal suspects for much longer than is permissible in the United States; access to counsel can be more delayed and restricted; telephone taps can be more easily obtained and kept in place longer; warrantless searches can be conducted more readily; evidence gathered illegally is rarely excluded from court; residents are required to carry special identity cards; and police are legally entitled to ask anyone to show them those cards. U.S. agents in Europe have been known to covet these powers, but they have also found that the Europeans' greater authority and discretion to question, detain, and search do not compensate for the restrictions on their ability to use the sorts of investigative methods that are regarded as so essential by U.S. agents. It is worth observing, however, that even as European drug enforcement has been becoming increasingly 'Americanized,' it is also possible to point to evidence of what one might call a 'Europeanization' of American law enforcement – albeit one in which the hands of the Europeans are nowhere apparent. In a series of U.S. Supreme Court decisions beginning in the 1980s and continuing into the 1990s, many of the European police powers coveted by the few DEA agents familiar with them have been legalized in the United States. The scope of warrantless searches has been expanded, the exclusionary rule narrowed, the right to counsel circumscribed, and the allowable period of detention lengthened.[9] The cumulative consequences of developments in drug enforcement on both sides of the Atlantic since the 1970s have been a convergence toward similar and greater police powers.

The 'Americanization' of European drug enforcement has also involved more than the changes in criminal investigative methods discussed in this chapter. Europeans have encountered many of the same sorts of illicit drug problems as the Americans encountered, albeit more belatedly and somewhat less dramatically. They responded, as in the United States, by imposing increasingly severe criminal sanctions beginning in the late 1960s.[10] During the 1970s, the movement to decriminalize the sale of small amounts of cannabis and the possession of small amounts of 'harder' drugs spread throughout much of Europe. During the 1980s, European legislatures renewed the trend toward broader and tougher sanctions, enacting stiffer penalties for illicit drug possession and distribution as well as laws designed to seize drug traffickers' assets, to identify and punish drug-related money laundering, and to better prosecute drug trafficking conspiracies.[11] More recently, rising frustration over the apparent lack of success of drug laws in stemming drug abuse, and growing concern over the spread of AIDS by illicit drug abusers, have sparked a renewal of calls for drug legalization, implementation of 'harm reduction' measures, and generally greater

---

9. This trend is critically analyzed in S. Wisotsky (1991), 'Not Thinking Like a Lawyer: The Case of Drugs in the Courts,' *Notre Dame Journal of Law, Ethics & Public Policy* 5, 651–692.
10. *See* European Committee on Crime Problems (1974), *Penal Aspects of Drug Abuse*, Strasbourg, Council of Europe; and H-J. Albrecht and A. van Kalmthout, eds. (1989), *Drug Policies in Western Europe, supra* note 4.
11. A. MacLeod (1989), 'Europe Plans Assault on Growing Drug Menace,' *Christian Science Monitor*, 14 September, 1.

reliance on public health approaches to the problems of illicit drug abuse. Since the early 1970s, the Netherlands has developed and quietly defended its more public health-oriented policies while Germany has taken the lead in advocating the more punitive criminal justice-oriented approaches emanating from the United States. Among the Scandinavian countries, Denmark's more lenient drug prohibition policies – in particular its toleration of the counter-culture communities of Christiania and Frøstrup-Lejren – have similarly upset its neighbors. Hard-liners throughout Europe were also hostile to Spain's revision of its drug laws in 1983, which introduced a Dutch-like distinction between 'soft' and 'hard' drugs and formalized the decriminalization of drug possession previously instituted by the courts. In all these respects one can find evidence of 'Americanizing' pressures, examples, and precedents, be it in the influence of the American counterculture on European youth and culture during the 1960s and 1970s, the Europeans' adoption of methadone maintenance programs developed initially in the United States, the trend toward decriminalization of cannabis during the mid-1970s, or the more prevalent trend toward tougher and broader criminal sanctions since the 1960s. Indeed, some of the countries that have been the most outspoken in advocating 'harm reduction' approaches to drug abuse and small-scale drug dealing have also been the quickest to adopt DEA-style approaches to investigating drug trafficking.

2. UNDERCOVER OPERATIONS

Aside from the low priority given to drug enforcement by most foreign governments until recently, the greatest challenge facing U.S. drug enforcement agents as they expanded their international operations during the late 1960s and 1970s was the widespread and deeply felt resistance to using undercover investigative methods. From the beginning of the post-war era until the late 1960s, and in many countries until well into the 1980s, most Europeans, including many police, viewed the use of undercover tactics by law enforcement agents as anathema. The very notion instantly conjured up images of the despised *agent provocateur* employed by governments in previous decades and centuries to discredit dissident political groups.[12] So great was the antipathy toward this tactic that the use of infiltrators not to provoke but solely to gather information was also cast into disrepute. To the greatest extent possible, Europeans preferred that police not disguise their identity in investigating crime. Resistance to police reliance on informants and other nonpolice agents to conduct undercover tasks was felt only slightly less strongly.

One reaction of European legal systems to their bitter experience with *agents provocateurs* was their preference for a strict interpretation of the legality

---

12. P. Chevigny (1972), *Cops and Rebels: A Study of Provocation*, New York, Pantheon Books, esp. chap. 10; and W.O. Weyrauch (1986), 'Gestapo Informants: Facts and Theory of Undercover Operations,' *Columbia Journal of Transnational Law*, 24, 553–596. Perhaps the finest description of the *agent provocateur* is by J. Conrad (1992), *The Secret Agent*, New York, Knopf.

principle and their rejection of a legal notion that has become central to proactive law enforcement in the United States, that '[a]cts which would be criminal when done by a private citizen are justifiable and not criminal when done by a government agent in the reasonable exercise of law enforcement power.'[13] In much of Europe, police could not even go through the motions of a criminal act. Undercover agents could not pretend to take or offer a bribe in order to catch a corrupt politician or public official; they could not play the role of a fence and purchase stolen goods in order to gather evidence against thieves; and they could not assume the guise of a drug trafficker interested in purchasing drugs. If agents performed any of these 'crimes,' they were as guilty as any criminal performing the same act for real. The same restrictions also applied, albeit not always as strictly, to informants and others acting at the behest of law enforcement agents.

Beyond the traditional association with *agents provocateurs*, the DEA also was obliged to overcome two other misperceptions. The first was the tendency of most Europeans to regard all undercover operations as an unacceptable form of entrapment. The second was the popular image of all undercover operations as 'deep cover' operations – those in which an agent becomes deeply enmeshed in a criminal organization or milieu and is obliged to play the role of a criminal virtually twenty-four hours a day for months at a time.[14] The reality of most undercover operations, at least those engaged in by DEA agents, is something quite different. The DEA, like most other U.S. law enforcement agencies, occasionally runs deep cover undercover operations. The vast majority of undercover operations involving DEA agents, however, are part-time affairs, in which the agent is able to return to his office or home after meeting someone in an undercover capacity. Few DEA operations require an agent to remain undercover for more than a few days at a time.

Despite European antipathies and restrictions, throughout the 1950s and 1960s American drug enforcement agents employed by both the FBN and the Army's Criminal Investigative Division routinely operated undercover and ran undercover informants.[15] Relying on personal contacts and an abundance of extralegal discretion to skirt the legal prohibitions on their U.S.-style tactics, the few FBN agents stationed in Europe pursued their cases without trying too hard to change the local systems.

With the expansion of the U.S. drug enforcement presence in Europe during the early 1970s, however, the U.S. agents began actively encouraging their

---

13. R.I. Blecker (1984), 'Beyond Undercover in America: Serpico to Abscam,' *New York Law School Law Review*, 28, 823, 855. The best overall discussion of undercover operations is in Gary T. Marx (1988), *Undercover: Police Surveillance in America*, Berkeley and Los Angeles, University of California Press, 1988. See also the essays collected in G.M. Caplan, ed. (1983), *ABSCAM Ethics: Moral Issues and Deception in Law Enforcement*, Cambridge, Mass., Ballinger.
14. A fine example of this type of operation is recounted in Joseph Pistone with Richard Woodley (1987), *Donnie Brasco: My Undercover Life in the Mafia*, New York, New American Library.
15. See the memoirs of Ch. Siragusa (1966), *The Trail of the Poppy*, Englewood Cliffs, N.J., Prentice-Hall; and of S. Vizzini (1972), *Vizzini: The Secret Lives of America's Most Successful Undercover Agent*, New York, Arbor House.

European counterparts to integrate undercover techniques into their own drug enforcement investigations. They were motivated not just by the proven effectiveness of undercover operations but also by their agency's institutional bias in favor of the technique. Electronic surveillance was also important, but many European police agencies already had developed their expertise in this area independent of U.S. influences. DEA efforts initially focused on familiarizing European police with undercover tactics.[16] As they developed a constituency for undercover operations among the police, the DEA agents extended their advocacy efforts to higher levels of European law enforcement systems. They briefed prosecutors, judges, and legislators regarding their investigative techniques and the changes in the law necessary to accommodate them. In particular, they sought to persuade high-level European law enforcement officials either that undercover operations did not clash with local laws or that local laws should be changed or reinterpreted to sanction such tactics.

Throughout much of Europe in the early 1970s, the straightforward 'buy and bust' tactic so fundamental to drug enforcement in the United States was regarded as either illegal or at best of questionable legality and rarely employed. An undercover agent who purchased drugs was, according to the dominant legalist interpretation, as guilty of violating the law as the illicit drug dealer from whom they were purchased. DEA agents working in Europe responded to this constraint by developing circuitous tactics on their own and by coopting local police and prosecutors in their efforts. One approach involved a slight modification of the 'buy and bust' technique, in which an undercover agent would set up an illicit transaction but not actually complete the purchase. For instance, agents might arrange with a trafficker to purchase some drugs, meet with the trafficker to inspect the drugs, and then either back out of the deal or excuse themselves for a moment – at which point the local police would introduce themselves and make the arrest. One problem with this approach was that it made it difficult to charge traffickers with anything more than possession since the agent, who was obliged to remain anonymous, could not offer evidence regarding the planned sale. In some countries, this limitation was partially remedied by creating a legal presumption that possession of a sufficiently large amount of drugs assumed the intent to sell them.

The receptivity of European prosecutors and judges to participating in these charades varied not just among countries but also among districts and even personalities. In Denmark, where undercover operations had been legally sanctioned but employed relatively infrequently for decades, DEA agents encountered little resistance – although the 1986 revision of the drug laws imposed greater judicial control over such tactics and prohibited the use of non-police agents and informants as undercover operatives.[17] In Italy, much depends upon the personal views of the investigating magistrate. Those who want to

---

16. Examples of DEA training lessons are provided by M.D. Moriarty (1990), 'Undercover Negotiating: Dealing for Your Life,' *Police Chief*, 57, 44–47; and G.E. Wade (1990), 'Undercover Negotiating: Flashroll Management,' *Police Chief*, 57, 48–49.
17. Section 754 (a-d) of the Code of Procedure, as formulated by Act No. 319 of 4 June 1986, discussed briefly in J. Jepsen (1989), 'Drug Policies in Denmark,' in: H-J. Albrecht and A. van Kalmthout, eds., *Drug Policies in Western Europe* (*supra* note 4), 107–141, esp. 114–115.

cooperate, one DEA agent observed, 'usually know an agent or informant has played a part, and they let it go if they can, but you can't slap the judge in the face with the facts.' In some countries, most notably the Netherlands, Germany and (somewhat later) Spain, certain prosecutors became specialists in drug trafficking cases and quickly learned to accommodate the DEA's methods. This in effect required keeping two sets of files on a case. The unofficial one, which was not necessarily compiled in any formal sense, would describe the investigation exactly as it had taken place. The official one, to be delivered to the judge, would present the charade according to which an unidentified participant in the transaction – the undercover agent or informant – 'failed to appear' or 'escaped.'[18] An arrest warrant might even be issued for that participant, although the name would likely be the alias used by the undercover agent or informant. If, however, the arrested trafficker were able to identify the undercover agent or informant by his real name, serious difficulties could result. On occasion, the police have been obliged to issue an arrest warrant for an undercover informant whose cover has been blown, although not without first warning the informant to leave the country.[19] When the accurately identified undercover operative is a law enforcement agent, it is highly unlikely that the informant will be charged. But on the rare occasions when an undercover agent is identified, courts are prone to dismiss the case as in clear violation of the prohibition against *agent provocateur* operations.

This charade continues to be integral to undercover drug investigations in a few countries, notably France, but it became far less of a necessity during the 1980s. The first to do away with it were the Germans, who adopted DEA models of investigation more quickly, and with fewer inhibitions, than any other Europeans. During the early 1970s, DEA agents stationed in Germany actively lobbied for the acceptance and use of undercover techniques. At first they conducted most undercover operations themselves, and virtually acted as informants for the German police. With relations among German police and prosecutors generally closer then than they are now, DEA agents also proved successful in persuading the latter of the merits of undercover techniques. As their resistance dwindled, the DEA agents, often in league with local police, gave presentations on undercover operations to judges. By the mid-1970s, some of the judges had not only gotten to know the U.S. agents but also come to view the fact that they were involved in a case as an indication that it should be taken more seriously. DEA agents also testified in German courts, which was a departure from the usual agency policy of maintaining as low profile a presence as possible. Since their testimony could prove helpful in protecting the identities of German police informants, German police were all the more grateful for DEA involvement.

---

18. E. Boutmans (1989), 'The Situation in Belgium,' in: H-J. Albrecht and A. van Kalmthout, eds., *Drug Policies in Western Europe* (*supra* note 4), 89–105, esp. 95, briefly refers to a number of court cases in which this ruse was employed: C. A. Antwerp, 2 Dec. 1977, *Rechtskundig Weekblad*, 1978–79, 875; *Corr. Tongeren*, 9 November 1977 and 13 July 1977, *Limburgs Rechtsleven*, 1978, 47, and 1979, 215.
19. There are a few cases in which informants whose covers have been blown have been obliged to spend years in virtual exile from their countries.

DEA's undercover tactics were quickly adopted by the BKA and by the LKA in Bavaria and Hesse. During the 1980s, resistance in other parts of Germany dwindled as the tactics became increasingly familiar and as drug enforcement assumed greater importance in German policing. By the late 1980s, few German drug enforcement units depended any longer on DEA agents to perform undercover tasks. The few exceptions were mostly investigations requiring an American undercover role, or an agent capable of posing as an Italian or Latin American, as a number of the Italian-American and Hispanic-American agents could.

From the late 1960s to the late 1980s, prosecutors, courts and legislators struggled to respond to the undercover initiatives of the police.[20] The Bundesgerichtshof ruled on the undercover issue numerous times without ever clarifying either the legal basis for undercover operations or the boundaries of permissable activity by an agent.[21] Debate over appropriate guidelines for undercover activities by police and informants was also a central issue of discussion at the periodic conferences of the interior and justice ministers of the German states.[22] In the fall of 1986, the ministers agreed to two sets of guidelines, one regulating the use of informants, the other regulating the employment of undercover police agents. But their lack of consensus was reflected in their appeal to the federal Ministries of Justice and the Interior to clarify the legal status of undercover agents and to create the legal basis for employing them. Only in 1991 were most of the legal issues resolved by federal legislation formally legalizing undercover operations but requiring that they be approved by a prosecutor and employed only when less intrusive tactics appeared not feasible.[23]

In Austria, a similar process occurred, albeit on a much smaller scale and more belatedly than in Germany. Throughout the mid-1970s, the Austrian police relied on the DEA to perform all undercover tasks. In 1977, a new activist chief of Austria's Central Narcotics Department, Herbert Fuchs, encouraged the resident DEA agents to train Austrian police in U.S. drug enforcement techniques. Shortly thereafter, the chief judge of the Salzburg region was persuaded to reinterpret the prohibition on undercover tactics in drug investigations. By

---

20. See K. Lüderssen, ed. (1985), *V-Leute: Die Falle im Rechtsstaat*, Frankfurt, Suhrkamp; and H. Körner (1985), 'Die Bekämpfung der organisierten Rauschgiftkriminalität durch V-Leute' ('The Fight Against Organized Drug Criminality by Undercover Agents'), *Taschenbuch für Kriminalisten*, 35, 29–113.
21. The rulings of the Bundesgerichtshof include BGH 10.6.1975, BGH 15.4.1980, BGH 21.10.1980, BGH 6.2.1981 and BGH 23.5.1984. See the discussions in H. Körner (1985), 'Die Bekämpfung' (*supra* note 20); A. Kreuzer (1982), 'Wenn der Spitzel lockt: Die Karlsruher Richter billigen fragewürdige Praktiken der Polizei' ('When the Informant Entraps: Judges of Karlsruhe Approve Questionable Police Practices'), *Die Zeit*, 29 January, 53; and in H-J. Albrecht (1989), 'Drug Policy in the Federal Republic of Germany,' in: H-J. Albrecht and A. van Kalmthout, eds., *Drug Policies in Western Europe* (*supra* note 4), 175–194, esp. 184–185.
22. See K. Rogall (1987), 'Strafprozessuale Grundlagen und Legislative Probleme des Einsatzes Verdeckter Ermittler im Strafverfahren' ('Criminal Trial Elements and Legislative Problems of Using Undercover Agents in Criminal Proceedings'), *Juristen Zeitung*, 42, 847–853.
23. See Section 110 of the 1991 Organized Crime Act.

creating a legal presumption that a person caught in possession of a large amount of drugs was intending to sell them, the contrary presumption that the sale had been 'provoked' by the undercover agent was negated. During the 1980s, more substantial legal support for undercover operations was provided by a 'legal interpretation' contained in a parliamentary report and by a number of supreme court decisions.[24] Until well into the 1980s, however, police and prosecutors generally continued to write up their reports as they had before the change in the law – that is, omitting any explicit mention of the undercover agent or informant. Only toward the end of the decade did the reluctance to be explicit about the use of undercover tactics gradually fade.

The Austrian situation regarding undercover operations is typical of much of the rest of Europe as well. In most countries, it remains a matter of controversy, but the general movement is in favor of increased use of the tactic; the European Commission for Human Rights bolstered this trend in 1986 when it declared that the use of undercover agents could be reconciled with Articles 6 and 8 of the European Human Rights Convention.[25] In Switzerland, where police agents trained by the DEA and the BKA have utilized undercover techniques in drug and counterfeiting cases, both the 1975 drug law and a 1986 judicial opinion by the Federal Tribunal have supported their use.[26] Drug enforcement agents in Spain do work undercover but typically must rely on the types of charades described above.

In Italy, Spain, and France, there is still substantial resistance to employing law enforcement agents in undercover capacities. The resistance, it should be noted, stems not only from the reluctance of prosecutors and judges to approve the use of such tactics but also from the unfamiliarity of the police with employing them. Exceptions do, however, exist. For instance, one DEA agent spoke of working closely during the late 1970s with an agent of Corsican origins on the Parisian police force who excelled at posing as a drug trafficker. Another agent, based in Spain, observed that it was relatively unusual for

---

24. *See* the discussion in M. Burgstaller (1986), 'Drogenstrafrecht in Osterreich,' in: J. van Dijk et al., eds., *Criminal Law in Action: An Overview of Current Issues in Western Societies*, Arnhem, Gouda Quint, 187, 189, 190. Burgstaller notes that the 1980 amendment has been challenged in the legal literature as conflicting with Section 25 of the Austrian Penal Code, which generally prohibits the police from committing a crime for the purpose of gathering information or implicating a criminal. For critical analyses of the legalization of undercover operations, *see* A. Pilgrim (1980), 'Die Kosten der Kriminalisierung des Drogenkonsums,' ('The Costs of Criminalizing Drug Consumption'), in: R. Mader and H. Strotzka, eds., *Drogenpolitik zwischen Therapie und Strafe* ('Drug Policy Between Therapy and Punishment'), Vienna, 117–148, discussed in J. Fehérváry (1989), 'Drug Policy in Austria,' in: H-J. Albrecht and A. van Kalmthout, eds., *Drug Policies in Western Europe* (*supra* note 4), 63–88, esp. 67–68. I have also relied upon information provided in a correspondence from Mag. Herbert Fuchs, 20 April 1990.
25. K. Rogall (1987), 'Strafprozessuale Grundlagen' (*supra* note 22).
26. *See* the brief discussion in H. Schultz (1989), 'Drugs and Drug Politics in Switzerland,' in: H-J. Albrecht and A. van Kalmthout, eds., *Drug Policies in Western Europe* (*supra* note 4), 361–381, which refers to Section 23 (2) of the 1975 Drug Law and the Federal Tribunal decision reported at BGE 112 (1986) 1a, 21, c. 3 and 4, which held that undercover operations were legal even in those cantons that had not explicitly authorized their use.

Spanish police to engage in undercover operations but that a number of agents of the National Police drug branch based in Madrid were very good and aggressive at working undercover.

By and large, however, police in southern Europe specializing in drug trafficking investigations do not view undercover operations as integral to their job. The fact that the courts remain reluctant – despite the lobbying efforts of the DEA – to permit any extended forms of undercover operations no doubt contributes to this view. In both France and Italy, for instance, an undercover agent cannot actually purchase drugs but can only do a 'knock-off' – that is, order the drugs and then seize them without paying. The principal difference between the Italian practice and the French and Spanish practice is that whereas the former are similarly leery of using informants in undercover roles, the latter have shown no such reserve.

In Belgium, U.S. drug enforcement agents of both the BNDD and the Army's Criminal Investigative Division began encouraging local police to recruit informants and work undercover during the late 1960s. Their efforts contributed to the creation of a special criminal intelligence unit, the Administration of Criminal Investigation (ACI) in the Ministry of Justice in 1971, which in turn prompted the Gendarmerie to establish their own criminal intelligence unit two years later. The ACI unit quickly integrated DEA-style tactics into their investigations but encountered resistance from prosecutors. Top Gendarmerie officials meanwhile resisted pressures by the DEA and the chief of the Gendarmerie drug unit, Captain François, to incorporate similar tactics into their investigations. Their resistance dwindled following a 1974 drug enforcement conference in which the U.S. ambassador praised François as a model law enforcement officer, and then increased when corruption in the drug enforcement unit, and a scandal involving François and an informant, were exposed to public view.[27]

During roughly the same time, the ACI was also shaken by a series of scandals. As a result, both drug enforcement units were dissolved and undercover work was gradually integrated into the regular criminal investigation branches of the Gendarmerie and the Police Judiciaire. As in Germany, the courts have struggled with defining the legal authority and limits of undercover operations, with the trend toward acknowledging the legitimacy of the basic technique.[28] During the 1980s, Police Judiciaire agents were more likely than agents of the Gendarmerie to work undercover, but their efforts similarly resulted in scandal when three top police officials in the drug enforcement brigade in Brussels were suspended by the Minister of Justice in 1990 for excesses related to the employment of undercover operations and informants.

In the Netherlands, the impetus for employing undercover operations was provided by the dramatic growth of the Chinese-dominated heroin trade in

---

27. C. Fijnaut (1983), *De Zaak Francois ('The Francois Case')*, Antwerp, Kluwer.
28. *See* esp. the June 1984 decision by the Tribunal Correctionnel, 24th Chamber of the State Court of Brussels, which acknowledged the legality of undercover operations and controlled deliveries; discussed in H. Körner (1985), 'Die Bekämpfung' (*supra* note 20), 39. *See* also E. Boutmans (1989), 'The Situation in Belgium' (*supra* note 18), 93–94, who notes a series of cases in which Belgian courts have struggled with the appropriate limits on undercover operations.

Amsterdam in the early 1970s. Totally unprepared for this development, the Dutch police turned to the DEA for assistance. DEA agents and their informants began working undercover, setting up drug busts and coopting Dutch police into the legal charades required to square DEA methods with Dutch law. Some local police reacted uneasily. 'One detective in the Drugs Squad,' Maurice Punch noted in his analysis of Dutch policing, 'was said to have had "sleepless nights and sweaty palms" about the "dicey" reports he had to write to cover certain operations and was relieved when he was transferred because in Dutch law the DEA men were as guilty as anyone else involved in a deal.'[29] On occasion, Dutch courts responded to these developments by dismissing cases in which the evidence had been gathered by undercover agents and informants and in which the police refused to reveal the identity of their informants.[30]

By the late 1970s, however, Dutch police officials were increasingly interested in integrating undercover operations into their own investigations. The willingness of the courts to grant a degree of legitimacy to undercover operations eased the process.[31] Particularly notable was the 1979 *Tallon* case, involving a DEA undercover investigation that had begun in the United States and culminated in arrests on Dutch territory, in which a court acknowledged that not all undercover tactics constituted entrapment. During the mid-1980s, the police chief of Amsterdam, Kees Sietsma, investigated the possibility of formally integrating undercover operations into Dutch criminal investigations, in part by participating in a Canadian undercover training program, and decided in favor. He was opposed, however, by the police chief of Rotterdam.[32] Two commissions set up to propose changes in the drug laws also debated whether and how undercover techniques should be employed.[33] In 1985, the Ministry of Justice formally authorized their use and the Amsterdam police force quickly established its own undercover unit. Virtually all undercover operations were initially employed in drug trafficking investigations. By 1990, however, almost half involved other sorts of crimes.

During the 1980s, public controversy over undercover operations and foreign drug enforcement operations focused not on the DEA but on German drug enforcement efforts. In one case, German police were publicly embarrassed when Dutch TV reporters posing as drug traffickers tricked German drug enforcement agents into conducting a unilateral law enforcement operation on

---

29. M. Punch (1985), *Conduct Unbecoming: The Social Construction of Police Deviance and Control*, New York, Tavistock Publications, 46.
30. *Ibid.*
31. *See* O. Anjewierden and J.M.A. van Atteveld (1989), 'Current Trends in Dutch Opium Legislation,' in: H-J. Albrecht and A. van Kalmthout, *Drug Policies in Western Europe* (*supra* note 4), 234–258, esp. 245–246, which refers to two Supreme Court decisions: HR 1 November 1983, NJ 1984, 586 and HR 3 January 1984, NJ 1984, 405.
32. 'Undercover Agents: gevaar en verleiding groter dan resultaten,' *Elseviers Magazine*, 11 May 1985; Carel Brendel and Theo Gerritse (1985), 'De undercover-agenten van commissaris Sietsma,' *Vrij Nederland*, 11 May, 1.
33. *See* the discussion in 'Politie, openbaar ministerie en bewijsverkrijging' ('Police, Public Prosecutors and Obtaining Criminal Evidence') (1982), *Handelingen der Nederlandse Juristen-Vereniging*, 112, 5–66.

Dutch territory and filmed them in the act. In other cases, tensions flared when German drug enforcement agents conducted undercover operations in the Netherlands, or used informants and private detectives to lure drug traffickers across the border, without notifying CRI officials in advance – although in a number of cases, local Dutch authorities consented to the operations but did not inform the CRI (the Dutch National Criminal Intelligence Service).

There is little question that European attitudes toward undercover operations have evolved greatly since the 1970s. At the one extreme are the BKA and some of the *Landespolizei*, who have followed increasingly in the DEA's footsteps. At the other extreme are the southern Europeans, who employ police agents in undercover operations relatively infrequently and who are still obliged to rely on charades to circumvent the legal restrictions. In between, one can discern a number of common attitudes regarding the use of the tactic.

As in the United States, European courts have struggled with where to draw the line between legitimate undercover techniques and those that qualify as entrapment; most continue to interpret entrapment far more broadly than do American courts. Even where undercover agents are able to purchase drugs legally, most countries still require that the seller be arrested at that time. The notion of an undercover agent making a series of undercover buys to establish one's credibility, to expand one's contacts, and to work one's way up the hierarchy of a drug trafficking organization, has yet to be accepted widely in Europe.

One also finds persistent resistance to the straightforward 'buy and bust' tactic so commonly employed by American drug enforcement agents. The notion, derived from the historical experience with *agents provocateurs*, that a police agent should not 'provoke' a crime remains quite powerful. An agent may properly be introduced into a situation in which a drug transaction is going to take place anyway, but he may not create the situation. More penetrative techniques, such as deep undercover operations, are exceptionally rare, and no European police agencies have yet followed the DEA's lead in employing 'reverse undercover,' or 'sell-and-bust,' operations.[34] One also finds a common disposition that undercover techniques should only be used as a last resort, when more traditional and less intrusive tactics have failed or offer no promise of success, and that they should be employed only in investigations of relatively serious offenses. With some exceptions, informants are generally freer than law enforcement agents to stretch some of the guidelines defining appropriate behavior in the service of the law. Many European drug enforcement units continue to rely heavily on DEA agents and the informants recruited by them to perform undercover tasks in major investigations; they also welcome the 'flashrolls' provided by the American agency, which can amount to as much as $5 million. And in most countries undercover agents are still used only or primarily in drug investigations. The general trend, however, is in the direction of expanded use of undercover operations throughout Europe. In short, the

---

34. These operations are discussed by Captain T.A. Raezer (1987), 'Needed Weapons in the Army's War on Drugs: Electronic Surveillance and Informants,' *Military Law Review*, 116, 1–65.

integration of undercover operations into European drug enforcement has progressed dramatically over the last two decades, but it has yet to approximate the extensive and aggressive use of undercover operations by U.S. drug enforcement agents.

3. CONTROLLED DELIVERIES

The technique of controlled delivery, in which drug enforcement agents 'let the drugs walk' – that is, allow a consignment of illicit drugs they have detected 'to go forward under [their] control and surveillance ... in order to secure evidence against the organizers of such illicit drug traffic,' is regarded by many drug enforcement agents as a particularly valuable tactic[35] – one that has been employed for decades.[36] During the 1970s, DEA agents and cooperative European agents continually found their efforts to investigate drug trafficking organizations hampered by the legality principle's requirement that the agents seize illicit drugs immediately upon identifying their location or coming into contact with them, and by customs regulations requiring that all imported goods be declared and cleared through customs. The result was that many investigations ended with the seizure of the drug consignment, or at best with the arrest of the 'mules,' or drug couriers, who often knew little about the organizations for which they worked. As with the evolution of undercover operations, DEA and European agents responded to the legal prohibition of a valuable investigative technique first by discreetly employing it anyway, then by persuading and pressuring prosecutors to sanction it, and ultimately by inducing judges and legislators to legalize it. Because so many controlled deliveries cross national borders, the control and legal status of this investigative technique have been addressed not just within the confines of individual European states but by the Council of Europe and various international associations and conferences of drug enforcement agents as well. Particularly influential was the inclusion in the United Nations Convention Against Illicit Traffic in Narcotic Drugs and Psychotropic Substances of provisions encouraging the use of controlled deliveries.[37]

In relying on controlled deliveries to investigate drug trafficking organizations, DEA agents first coopted those local agents willing to bend the law for legitimate investigative goals. Prosecutors were kept in the dark, as were other

---

35. P.D. Cutting (1983), 'The Technique of Controlled Delivery as a Weapon in Dealing with Illicit Traffic in Narcotic Drugs and Psychotropic Substances,' *Bulletin on Narcotics*, 35, 15–22.
36. The annual report of the FBN in 1931 discusses an investigation of an opium shipment from Istanbul destined for the United States via Amsterdam and Hamburg in which Dutch officials agreed to allow the opium to pass through its port so that the drug traffickers could be identified and arrested in Hamburg. See U.S. Treasury Department (1932), *Traffic in Opium and Other Dangerous Drugs for the Year Ended December 31, 1931*, Washington, D.C., Government Printing Office, 43.
37. See Art. 11 of the U.N. Convention Against Illicit Traffic in Narcotic Drugs and Psychotropic Substances, 1988.

law enforcement agents, particularly customs officials, who might not be inclined to cooperate with the drug agents; the likelihood that customs officials would find the drugs crossing the border without a tip from the drug agents was slight. The same held true for foreign law enforcement and customs agents, who might seize the drugs either because they felt bound by the legality principle or customs regulations or because they wanted the credit for the seizure. Whoever was not essential to conducting the controlled delivery was simply not informed. According to the recollections of DEA agents who had worked in France and Italy, for instance, police would allow the drugs 'to walk' if they had found out about the drug delivery from an informant or by monitoring an illegal wire-tap. But if the tap had been legally authorized by a prosecutor, who would have access to the transcripts of any recorded conversations, the police would carry out their official duties and arrest the drug courier. Although prosecutors were highly unlikely to actually prosecute drug agents for conducting unauthorized controlled deliveries, the agents generally refrained from defying the prosecutors' authority.

Since the mid-1980s, however, prosecutors in almost every European country have begun to play at least some role in authorizing, supervising or informally shielding controlled deliveries. This has involved first circumventing, then bending and ultimately redefining the legality principle to accommodate controlled deliveries. Initially prosecutors agreed to ignore or wink at the legal charades engaged in for their benefit by the police. It has since progressed to the point where prosecutors can legally authorize a controlled delivery, impose certain constraints on its conduct, and demand certain assurances from the police. They may require the police to guarantee that they will not lose the drugs once they walk; they may insist upon an assurance that the courier will be prosecuted in the destination country; they may prefer that the courier be flipped before proceeding with the controlled delivery; and they may prefer that the drugs be discreetly seized and that only a small portion of the drugs, combined with some innocuous white powder, be substituted for the original package in the controlled delivery. From the perspective of the police, the importance of the prosecutors' growing role stems less from their oversight functions than from their ability to authorize, and in effect legalize, an essential investigative technique. Controlled deliveries are now regarded as legal throughout most of Europe even if their changed status has yet to be codified in the assorted codes of criminal procedure.

Responsibility for reinterpreting the legality principle to allow controlled deliveries has fallen not just to the prosecutors and the courts but also to legislators, interior and justice ministers, and international working groups. The courts have responded by relaxing customs regulations and the requirements of the legality principle to allow broader use of controlled deliveries. Legislators under increasing pressure during the 1980s to enact tougher drug legislation have enacted laws explicitly authorizing the investigative technique. In Austria, efforts by DEA and local drug enforcement agents to employ controlled deliveries along the notorious 'Balkan connection' raised the same sorts of legal disputes that had hampered the introduction of undercover operations.[38] When those were resolved favorably by the Austrian supreme court, debate focused on customs regulations requiring that all goods imported into Austria be declared and cleared; a 1985 amendment to the customs laws removed this obstacle and further allowed for the reexport of illicit drug shipments provided they remained under surveillance.[39] The practice is much the same in France, where controlled deliveries from Spain to the Netherlands are not unusual; magistrates will authorize a controlled delivery but insist that the police arrest the couriers and seize the drugs if they think there is a chance they will lose track of either. In Denmark, controlled deliveries have been regarded as entirely legal; Dutch and Danish police cooperate frequently, particularly on shipments passing through Denmark en route to Sweden. In Germany, the interior and justice ministers of the *Länder* appointed working groups to devise national guidelines for conducting controlled deliveries. In 1983 and 1986, for instance, the Northern Working Group on the Suppression of Drug Trafficking, which includes police representatives from the Netherlands and the Scandinavian countries, the German border control and customs agencies, and Hannover, Bremen, Hamburg, Berlin, and Kiel, conducted controlled delivery exercises – codenamed Baltica 83 and Baltica 86 – to test the capacity of the police to transfer surveillance across national borders.[40] Elsewhere, legal formalities continue to pose substantial problems. In Spain, for instance, a South American informant employed by the DEA on a controlled delivery from Bolivia to Spain in 1988 was arrested by Spanish customs because the DEA and Spanish police had failed to notify the proper customs authorities; two years later, the unfortunate informant remained incarcerated in a Spanish jail. Throughout much of Europe, however, pressures to better coordinate controlled deliveries – generated in part by the elimination of border checks in 1992 – are certain to lead to greater harmonization of the laws and guidelines regulating uses of the technique.

4. WIRE-TAPPING

Among the various investigative techniques best suited to drug trafficking investigations, wire-tapping was the one with which most European police agencies were most familiar when American drug enforcement agents began fanning out through Europe in the 1960s and 1970s. Indeed, many relied on electronic surveillance with substantially greater frequency than was the case in the United States. As in the United States, however, the investigative technique generated substantial political and legal controversy. Some forms of electronic surveillance, such as pen registers (which reveal only the telephone number that

---

38. The disputes, which focused on Section 25 of the Austrian Code of Criminal Procedure, are briefly discussed in J. Fehérváry (1989), 'Drug Policy in Austria' (*supra* note 24), 68.
39. The information is in correspondence from ACND chief Herbert Fuchs to the author, 20 April 1990. *See* Art. 121 of the 1955 Austrian Customs Law, as amended on 10 May 1985.
40. W. Tabarelli (1987), 'Baltica 86; An International Exercise on Controlled Deliveries,' in: C.J.C.F. Fijnaut and R.H. Hermans (*supra* note 6), 79–84.

one has dialed), are relatively less invasive as such techniques go. Wire-taps on telephones, and listening devices ('bugs') in people's homes, offices and cars, are far more intrusive. Most governments authorize but strictly control the use of such devices by law enforcement authorities.[41] The principal exception is Belgium, which absolutely forbids their use, although information obtained abroad from a legal wire-tap is admissable in Belgian courts.[42] Others routinely rely on them in conducting criminal investigations. In a few countries, the police make frequent use of illegal wire-taps. The broad exception to all restrictions on electronic surveillance is national security. In much of Europe, wire-tapping by the intelligence agencies is subject to even less vigorous scrutiny and oversight than it is in the United States, although occasional media exposés, most notably in Germany and Britain, have generated intense debate about the use of such techniques and how they should be regulated.[43]

5. CONCLUSION

The central paradox of international law enforcement is the need for law enforcement agents to perform outside their nation's borders a function that relies primarily on the sovereign powers of the state. Aside from simple liaison functions, much of what is expected of a DEA agent working abroad does not mesh neatly with the requirements of U.S., foreign, and international law. DEA agents accordingly rely on the exercise of substantial discretion in carrying out some of their tasks unilaterally or in informal cooperation with foreign counterparts. This was especially true before the late 1960s, when the few FBN agents overseas cultivated personal relationships with foreign police, took advantage of Interpol to obscure their national identity, and focused on the traditional tasks of criminal investigation. But with the expansion of the BNDD's international presence during the late 1960s and early 1970s, and the institutionalization of the DEA's global presence thereafter, U.S. drug enforcement agents devoted greater efforts to persuading foreign police to develop their own drug enforcement capabilities and to model them after the DEA's model. The 'Americanization' of foreign drug enforcement came to be seen as a useful means of sharing the burden of international drug enforcement, improving the capacity of foreign criminal justice systems to assist U.S.-based investigations, and easing the DEA's ability to carry out its own investigative functions abroad. Stated otherwise, the transnational law enforcement organization recognized that the key to its success abroad lay not in expanding its own freedom of operation in foreign territories but in developing vicarious capabilities within and among foreign police agencies.

---

41. Council of Europe (1982), Legal Documentation and Research Division, *Telephone Tapping and the Recording of Telecommunications in Some Council of Europe Member States*, Legislative Dossier No. 2, Strasbourg.
42. Cass. 24 May 1983, *Rechtskundig Weekblad*, 1984, 1701, cited in E. Boutmans (1989), 'The Situation in Belgium' (*supra* note 18), 97.
43. *See* Note (1981), 'Secret Surveillance and the European Convention on Human Rights' (*supra* note 7).

ETHAN A. NADELMANN

In developing their drug enforcement capabilities, most European criminal justice systems have been motivated less by the DEA than by their own need to respond to significant increases in domestic illicit drug trafficking. Indeed, it is reasonable to assume that even in the absence of an agency such as the DEA, European police would have developed their own drug enforcement capabilities and adopted many of the proactive investigative techniques identified with the DEA once the limitations of their customary methods of criminal investigation became apparent. But there can also be little doubt that the DEA has played a central role in hastening and shaping the evolution of European drug enforcement. The U.S. agency provided a substantial impetus for the initial creation of specialized drug enforcement units within European police agencies; it has provided much of the intelligence on local involvement in transnational drug trafficking needed to stimulate local concern and enable local police to target local drug traffickers; it has served as an advocate for the integration of undercover operations, controlled deliveries, and new means of recruiting informants into European drug enforcement; and it has provided a role model and mentor for European drug enforcement units. Not since the European powers trained colonial police forces has one nation's police agency exerted such a powerful international influence.

The integration of DEA-style methods into European drug enforcement has required metamorphoses not just in the *modus operandi* of European police but in the laws regulating their behavior as well. Changes in the laws of criminal procedure can be seen as responses to both changing public demands on the police and changing police practices. Courts, legislators and the authors of internal police guidelines tend to respond to perceived police excesses by restricting the power and discretion of the police, and to perceived inadequacies by expanding their power and discretion. In the latter case, the pressures often arise from the need to legalize and regulate what the police have already begun to do 'extralegally' or illegally. The evolution of European drug enforcement over the past two decades has been characterized by exactly this process. Where once most bargaining between European police and informants was both informal and illegal, today prosecutors in many countries can legally offer drug dealers who have been arrested the possibility of reduced charges or even immunity in return for their cooperation. Where once European police agents relied on their informants or DEA agents to perform undercover tasks illegally, today European drug enforcement agents are increasingly able to conduct legal undercover operations themselves. Where once police were obliged to reach into their own pockets to pay informants small amounts of money, today many police agencies in Europe can legally pay their best informants many thousands of dollars. And where once all sorts of charades were necessary to keep prosecutors and judges in the dark about the exact nature of drug trafficking investigations, today many of the techniques drug enforcement agents rely on are both legal and supervised by prosecutors. To be sure, no European criminal justice system has legalized all of the drug enforcement tactics that are legal in the United States, and many Europeans still cling to their traditional views of the legality principle and the ban on *agents provocateurs*, but the trend in most of Europe seems to favor continuing in American footsteps. European drug enforcement, and in certain respects European criminal procedure as well, are becoming increasingly 'Americanized.'

Throughout this chapter, I have portrayed this evolution as both a process and a consequence. From the perspective of U.S. drug enforcement agents, the 'Americanization' of European drug enforcement has represented not an end in itself but rather a means of improving their own capacity to immobilize drug traffickers. Even as DEA agents have spoken with pride of the changes in European drug enforcement stimulated by their efforts and examples, they also have observed that the changes are of significance only insofar as they represented vicarious extensions of the DEA's own objectives and capabilities. Europeans, however, have viewed those same transformations as significant consequences in their own right. Harmonization, from their perspective, has involved not just regularization of relations with the U.S. Drug Enforcement Agency but also accommodation and adaptation to American methods.

Nikos Passas* and Richard B. Groskin** | **International Undercover Investigations**

1. INTRODUCTION

This chapter focuses on international operations and employs two case studies, Operation C-Chase and Operation Exodus, as points of reference for a discussion of undercover methods, procedures, difficulties, and risks. These operations targeted the laundering of drug proceeds and illegal arms trafficking, two areas of major interest to U.S. and global law enforcement with wide implications for public and foreign policy. These cases both sparked controversy and highlight several problems in this type of operation. Finally, primary documents relative to these operations had been collected by the first author in the course of his other research projects (so, reliable data were readily available for the present purposes).

The increasing ease of the movement of people, capital, goods and services across borders has facilitated the internationalization of trade and its corollary, the business of crime (Edelhertz, 1980; Passas, 1991; Passas and Nelken, 1991, 1993; Pearce and Woodiwiss, 1992; Punch, 1991; Reiss, 1993; Williams, 1994). In many fields, the *de facto* internationalization of trade has taken place without a *de jure* framework. As new and wider markets develop, supply usually meets the demand for both legitimate and illegitimate commodities. As businesses, governments and international bodies face the challenges of a 'new world order' and a global economy, criminal organizations exploit opportunities across national borders and move their proceeds through electronic funds transfer systems evading detection.

---

[*] Associate Professor, Department of Criminal Justice, Temple University, Philadelphia, United States. Nikos Passas is solely responsible for the presentation and analysis of the two case studies, which are based on primary data he has collected and interviews he conducted with investigators, prosecutors, defendants and their lawyers. All other information discussed here was obtained from public record sources.

[**] Resident Criminologist, General Accounting Office, Washington D.C., United States. The views of Richard B. Groskin do not represent the official position of the U.S. General Accounting Office.

Consequently, control efforts are also increasingly internationalized. In the U.S., this trend is reflected in substantial increases in training of personnel on cross-border financial crime and a rise in international travel by federal agents. While some multinational operations are mounted, more often law enforcement practices from one country are extended to cover other countries or are exported to foreign jurisdictions.

This internationalization of law enforcement is fueled not only by international crime (violations of international law, treaties or conventions) or transnational crime (violations of the laws of more than one country) (*see* Bossard, 1990; Smith, 1989), but also by domestic crime concerns. Offenders often operate from, or flee to, different countries – although concrete figures are hard to establish, fugitive cases in the U.S. have risen in recent years. Offenses perpetrated overseas frequently have serious domestic repercussions, especially those involving illicit trade in drugs, weapons or technology.

Yet, control agencies are often hampered by political and legal barriers in their fight against serious criminal activities. One of these barriers relates to the interpenetration of foreign policy and criminal justice issues, which is evident in state-organized law violations (Chambliss, 1988; Walsh Report, 1993), U.S. extra-territorial law enforcement practices (Nadelmann, 1993; Piñera-Vasquez, 1988), the war on drugs (Bullington and Block, 1990), the illicit arming of Iraq (Cowley, 1992; Friedman, 1993), or the BCCI affair (Passas, 1993). A consequence of the pursuit of distinct and often conflicting political objectives by various governments, combined with the lack of an adequate and widely accepted normative framework at an international level, is that cooperation among controllers from different countries is commonly on an ad hoc basis or limited to specific offenses or offenders.

The case-by-case approach also characterizes undercover operations, whose importance and use has increased (Marx, 1988; Stavsky, 1985; Stephens, 1986), even in countries that resisted such methods in the past (Nadelmann, 1993). This increase is chiefly due to the growing sophistication of crimes that cannot be detected through traditional methods, but also to the unwillingness or inability of foreign agencies to cooperate in cases or activities of grave concern to other countries.

Undercover investigations constitute a semi-covert implementation of public policy aimed at finite control objectives, such as discovering funds transfer methods used to secretly move the proceeds of criminal activities and novel accounting procedures which involve fraud against depositors and investors in financial institutions. Another example is infiltrating a drug trafficking network with operatives posing as drug smugglers or financiers, in order to learn the identities of persons higher-up in a criminal enterprise, eventually getting close enough to the leadership to determine how best to intervene and immobilize the organization (O'Brien, 1990). A third example could be enlisting the cooperation of a fringe member of a support group for a terrorist organization and establishing an information-gathering capability or 'listening post,' to attempt to learn of the terrorist group's plans or sources of funding and logistical support.

Among the more successful investigations was Operation Greenback, a U.S. Customs-Internal Revenue Service probe into the huge cash excess in the

Florida economy. This operation documented the laundering of $2.1 billion through seven organizations over a period of 30 months and led to about 140 indictments (U.S. Senate Committee of Government Affairs, 1983, 285–286). Operation Green Ice targeted drug trafficking and money laundering networks, revealed the use of Swiss banks by Latin American launderers, and exposed intriguing international alliances of convenience among different criminal enterprises. Nevertheless, undercover work is hardly problem-free and has its limitations. Despite bringing together control agencies in eight countries, Green Ice led to the seizure of only $50 million and 700 kilogrammes of cocaine (Labrousse, 1994, 10). Some of the problems are common to any undercover operation, but additional problems appear with multi-agency or international investigations.

2. OPERATION C-CHASE

C-Chase aimed at Colombian drug trafficking and money-laundering networks. It involved a joint investigative team composed of Customs and Internal Revenue Service's Criminal Investigative Division (IRS-CID) Special Agents. Undercover agents posed as investment fund managers offering professional money laundering services to drug traffickers. C-Chase was funded and operated under the Organized Crime and Drug Enforcement Task Force Program (OCDETF), which was designed to facilitate coordination and sharing of law enforcement resources across organizational boundaries to prevent the usual turf battles and jealousies (GAO, 1991). The OCDETF was led by the U.S. Attorney's Office for the Middle District of Florida. Ultimately, C-Chase came to involve the FBI and the DEA, as well as a number of foreign, state, and local agencies. However, the role and contributions of the FBI and DEA in C-Chase were inconsequential, other than possibly in monitoring what Customs and IRS were doing.

Robert Musella (the Customs agent's alias), established an impressive business front, involving a financial consulting firm, a mortgage brokerage firm, a small charter airline, and a series of jewelry retail outlets. Through an informant, he approached members of a Medellín drug ring to interest them in money laundering services through his organization. Gradually, drug cartel members came to trust Musella and provided him with substantial amounts of money to launder.

Several U.S. banks were approached to ensure their cooperation. Although its collaboration had not been sought out, the Bank of Credit and Commerce International (BCCI) was also used by undercover agents as it was an international bank with a presence in Tampa, Miami, and Panama. Musella opened a checking account with BCCI in the name of a Panamanian shell corporation. Through a complex series of transactions the money was laundered and made available to drug traffickers in Latin America.

Here is an illustration of the route money would take: Cash picked up in Detroit would be wire transferred to Florida National Bank, then via First American Bank to the Banque de Commerce et de Placements, a BCCI affiliate. The funds would be deposited in 90-day certificates of deposit that would be used as collateral for a loan issued to a shell corporation in Panama at BCCI's branch. On paper, the loan was issued by BCCI's Panama branch and the real collateral would be hidden. Then, it would be transferred to the checking account of a second shell corporation's account in Panama. Musella would then write checks (leaving the amount blank) that were eventually cashed for the traffickers in South America. More complex schemes were also employed and involved BCCI bankers and branches in Luxembourg, France, Britain, and Grand Cayman.

Gradually it became clear that BCCI's money laundering activities constituted but a small piece of a huge jigsaw puzzle of illegalities. C-Chase closed down in October 1988 in Tampa with many arrests and indictments against BCCI, BCCI officials and other participants in the scheme. The close-down took place at that time despite the strong wishes of line agents to continue the investigation in the hope of implicating higher-level figures at BCCI. Other officials, however, justified the timing by pointing out that press leaks and suspicions among drug traffickers had increased the risks to the lives of undercover operatives.

The first Tampa case ended with a plea bargain agreement with the bank. BCCI forfeited about $15 million ($14 million that had been seized at the close-down plus accrued interest), agreed to cooperate in other investigations, and was placed on probation under a cease and desist order for five years. Five BCCI officials were convicted after trial and received prison sentences of 37 to 144 months and three years of supervised release upon release from confinement. In addition, one of them received a fine of $100,000. The sentences of three BCCI officials were later reduced in exchange for their cooperation with authorities, and the conviction of one of them was reversed on appeal (*U.S.* v. *Awan et al.*, 966 F.2d 1415 (11 Cir. 1992)).

These results were hailed by Customs and the Justice Department as a major success. After all, these were record penalties for money laundering, and this was the first time a major international bank was convicted of money laundering. However, given that the investigation developed additional leads that were not aggressively pursued and the plea agreement with BCCI precluded further prosecutions of BCCI in that district, critics did not consider the case a success (for details on these aspects *see* Passas and Groskin, 1993).

3. OPERATION EXODUS

This case illustrates complications and diplomatic tensions that may arise from aggressive international operations. U.S. Customs Service's Operation Exodus, which has been targeting arms trafficking networks for more than a decade, has had some embarrassing results in recent cases that 'have drawn protests from the government of Canada, Uganda and Poland ...' (Fialka, 1994, A12). One of the Canadian cases is that of Kenneth Walker, an Ontario business broker who is now suing the U.S. government and the Bank of New York for $9.5 million charging fraud, deceit, breach of fiduciary duty, and abduction.

In the spring of 1989, a New York-based trader, Barry Brokaw, asked Walker's assistance in arranging the purchase of 1,000 handguns. After many conversations about other potential business and thanks to Brokaw's persistence,

Walker agreed to source 1,000 chrome-plated Smith & Wesson pistols, which were legal and obtainable in the U.S., but were back-ordered. Brokaw then brought in other individuals, including U.S. Customs undercover agent Ken Prince, who told Walker that the pistols would go to Ecuador, a destination not prohibited by the Arms Export Control Act. There were additional reasons for Walker to believe that the transaction was legal: these pistols could not be supplied without the help of a broker due to the short supply in the U.S. market; in addition, he thought these reflective chrome-plated pistols were useful for ceremonial rather than military purposes.

Prince presented himself as a representative of China Trade Inc. and its affiliate, Tagell Ltd. Their account was held at the Bank of New York. Walker contacted the account officer who confirmed that information, but Walker got worried when Prince suggested that the pistols, after Ecuador, might end up in Chile. Chile was a banned destination under U.S. law at the time. Prince also expressed surprise at the price Walker quoted to him because it was not inflated.

Walker contacted then the Senior Vice-President of the bank to convey his concern that their client may be involved in illegal transactions. According to the statement of claim, the Senior Vice-President of the Bank of New York acknowledged the seriousness of his concerns and:

> undertook and agreed: (a) to instruct The Bank's investigation department to investigate the business background of Prince, Tagell and China Trade; (b) to refuse to issue the letter of credit [which was necessary for the proposed transaction] and close the account if any irregular conduct whatsoever was discovered; (c) to contact the appropriate law enforcement agencies of the United States on behalf of Walker in the event any illegal or irregular conduct was suspected; and (d) to inform Walker of anything that might adversely affect his dealing with Tagell and associates so that he could make an informed business decision with respect to further dealings with Prince, Tagell and China Trade, or any of them (*Walker et al.* v. *The Bank of New York et al.*, Ontario Court, Court File No. 92–CQ–23136, 13).

The bank did not get back to him, but Prince told him a few days later that he knew of that conversation, the bank's scrutiny took place and there was no problem, and the bank was now willing to issue the letter of credit. He also invited Walker to New York for a meeting, but Walker declined the invitation. Eventually, Walker agreed to meet with him and the prospective purchaser of the pistols in the Bahamas (in subsequent conversations, Prince told Walker that the potential customer was also interested in buying commercial helicopters). Tagell would cover the travel expenses.

Prince and his colleagues arranged for the ticket to be issued at a time close to the departure time and to be ready for pick-up at Pearson International Airport (in Ontario) before the flight. The flight was routed through New York and involved a change of planes at La Guardia airport, where Walker was arrested by Customs agents and charged with conspiracy to violate U.S. law prohibiting the sale of arms to Chile. Also arrested were Brokaw and another

American broker who were released on their own recognizance. The second American disappeared shortly thereafter and so did his family.

Walker alleges that he was told that the agents were not really after him, but wanted his cooperation to get others, that they wanted him to join 'Team America,' a loosely organized network of undercover agents. He refused to cooperate and provide the requested services in Canada. On his counsel's advice, he pleaded guilty on the understanding that he would be released before sentencing and would be allowed to join his wife and three children in Canada after the three and a half months he had already spent in jail. Upon his return to Toronto, Walker filed a motion to withdraw the guilty plea. This issue is still pending, however, given that his presence for a hearing is required in New York; if he does go to New York, however, he faces arrest.

In Canada, Walker is pursuing all possible legal channels to substantiate his claims of wrongdoing on the part of undercover agents and repair the damages he and his family have allegedly suffered. His case has drawn the attention of financial and legal news reporters who do not see in it an isolated incident of inappropriate law enforcement action (Beaufoy, 1993; Fine, 1992; Francis, 1992a, 1992b, 1993, 1994; Reguly, 1992). His perseverance has been rewarded with favorable rulings by Canadian courts against a variety of motions filed by the defendants (e.g., *Walker et al.* v. *Bank of New York Inc. et al.*, (1994) 15 O.R. (3rd) 596), whose claim to state immunity was unsuccessful. However, the Ontario Appeal Court ruled that, under the State Immunity Act, U.S. defendants could not be sued because the alleged injury did not occur in Canada. Walker has taken the case to the Supreme Court, where it is still pending (as of 15 August 1994, the case remains unresolved). However, his charges are taken seriously enough for Canada to refuse an extradition request from the U.S.A. In addition, the Attorney General of Canada has applied to intervene before the Supreme Court on his behalf. Walker has also gathered strong support for his case from the International Human Rights Law Clinic in Washington, the Canadian Council on International Law and many lawyers, academics and others who have provided numerous affidavits in support of his appeal.

Both of the above cases highlight issues and risks relative to the preparation, coordination and close-down of international undercover operations. We now consider these issues and risks (for a summary, *see* table 1).

4. PREPARING INTERNATIONAL OPERATIONS

All undercover investigations require elaborate strategic and tactical planning, special equipment and personnel under designated control agents, and secure communications. When it comes to international operations, such as C-Chase and Exodus, these requirements become more complicated. In both of the above cases, agents and targets operated in several countries. This made the planning for possible contingencies, coordination, and protection of the undercover efforts and agents far more challenging than for domestic cases. There was also a need for additional skills, such as knowledge of foreign languages, familiarity with other legal and regulatory cultures, international law and banking practices, monetary instruments, and methods of executing financial transactions (*see* table 1). New skills may need to be developed. For example, the mid-1980s witnessed a growth of criminal activities directed at classical paintings and artifacts. With many enforcement agencies unprepared to deal with theft and forgery of rare art, consultants were at first used, but additional expertise was necessary in order to track down transactions of well-heeled international patrons. This led to the emergence of a new forensic specialty that drew on the knowledge and technical capabilities of several organizations.

Table 1. Comparison of Domestic and International Undercover Investigations

Domestic	**International**
Single agency more often than multi-agency	Multi-agency more often than single agency requiring greater attention to coordination of participating teams
Elaborate strategic and tactical planning	Elaborate strategic and tactical planning. Greater planning to counter unexpected contingencies
Use of specialized equipment and personnel	Use of specialized equipment and personnel with advance matter expertise operating under designated control agents with personnel operating within tight command and control frameworks to ensure smooth coordination of sub-teams
Secure communications	Extended and more protected communications and logistical support networks
Familiarity with international banking practices is not always necessary	Familiarity with international banking practices is indispensable
Covert methods not as complex	Greater complexity of covert methods
Comparatively lower budget	Comparatively higher budget
Context is familiar	Context is unfamiliar, requiring special training to cope with differences in language and customs, legal procedures, law enforcement methods, techniques of recruitment and management of informants
Few, if any, international law issues arise	International law issues arise very often
Few, if any, diplomatic complications	Diplomatic complications are frequent

Knowledge of the investigation is limited to a relatively small circle of persons who have a 'need to know' and are in a position to assist, monitor and control the participants in the operation. By 'need to know' we refer to the strategic, tactical or operational necessity to provide one or more parties with non-public information obtained through covert methods. Information sources may be compromised if, for example, an investigator probes someone without knowing that the latter is an informant for another agency.

In order to enhance the chances of success and minimize the risks for the agents involved, fronts are set up before the undercover phase of the operation gets underway. In doing so, it is essential to ensure the cooperation of additional actors, such as financial institutions, informers, and contact persons who can introduce the undercover agents to criminal networks. In the Walker case, the role of the Bank of New York was vital in making him believe that the agents were good faith traders. In C-Chase, U.S. banks from different states had been enlisted for the deposit of cash money from drug sales, which was then wire transferred to BCCI. One of these banks, Florida National Bank, also provided a reference for Musella when BCCI officials checked his credentials.

Defendants in both cases have alleged that pressures have been put on them to provide information and future services in exchange for a better deal or even dropping all charges and getting them into the Witness Protection Program. Regardless of whether Walker's allegation about 'Team America' is true, it is consistent with the Customs' policy to use 'cooperating defendants' from prior 'successful' cases to set up subsequent sting operations (Fialka, 1994).

Although there are advantages in this practice, some critical points must be made. What case qualifies as 'successful' is not a settled question. Conviction of important offenders and sizable forfeitures are criteria used by control agencies. However, a former Senate investigator argues that, especially in the arms business, successes are against 'basically low-rent types who are wandering around on the margins of it' (quoted in Fialka, 1994). In order to present its cases as big successes, an agency may exaggerate their significance or the importance of those arrested. Furthermore, pressures are thus generated and passed down the chain of command to obtain good results (or better than those of competing agencies) as quickly as possible. Such organizational pressures may spring from budgetary concerns, over-commitment to an agency's goals, or personal agendas. These pressures, combined with the military-like culture promoted by the 'war on crime,' can be counterproductive and lead to excesses both in domestic (Skolnick and Fyfe, 1993) and international cases.

An issue that emerged in the Walker and many other cases is whether the most appropriate area to apply law enforcement resources is the temptation or trickery into the commission of crimes on the assumption that upstanding citizens will not succumb (Marx, 1982, 170–172). In many instances, undercover operations produced evidence against defendants who may not have committed any offense, had government agents not interfered. U.S. courts have supported these practices ruling that what matters is the defendants' predisposition to commit the crime (*see* Stephens, 1986; *United States* v. *Russell*, 411 U.S. 423 (1972); *Hampton* v. *United States*, 425 U.S. 484 (1975)).

Underlying such practices and rulings is the positivist assumption that there is a clear distinction between criminals and law-abiding citizens. Effectively, this positivist influence has helped shift the question from 'Is he corrupt?' to 'Is he corruptible?' (Marx, 1992, 154), a question that seems to apply to Walker's case and a series of botched stings. Despite the Customs Commissioner's triumphant announcement of the conclusion of Operation Flying Kite, the prominent Yugoslavians who were accused of money laundering were acquitted by a jury and were consoled by the judge for their ordeal (Rushford, 1989).

Undercover operations may also create or widen illegal markets. Much debate has been sparked, for example, by reported arrests of smugglers of nuclear material from Russia as a result of German undercover operations. Russian officials, press, and experts denounced the reports as slander and politically motivated. In one case, the agent who handed a slightly radioactive smoke detector component to a reporter has been disowned by police and secret service agencies, although federal police admitted that he had been recruited two years before as official agent (Parkes, 1994). More to our point, a German security official noted that it 'may be that undercover agents and headline-hungry journalists are *offering smugglers deals they can't resist*' (Saffron, 1994; emphasis added). The anomic conditions following the disintegration of the USSR justify serious concerns about arms proliferation (Hersh, 1994). Overemphasizing the risk from Russia, however, may divert attention from Western and other sources known to contribute to this problem (*Economist*, 1994a; Hartung, 1994).

5. COORDINATION WITH DOMESTIC AGENCIES

Differences in language, customs, law enforcement practices, and procedures for recruiting and managing informants make single-agency, aggressive investigations difficult to mount and sustain in foreign law enforcement environments. When they are mounted, problems such as those seen in Operation Exodus are likely to occur. Multi-agency efforts require additional attention to command and control frameworks to ensure coordination of sub-teams. The strengths and weaknesses in one agency may be counterbalanced by those of another agency. For example, the IRS-CID has superb financial crimes investigators and methods, but lacks a network of working counterparts in other countries where tax law enforcement is not as highly prioritized. The Drug Enforcement Agency (DEA), on the other hand, has only more recently developed comparable investigative skills, but devoted considerable efforts to developing and maintaining a large network of informants and points of contact in law enforcement agencies around the world. Multi-agency teams function as components of a larger organization which is usually disbanded after completion of specific assignments.

C-Chase illustrates the difficulties of bringing together several agencies. Although it was an OCDETF (Organized Crime and Drug Enforcement Task Force) case, problems arose in the coordination of efforts and sharing of evidence even among U.S. agencies. Some of the problems are inherent to the nature of an undercover operation and the fact that it must end at some point. As many operations take place at the same time, the close-down of one can negatively affect those still ongoing. For instance, there were serious concerns for C-Chase agents when DEA's operation Pisces ended. Named (but not charged) in the indictment was one of C-Chase's primary targets, a money launderer who would subsequently have to keep a lower profile and might be less trusted by the drug traffickers. Pisces had used methods similar to those in

C-Chase, which meant that many procedures and plans would have to be rethought in order to minimize the targets' suspicions. Finally, assets were frozen at several banks in Panama, the place chosen by Musella for his operations. Bank clients with suspect business could shift their funds elsewhere because of reasonable fears that more regulatory attention would be brought to Panamanian branches.

Pisces was only one of the undercover operations that closed down in the two-and-a-half years C-Chase was going on. The FBI's operation Expressway and the DEA's operation Polar Cap were among others that generated additional complications for C-Chase.

Moreover, it subsequently emerged that Customs, IRS, DEA, FBI and other agencies' files contained a wealth of intelligence concerning illegal activities of BCCI clients and officials. It would have been beneficial to C-Chase team members and the prosecutors to have this information; it could have widened the scope of their investigation. Yet, this was not done due to the diverse organizational objectives of the bodies holding the information, as well as lack of communication and adequate analysis of the intelligence, and a degree of inertia. Inter-agency conflicts and antagonism were also evident in the BCCI investigations in that at least one witness was asked by investigators not to tell other agencies what he had told them. These problems are not unique. A variety of narcotics task forces, anti-money laundering, international financial fraud, and counter-terrorism initiatives involving multiple agencies have functioned in this manner since the early 1980s.

Conflicts do not arise only among law enforcement agencies, but also with intelligence services. Targets of investigations often turn out to be secret agents or cutout organizations that receive special protection and are not prosecuted. In the Matrix Churchill affair, involving the illegal trade of military-useful material and technology to Iraq, the prosecution's case collapsed and charges were dropped when it was revealed that the main defendant, a top corporate executive, was working for British intelligence for many years and the transactions had taken place with the knowledge and consent of government ministers (Leigh and Norton-Taylor, 1993). More often, scandals like this do not develop because cases are abandoned before the start of a trial, charges are not brought at all or get dropped.

Even when these conflicts are quietly resolved, however, frustrations and tensions among committed law enforcers are hard to avoid. Richard Gregorie, a most effective narcotics federal prosecutor, resigned in 1989 because the State Department opposed his efforts and made it impossible for him to get to top cocaine bosses. In an NBC interview, he said: 'We are not being allowed to win this war [on drugs]' (cited in U.S. Senate Committee on Foreign Relations, 1989, 123). Another case of protection of 'friendly' or useful people and organizations is the Iran-Contra affair with its list of shady characters and organizations (*ibid.*, 124–125).

Although it is hard to gauge their precise impact on prosecutors, such relationships can also be found in C-Chase and Exodus cases. The CIA, for instance, held accounts at BCCI and First American Bank, although it knew of money laundering and other activities at BCCI, and despite its conclusion that BCCI secretly controlled First American. BCCI was also used for payments of intelligence operatives in Europe, for some Iran-Contra transactions and for covert fund transfers to the Afghani rebels during the civil war. A number of foreign secret services also used BCCI services or monitored some of its clients with or without the knowledge of bank managers (Passas, 1993; Truell and Gurwin, 1992). Walker, on the other hand, was introduced into business networks of persons investigated in the Iran-Contra and October Surprise affairs (the latter refers to allegations of a deal to delay the release of U.S. hostages held in Teheran until after the Presidential elections, in order to enhance Ronald Reagan's chances; *see* Parry, 1993).

6. COORDINATION AND COLLABORATION WITH FOREIGN AGENCIES

It is rare for a law enforcement agency to conduct international investigations without informing some government official in each country affected. In C-Chase, the need for some cooperation with foreign agencies was highlighted when Musella was arrested in London for using a forged passport. He was released, to the surprise of local law enforcement agents, after he made a call to his U.S. contact in Britain. Such incidents are inevitable in view of the need to keep knowledge of undercover investigations as restricted as possible.

When assistance requests require commitment of local personnel and resources in foreign countries, they sometimes are made through Interpol (Fooner, 1989). As many as 141 countries are signatories to Interpol and routinely share information on wanted persons and cross-border criminal activities, such as art theft, money laundering, fraud, and terrorism. Interpol serves as a major communication network linking police and criminal investigative agencies through high-speed telecommunications and information systems. For example, if a serious offender flees the country before conviction, the country in which the fugitive is wanted can request assistance from agencies in countries where s/he is suspected to have fled. This can take the form of requests for surveillance of locations where the fugitive is believed to be, telephone intercepts or examination of financial transactions. It may also involve requests to arrest him/her when there is a proper arrest warrant, provided that the source country intends to request his/her extradition. The requesting agency will have to explain the reasons for the query to assure the requested agency that it is legitimate and initiated for law enforcement purposes falling within the boundaries of the Interpol charter. If the assistance is routine and consistent with the laws and traditions of the assisting country, responses can be quick and effective.

When the nature of the activity under investigation requires more than incidental requests and queries, a joint investigation may be established. Multinational undercover investigations are rare and of a limited scope. This is because they would require an agreement on objectives, methods and targeted activities at a very early stage when suspicions or allegations are not quite substantiated. Lack of good evidence means that suspicions may not be confirmed, which exposes participating agencies to embarrassment, political and other risks. This renders multinational-from-the-start efforts unlikely. Most often, objectives are set by the lead agency with collateral objectives agreed to by participating foreign organizations. Typically, such cases grow out of a single investigation that identifies international activities or offenders. When investigators are unable to follow specific transactions or subjects in or out of the country, they reach out to other law enforcement agencies with jurisdiction to function in other countries (e.g., DEA), or which have a liaison capability (e.g., FBI), to facilitate the process. A first step in such cases would involve investigators from the requesting country reaching out to investigators in other locations with whom they have an established level of trust and cooperation from prior cases. Where such professional relationships exist, informal communications channels are utilized as often as possible to avoid red tape and diplomatic complications. In other cases, more formal communication channels are activated to coordinate the response with other government organs (e.g., when a search warrant is needed). Higher level clearance and sanction must be obtained when informal channels of communication are insufficient for conducting an international investigation.

Bilateral treaties provide the framework for establishing a working relationship based on common purposes or goals. Multi-lateral treaties, on the other hand, are geared more to authorizing joint or mutual assistance efforts, rather than prescribing how it will be done on a day-to-day basis. Where more than two countries are involved, a coordinating committee or joint command and control unit is organized to ensure that each law enforcement unit understands what is needed and plans in concert with the others. The extent of coordination is contingent on an agreed division of labor and the legal or political constraints under which each party operates.

7. DIVERSITY OF METHODS AND PROCEDURES

Many investigative techniques have been improved and modernized thanks to advances in forensic sciences, physics, engineering, pathology, data processing, and cybernetics. While there are few differences among Western societies in the availability of enhanced technologies, there are variations in how, or the extent to which, they are applied because of (a) differences in governmental structure, (b) organizational placement of law enforcement agencies within the governmental structure and (c) cultural or legal traditions regarding investigative policies and procedures on cross-border crimes.

There are numerous differences in investigative *modi operandi*, but these become of less concern when the different parties share common strategic and operational objectives. When these matters are not resolved, joint investigations do not get off the ground. The efforts that seem to work best place emphasis on a division of labor based on available expertise, opportunity to implement covert or overt practices, and permissibility of certain methods. For example, the use of telephone wire taps may present some difficulties to one country, proper warrants notwithstanding, but may be allowed in the country where the target resides. Anti-money laundering statutes and currency restrictions may offer an avenue for inquiries into the source country, but have little potential benefit in the target's country, where such law enforcement tools are not available. The resolution of procedural and jurisdictional matters can also be achieved through treaties and conventions (Kritz, 1992; Nadelmann, 1993), as well as through more informal methods, such as the use of special, single-purpose task forces, and the use of 'technical advisers' who merely recommend actions to be taken by others.

Different legal cultures can provide advantages as well as generate constraints on the scope of an international investigation. While sting operations in the U.S. have stood the test of court battles on the question of entrapment, in other countries they are considered an unacceptable invasion of privacy and a violation of due process (Nadelmann, 1993). Yet, the question is resolvable most often depending on where the sting is carried out, not on the nationality of the persons who participate as actors in the undercover scheme. In some countries, the enforcement agencies are permitted to 'second' an official to the authority of another investigative agency and he or she functions under the laws and legal precedents binding the latter organization. Elsewhere, undercover operations are allowed provided the agents do not themselves break the law (e.g., in Germany).

8. DIVERSITY OF SUBSTANTIVE LAWS

Differences in governmental structures, ideologies, political aims, and legal systems affect the manner in which countries respond to assistance requests or join multinational operations. As long as there is no commonly accepted international normative framework and no permanent international criminal tribunal is established, little consistency in investigative initiatives (covert or overt) can be expected.

When it comes to money laundering, for example, some agreement and convergence of views has been achieved, but only for drug-related funds. Even on this front, there is not yet legal harmonization. The *Economist* (1994b) has reported that only half of the Financial Action Task Force (FATF) members have ratified the 1988 Vienna Convention against drug trafficking and money laundering. Turkey, although a FATF member, still has not criminalized drug money laundering and its banks hold anonymous accounts. Furthermore, proceeds from tax evasion, corruption, capital flight, arms trafficking or various types of smuggling are usually left out of treaties and conventions. Legal provisions are so diverse as to preclude an agreement in these fields in the near future.

In both our case studies, some outlawed activities in the U.S. were legal elsewhere. BCCI bankers assisted in the structuring of transactions in order to ensure the anonymity of their clients. By other countries' standards (where the convicted bankers had worked before moving to BCCI's Florida agencies), what they did was not a criminal offense, but common banking practice. Foreign secrecy laws prevented the cooperation of overseas authorities in several BCCI cases. Walker, on the other hand, would have committed no crime in Canada, even if all U.S. charges against him were true. Even if he was not going to do his due diligence in the Bahamas, even if he was going to broker the sale of pistols to Chile rather than Ecuador, no Canadian law would have been violated.

This is what makes Walker argue fervently that U.S. authorities' role is neither to police the world under U.S. law nor to lure foreigners, who have broken no law in their country, into the U.S.

Ideologically motivated crime, where one country's freedom fighter or immunity-worthy government agent is another's terrorist, is the best illustration of cross-border legal and political discrepancies. When an offense is committed by an indigenous non-governmental organization against domestic targets, international cooperation is very limited and politically suspect, unless the terrorist acts are considered crimes in the countries from which information and assistance is requested. International terrorism, on the other hand, attracts more support and cooperation. A terrorist group may act against targets in other countries to achieve political ends of domestic concern, but which threaten the safety and integrity of institutions abroad. International terrorist groups which operate with relative impunity tend to engender the greatest degree of cooperation among countries with similar institutions and traditions. This may lead to joint training and sharing of technology, information and communications systems.

This is less likely in cases of state terrorism, where a government or its leaders employ terrorism as an instrument of domestic or foreign policy. In the UN-promoted 1991 Draft Code of Crimes against the Peace and Security of Mankind, only state-sponsored terrorism against other states has been criminalized. Episodes such as the bombing of the Greenpeace boat 'Rainbow Warrior' by French undercover agents in Auckland, or U.S.-U.K. tensions over extradition requests of IRA suspects put in relief the lack of consensus even among Western democracies and allies – whose positions became, nonetheless, flexible on suspected Libyan terrorists (McCormack and Simpson, 1994).

Where the law enforcement environment in the target's country does not welcome foreign investigations, undercover operations may be perceived as the only way to gather information and evidence. This can take the form of recruiting informants to report back to control agents, sponsoring a team of investigators to obtain documentation and evidence from knowledgeable third parties, and use of deception and misdirection to induce the targets to divulge incriminating facts about themselves or their associates (international fugitive investigations frequently proceed in this fashion).

9. OTHER POLITICAL CONSIDERATIONS

Cross-border undercover activities present a number of challenges to those in charge of diplomatic relations. On the political front, undercover investigations are viewed as a necessary evil and best done where targets have little or no political following in both the target and source countries. Where this is not achievable for all sides concerned, plausible deniability becomes the 'next best thing.' For example, the President of a South American country may publicly decry the use of deception by foreign investigators in entrapping a prominent citizen from that country, but privately condone these methods when such a person poses an independent threat to that leader's political power base.

The situation is much more difficult when the targets of the investigation can manipulate political power elites. This should not be confused with corruption of political figures, which tends to be driven more by economic motives than the corruptor's desire for political power. In the latter situation, it is more an alliance of convenience based on shared economic rewards, with political goals and objectives being of secondary importance. However, where the investigative target holds political power, the thrust of an international investigation may well resort to methods which are known to only a select few in the target's country of residence or business. Recruitment of local resources and support is carefully done to give a wide birth to political factions allied with the target or which could make political gains by siding with the target. Conversely, persons and organizations politically, morally, or legally opposed to the target's activities are likely to be constructive and responsive to investigative efforts directed at a common enemy. This is very shaky ground and most law enforcement agencies do not have the requisite knowledge or expertise to assess such nuances from a distance. For these and other reasons, cooperating but politically neutral professional law enforcement officials in the target's country can prove invaluable in negotiating political minefields.

Where legal systems militate against any of the above forms of cooperation and mutual assistance, personnel from the private sector can be and have been employed. Like subcontractors, they fulfill a designated set of roles and carry out tasks that government agencies are unable or unwilling to undertake. Private agencies may spring up as a result of constraints on government bodies that are perceived as unreasonable. A private intelligence-gathering agency, Western Goals, for example, in its fund-raising literature stated in 1983 that it would be 'the first and only public foundation to enter this area and fill the gap caused by the crippling of the FBI, the disabling of the House Committee on Un-American Activities and the destruction of crucial government files' (quoted in Chevigny, 1984, 782).

One drawback is the difficulty of achieving control over the private support group, ensuring security of its activities and loyalty of personnel. Past experiences with excesses exposed in the Iran-Contra affair (U.S. Senate Committee on Foreign Relations, 1989; Walsh Report, 1992) and confused identities or roles of various parties in the BCCI (Kerry Report, 1992; Passas, 1993, 1994a; Truell and Gurwin, 1992), Matrix Churchill (Leigh and Norton-Taylor, 1993) and BNL-Iraqgate (Friedman, 1993; see also the numerous U.S. House Banking Committee hearings) scandals make this a problematic area. There is also the serious risk of scapegoating when the operation is discovered and those chiefly responsible escape accountability or hide behind the pre-designed plausible deniability. Nevertheless, the trend has been toward more, not fewer, private non-governmental undercover investigations, where a government agency obtains information almost as a by-product of routine due-diligence legal work of firms with multinational corporate clients.

10. TIMING THE CLOSE-DOWN OF UNDERCOVER OPERATIONS

Given the substantial costs of setting up credible fronts and running undercover operations, it is unwise to close them down too soon – that is, before significant results are achieved. Although a time schedule may exist at the start of an operation, it is possible that unexpected leads may develop that require more time and resources. This is exactly what happened in C-Chase, when the opportunity arose to widen the scope of the investigation and pursue serious offenses perpetrated through BCCI. On the other hand, lengthy operations increase the risks taken by the undercover agents, may stress them out (Girodo, 1984), and facilitate too much crime. It is hard to tell exactly how much crime should be allowed to occur with the help of undercover agents. There comes a point, however, when such crime facilitation exceeds policy bounds and becomes unnecessary or disproportionate to potential benefits to society. In the meantime, agents' relations with each other or their families may become strained. The task for married agents is even harder. Musella was able to pay occasional visits to his wife. A female undercover agent posed as his fiancé, which served to avoid the problem encountered by colleagues in the past when they had women offered to them by the targets of their investigations. Nonetheless, undercover work that goes on for years is anything but easy in this respect. Agents may also start liking or bonding with their targets. Finally, long operations are more vulnerable to leaks to the press or the anti-law enforcement activities of the criminal entrepreneurs. C-Chase agents experienced both of these problems, as botched law enforcement surveillance raised suspicions among drug traffickers and media reporters were notified of the operation weeks before its closedown.

These risks must be balanced against the value of substantial asset seizures and arrests of serious offenders. Unfortunately, other calculations may also drive the timing of close-downs. C-Chase, for instance, ended during a U.S. Presidential campaign, despite the willingness and desire of undercover agents to continue. This led to speculations that it was intended to produce a 'major success' in the war on drugs for the benefit of the Bush administration (Adams and Frantz, 1992). Budget considerations also play a role, as agencies need 'results' at the end of budget years in order to justify or fight over new resources (Blum, 1993). Ironically, such budgetary concerns militate against complex and long-term investigations, precisely the ones most likely to bear the best results.

11. ARRESTS AND PROSECUTIONS

Whenever undercover operations lack foreign support and future assistance is not guaranteed, suspects can be arrested only if they are brought to the U.S.A. Occasionally, attempts to do so by force or deceit backfire and defendants, like Walker, charge kidnapping and unlawful extra-territorial jurisdiction (Fialka, 1994). The abduction of a Mexican doctor, which was organized by DEA agents, caused a lot of diplomatic heat and became more controversial when the U.S. Supreme Court did not find it unconstitutional (*U.S.* v. *Alvarez-Machain*, 112

S.Ct. 2188 (1992); Glennon, 1992; Heymann and Gershengorn, 1993; Levine, 1993; Organization of American States, 1992). Terrorism suspects have also been abducted from Central and South American countries to stand trial in the U.S.A. (Findlay, 1988).

In C-Chase, most of the suspects were invited to attend a fake wedding between Musella and his fiancé, another Customs undercover agent. The arrests were made as the guests were on their way to a bachelor's party. C-Chase started as a U.S. operation, but ultimately involved British and French authorities which arrested and tried other suspects. Cooperation in this and subsequent BCCI cases was achieved largely because many countries' own interests converged and usual jurisdictional and legal problems, such as bank secrecy laws, were overcome (Raphaelson, 1993). Although the BCCI case illustrates the recent trend of convergence of interests in attacking drug money laundering around the world, international cooperation was not at all easy before the end of the Gulf war – the fear of alienating the ruler of Abu Dhabi, the owner by that time of BCCI and an ally against Iraq, affected the thinking and actions of regulators and other policy makers, at least in Britain (Bingham Report, 1992). As is common in cases where suspects are located in different countries, problems on who will prosecute which part of the network of offenders and under what laws (Passas, 1991) arose in the aftermath of C-Chase and the closure of BCCI. This was seen most publicly when a witness who cooperated with New York State prosecutors, was given immunity and testified in two U.S. trials, but was subsequently prosecuted by the British Serious Fraud Office and sentenced to prison.

12. CONCLUSION

The decreasing ability of nation states to control criminal activities on their own territory and the serious threat from sophisticated illegal traders suggests that international undercover operations are here to stay. Unilateral efforts are fraught with difficulties and can result in diplomatic rifts. The frequent lack of international cooperation, however, combined with a dissatisfaction with the current lack of consensus on laws and procedures, means that some of these investigations will not enjoy the full support or consent of countries where targets reside and operate. Pressures placed on law enforcement agencies to achieve certain targets, quantitative or otherwise, may mean that undercover operations will be mounted without attending to the problems we discussed and without seriously considering long-term objectives. Whenever demands on law enforcers are high or unreasonable, such problems are largely inevitable (Reuter, 1983). High expectations and over-commitment to domestically defined goals also lead to unacceptable exercises of extra-territorial jurisdiction and breaches of international law.

Yet, it is becoming commonplace to note that cosmopolitan offenders cannot be countered by parochial controllers (Passas, 1994b). Merely engaging in cross-border investigations does not make controllers cosmopolitan. If the mentality is unchanged, foreign and international law selectively observed, and general principles shunned, international operations may produce adverse consequences, such as more unwillingness to cooperate in future cases. There is, in other words, a need to collaborate on a multilateral or even supranational level.

The likelihood of effective cooperation ultimately depends on a realistic 'fear of reprisal,' the existence of unambiguous treaties on 'universally recognized crimes,' a practice of mutual assistance or informal arrangements, the cost of cooperation for the concerned states or authorities, and the compatibility of the respective legal systems. As Heymann (1990) has pointed out, one may discern two general approaches to cooperation in international criminal cases. The approach to which the U.S. subscribes is a preference for ad hoc missions characterized by informality, trust, no specific obligations or exceptions, that allows for limited and relatively unintrusive self-help. This is a model that can only work on a bilateral or small-group basis. Therefore, pragmatic structures need to be created to serve mutual assistance needs, even if these are intellectually incomplete (Heymann, 1990, 102–104). The problem with this approach and what is often perceived as unwarranted or illegal extraterritorial jurisdiction is that the U.S. may thus undermine its own principles of legality as well as the legitimacy of international bodies and norms (to which the U.S. generally subscribes and relies on for its overt actions).

The other approach is carefully designed to accommodate disparate political views, carefully negotiated agreements, specification of cases when assistance may be denied, and definition of state responsibilities. So, judges, lawyers and scholars would be invited to come up with a comparatively coherent and seamless structure of international law that complements domestic law. Sovereignty is accorded higher importance and efforts would be made to ensure that no serious offender escapes sanction by taking advantage of national borders (Heymann, 1990, 104–105).

The bottom line in international cooperation, however, is that there must be recognized common interests that converge in the containment of specified acts. There has to be a degree of consensual knowledge before the creation of international regimes and agreement on general and enforceable principles can be more realistic (Haas, 1980; Keohane, 1984; Krasner, 1983).

In the absence of international structures and general principles guiding control practices, even allied countries find their positions occasionally at loggerheads. Practical interim remedial steps can include pre-operational planning and joint training of personnel from different countries. Frequent contacts and exchange of views among professionals can sensitize them to each other's traditions and views. Dialogue at administrative and political levels in the UN or other supranational fora is essential, if the objective is to reach a better level of understanding and gradually move towards a degree of harmonization of crime definitions, crime-fighting procedures, and sanctions.

From a domestic perspective, most important is the establishment of a system of internal and external controls, with checks and balances to prevent unilateral deployment of tactical resources from a co-team task group that might compromise the undercover status of the overall effort. The objectives of undercover operations need to be clear and focused. Statutory and procedural rules have to be observed and effective management controls to monitor activities need to be established. All this requires training and education, strong in-group identification and *esprit de corps*, and the existence of reward systems and other incentives for adherence to high ethical standards. Given the high risks of private operations, they are to be avoided. Also, more flexibility on the close-down timing must be allowed, following consultation with line agents.

Finally, our knowledge of the mechanics and problems in international undercover investigations is rudimentary. No systematic or detailed data and figures on such operations are published. We do not know what proportion of international investigative efforts are covert. We do not know how many operations never got off the ground, never resulted in prosecutions, at what stage and for what reasons they were aborted, what techniques were employed but failed. There is a need for systematic research and analysis of information that is spread across different agencies and countries. In order to arrive at more concrete and useful policy recommendations, further empirical research into multi-agency operations, trends and patterns is indispensable.

REFERENCES

Adams, J., Frantz, D. (1992), *The Full Service Bank*, New York, Pocket Books.
Beaufoy, J. (1993), 'Toronto Man's Court Victory Stymied by Boyd's Decision Not to Get Involved,' *Law Times*, 22 November.
Blum, J. (1993), 'BCCI, International Business Crime, and the Criminal Justice System,' in: *Symposium on Cross-Border Banking Offenses and Regulation; Policy Lessons from the BCCI Affair*, Temple University (November).
Bossard, A. (1990), *Transnational Crime and Criminal Law*, Chicago, Office of International Criminal Justice.
Bullington, B., Block, A. (1990), 'A Trojan Horse; Anti-Communism and the War on Drugs,' *Contemporary Crises*, 14, 1, 39–55.
Chambliss, W.J. (1988), *On the Take; From Petty Crooks to Presidents*, Bloomington, Indiana University Press.
Chevigny, P.G. (1984), 'Politics and Law in the Control of Local Surveillance,' *Cornell Law Review*, 69, 735–784.
Cowley, C. (1992), *Guns, Lies and Spies: How We Armed Iraq*, London, Hamish Hamilton.
Economist (1994a), 'The Covert Arms Trade,' 12 February, 21–23.
Economist (1994b), 'Money Launderers on the Line,' 25 June, 81–82.
Edelhertz, H. (1980), 'Transnational White-Collar Crime; A Developing Challenge and a Need for Response,' *Temple Law Quarterly*, 53, 1114–1126.
Fialka, J.J. (1994), 'Customs Service's "Stings" to Curtail Arms Sales Draw Blood (Its Own) as Cases Collapse in Court,' *Wall Street Journal*, 18 March, A12.
Findlay, D.C. (1988), 'Abducting Terrorists Overseas for Trial in the United States,' *Texas International Law Journal*, 23, 1–54.
Fine, S. (1992), 'Fugitives May be Snatched from Canada,' *Globe and Mail*, 19 June, A1, A10.
Fooner, M. (1989), *Interpol; Issues in World Crime and International Criminal Justice*, New York, Plenum.
Francis, D. (1992a), 'Canada Must Get Tough With U.S. Bounty Hunters,' *The Financial Post*, 14 July.

Francis, D. (1992b), 'No Way to Treat Neighbors; U.S. Customs Officials Entrapping Unsuspecting Canadians,' *The Financial Post*, 27 January.
Francis, D. (1993), 'Conspiracy Victim Continues his Fight With U.S.,' *The Financial Post*, 28 December.
Francis, D. (1994), 'Liberals Should Come to Ken Walker's Aid,' *The Financial Post*, 10 March.
Friedman, A. (1993), *Spider's Web; The Secret History of How the White House Illegally Armed Iraq*,' New York, Bantam Books.
GAO (1991), *Money Laundering*, NSIAD-91-130, May.
Girodo, M. (1984), 'Entry and Re-Entry Strain in Undercover Agents,' in: Allen, V.N., v.d. Vliert, E., eds., *Role Transitions*, New York, Plenum, 169-179.
Glennon, M.J. (1992), 'State-Sponsored Abduction; A Comment on United States v. Alvarez-Machain,' *American Journal of International Law*, 86, 746-756.
Haas, E.B. (1980), 'Why Collaborate? Issue Linkage and International Regimes,' *World Politics*, 32, 357-405.
Hartung, W.D. (1994), *And Weapons For All*, New York, HarperCollins.
Hersh, S.M. (1994), 'The Wild East,' *The Atlantic Monthly*, June, 61-86.
Heymann, P.B. (1990), 'Two Models of National Attitudes Toward International Cooperation in Law Enforcement,' *Harvard International Law Journal*, 31, 99-107.
Heymann, P.B., Gershengorn, I.H. (1993), 'A Missed Opportunity,' *Criminal Law Forum*, 4, 1, 155-175.
Keohane, R.O. (1984), *After Hegemony; Cooperation and Discord in the World Political Economy*, Princeton, Princeton University Press.
Kerry Report (1992), *The BCCI Affair*, Washington, D.C., GPO.
Krasner, S.D., ed. (1983), *International Regimes*, Ithaca, Cornell University Press.
Kritz, G.J. (1992), 'International Co-operation to Combat Money Laundering; The Nature and Role of Mutual Assistance Treaties,' *Commonwealth Law Bulletin*, 18, 723-734.
Labrousse, A. (1994), 'Géopolitique de la drogue; Les contradictions des politiques de "Guerre à la Drogue",' *Futuribles*, 185, 9-22.
Leigh, D., Norton-Taylor, R. (1993), *Betrayed; The Real Story of the Matrix Churchill Trial*, London, Bloomsbury.
Levine, M. (1993), 'I Volunteer to Kidnap Oliver North,' *Crime, Law and Social Change*, 20, 1-12.
Marx, G.T. (1982), 'Who Really Gets Stung? Some Issues Raised by the New Police Undercover Work,' *Crime and Delinquency*, 4, 165-193.
Marx, G.T. (1988), *Undercover; Police Surveillance in America*, Berkeley, University of California Press.
Marx, G.T. (1992), 'Under-the-Covers Undercover Investigations; Some Reflections on the State's Use of Sex and Deception in Law Enforcement,' *Criminal Justice Ethics*, Winter/Spring, 13-24.
Marx, G.T. (1992), 'When the Guards Guard Themselves: Undercover Tactics Turned Inward,' *Policing and Society*, 2, 151-172.

McCormack, T.L.H., Simpson, G.J. (1994), 'The International Law Commission's Draft Code of Crimes Against the Peace and Security of Mankind; An Appraisal of the Substantive Provisions,' *Criminal Law Forum*, 5, 1, 1–55.
Nadelmann, E.A. (1993), *Cops Across Borders; The Internationalization of U.S. Criminal Law Enforcement*, University Park, Pennsylvania State University Press.
O'Brien, P.T. (1990), 'Tracking Narco-Dollars; The Evolution of a Potent Weapon in the Drug War,' *Inter-American Law Review*, 21, 3, 637–677.
Organization of American States (1992), *Legal Opinion on the Decision of the Supreme Court of the United States of America*, OEA/ser. G/CP/doc 2302/92.
Parkes, C. (1994), 'Germany's Plutonium Smuggling Saga Turns into Farce,' *Financial Times*, 20–21 August, 24.
Parry, R. (1993), *Trick or Treason; The October Surprise Mystery*, New York, Sheridan Square Press.
Passas, N. (1991), *Frauds Affecting the Budget of the European Community* (Report to the Commission of the European Communities).
Passas, N. (1993), 'Structural Sources of International Crime; Policy Lessons from the BCCI Affair,' *Crime, Law and Social Change*, 20, 4, 293–305.
Passas, N. (1994a), 'I Cheat, Therefore I Exist? The BCCI Scandal in Context,' in: Hoffman, W.M., Kamm, J., Frederick, R.E., Petry, E., eds., *Emerging Global Business Ethics*, Newport, CT, Quorum Books, 69–78.
Passas, N. (1994b), 'European Integration, Protectionism and Criminogenesis; A Study on Farm Subsidy Frauds,' *Mediterranean Quarterly*, 5, 4, 66–84.
Passas, N., Groskin, R.B. (1993), 'BCCI and the Federal Authorities; Regulatory Anesthesia and the Limits of Criminal Law,' *Society for the Study of Social Problems*, Miami Beach, Annual Meeting.
Passas, N., Nelken, D. (1991), 'The Fight Against Fraud in the European Community; Cacophony Rather Than Harmony,' *Corruption and Reform*, 6, 237–266.
Passas, N., Nelken, D. (1993), 'The Thin Line Between Legitimate and Criminal Enterprises; Subsidy Frauds in the European Community,' *Crime, Law and Social Change*, 19, 3, 223–243.
Pearce, F., Woodiwiss, M. (1992), *Global Crime Connections; Dynamics and Control*, London, Macmillan.
Piñera-Vasquez, S.B. (1988), 'Extraterritorial Jurisdiction and International Banking; A Conflict of Interests,' *University of Miami Law Review*, 43, 449–491.
Punch, M. (1991), 'Tough or Tame? The Contextuality of Tackling Business Crime in Three Societies,' *Corruption and Reform*, 6, 211–235.
Raphaelson, I.H. (1993), 'BCCI: Its Place in History,' *Symposium on Cross-Border Banking Offenses and Regulation: Policy Lessons from the BCCI Affair*, Temple University, November.
Reguly, E. (1992), 'Banking and Sting Operations Don't Mix,' *The Financial Post*, 14 February.
Reiss, A. (1993), 'Detecting, Investigating and Regulating Business Lawbreakers,' in: Grabosky, P., Braithwaite, J., eds., *Business Regulation and Australia's Future*, Canberra, Australian Institute of Criminology, 189–200.

Reuter, P. (1983), 'Licensing Criminals; Police and Informants,' in: Caplan, G.M., ed., *ABSCAM Ethics; Moral Issues and Deception in Law Enforcement*, Washington, The Police Foundation, 100–117.

Rushford, G. (1989), 'Botched Customs Sting May Spark Hill Inquiry,' *Legal Times*, 8 September, 6–7.

Saffron, I. (1994), 'Russia Rejects Germany's Nuclear Smuggling Claims,' *Philadelphia Inquirer*, 19 August, A25.

Skolnick, J.H., Fyfe, J.J. (1993), *Above the Law; Police and the Excessive Use of Force*, New York, Free Press.

Smith, H.E., ed. (1989), *Transnational Crime; Investigative Responses*, Chicago, Office of International Criminal Justice.

Stavsky, M.M. (1985), 'The "Sting" Reconsidered; Organized Crime, Corruption and Entrapment,' *Rutgers Law Journal*, 16, 937–989.

Stephens, J.B. (1986), 'Setting the Sting; Minimizing the Risk,' *Criminal Justice*, Summer, 14–17, 38–39.

Truell, P., Gurwin, L. (1992), *False Profits*, Boston and New York, Houghton Mifflin.

U.S. Senate Committee on Foreign Relations (1989), *Drugs, Law Enforcement and Foreign Policy; Report of the Subcommittee on Terrorism, Narcotics and International Operations*, Washington, D.C., GPO.

U.S. Senate Committee on Governmental Affairs (1983), *Crime and Secrecy; The Use of Offshore Banks and Companies; Hearings before the Permanent Committee on Investigations*, Washington, D.C., GPO.

Walsh, L.E. (1993), *Final Report of the Independent Counsel for Iran/Contra Matters*, Washington, D.C., U.S. Court of Appeals for the District of Columbia Circuit.

Williams, P. (1994), 'Transnational Criminal Organisations and International Security,' *Survival*, 36, 1, 96–113.

Gary T. Marx*

Undercover: Some Implications for Policy

The preceding articles have covered different countries and issues. Yet all of them imply ambivalence about the use of covert means and identify potential problems. In this article I (1) suggest some criteria to use in considering whether or not the tactic is justified, (2) identify some assumptions about the empirical world that should be met before the tactic is used, (3) note some types of undercover operations and some dimensions along which they may vary and (4) note some tensions that accompany even the most clearly and carefully developed policies.[1]

Ethical Considerations

It is clear that there are significant opportunities for effective law enforcement, as well as grave risks, associated with the use of covert means. Neither the unleashing of these tactics, nor their total prohibition seems wise. Yet if they are to be used effectively and justly according to democratic standards, they must be used cautiously and only after careful consideration of alternatives and risks.

In thinking about the ethical status of undercover tactics we must ask four questions: First, can undercover practices be ethical? If the answer to this is 'Yes,' we are led to a second and third question: under what conditions are they ethical – as a broad strategy, and as tactically implemented? If we can resolve these matters, there is still a fourth question: in any given case, to what extent do the conditions for ethical use hold?

A number of arguments for and against covert means can be identified. The following arguments do not carry equal weight, but they reflect the range of ideas heard in current discussions. Any decision to use or not use undercover tactics must come to terms with them.

---

* Professor of Sociology, University of Colorado, Boulder, United States.
1. The four sections here summarize material in G.T. Marx, *Undercover*, chs. 4, 5, 6, and 9.

For Use of the Tactic:

1. Citizens grant to government the right to use exceptional means.
2. Undercover work is ethical when used for a good and important end.
3. Enforce the law equally.
4. Convict the guilty.
5. An investigation should be as nonintrusive and noncoercive as possible.
6. When citizens use questionable means, government agents are justified in using equivalent means.
7. Undercover work is ethical when there are reasonable grounds for suspicion.
8. Special risks justify special precautions.
9. Undercover work is ethical when the decision to use it has been publicly announced.
10. Undercover work is ethical when done by persons of upright character in accountable organizations.
11. Undercover work is ethical when it is undertaken with the intention of eventually being made public and judged in court.

Against Use of the Tactic:

1. Truth telling is moral; lying is immoral.
2. The government should neither participate in, nor be a party to, crime nor break the law in order to enforce it.
3. The government should not make deals with criminals.
4. The government should not offer unrealistic temptations or tempt the weak.
5. Do no harm to the innocent.
6. Respect the sanctity of private places.
7. Respect the sanctity of intimate relations.
8. Respect the right to freedom of expression and action.
9. It is wrong to discriminate in target selection.
10. The government should not do by stealth what it is prohibited from doing openly.

It is clear that covert practices in a democratic society involve conflicting principles. One solution to the problem of conflicting principles is to weigh them. In the criminal justice system, effectiveness often conflicts with humaneness, decency or fairness. A democratic society gives significant weight to fairness and, thus, formally rejects the notion that the end justifies the means. Ethics attach to means as well as to ends, and some means are just too abhorrent to use. Police are prohibited from torturing people, pumping their stomachs to discover drugs, or harming innocent friends or relatives of the accused. These tactics are seen as so unethical that they are categorically rejected. The moral distinction between crime and criminal justice is maintained only by such restrictions.

However, few persons would argue that undercover means ought to be categorically prohibited or that they should be used indiscriminately without restrictions and guidelines. Given an intermediate position, where and how should the lines be drawn? In answering the question 'is undercover work ethical?', we can learn from the response of a wizened old stationmaster who, when asked whether or not the train would be on time, looked down at his watch, hesitated and then said, 'That depends.' When asked 'What does it depend on?', he hesitated again and replied, 'That depends too.' So it is with undercover work. Whether or not it is ethical 'depends.' I think much of what it depends on should be determined by answers to the following questions:

- *Seriousness:* is the use of undercover work proposed for crimes of a seriously harmful nature?
- *Alternatives:* are alternative nondeceptive means unavailable for obtaining the same end?
- *Democratic decision making:* has granting police the option to use undercover means been subject to a degree of democratic decision making, however indirect, and has it been publicly announced that such means will be used?
- *Spirit of the law:* is use of the strategy consistent with the spirit, as well as the letter, of the law?
- *Prosecution:* is the goal of the strategy eventually to invoke criminal justice processing and hence make the deception publicly subject to judgement, rather than to gather intelligence indiscriminately, to harass, or to coerce cooperation from an informer?
- *Clarity of definition:* is its use proposed for crimes that are clearly defined, or, if not, can a tactic be devised that insures that the target is well aware of the criminal nature of the behavior?
- *Crime occurrence:* are there reasonable grounds for concluding that the crime that occurs as a result of the undercover operation is not an artifact of the method of intervention?
- *Grounds for suspicion:* are there reasonable grounds for concluding that the particular target of an undercover operation has already committed or is likely to commit an equivalent offense, regardless of the government's undercover effort?
- *Prevention:* are there reasonable grounds for concluding that the undercover operation will prevent a serious crime from occurring?

The greater the number and strength of affirmative answers, the more ethically defensible a general undercover strategy is. Questions must also be raised about the ethics of particular activities within the investigation. (It may be ethical as a broad strategy, even when specific aspects are unethical.) The following questions deal with the actual organization and dynamics of an operation.

- *Autonomy:* does the tactic permit a high degree of self-selection and/or autonomy on the part of the suspect in breaking the law?
- *Degree of deception:* does use of the tactic involve minimal or extensive deception, and is the amount involved only that which is necessary to carry out the investigation?
- *Bad lessons:* how far does the tactic go in casting the state in the role of teaching a bad moral lesson?

- *Privacy and expression:* will use of the tactic sufficiently respect the sanctity of private places, intimate and professional relations, and the right to freedom of expression and action?
- *Collateral harm:* how great is the potential for exploitation, corruption, perjury, or abuses and harm to police, informers, and unwitting third parties? Can these be adequately controlled or compensated for?
- *Equitable target selection:* are the criteria for target selection equitable?
- *Realism:* does the undercover scene stay reasonably close to real world settings and opportunities?
- *Relevance of charges:* are the charges brought against a person directly connected with criminal harm, or do they reflect mere procedural violations?
- *Actors:* does the undercover investigation involve sworn agents playing central roles rather than informers?

Asking such questions is important if one accepts Sissela Bok's (1978) position that lying is not neutral and that there should be a presumption against it. To use undercover tactics will require greater justification than is the case for more conventional police methods. The situation is analogous to the greater justification required for, and stricter controls around, the use of force. The greater the extent of the affirmative or 'harm-avoiding' answers to the above questions, the more justified an undercover operation is.

The two sets of questions presented above should be seen as navigational aids and not as a flight plan. They are skill-honing devices that can increase the sensitivity of the judgments made by agents, police supervisors, criminal justice officials, and concerned citizens. In noting that some resolution of the disagreements around secret police tactics is possible, our optimism (for both the resolution and the tactic) must remain qualified and guarded. Virtue is often intertwined with evil.

Calling something a necessary evil does not get around the problem of conflicting principles, even when an operational solution is found. The hallmark of a moral dilemma, of course, is that there is no way out. This is part of the topic's fascination and why persons of good will strenuously disagree. We can not reach an easy general conclusion about whether undercover tactics should be prohibited or justified on ethical grounds. Paradoxically, no matter what action is taken, there are moral costs. There are clear costs whenever the government uses deceit, and still other costs are at risk. But not to use the tactic can have costs too, whether inaction and inequality in law enforcement in the face of serious crime, or the greater costs that may accompany use of some other tactic.

In dealing with such moral dilemmas, the problem is not only whether we can find an acceptable utilitarian calculus, but that the choice always involves competing wrongs. The danger of automatically applied technical, bureaucratic, or occupational subcultural formulas lies in their potential for generating the self-deluding and morally numbing conclusion that a cost free solution is possible.

Some Empirical Assumptions

Even if we conclude that the tactic is on balance ethical, that is not enough to justify it. There should also be grounds for thinking that the following often tacit empirical assumptions that usually accompany its use are correct.

1. The world in question is clearly divided between criminals and non-criminals.
2. The supply of and demand for illicit goods and services are limited.
3. Undercover practices can have a major impact in reducing crime, apprehending criminals, and recovering stolen property.
4. Those arrested in undercover operations are repeat offenders who might otherwise avoid arrest.
5. The not guilty (this time) assumption.
6. Undercover operations are independent of each other.
7. Undercover operations can control their environment.
8. Undercover operations do *not* amplify crime as a result of
   a. generating a market for the purchase or sale of illegal goods and services or indirectly generating capital for other illegality;
   b. generating the idea and motive for the crime;
   c. using coercion, intimidation, trickery, or persuasion of a person not otherwise predisposed to commit the offense;
   d. offering a seductive temptation to a person who would not otherwise encounter it;
   e. providing the contraband or a missing resource or ingredients essential for the commission of the crime;
   f. providing the context for false records and framing;
   g. generating a covert opportunity structure for illegal actions on the part of the undercover agent or informant;
   h. generating retaliatory violence against informers;
   i. stimulating a variety of crimes on the part of those who are not targets of the operation.

Types and Dimensions

For purposes of both policy and understanding we must recognize that there are different kinds of undercover activity and even the same kinds may differ according to many dimensions. There is a need to disaggregate and to consider the particular forms in question. What applies to one form of investigation may not apply to another.

A basic distinction is between intelligence, preventive, and facilitative operations. Intelligence operations use covert and deceptive tactics to gather information about crimes that have already occurred, are or might be planned, or are in progress. The agent's role tends to be relatively passive, involving observation and questioning, rather than an effort to direct the interaction. Events that have occurred or are under way are postliminary, while those believed to be planned are anticipatory. Preventive operations seek to either prevent a crime from occurring or to prevent harm if it does occur. In contrast, facilitative operations seek to encourage (or at least not to prevent) the commission of an offense. The undercover agent can play the role of co-conspirator or victim.

Investigations also differ depending on:

1. the grounds for initiation;
2. the specificity in target selection;
3. the degree of self-selection;
4. the correspondence to real-world criminal behavior;
5. natural or artificial criminal environments;
6. intent and autonomy;
7. whether or not the offense is carried out;
8. whether a sworn state agent or informer plays the role;
9. whether they involve 'deep' or 'light' cover;
10. the use of the results.

The three types of operation and various dimensions are of more than academic interest; they can also help us in considering the desirability of various types of undercover activity. From my analysis of the ethical and operational aspects, the following conclusions seem warranted.

Postliminary (after-the-fact) intelligence operations raise fewer problems than anticipatory investigations because they are likely to be more bounded. Furthermore, because the crime has already occurred, intent, discriminatory enforcement, and entrapment are less likely to be issues.

With respect to anticipatory investigations, those of a preventive nature may forestall harm but sometimes leave doubts over whether the criminal action would actually have been carried out. Among those of a facilitative nature, there is always the danger of entrapment.

In general, the providing of a target for victimization is likely to raise fewer problems than co-conspiratorial operations. Undercover operations organized on the basis of prior intelligence or complaints that stay close to real-world criminal conditions are superior to random integrity testing or to the creation of an artificial criminal environment with unrealistically attractive temptations. Covert investigations should mimic actual criminal settings as much as possible given the constraints, and the emphasis should be on a recognized crime problem. The goal of an investigation should be to determine if there is sufficient evidence to warrant judicial proceedings.

Operations directed against persons who have behaved autonomously, where the opportunity for self-selection is maximized, where the nature of the criminal activity is clear, and where the undercover agent's role is passive or, at least, not highly facilitative are preferable to their opposites. Light undercover operations and those where the major role is played by a sworn agent are likely to raise fewer problems than deep undercover operations and those where the major role is played by a witting, or worse, an unwitting informer.

Because at their worst undercover tactics are so troubling and at their best so filled with ethical and operational dilemmas, they must be used with extreme caution, and only after consideration of alternative means and the cost of taking no action.

Some Paradoxes of Undercover Work

Undercover work involves some unavoidable trade-offs and risks. Undercover operations involve a number of paradoxes: doing good by doing bad (lies, deceit, and trickery); to see police act as criminals and criminal informers act as police; to seek to reduce crime and, in fact, to increase it; to see restrictions on police coercion result in increased police deception.

Other operational paradoxes involved in efforts to manage and control covert investigations are related to conflicts between gathering intelligence and taking action that gives the intelligence away; between bureaucratic control and innovation; between prevention and apprehension; and between secrecy and open communication. The very power of the technique also can be its undoing. These tensions can be stated as the following hypotheses:

1. The goal of equal law enforcement (in the sense that different categories of serious offenses have roughly equivalent chances of being prosecuted) may conflict with our expectation that there be some grounds for suspicion before an investigation can be carried out. Random integrity tests may create equity, but at a cost of violating the latter principle. Conversely, the more stringent the criteria for initiating an operation and the more formalized and routinized the controls, the greater the difficulty of apprehending the highly skilled offender and those involved in offenses where there is no complaint. The solution to this is a less stringent standard for them, but this solves one equity problem at the expense of creating another.
2. Elaborate legislative controls on undercover operations with strong sanctions for violations would reduce abuses but might also unintentionally inhibit legitimate uses.
3. The higher the level of supervision, the poorer the quality of information available for decision making and the greater the time required for a decision.
4. The more extensive the controls, the greater the likelihood of leaks and the greater the cost of the operation.
5. The further the undercover agent is socially and organizationally from the target, the more objective and hard-hitting the investigation is likely to be, even as there may be less understanding of the subtleties involved and greater difficulty of access. Put another way, it takes one to know one, but with firsthand knowledge there can be added restraints.
6. Electronic surveillance offers a means of documenting transactions and enhancing safety, but it also increases the risk of discovery. The most crucial meetings may be the initial ones, which are least likely to be recorded for security reasons. Later taped meetings may simply refer to 'our understanding' or 'our deal.'
7. A sophisticated cover story may be required to gain access, but its very complexity may mean that the agent has trouble remembering it and that he is more vulnerable to discovery via checking.
8. Multiple agencies/agents playing undercover roles can serve as a check on each other, but this also increases the risk of their becoming unknowingly ensnared in each other's investigations.

9. The closer an operation comes to the real-world context in which the violation occurs, the less the concern that the offense is solely an artifact of the investigation or of government overreaching, yet the greater may be the threat to the officer's safety, the difficulty of obtaining documentary evidence, and the harm done from the crime.
10. A requirement that operations stay close to real-world criminal situations may conflict with other moral or legal requirements to make clear the illegal nature of the transaction, not to mix legitimate objectives and criminal opportunities, and not to use coercion, intimidation, or manipulation to gain compliance.
11. A policy of avoiding juveniles in property stings and related efforts may help the public image of an operation and keep some weak and immature youths from going astray. But it also means avoiding a group that disproportionately contributes to street crime.
12. New recruits may be successful in gaining initial entry because they are not known and don't seem like 'cops,' but their inexperience can mean an increased vulnerability to problems. However, aside from greater difficulty of access, there also may be a point at which too much experience is dysfunctional for the individual agent and the agency.
13. The more involved in crime an informer is, the more useful he is likely to be, yet the more difficult he may be to control, the weightier the ethical issues, and the greater the potential damage to public image.
14. Unwitting informers can be a means of penetrating inaccessible criminal milieus and may protect authorities against charges of political targeting, but because they are not knowingly a part of the investigation, they cannot be directly controlled.
15. From a prosecutive viewpoint, the less paid the informer the better, and payment must not be tied to the number or identity of subjects, but this runs contrary to the basic expectation that performance and reward will be linked and the need to motivate informers for difficult and dangerous work.
16. For both moral and pragmatic reasons 'you need to treat informers like human beings with dignity.' The friendship and guidance the agent offers, along with leniency or a degree of protection for minor violations, is likely to mean a more productive and reliable informer. But the line between such friendship/reciprocity and the agent being compromised can be thin.
17. For local police, a significant expansion of undercover activities is likely to mean fewer visible police patrols (which many citizens find reassuring) and fewer police to respond to citizen requests.
18. Within police departments and other organizations, internal investigative mechanisms, such as random integrity tests and the use of unidentified 'field associates' who secretly report on the misbehavior of their peers, may increase the amount of corruption discovered, but they communicate distrust and may lead to lower morale and have a negative labelling impact – all factors conducive to corruption.
19. Law-enforcement media representatives face a conflict between the need to protect an ongoing investigation and their task of honestly keeping a free press informed. If the representative is uninformed, agency interests

will be protected, although journalists will seek out other sources. If the representative is knowledgeable, there is the danger of disclosure or lying to the press.
20. The exemplary straight-arrow image of a law-enforcement agency that inspires citizen respect and cooperation is likely to undergo erosion, the greater the resort to covert and devious methods.
21. Some of the personality characteristics that draw people to undercover work and make for successful presentations are also associated with an increased risk of undesirable personality and behavior changes when they leave undercover roles.
22. Up to some reasonable point the longer an operation goes on, the more damage it may do (in the failure to prevent harm or actually stimulating or contributing to it): logistical problems with witnesses and evidence may be greater, suspects may flee, and the individual's right to a speedy trial may be denied. But in addition, the greater the certainty about the occurrence of the crime, the higher the level of offender likely to be arrested and the better the evidence. The requirements of prevention and facilitation may conflict.
23. Concluding an operation, even with quality arrests, usually will necessitate divulging the identity of the agents and the tactics used. This is the classic dilemma of acting on the information received from spying. Not to act risks damage to your side, but to act may alert your adversary to your means of collecting information. Like a bee that dies after using its sting, police stings (to a greater extent than other means) have a self-destructive quality. Within the same locale, the very success of the tactic can be its undoing. Agents cannot rest on a proven method but must continue to be inventive.
24. In principle, a major advantage of anticipatory or preemptive undercover police action is the greater opportunity for planning, deliberation, and control relative to situations in which police behave reactively, for example, calls about crimes in progress, hot pursuits or having to respond to whatever event occurs, when and where it occurs. Yet the rational impulse presupposes adequate information on which to make decisions.

When Robert Burns wrote that our best laid plans 'gang aft agley,' he didn't have the confounding effects of secrecy in mind. In many undercover situations it may not be clear who the players are, or even what the game is. In undercover work, for things to go as anticipated may mean they do not go as planned. The unknowns and the emergent nature of the process often result in unpredictable events that can severely undermine the effort to plan ahead. Some investigations resemble Greek tragedies more than strategic game plans. Circumstances that agents thought they could control may come to control them.

It is easier to describe the above paradoxes than to solve them. But awareness can at least mean better-informed choices. In calling attention to the problems and limits of undercover means, I am not arguing for the fashionable notion that nothing works. It is true that there are no easy answers, but the choice is hardly between perfection and abject failure. As we have noted, there is great variation across undercover situations. Sound policy and planning can make a difference in both protecting liberty and maintaining order.

Gary T. Marx* | # Undercover in Comparative Perspective: Some Implications for Knowledge and Social Research[1]

Research projects, even when exploratory and largely descriptive as this undertaking is, always involve at least tacit theoretical expectations. This project is no exception.

In my study of undercover practices in the United States I argued that social control was changing in important ways. As we note in our introduction, a remarkable expansion in undercover tactics occurred in the decades following J. Edgar Hoover's death. The increased prominence of undercover methods was accompanied by an increase in other (often covert) forms involving video and audio surveillance and electronic location monitoring, computer dossiers, and a variety of biometric measures such as drug testing and DNA analysis. Rather than being alternatives, these often bolstered each other and can be seen to reflect a cult and culture of surveillance.[2]

The new surveillance and the 'maximum security society' seen in the United States reflect broader changes associated with the modern state. These changes in social control go beyond government and law enforcement to commerce, the workplace and even interpersonal relations. As a sociologist looking at the big picture, I hypothesized that these changes were not idiosyncratic to the United States and that many of the same broad factors operating to produce them would be found in other industrial democratic societies. Among reasons for thinking this were:

1. Common cultural and structural factors associated with the development and organization of the modern state such as ideas of science, rationality and citizenship and the interdependence and complexity of mass society, with its impersonality, mobility and bureaucratic organization.
2. Functional needs – modern complex societies face many common problems and may reach similar conclusions about how to best deal with them

---

* Professor of Sociology, University of Colorado, Boulder, United States.
1. I am grateful to Albrecht Funk, Richard Leo and Fred Pampel for their comments.
2. An analysis of the cultural imagery around surveillance can be found in Marx (1995).

(e.g., radar and driving under the influence of alcohol tests for traffic enforcement; covert tactics for offenses without a complainant; testing and quarantine for public health emergencies; a common forensic science for dealing with ballistics and DNA evidence; and the internationalization of crime which requires cross border cooperation). This might be seen most clearly where risks are the greatest, as with control practices found at nuclear power plants or airports.
3. Aggressive entrepreneurship by countries such as the United States and France seeking to export their control practices. This is done by government agents seeking influence and by private sector entrepreneurs seeking profits.
4. Fads and fashion. In democratic societies, social interventions into complex social problems such as crime are generally only partly successful. There is a constant search for new and presumably better ways. A related aspect is simply symbolic – the desire of countries to appear modern and proessional by using the latest means.
5. Increased communication between countries and new cross border social control efforts involving bi- and multi-lateral treaties, international law, and new organizations and forms of cooperation such as Europol and Trevi and Schengen. Common security practices at borders and airports as a result of international standards are one example. The weakening of borders in Europe (and between the United States and its immediate neighbors) suggests that cooperative efforts and common practices will become more prevalent. For example, in 1995 the DEA had agents in 50 countries and the FBI and customs in 25.
6. Competitive pressures in a global political and economic system and/or a desire to increase efficiency and control in which a tactic perceived to offer an advantage (such as new, more comprehensive forms of work monitoring or satellite surveillance) would be adopted out of self-interest.

Such social forces are certainly operative. Yet regardless of how important the United States is as a political and economic superpower and exporter of its culture through powerful international mass media and governmental bodies and marketing channels, it is premature to conclude that a standard, technocratic, anticipatory, velvet glove, paradigmatic American social control model is taking over the western democratic world. If that were the case the main thing left to study would be the process of its diffusion.[3]

While Coca Cola and basketball may be quickly imported, new undercover police tactics and intrusive surveillance technologies may be rejected (as seems to be the case in Europe with most drug testing and technologies for electronic

---

3. If the model of a dominant United States social control paradigm is wrong, there may still be a move toward a more standardized, democratic, industrial society model which involves amalgamation and convergence. These contrast with a model of continued and perhaps even increasing differences. These should be seen on a continuum and can be broken down into a number of dimensions. We are certainly far from the ideal-type end points of the continuum. The key question involves developments over time and whether general movement in a consistent direction can be observed.

monitoring of prisoners, children and workers). If accepted they will be adjusted and changed to meet a country's social contexts, culture and needs.

Certainly the new forms of surveillance have come to Europe. Some changes represent a radical and sudden break with the recent past. In recent decades new enabling legislation has been passed, courts have offered new supports, special units (particularly for drugs and organized crime) have been created and covert activities have expanded in Germany, France, the Netherlands, Belgium, Russia and elsewhere. But this has not happened to the same degree, or with the same force and energy, as was the case for criminal and non-criminal uses in the United States. Europeans have far more stringent protections from personal data collection, and seem to go to greater lengths to maintain physical privacy in the face of greater density.

Holding apart counter-terrorist and state security uses, the main European use is for drugs. Property stings, street decoys, anti-corruption, environmental and endangered species protection uses were rare, or non-existent. To be sure, there are idiosyncratic uses, (e.g., in Britain against soccer hooliganism and contract homicides, in Italy to recover stolen art and against the Mafia), but I had anticipated that the tactics would be used more extensively and intensively than they appear to be. Of course with time this may change.

There is of course great variation within the world outside the United States. For example, Germany makes far more extensive use of computer dossiers and artificial intelligence systems and has a more developed ethos of prevention than do other countries in Europe. Britain appears to make more extensive use of public video cameras, of telephone hot lines for secret citizen reporting and of neighborhood watches. France makes extensive use of political dossiers, while showing great contempt for informers. Italy relies upon mafia informers (*pentiti*) with new identities. Given its size, Canada may be the leader in wire-tapping.[4] The European country that seems closest to the United States in the use of these tactics is the Netherlands. It is interesting that the country often seen as one of Europe's most permissive and tolerant is closest to United States both in that regard and with respect to its surveillance practices. One factor is its importance as a transit area for drugs and for organized crime. Moreover, as in the United States, there may be the irony of greater restrictions on overt police leading to the greater use of covert means. The greater openness of the society may also generate greater citizen fear of crime and disorder and hence generate pressure for greater surveillance.

There are interesting historical differences between Britain and the United States, as Miller (1977) notes. Yet one might have thought Britain would be closest to the United States, given the many similarities and the absence of a strong centralized state tradition. Yet for criminal matters, it appears to make less use of covert means than its continental neighbors. With the divergence from its American offspring, it may no longer be possible to talk about a common Anglo-American fear of 'continental despotisms.'

---

4. Brodeur (1992) notes that for its size Canadian police appear to resort to electronic surveillance twenty times more often than police in the United States.

Finally, it would be wrong to necessarily conclude that the absence of the new surveillance technologies necessarily implies very much about how closely watched individuals are, or feel (at least in the conventional ways). The cloying eyes and elongated ears of the small village make that clear. While they don't know from data-base predictive profiles or DNA, community memories about character or family illnesses may overlap these.

The ratio of human to machine surveillance is an interesting issue. It would be wrong to conclude that a higher ratio necessarily means less overall surveillance. For many purposes video and the other forms of electronic surveillance are certainly more efficient than using the unaided senses. Yet their absence need not mean less intense surveillance. Anyone who has traveled in poor, less developed, but more labor-intensive countries, is aware of the many guards, door and floor persons, and hangers-on, whose monitoring function may not be immediately clear.

While such persons are functional alternatives to electronic surveillance, they are not necessarily opposites. One interesting issue is whether the number of persons engaged in surveillance activities actually declines or even increases as hi-tech means are adopted. Machines require people to design, manufacture, install, repair and interpret results. In addition, results can generate new needs to investigate. This may be a bit like the number of restaurants on a block, in which contrary to common sense, up to a point, the more restaurants there are, the more people eat out. It may be the same for surveillance. Information begets a desire for still more information.

Cultural Attitudes

Cultural attitudes toward privacy, individual rights, community and government are relevant as both conditioners and reflectors of history and social structure. A more public and open ethos in the United States may mean greater acceptance of state requests for information (e.g., high rates of income tax and census request compliance), particularly when balanced by expectations that to the extent possible, the state will be open about its practices as well. This may also mean strong support for individuals and private organizations to use surveillance technologies for their own ends. There may be a kind of perverse and reciprocal tolerance involving a stand-off that is lacking in Europe where individualism is weaker and the state less trusted.

One indicator of possible cultural differences (at least at the level of attitudes) is to ask: what does the foreign observer find noteworthy? For example, when I taught in Austria my students were shocked by the extensive American police requests for information from citizens via hotlines. They felt that it was the job of police, not citizens, to locate crime and criminals and that 'it doesn't feel right' and 'it's not my business to report.'

Support for citizen review of police actions, citizen's rights against the state and the expectation that government actions should be as transparent as possible is not strong in Germany. On the other hand, the Germans have a constitutional protection for human dignity which appears to prohibit many of the kinds of surveillance found in the United States (where acceptability or rejection is based on the particular technology, not a general principle). In Germany I encountered surprise and even indignation at the United States' use of systems for the electronic and video monitoring of those subject to home arrest (one colleague shook his head in disgust and said 'it's shocking, it's a different culture'). Another colleague thought it was 'an absolute insult to privacy' that in the United States detailed telephone records were kept, and for billing purposes mailed at the end of the month. He said: 'I don't want to know who my wife calls or for her to know who I call.' This individual found it amazing that on visiting the United States he could not check into a hotel or rent a car without a credit card. The French were wary of private police and the Germans of the various forms of citizen involvement and oversight found in the United States, Britain and the Netherlands.

On the other hand I found it of interest that the French are so accepting of the intelligence-gathering activities of the *Renseignements Généraux* which regularly monitors lawful political behavior, interviewing all political parties and trade unions several times a year – among its dossiers is a list of 600,000 serious gamblers. I was also surprised at the often close relationship between building concierges and police and that the French put significant reliance on handwriting as a key to character.

I was struck by the massive 1983 protests in Germany against a national census which asked questions far less invasive than those routinely asked by the U.S. census. I found it curious that only phone numbers, not addresses, were found in the German telephone books I consulted (although the proportion of unlisted phone numbers appears much greater in the United States). I was astonished that even among national civil liberties leaders in Belgium and other countries with a Napoleonic tradition, there seems to be little opposition to the national identification cards which all must carry and present. My European colleagues in these countries take that, along with the traditional police habit of visiting hotels each night to see the passports or identity cards of residents for granted. In some countries such as the Netherlands, hotel registration can now be remotely accessed via computer. The small size and communal nature of countries such as Belgium and the Netherlands also support this.

Architecture reflects and reaffirms attitudes. The North American visitor is often struck at how much more closed, private and less visible European life seems to be (although an exception to this is the centuries old vital and active public street life). Indications of this are more formal self-presentations and public dress, the high walls, human monitors controlling building access or locked doors of ostensibly public places such as offices and apartment buildings, and houses without inviting porches. Once inside it is often dark, there may be labyrinthine entry ways that would do Franz Kafka proud, with doors, double doors (often a sign of high status), and closed shutters or layers of draperies.

In North America architecture in general seems more open and inviting (indeed design principles now even stress creating visibility as a crime deterrent). Of course the age of a city and building are factors, but I think it goes beyond this. In America office doors, particularly of clerical and staff persons, are usually open. My experience in European universities and other offices suggests that these are more likely to be closed. Once when I was alone using the office of a colleague he went out and closed the door and on returning a few minutes later he knocked on his own door. On numerous occasions as a house guest in several European countries, I left the door to my room open on leaving for the day, only to find the door closed when I returned. I had left the door open unreflectively, perhaps for air or as a symbol that I didn't want to suggest a barrier between my space and my hosts. They obviously felt differently, whether to protect my privacy or theirs, or both.

Some of the general confusion around the broad topic of government information collection has to do with different histories and conceptions of government. This is illustrated by attitudes toward informing. While every culture has negative terms for this such as snitch, there are important national differences, particularly with respect to attitudes toward cooperating with government.

There are at least two informer traditions. In the democratic, anglo-saxon version, a degree of responsibility for community well-being and reporting misdeeds is viewed as a high form of citizenship. Local, limited government is favored and it is believed to grow out of the people and to be accountable to them. In reporting, individuals are believed to be helping themselves and their community. This contrasts with a tradition of unpopular and/or colonial government imposed from the outside. In order to rule, such governments rely on buying and coercing informers who are viewed as selling out their own people. Informing is a way of destroying rather than sustaining community. The ultimate case is the boy hero of the former Soviet Union who turned in his father for anti-state attitudes.

This second tradition helps explain the Italian view of informers (in which retaliation is sometimes sought even against family members of the informer). Part of the French opposition to community police and citizen involvement in law enforcement is that this is believed to turn all citizens into informers. With historic and recent memories of authoritarian rule, Europeans in general want a clearer line between the police and public than is the case in Britain and the United States. This also helps account for the generally more favorable attitudes toward police in those countries. In an interesting contrast, East Germany continued with neighborhood watches after the war was over, but not West Germany.

A related aspect involves cultural differences in imposing (rather than taking) information. Countries show considerable (although perhaps lessening) differences in where they draw the line between one person's liberty or freedom of expression in a public place, and another's right to be left alone. Thus Americans are often shocked by the public displays of urination, nudity, and romantic expression seen in Europe, while Europeans are often surprised at the playing of loud music in public places and the extent to which Americans use first names and reveal personal information about their work, health, life style and religious and political beliefs to persons they hardly know. While Britain has its tabloids and Italy its *paparazzie*, in general it appears that Europeans are less likely to publicize the peccadillos of public figures. They are also less likely to share personal details with those they do not know well.

A number of diverse behaviors may be subsumed under a broad variable involving degree of openness. For example, activities can be contrasted with respect to the extent to which they are public. This involves being seen and heard, and the revelation of personal, organizational and governmental information involving both informal expectations and formal law. There is a strain toward consistency in this, at least when we compare societies. It thus may not be surprising that the United States, on the far end of the continuum, would be a more receptive environment than Europe for technologies for discovering information.

We also of course can identify considerable variation within countries (e.g., between the many different police agencies and the divisions within an agency) such as in France between the National Police, the Gendarmerie and Customs, or in the United States between the FBI and DEA or local police. This alerts us to the need for caution in making broad comparative statements. General statements require a level of abstraction that is likely to mask much internal variation. Even with broad conclusions such as that the new surveillance tactics are in general less prevalent in Europe than in the United States and that there is significant variation within Europe, we cannot say much with precision. The data that would permit us to do that has simply not been gathered and may not be possible to gather. Nor do we have adequate analytic categories for parsimonious comparisons.

The Need for Research

Perhaps the strongest conclusion we can reach is how little we know that would permit a detailed assessment contrasting continents, specific regions and countries or functional areas. While this book contains work by many of the leading police scholars in Europe, they are generally forced to rely on the occasional government report of a scandal, court records, historical and mass media accounts, and their experience as citizens. Their task has also been to describe their country, rather than to work comparatively.

It is far easier to ask questions about social control than to answer them. The United States is distinctive, not only in the relatively large number of social scientists and journalists concerned with these questions, but with its degree of openness. In most European countries, perhaps reflective of the tradition of the strong state, citizens do not have the 'right to know' which is taken for granted in the United States. In much of Europe a special (and rare) parliamentary request is required to discover things such as how many official wire-taps are done each year, while in the United States an annual report detailing this is published by the Justice Department. The major federal police agencies must testify before Congress in budget and oversight hearings and Freedom of Information Act requests are often revealing. United States police agencies (along with those in the Netherlands) are also more open to social science researchers.

In mulling over these materials for several decades I have the feeling of working with a gigantic jigsaw puzzle, or perhaps better, one in which the pieces from a number of puzzles have been mixed together. There are partial fits, areas that appear to belong together and a glimpse of what the whole might look like, but there are also numerous pieces that don't seem to fit at all. Consistency and anomaly seem forever linked within and between areas. It is not clear whether (in Kipling's terms) we are simply looking at different parts of the same elephant or at entirely different species.

GARY T. MARX

There is a great research need for standardized, quantitative trend data within and across countries, on the information collection and use practices shown in Table 1. There is much conceptual and empirical work to be done with respect to just what it is we wish to account for. We also need to specify the appropriate level of analysis. This is dependent on the type of question asked and level of granularity sought. For example, does one contrast techniques for collecting information by national, geographical or cultural borders, types of police and legal system, or by functional area of enforcement? Latent patterns or clusters may be identified which do not correspond to any of these. Rather than starting with presumed causes, we might start with outcomes and ask what the correlates of different patterns of control are. But to do this we need to be able to classify according to the variables in Table 1.

Table 1 Some Social Control Discovery Mechanisms*

| undercover | intelligence operations | |
| | facilitative operations | a. co-conspirators
b. victims
c. preventive operations |

| participatory and non-participatory informers |
| disguised observers |
| hotlines and other procedures for citizen reporting; anonymous reporting |
| neighborhood watches |
| private police |
| electronic surveillance – video and audio (wire-taps, bugs etc.), location monitoring, monitoring of computer usage and computer generated data, visual |
| computer data bases (including suspects, arrest and convictions) and artificial intelligence systems and computer matching and profiling |
| biometric measures – polygraph, voice stress and handwriting analysis, DNA, finger, hand geometry, voice and olfactory prints, hair, blood etc. |
| detention; interrogation techniques |
| traditional physical searches and seizures |
| national id card and various police registries, census |
| drug and alcohol testing |
| psychological tests for honesty and other characteristics |
| work monitoring |
| consumer behavior monitoring |
| health monitoring |

* This list is meant to be illustrative and could be greatly extended.

For any discovery mechanism we need to ask:

1. Who can use it (police, private organizations, any citizen)?
2. For what purposes and under what conditions (as defined by law, policy or custom) can it be (and is it) applied and used?
3. How intensive, extensive, invasive, engineered and invisible is the data collection?
4. To what extent do individuals engage in self-surveillance or voluntarily cooperate with the data collection? What incentives (rewards, immunity, reduced sentences, witness protection) are offered for reporting and other forms of cooperation?
5. Are certain places, activities, persons or relationships given particular protections (e.g. private places or churches and universities, political activities, family relations)?
6. How is the data treated once it has been collected with respect to things such as validation, security, sharing and retention?
7. What types of oversight and sanction exist for misuse?
8. How integrated are the various discovery mechanisms across techniques and areas of life such as citizenship, work, consumption, health and leisure?

Some Additional Explanatory Variables

Even without data called for in Table 1, it is clear that American style undercover work and surveillance practices have not taken hold to the extent that one might have predicted. Just as we can identify factors presumed to create this, we can identify factors presumed to create differences between countries.

The lesser use of these tactics in Europe is likely related to a number of factors. Memories of 20th century totalitarianism offer some continuing inoculation, as may Britain's historic fear of an invasive central authority.

The degree of concern over crime is in general not as great in Europe as in the United States and there is less pressure on police to find innovative and intrusive means to deal with it. In general Europe does not criminalize drugs, alcohol, gambling and the sexual practices of consenting adults to the extent that the United States does. There is thus less demand to use covert means for gathering evidence regarding such consensual behavior. This is part of a broader variable involving the seriousness and prevalence of violations in which it is difficult to identify offenses, offenders and complainants. Perhaps related to this is that prison overcrowding is not a problem and hence there are fewer pressures to turn the community into a carceral environment.

One of the central arguments of *Undercover* (Marx, 1988) is that in a democracy covert surveillance is a functional alternative to restrictions on overt police powers both before and after arrest. In Japan, for example, there is almost no undercover work, wire-tapping or plea bargaining, but police can hold suspects for up to 21 days with minimal cause. European police also tend to have greater powers than is the case in the United States with respect to search and seizure, arrest, interrogation, and self-incrimination. They do not have an exclusionary rule. They may often interrogate without a defense attorney present. In most of Europe, citizens are required to carry ID cards and to register their residences with police. The greater power of European police to overtly intervene in citizen's lives may mean there is less perceived need for new surveillance tactics.

A corollary hypothesis is that where the ability of police to gather information is relatively strong (whether to induce confessions or to search), other means of information gathering such as through forensic science will be weaker. This is consistent with the very well developed crime labs found in the United States.

Other differences in legal culture are also relevant. In most continental countries it was traditionally a crime for police to engage in a crime, even for a worthy end. Police, in principle at least, had far less formal discretion with respect to whether to report an offense and to arrest and were bound to compulsory prosecution. Such factors obviously worked against undercover practices for conventional crime and the 'turning' of suspects and led to innovations such as the pseudo-buy.

Apart from the law's encouragement or inhibition and even prohibition, another relevant factor would appear to be the sheer number of laws police are expected to enforce. We might expect that the more police are expected to do, the more developed will be their arsenal. While I don't know of any good data on this, a popular saying holds that 'in England and the United States all that is not legally prohibited is allowed. In Germany all that is not legally allowed is prohibited. In Austria and the countries of the Mediterranean all that is legally prohibited is allowed.'

General societal attitudes toward fate, temptation and technology may also be relevant. For example, in Catholic countries where individuals may be believed to be prone to sin and vulnerable to temptation, it does not make sense, or seem fair, to test them with undercover opportunities, while in Protestant countries individuals' expectations about self-control and responsibility for one's own fate are stronger. Where fate is believed to be important to human affairs, there may be less interest in anticipation and intervention and less may be expected of the individual. The European humanistic spirit is more skeptical of technology than is the case in the technophilic United States. While there is variation (e.g., Southern v. Northern European countries), Europeans have been slower to develop and adapt to technical changes.

Climate and geography are additional factors which may have an indirect effect on what is available to be observed without special efforts or technology. Thus, before the advent of modern building materials and better means of heating, structures in cold climates with fewer and smaller windows, smaller rooms, more enclosed areas, and thicker walls were less open to public view.

Some additional factors that we might expect to be correlated with surveillance practices are:

- a civil or common law tradition,
- an adversarial or inquisitorial legal process,
- a national or federal criminal justice system,
- significant or minimal role for judicial review of executive and judicial actions,

- clearly codified Bill of Rights,
- a single or multiple police system,
- the degree of police officer heterogeneity within systems,
- police as part of a civil or military bureaucracy,
- an Anglo-American community or a strong state model of policing,
- Mediterranean Catholic or Northern European Protestant traditions,
- imposed or indigenously developed democracy,
- a colonial power or not,
- feudal tradition or not,
- monarchy or republic,
- greater or lesser importance placed on citizen actions to mobilize the law,
- greater or lesser role for private sector social control for both individuals and organizations,
- greater or lesser importance placed on anticipatory police actions.

The above of course may be intertwined (e.g., feudal, Catholic, strong state, national, inquisitorial or common law, civil bureaucracy, community, federal). Having once defined what we wish to account for from Table 1, we can move to explore clusters of causal variables as above.

While there is an extensive English language literature on police in various countries, in general it is neither very analytic nor comparative.[5] My purpose here is only to indicate the kinds of variables that ought to be explored in moving to the next stage of understanding, rather than to offer hypotheses about surveillance and democratic societies. However, some hypotheses leap off the page, such as the greater the perceived crime threat, the greater the overt police power, the stronger the state tradition, the weaker organized labor, the greater will be the surveillance, other factors being equal (which they rarely are). Similarly, formal surveillance might be thought to be taken further within adversarial and judicial review systems, or within systems that have a higher likelihood of identifying government over-reaching as a result of external watchdog agencies, inspectors-general, and legislative and judicial oversight. In such settings there may be less concern that these tactics will be misused because of the likelihood of discovery.[6]

Moreover, there are some standard sociological variables that should be considered:

1. degree and types of inequality,
2. degree and types of heterogeneity and homogeneity,
3. degree of differentiation,
4. degree of legitimacy granted authority,
5. degree of consensus on the rules,

---

5. Some exceptions to this include Miller, 1977; Punch, 1985; Brewer *et al.*, 1988; Bayley, 1985, 1994; Mawby, 1990.
6. This is part of a more general policy dilemma regarding discretion and risky tactics. The legalistic and bureaucratic response to codify them means restricting, but also legitimating them. Absent this, there may be greater risk to authorities in their use (and hence more discretion), since a mandate is lacking for the use of controversial tactics.

6. degree of self-control,
7. degree of expectation and willingness of citizens to control each other,
8. population size and density,
9. degree of geographical mobility.

The implications of many of these are clear. Thus large size, impersonality, less consensus and legitimacy suggest there will be greater surveillance. But some of these factors pull in opposite directions – for example perceived crime seriousness and weak state traditions.

Some single variables permit opposite inferences. Should a high degree of homogeneity lead one to expect higher or lower surveillance? One can argue it both ways. Thus the homogeneity might suggest that there would be greater intolerance of difference and hence support to root it out. On the other hand deviant behavior may be seen as non-threatening because it is statistically insignificant and deemed not worthy of attention. In more heterogenous settings, there may be norms of mutual tolerance out of self-interest, or civil strife which would call forth enhanced surveillance. It is also important to specify the type of homogeneity.

Furthermore, when one gets down to cases and looks concretely, each local context is so rich, distinctive and often changing, that an easily identifiable impact for any single variable is usually difficult to show. We also need to separate the formal (more easily measured indicators) from actual behavior. The mere presence of a law or a formal structure is not a sure guide to behavior, any more than their absence means that behavior consistent with them will not be found. The informal can be seen only through fine-grained observational analysis.

This raises a broader question regarding what type of understanding students of comparative social control should seek – that of the social historian or journalist who describes, or that of the positivist sociologist who looks for explanations and general laws. For the former, an important rule of social inquiry is 'beware of sociologists bearing broad generalizations.' For the latter, the rule 'find variation and account for it' is equally important. Yet if we qualify our generalizations by factors such as social context, time and place, and identify different types of the phenomena of interest, we can avoid the contradiction. A little humility and a tentative approach to a dynamic world also helps.

My own position is somewhere in the middle. I think we must seek the explanatory and the general, but am not very optimistic about obtaining them. We will do better at offering reasonable, and sometimes disprovable, explanations regarding particular contexts and events, than general laws. When we find the latter they will often be bland and the kind of simple observations that can give sociology a bad name. We do not want our efforts to amount (in novelist Allison Luria's words) to offering 'explanations of the obvious by the devious.' We must reach for the moon, knowing that if we miss we may still grab a few stars. The observations throughout the book and in this section are far more impressionistic than I would like. But they do identify empirical patterns, relevant variables and some hypotheses for more systematic future assessments.

This discussion has sought to understand differences in the use of covert surveillance among democracies. The study of the relationships between covert and overt forms of surveillance and their correlates is one part of a broader interest in the forms, processes and powers of contemporary social control.

Our inquiry is part of a larger intellectual tradition concerned with convergence and divergence among ostensibly similar, economically developed democratic nations. Consistent with our findings, the comparative literature has generally found that in spite of the presence of apparently common structures, functional needs, communication and interaction patterns and regional and global pressures, distinctive national environments shape these common factors into at least somewhat distinct national behaviors. Yet there are patterns as well.

For several decades research has sought to understand the effect of broad social, political and cultural factors on public policy and behavior among economically developed democratic nations. Much of the literature on the topic has been concerned with three broad clusters of variables or dimensions which differentiate among nations. While various authors emphasize slightly different factors, Hicks and Swank (1992) identify these as left corporatism, state centralization and bureaucratic paternalism.

It would be useful to develop systematic empirical indicators of the surveillance and control practices from the items in Table 1 and to relate them to each other and to the three dimensions above. Would the pattern for surveillance be similar to that found for economic performance, welfare state policies, internal conflict and demographic patterns? (See for example Liphart and Crepaz 1991; Hicks and Misra 1993; Huber *et al.* 1993; Schmitter 1979; and Pampel 1993.) Will these conceptualizations also help account for national differences in attitudes and practices involving surveillance, privacy and civil liberties? Will they help account for more general differences in social control?

My hunch is that the relationships would be weaker because additional elements are present. In fact there is likely need for a distinct multi-faceted social control dimension reflecting a realm of social values and characteristics separate from (if related to) political values. Determination of the linkages among the many variables discussed in this chapter and hopefully their reduction to a much smaller number of broad dimensions is an important task for future work.

New Directions in Social Control

While the comparative observations in this chapter are tentative, the new surveillance has not yet (and may never) come to Europe to the degree it has in the United States. Yet I think it is equally clear that social control is changing.

While there have been ebbs and flows, in chapter 1 we argued for the normalization of undercover tactics. By that we meant that the secret and unobtrusive collection of information, particularly for political reasons, has been in use for centuries. Covert information collection, undercover interventions and disguised surveillance are fundamental social processes. In that sense the further development of these tactics in the United States in the last three decades and their spread to Europe in the 1970s and 1980s is not surprising.

Yet it would be a mistake to conclude from our historical review which notes some continuities, that there is nothing really new here. The normalization thesis is inadequate to account for the rapid changes that occurred and our occurring.

The technology is certainly new and it can probe much more efficiently, silently, intensively and extensively than human informers alone can. But beyond that there is a new, or at least much more clearly defined ethos or philosophy of modern social control[7] which involves:

1. prevention rather than responding after the fact with a reliance on engineering of physical and social environments to preclude violations or identify violators (Marx, 1995),
2. a 'rational' strategy of categorical rather than individual suspicion and treatment of persons,
3. an interest in general problem solving and system intelligence rather than in specific cases involving a particular violation or violator,
4. a decentralized increased reliance on citizens to mobilize the law and to control themselves and others, rather than waiting for state agents to do this,
5. the extension of law and policy to tactics that had once been ignored and unregulated.

Technology is of course fundamental to much of this. But the technology exists in a cultural context and is congruent and supportive of prior human goals and conceptions, even as it suggests new possibilities.

The European concept of 'high policing' which traditionally relied on covert means was focused on political threats to the state and tended to be beyond the law. Nineteenth century European and American legal reforms were in opposition to this. They stressed using the state's police power in a restrictive fashion to respond to legally defined dangers and to focus on concrete crimes.

There was a bifurcation. The rule of law was increasingly applied to garden variety crimes. Abusive police techniques, whether through searches and arrests or in interrogation, appear to have declined in the aggregate (Leo, 1992). Yet as our review and the articles in this book indicate, to a significant extent, the policing of politics continued to be excluded from this. In some relative sense that is still true. Yet the covert, anticipatory and encouragement techniques of high policing have become more normalized in their application to ordinary crime, while the policing of politics is no longer so far beyond the rule of law. Perhaps there is a golden (or depending on your point of view) tarnished mean here.

---

7. Social control is a broad term and its various components are not equally affected by these changes. For example, these observations apply more to efforts taken to deter or prevent violations and to the discovery of information on violations and violators (whether initial social control mobilization or subsequent interrogation of suspects) than to the creation of rules for enforcement, adjudication, mediation, or sanctioning.

The American writer Mark Twain once said of an erroneous obituary: 'the report of my death was an exaggeration.' The same thing might be said of the death of clearly distinct national surveillance practices in the face of a homogenizing international system of modern social control. However, the report of Twain's death *eventually* was correct.

REFERENCES

Bayley, D.H. (1985), *Patterns of Policing: A Comparative International Analysis*, New Brunswick, Rutgers University Press.
– (1994), *Police for the Future*, New York, Oxford University Press.
Bok, C. (1978), *Lying: Moral Choice in Public and Private Lives*, New York, Vintage Books.
Brewer, J.D. et al. (1988), *The Police, Public Order and the State*, London, Macmillan.
Brodeur, J-P. (1992), 'Undercover Policing in Canada: Wanting What is Wrong,' *Crime, Law and Social Change*, 105–136.
Hicks, A.M. and Swank, D.H. (1992), 'Politics, Institutions, and Welfare Spending in Industrialized Democracies, 1960–82,' *American Political Science Review*, 658–674.
Hicks, A.M. and Misra, J. (1993), 'Political Resources and the Growth of Welfare,' *American Journal of Sociology*, 668–710.
Huber, E., Ragin, C. and Stephens, J. (1993), 'Social Democracy, Christian Democracy, Constitutional Structure and the Welfare State,' *American Journal of Sociology*, 711–749.
Leo, R. (1992), 'From Coercion to Deception: The Changing Nature of Police Interrogation in America,' *Crime, Law and Social Change*, 33–60.
Lijphart, A. and Crepaz, M.L. (1991), 'Corporatist and Consensus Democracy in Eighteen Countries,' *British Journal of Political Science*, 235–256.
Marx, G.T. (1988), *Undercover: Police Surveillance in America*, Berkeley, University of California Press.
– (1995a) 'Electric Eye in the Sky: Some Reflections on the New Surveillance and Popular Culture,' in: D. Lyon and E. Zureik, eds., *New Technology, Surveillance and Social Control*, Minneapolis, University of Minnesota Press.
– (1995b) 'The Engineering of Social Control: The Search for the Silver Bullet,' in: J. Hagan and R. Peterson, eds., *Crime and Inequality*, Stanford, Stanford University Press.
Miller, W.R. (1977), *Cops and Bobbies: Police Authority in New York and London, 1830–1870*, Chicago, University of Chicago Press.
Pampel, F.C. (1992), 'Relative Cohort Size and Fertility: The Socio-political Context of the Easterlin Effect,' *American Sociological Review*, 496–514.
Punch, M. (1985), *Conduct Unbecoming: The Social Construction of Police Deviance and Control*, London, Tavistock.
Schmitter, P.C. (1979), 'Intermediation and Regime Governability in Contemporary Western Europe and North America,' in: P.C. Schmitter and G. Lehmbruch (eds.), *Trends Toward Corporatist Intermediation*, London, Sage, 285–327.